INSTANT POT PRESSURE COOKER COOKBOOK

525 TASTY & HEALTHY EVERYDAY RECIPES – GET MORE ENERGY AND BECOME MORE PRODUCTIVE ENJOYING YOUR INSTANT POT

BY DEANA DOUGLAS

Copyright © 2018 by Deana Douglas - All rights reserved.

This document is geared towards providing exact and reliable information in regards to the topic and issue covered. The publication is sold with the idea that the publisher is not required to render accounting, officially permitted, or otherwise, qualified services. If advice is necessary, legal or professional, a practiced individual in the profession should be ordered.

From a Declaration of Principles which was accepted and approved equally by a Committee of the American Bar Association and a Committee of Publishers and Associations.

In no way is it legal to reproduce, duplicate, or transmit any part of this document in either electronic means or in printed format. Recording of this publication is strictly prohibited, and any storage of this document is not allowed unless with written permission from the publisher. All rights reserved.

The information provided herein is stated to be truthful and consistent, in that any liability, in terms of inattention or otherwise, by any usage or abuse of any policies, processes, or directions contained within is the solitary and utter responsibility of the recipient reader. Under no circumstances will any legal responsibility or blame be held against the publisher for any reparation, damages, or monetary loss due to the information herein, either directly or indirectly.

Respective authors own all copyrights not held by the publisher.

The information herein is offered for informational purposes solely and is universal as so. The presentation of the information is without a contract or any type of guarantee assurance.

The trademarks that are used are without any consent, and the publication of the trademark is without permission or backing by the trademark owner. All trademarks and brands within this book are for clarifying purposes only and are the owned by the owners themselves, not affiliated with this document.

CHAPTER 1: INSTANT POT OPTIONS AND BASICS...15

INSTANT POT OPTIONS 15

INSTANT POT TERMINOLOGY 16

BEYOND THE BASICS 16

CHAPTER 2: BREAKFAST RECIPES 18

ON-THE-GO EGG CUPS 18

CHEDDAR BACON POTATO 18

BROCCOLI EGG MORNING 19

WHOLESOME BREAKFAST EGGS..20

BROCCOLI BREAKFAST FRITTATA..20

MUSHROOM OYSTER FRITTATA 21

SAUSAGE CABBAGE MORNING..22

CAULIFLOWER BREAKFAST PUDDING 22

SAUSAGE EGG QUICHE..22

WHOLESOME BACON MUFFINS 23

AVOCADO EGG MORNING..24

BAKED BACON EGG 24

RAISIN FARRO BREAKFAST...25

CLASSIC APPLE OATS 26

BERRY CHIA OATS...26

CINNAMON SPICE VEGETABLE OATMEAL 27

CHAI SPICED RICE PUDDING 28

INSTANT HOT CHOCOLATE 28

BUCKWHEAT WALNUT PORRIDGE 29

INSTANT SPICED PILAF..30

INSTANT FRUIT COBBLER 30

NUTTY BANANA OATS 31

BLACK BEAN QUINOA..32

PUMPKIN SPICED ESPRESSO 32

RAISIN VEGGIE OATS..33

HEALTHY APPLE BUTTER 34

INSTANT QUINOA CORN 34

WHOLESOME PEACH OATS 35

VANILLA WALNUT OATS 35

POTATO BERRY BREAKFAST...36

SOY MILK APPLE QUINOA 37

SAUSAGE EGG PIE 38

CREAMY KALE EGGS 38

OATS APPLE BREAKFAST CAKE 39

CHEESE TOMATO OMELET 40

HAM EGG FRITTATA..40

SPINACH OMELET MORNING...41

SPICED HAM EGGS 42

BACON BRUSSELS SPROUTS..42

BREAKFAST FRUIT BOWL 43
BREAD ROLL EGG MORNING 43
CINNAMON BANANA SMOOTHIE.. 44
WATERMELON CHIA SMOOTHIE 44
CUCUMBER PINEAPPLE SMOOTHIE 45
SPINACH AVOCADO BREAKFAST CHICKEN 45
INSTANT PORK & EGGS... 46
SAUSAGE CHEDDAR BREAKFAST 46
CREAMY EGGS & BACON 47
CHICKEN HERBAL BREAKFAST.. 48
SPINACH EGG BREAKFAST RAMEKINS 48
CLASSIC BUCKWHEAT PORRIDGE 49
CLASSIC HASH BROWN FRITTATA 50
YOGURT OATS MORNING 50
BERRY QUINOA MORNING 51
SWEET POTATO HASH MORNING 51
SQUASH CINNAMON PORRIDGE 52
CHERRY APPLE RISOTTO 53
PISTACHIO QUINOA MORNING 53
BACON EGG MUFFINS... 54
CRANBERRY OATS... 55
FRENCH TOAST BAKE 55
SPINACH EGGS MORNING 56
PEAS TOMATO EGGS 56
FRESH CHEESE & TOMATO 57
SWEET POTATO BACON & EGG BREAKFAST 57
ALMOND HONEY PANCAKES 58
PECAN BANANA TREAT 58
APPLE CAULIFLOWER BREAKFAST 59
CARDAMOM FLAX MORNING 59
SPINACH TOMATO QUICHE 60
FLAX MEAL STRAWBERRY BREAKFAST.. 60
PUMPKIN OATS MORNING 61
BROCCOLI WITH EGGS 61
BARLEY PEPPER BREAKFAST 62
WHOLE GRAIN TOAST... 62
PEACH TURKEY BREAKFAST.. 63
APPLE ALMOND RICE MEAL.. 63
MULTIGRAIN RISOTTO... 64
GARLIC BEAN RICE MEAL.. 65
AVOCADO RICE SALAD... 65
SPINACH CHICKPEA RICE MEAL 66
SORGHUM PUMPKIN MEAL 67
SPINACH MUSHROOM RISOTTO 67
GREEN TEA RICE RISOTTO 68
TOMATO COUSCOUS... 69

SALMON GREEN BREAKFAST 69
BANANA BUCKWHEAT PORRIDGE 70
CARROT CAKE OATMEAL 70

CHAPTER 3: BEANS & GRAINS 71
SOUTHERN SUCCOTASH 71
BUTTERY POLENTA 71
KIDNEY BEAN SAUSAGE RISOTTO 71
TANGY ASPARAGUS RISOTTO 72
SPICED CHICKPEA CURRY 73
BROWN RICE HAM TREAT 74
BBQ LENTIL MEAL 74
MEXICAN BEAN AVOCADO RICE 75
HAM & RICE TREAT 76
POTATO LENTIL RICE 76
OREGANO POLENTA 77
CHEESY ASPARAGUS RISOTTO 77
CHICKPEA AVOCADO SALAD 78
ZUCCHINI BULGUR MEAL 79
BROCCOLI CREAM PASTA 79
PURE BASMATI RICE MEAL 80
MUSHROOM SPINACH CASSEROLE 80
CAULIFLOWER PASTA 81
TOMATO ONION RICE 81
COCONUT MILK RICE 82
MUSHROOM RICE MEAL 82
ONION PENNE PASTA 83
CHICKPEA EGG BOWL 83
TANGY SPINACH PASTA 84
CAJUN DIRTY RICE 84
ESCAROLE AND BEANS 85
CINCINNATI CHILI 85
BOSTON BAKED BEANS 86
SUPERFOOD QUINOA SALAD 86
CREAMY POLENTA 87

CHAPTER 4: VEGETABLES & SIDES 88
SWEET POTATO CASSEROLE 88
SWEET BRUSSELS 88
PAPRIKA POTATO APPETIZER 89
EGGPLANT GREEN SIDE 89
ASPARAGUS LEMON SIDE 90
BACON GREEN APPETIZER 90
CHEESY EGGPLANT 91
BACON HONEY SPROUTS 92
GREEN BEAN & BACON 92
CHEESY ASPARAGUS 93
CREAMY PEPPER & CORN 93

MASHED CAULIFLOWER 94
CREAM & ONION MUSHROOM 94
WHOLESOME ASPARAGUS APPETIZER 95
SWEET SPICED RIBS 96
SHRIMP & ASPARAGUS SIDES 96
PINE SPINACH APPETIZER 97
MINTY VEGGIE APPETIZER 97
MUSHROOM RISOTTO SIDES 98
GARLIC TUNA APPETIZING PATTIES 99
QUICK CORN ON THE COB 99
GREEN BEANS ALMONDINE 99
SOUTHERN COLLARD GREENS 100
SCALLOPED POTATOES 100
POTATO SALAD WITH EGGS 101
ZUCCHINI POTATO APPETIZER 101
EGGPLANT TOMATINO 102
SPINACH TOMATO APPETIZER 103
CHILI GARLIC OKRA 103
TOMATO EGGPLANT SPREAD 104
POLENTA SNACKY BITES 105
CINNAMON PEANUT SNACK 105
CASHEW SNACK DIP 106
ARTICHOKE COCONUT DIP 106
ORANGE BRUSSELS SPROUTS 107
INSTANT MUSTARD CABBAGE 107
CLASSIC BEAN & PEPPER 108
JUST JALAPENO BEANS 109
CAULIFLOWER POTATOES 109
MAPLE BACON BRUSSELS SPROUTS 110
BEET SALAD 110

CHAPTER 5: SAUCES & SPREADS 112
APPLE MANGO SPREAD/CHUTNEY 112
BBQ SAUCE 112
OREGANO TOMATO SAUCE 113
ZUCCHINI SPICED SAUCE 114
TANGY CRANBERRY SAUCE 114
GARLIC TOMATO SAUCE 115
PUMPKIN BUTTER 115

CHAPTER 6: FISH & SEAFOOD 117
FOIL-STEAMED TILAPIA 117
CHEDDAR CREAMY HADDOCK 117
BANANA MACKEREL 118
BASIL HERBED SALMON 118
ROSEMARY BUTTERY FISH MEAL 119
VEGETABLE SALMON DELIGHT 120
WINE MARINATES SHRIMPS 120

BEAN SHRIMP RICE MEAL 121
TANGY ORANGE TROUT 122
SHRIMP ZOODLES MEAL 122
SHRIMP SAUSAGE MEAL 123
HERBED TROUT FILLET 123
GARLIC SHRIMP WITH RICE 124
RASPBERRY SALMON 125
ZESTY SALMON BURGER 125
SEASONED MAYO FISH MEAL 126
ALMOND CHEDDAR TUNA 127
MAHI MAHI CHILI 127
POACHED SALMON WITH RELISH 128
MILKY WHITE FISH CURRY 128
COCONUT MILK SALMON 129
CLASSIC SHRIMPS 129
SOUTHERN SHRIMP AND GRITS 130
SWEET SOY SALMON 131
ORANGY COD DINNER 131
BROCCOLI SALMON MEAL 132
SHRIMP PASTA MEAL 132
FISH COCONUT CURRY 133
GARLIC CHILI SALMON 134
WINE BRAISED COD 135
JALAPENO PEPPER SHRIMP 135
WHITE WINE HADDOCK 136
TANGY CRABS 136
MUSSELS TOMATINO 137
SWEET CARAMEL SALMON 137
ROSEMARY SALMON 138
TANGY LIME SALMON 138
OLIVE COD MYSTERY 139
CLASSIC GARLIC SHRIMP 140
ORANGE GINGERY FILLETS 140
ASPARAGUS TOMATO CLAMS 141
BROCCOLI SALMON VEGGIES 141
WONDER WINE CLAMS 142
MAYONNAISE LEMON FISH 142
CRAB ONION PATTIES 143
CREAMY SHRIMP PASTA 143
SALMON PEAS MEAL 144
SHRIMP GREEN CURRY 144
BLACK BEAN SHRIMP MEAL 145
YOGURT FISH PATTIES 146
SWORDFISH FRA DIAVOLO 146
CAJUN CRAB ETOUFFEE 146
CHINESE TAKEOUT SHRIMP FRIED RICE 147

SEAFOOD PAELLA..148
CAPE COD LOBSTER BAKE...148
NEW ORLEANS GUMBO...149

CHAPTER 7: MEATLESS MAINS..**150**
BLACK BEAN BURGERS...150
MASALA KIDNEY BEANS...150
SPINACH JALAPENO LENTIL CURRY....................................151
CREAMY LIMA BEANS..152
INSTANT PEAS RISOTTO...152
TOFU VEGGIE TREAT...153
MUSHROOM ZUCCHINI PASTA...153
POTATO MUSTARD SALAD..154
CHICKPEA BURGER...155
SPINACH PASTA TREAT..155
MEXICAN STYLE VEGAN RICE...156
WHOLESOME LENTIL TACOS...157
PUMPKIN BEAN STEW..157
MUSHROOM BEAN FARRO...158
SORGHUM RAISIN MEAL..159
SQUASH EGGPLANT MANIA...160
ZUCCHINI EGGPLANT MEAL..160
JALAPENO BEAN MEAL...161
WHOLESOME CAULIFLOWER MEAL......................................161
FARO PEAS COLLARD WRAPS..162
CHILI BEAN TACOS...163
CHICKPEA CURRY..164
REFRIED BEAN ENCHILADAS..164
BROWN RICE STUFFED PEPPERS.......................................165
"BAKED" ZITI..165
QUICK MAC & CHEESE..166
PASTA PRIMAVERA...166
EGGPLANT PARMESAN..167
VEGETARIAN SHEPHERD'S PIE..167

CHAPTER 8: POULTRY...**169**
CREAMY CHICKEN AND RICE CASSEROLE............................169
ROSEMARY CHICKEN..169
TANGY POTATO CHICKEN..170
OREGANO PASTA CHICKEN..170
CHICKEN SOY TORTILLA..171
NUT & DATE CHICKEN...172
MAPLE TOMATO CHICKEN..172
COUPLE'S BBQ CHICKEN..173
MEXICAN STYLE PEPPER TURKEY......................................174
TANGY OLIVE CHICKEN...174
LEMONGRASS COCONUT CHICKEN.....................................175
COLA CHICKEN WINGS..175

BBQ CHICKEN 176
TURKEY TOMATO MEAL 177
OREGANO PASTA CHICKEN 177
TANGY CRANBERRY TURKEY 178
ROSEMARY GARLIC CHICKEN 178
TANGY POTATO CHICKEN 179
LEMONGRASS COCONUT CHICKEN 180
COLA CHICKEN WINGS 180
POTATO CHICKEN ROAST 181
COCONUT CURRY CHICKEN 181
GARLIC SALSA CHICKEN 182
CHICKEN YOGURT SALSA 183
CHICKEN ROSEMARY CONGEE 183
CREAMY CHEESE CHICKEN 184
SPAGHETTI TURKEY MEAL 184
SESAME SHERRY CHICKEN 185
COCONUT CHICKEN DELIGHT 185
CLASSIC SPICED CHICKEN 186
OREGANO CHICKEN STRIPS 187
SOY TURKEY MEATBALLS 187
CLASSIC BBQ CHICKEN 188
TURKEY TOMATO MEAL 189
OREGANO PASTA CHICKEN 189
FRESH VEGGIE TURKEY 190
CLASSIC HONEY TURKEY 190
CASHEW CHICKEN CHILI 191
SWEET POTATO TURKEY MEAL 191
CLASSIC LEMON COCONUT CHICKEN 192
LEMONGRASS CHICKEN TREAT 193
CHICKEN MARSALA 193
CAJUN CHICKEN MEAL 194
BROCCOLI CHICKEN PASTA 194
TURKEY CAULIFLOWER MEAL 195
CHICKEN PEAS RICE 195
CHICKEN MEATBALLS WITH SAUCE 196
CHERRY TOMATO CHICKEN 196
BROCCOLI CHICKEN TREAT 197
CHEESY BACON CHICKEN 197
GARLIC SPICED TURKEY 198
CHICKEN DRUMSTICKS 199
WHITE WINE MUSHROOM TURKEY 199
PUMPKIN HOT CHILI 200
CHEESE JALAPENO CHICKEN 201
INSTANT LEMON CHICKEN 201
CREAMY TURKEY CHICKEN 202
MEXICAN STYLE CREAMY CHICKEN 202

BACON CHICKEN 203
ROSEMARY TURKEY 204
TURKEY APPLE CURRY 204
BACON CREAM CHICKEN 205
TURKEY ASPARAGUS MEAL 205
BROCCOLI CHICKEN MEAL 206
MUSHROOM TURKEY MEAL 206
CREAM CHICKEN QUICHE 207
TURKEY RICE BOWL 208
CHICKEN COCONUT CURRY 208
CLASSIC LEMON CHICKEN 209
CHICKEN AND DUMPLINGS 209
TENDER CORNISH HENS WITH GRAVY 210
MIDWESTERN BARBECUE PULLED CHICKEN 210
GAME DAY BUFFALO WINGS 211
TEXAS CHICKEN TAMALES 211
CHICKEN RAGOUT 212

CHAPTER 9: BEEF & PORK 213

SOY SAUCE PORK BELLY 213
BEEF STROGANOFF 213
GARLIC ROAST 214
SPICY VINEGAR LAMB 214
SWEET POTATO STEAK 215
PORK & BACON DINNER MEAL 216
OREGANO SPICED BEEF CHOPS 216
MILKY BEEF ROAST 217
BEEF AVOCADO BOWL 217
BROCCOLI BEEF WITH GARLIC TWIST 218
BEEF BROCCOLI CURRY 219
PARMESAN BEEF MEATBALLS 219
PORK CHOPS TOMATINO 220
WINE BRAISED BEEF ROAST 220
CREAMY PORK TREAT 221
BUTTERY GARLIC LAMB SHANKS 222
SPICED CREAM LAMB 223
PINEAPPLE PORK 224
GREEN CHILI BEEF 224
BEEF RED POTATO STEW 225
SPICED POTATO LAMB DINNER 226
PORK MEATBALL CURRY 226
SQUASH WINE LAMB MEAL 227
ARTICHOKE MAYO BEEF 228
APPLE PORK ROAST 228
GARLIC PULLED PORK 229
SAUCY PORK MEATBALLS 230
OREGANO LAMB SHANKS 230

HONEY GLAZED PORK ROAST 231
CLASSIC BEEF BOURGUIGNON...231
TERIYAKI PORK MEAL 232
BEEF MEATLOAF DINNER 233
PINEAPPLE STEAK MEAL 233
CHIPOTLE BEEF ROAST 234
CORN POTATO BEEF 235
BEEF PENNE MEAL 236
CLASSIC OREGANO TENDERLOINS 236
WORCESTERSHIRE PORK TENDERLOINS 237
CHEESY MEAT PASTA 238
HONEY SPICED BEEF RIBS 238
GLAZED PEPPER PORK 239
OREGANO SPICED BRISKET...239
CLASSIC TOMATO PORK RIBS..240
LIME CHILI ROAST 240
CLASSIC LAMB & FIGS 241
SMOKY PORK ROAST 242
GOAT TOMATO CURRY...242
BEEF TOMATO MEATBALLS..243
TOMATO CHILI PORK 244
BEEF GREEN BEANS..244
ROSEMARY LAMB 244
BEEF CORN CHILI 245
MUSHROOM BEEF MEAL 246
SAUSAGE RICE MEAL...246
LEMON BEEF MEAL...247
SWEET POTATO BEEF...247
PORK POTATO LUNCH...248
VEAL CHEESE MEAL 248
BEEF ASPARAGUS SALAD..249
HEARTY BEEF STEW..249
YANKEE POT ROAST..250
AMERICAN CHOP SUEY..250
SUNDAY BEEF BRISKET...251
APPLESAUCE PORK CHOPS...251
PORK CARNITAS...252
BARBECUE PORK RIBS..252

CHAPTER 10: WARM SOUPS & STEWS...253
SEAFOOD MIX STEW..253
PORK VEGGIE SOUP..253
KALE LENTIL VEGETARIAN SOUP 254
SQUASH CHICKEN MUSHROOM SOUP 255
VIETNAMESE CHICKEN SOUP...256
CREAMY LENTIL STEW...256
TURKEY BROWN RICE SOUP 257

CHICKEN BEAN SOUP 257
MIXED BEAN CHICKEN STEW 258
BEAN PEPPER SOUP 259
TURKEY BEAN SOUP 259
MUSHROOM STEAK SOUP 260
CORN CREAM SHRIMP SOUP 261
CHICKEN COCONUT SPINACH SOUP 262
HERBED TURKEY STEW 262
GREEN BEAN BEEF STEW 263
FISH CREAM STEW 264
CHEESY LEEK SQUASH SOUP 264
BEEF CARROT SOUP 265
CHEESY CHICKEN SOUP 266
SLOW COOKED SPICED SQUASH SOUP 266
YUMMY ASPARAGUS HAM SOUP 267
CREAMY TOMATO SOUP 267
SPINACH LENTIL SOUP 268
CHEESY TOMATO SOUP 269
ITALIAN SAUSAGE CREAM SOUP 269
MARINARA TURKEY SOUP 270
CHICKEN SPICED TROPICAL SOUP 271
WHOLESOME VEGGIES SOUP 272
KALE BEEF STEW 272
PORK CABBAGE SOUP 273
CASHEW RICE SOUP 273
CORN CHICKPEA CURRY 274
WHOLESOME BROCCOLI SOUP 275
CASHEW CARROT SOUP 276
SPINACH VEGGIE SOUP 277
QUINOA MIXED BEAN SOUP 277
BROCCOLI BEAN SOUP 278
CORN PEPPERY CHOWDER 279
SWEET POTATO LEMONGRASS SOUP 280
CLASSIC LENTIL POTATO STEW 280
BROCCOLI CASHEW SOUP 281
KALE SQUASH STEW 282
ZUCCHINI GARLIC SOUP 283
CAULIFLOWER CHICKPEA SOUP 283
ZUCCHINI INSTANT VEGGIE SOUP 284
TOMATO VEGGIE SOUP 285
SQUASH CRANBERRY SOUP 286
WHOLESOME BEAN POTATO CURRY 287
ZUCCHINI COCONUT SOUP 287
MUSHROOM LENTIL SOUP 288
INSTANT CARROT SOUP 289
CHICKEN GINGER SOUP 289

MINESTRONE PASTA SOUP 290
SPICED BLACK BEAN SOUP 291
SWEET POTATO CHICKEN STEW... 291
CARROT COCONUT SOUP 292
TURKEY CHILI STEW... 293
SWEET POTATO FISH STEW 293
BEEF MUSHROOM STEW... 294
BEET CARROT SOUP 295

CHAPTER 11: SNACKS & APPETIZERS..296

QUESO SAUCE WITH CHORIZO... 296
ARTICHOKE DIP WITH NACHOS 296
CHEESY ASPARAGUS 297
OREGANO BLACK BEAN 297
CLASSIC POTATO FRIES 298
CHICKPEA HUMMUS... 298
SOY SAUCE TOFU 299
HONEY CARROTS 300
POTATO BUTTERMILK APPETIZER 300
ORANGE GLAZED POTATOES... 301
BROCCOLI SPINACH GREENS 302
CHEESY ARTICHOKES 302
BEAN JALAPENO DIP.. 303
CASHEW HUMMUS... 303
SEASONED PEANUT MANIA 304
CHEDDAR CHICKEN DIP 304
ZUCCHINI BITES.. 305
BOILED CHEESE PEANUTS 305
ALMOND ZUCCHINI BALLS 306
TURKEY MEATBALL SNACK.. 306
TANGY CASHEW HUMMUS... 307
GARLIC BRUSSELS SPROUTS 307
SCRUMPTIOUS COCONUT COOKIES.. 308
MAYO HORSERADISH SNACK 309
SPINACH BACON DIPS.. 309
CLASSIC TURNIPS STICKS 310
RADISH LEMON SNACK 310
SWEET POTATO LEMON SPREAD 311
GARLIC MUSHROOM SNACK 311
CINNAMON ALMOND... 312
LOADED POTATO SKINS 312
CHEESE FONDUE... 313
CURRIED CAULIFLOWER BITES WITH DIJONNAISE.. 313
COCKTAIL MEATBALLS 314
DEVILED EGGS.. 314
STUFFED MUSHROOMS 314

CHAPTER 12: DESSERTS...316

RAISIN BREAD PUDDING..316
FUDGY BROWNIES...316
CINNAMON RICE PUDDING 317
NEW YORK CHEESECAKE...317
APPLE CRISP 317
FRUITY DESSERT BOWL...318
TANGY TAPIOCA TREAT 318
BANANA PIE..319
THE RED PEARS..319
NUTTY CHOCOLATE FUDGE BALLS..320
MOUTHWATERING RAISIN APPLES 320
CHOCOLATE RAMEKINS..321
WONDER WINE PEARS...321
TANGY BLUEBERRY LEMON DELIGHT 322
COCOA PUDDING DESSERT 323
AVOCADO CHOCO TREAT 323
CHOCO ALMOND PUDDING 324
CASHEW TAPIOCA PUDDING 324
STUFFED DESSERT APPLES 325
BERRY DESSERT MYSTERY...325
BUCKWHEAT BANANA TREAT...326
CARDAMOM RICE PUDDING 326
INSTANT FRUIT BOWL 327
YUMMY WINE FIGS 328
BERRY DESSERT CUPS...328
CHERRY PECAN MOUSSE..329
CREAMY STRAWBERRY PUDDING..329
CHOCOLATE CAKE...330
VANILLA ORANGE MUFFINS 331
ORANGE CHOCO MUFFINS 331
PURE PEAR BERRY CAKES...332
INDIAN PUDDING...333
CREAM BRULEE..333
COCOA ALMOND CAKE...334
BASIC YOGURT RECIPE..334
STRAINED GREEK YOGURT 335
HERBED YOGURT CHEESE 335
DRINKABLE YOGURT SMOOTHIES..335
COCONUT MILK YOGURT...336
VANILLA FROZEN YOGURT RECIPE..336
ORANGE HONEY YOGURT PANNA COTTA 337

Chapter 1: Instant Pot Options and Basics

Instant Pot Options

Instant Pot, the most popular multi-purpose electric pressure cooker brand in North America, currently offers three different models of their product: Lux, Duo, and Smart. All of these are impressive and largely similar machines, but each has certain qualities that differentiate it from the others.

Lux

Lux is the second model Instant Pot introduced, right after their now-discontinued first model, CSG. It offers six distinct functions: pressure cook, slow cook, steam, make rice, saute, and keep warm. While these six functions make the Lux Instant Pot a highly useful machine, it lacks a few features that were introduced in later models. Namely, it doesn't have a low-pressure setting or a yogurt-making setting. You can technically still make yogurt in the Instant Pot using the slow cooker function, but this MacGyver takes considerably more guesswork than the built-in yogurt- making function in the later models. That means that the Lux model is probably not the right choice for anyone who has her heart set on making perfect yogurt in the Instant Pot.

Duo

The Duo is the third model Instant Pot released, and it remains their most popular. The Duo Instant Pot boasts seven functions — all of the six that are included in the Lux model plus yogurt- making. In addition, the pressure cooker function in the Duo offers both high and low-pressure settings. There's even a new ergonomic design feature on the pot itself: the handles feature slots that the detachable lid can latch onto, so you can latch the lid on the handles instead of setting it on the counter and getting drips all over your granite.

Smart

The Smart is the latest, most cutting-edge version of the Instant Pot. In addition to the seven functions included in the Duo model, the Smart features precision temperature setting, which means that you can use it to bring your food to specific temperatures. The effect of this function is similar to that produced by sous vide ovens, which have long been renowned for their ability to cook Platonically ideal steaks and other dishes. You can even program the Smart to reach one precise temperature, hold it for a specific amount of time, and then move on to another temperature. These programmed sequences are called "recipe scripts" and allow you to use your Instant Pot to make things like cheese and yeasted doughs. The Smart also has Bluetooth capability, so it can send notifications to your phone using a paired application. It's an amazingly powerful piece of technology, but it may be a little complex for people who just want a way to combine several familiar appliances into one tool.

Instant Pot Terminology

Here are a few vocabulary words that will come in handy as you read through this book and get acquainted with the Instant Pot world.

Quick release (QP) - Open the pressure valve to quickly release the steam inside. Natural release (NP) - Leave the valve closed, so the pressure will slowly drop on its own terms. Also called "natural pressure release" (NPR).

Seal - The silicone ring around the lid that seals the unit closed, allowing the pressure to increase.

Pressure valve - The knob on the lid that controls the pressure cooker function. You can turn it to seal to increase the pressure or vent to decrease the pressure.

Recipe script - A program that tells the Instant Pot to reach a series of preset temperatures for a series of preset times. This applies specifically to the Smart Instant Pot model.

.

Beyond the Basics

- Use the yogurt setting for anything else that requires fermenting, from yeasted bread doughs to kimchi.

- Don't think you have to use just one cooking setting per meal. Go ahead and move

16

from saute to steam to slow cook if you need to.

- Use the precision temperature setting on your Instant Pot to get the same picture-perfect results you'd see in a sous vide setup. For example, you can set the temperature to 140°F for a flawless steak.

- You can put pots inside your inner pot! This is called pot-in-pot cooking by those in the know and is useful for any recipes that require the ingredients to stay inside a container, such as custards and casseroles. Don't think you're required to stay within the confines of the inner pot.

- For clever Instant Pot meal prep, freeze prepped ingredients inside freezer bags lining containers that fit inside the inner pot. When it's time to cook your freezer meal, just cut the bag off the frozen ingredients, put them in the pot, and wait for your no-effort home- cooked dinner.

- Be creative! The world won't end if you make one unsuccessful dish. Use the tips and tricks included with these recipes to develop your own brand-new Instant Pot menu.

Chapter 2: Breakfast Recipes

On-the-Go Egg Cups

Prep Time: 8-10 min.
Cooking Time: 5 minutes
Number of Servings: 6
Ingredients:
- 6 eggs
- 2 tablespoons half and half
- 1/2 teaspoon salt
- 1/2 teaspoon black pepper
- 1 tablespoon chives or your favorite herbs and spices

Directions:
1. Beat together eggs, half and half, salt, pepper, and chives.
2. Pour egg mixture into silicone molds or small custard ramekins.
3. Pour 1 cup of water into the Instant Pot. Place the steamer basket above the water and set the egg cups in the basket.
4. Close the lid and set the cook time for 5 minutes on high pressure.
5. Cool slightly before serving.

Cheddar Bacon Potato

Prep Time: 8-10 min.
Cooking TIme: 7 min.
Number of Servings: 2
Ingredients:
- 1/2 teaspoon garlic powder
- 1 1/2 ounces cheddar cheese, grated
- 1 ounces ranch dressing

- 1 teaspoon parsley, dried
- 1/2 pound red potatoes, make medium size cubes
- 1 bacon strip, chopped
- A pinch of pepper and salt
- 1 tablespoon water

Directions:
1. Take your 3-Quart Instant Pot; open the top lid. Plug it and turn it on.
2. In the cooking pot area, add the bacon, parsley, salt, potatoes, pepper, garlic powder, and water. Using a spatula, stir the ingredients.
3. Close the top lid and seal its valve.
4. Press "MANUAL" setting. Adjust cooking time to 7 minutes.
5. Allow the recipe to cook for the set cooking time.
6. After the set cooking time ends, press "CANCEL" and then press "QPR (Quick Pressure Release)".
7. Instant Pot will quickly release the pressure.
8. Open the top lid, add the cooked recipe mix in serving plates. Mix in the cheese and dressing.
9. Serve and enjoy!

Broccoli Egg Morning

Prep Time: 5-8 min.
Cooking Time: 5 min.
Number of Servings: 2
Ingredients:
- 3 eggs, whisked
- ½ cup broccoli florets
- A pinch garlic powder
- 2 tablespoons tomatoes
- 1 clove garlic, minced
- ½ small yellow onion, chopped
- ½ red bell pepper, chopped
- 2 tablespoons cheese, grated
- A pinch chili powder
- 2 tablespoons onions
- 2 tablespoons parsley
- Pepper and salt as needed

Directions:
1. Take your 3-Quart Instant Pot; open the top lid. Plug it and turn it on.
2. Open the top lid; grease inside cooking surface using a cooking spray.
3. In a bowl, whisk the eggs.
4. Add the remaining ingredients except the cheese. Season with Pepper and salt.
5. In the cooking pot area, add the mixture.
6. Close the top lid and seal its valve.
7. Press "STEAM" setting. Adjust cooking time to 5 minutes.

8. Allow the recipe to cook for the set cooking time.
9. After the set cooking time ends, press "CANCEL" and then press "QPR (Quick Pressure Release)".
10. Instant Pot will quickly release the pressure.
11. Open the top lid, add the cooked recipe mix in serving plates. Top with the cheese.
12. Serve and enjoy!

Wholesome Breakfast Eggs

Prep Time: 8 min.
Cooking Time: 15 min.
Number of Servings: 2-3
Ingredients:
- ¼ teaspoon cumin, ground
- 4 eggs
- ½ teaspoon sea salt
- ¼ teaspoon ground cayenne
- 1 teaspoon thyme leaves
- 2 garlic cloves, peeled and chopped finely
- ½ cup parsley, chopped
- ½ cup cilantro, chopped
- 2 tablespoons butter
- 1 tablespoon coconut oil

Directions:
1. Arrange your Instant Pot over a dry, clean platform. Plug it in power socket and turn it on.
2. Now press "Saute" mode from available options. In the cooking area, add the butter, oil, and garlic; cook for 2-3 minutes to soften the added ingredients.
3. Add thyme and cook for a minute. Mix in the parsley and cilantro and cook until it starts to crisp for around 2-3 minutes.
4. Take the eggs and break into the pan; do not to break the yolks.
5. Close the lid and lock. Ensure that you have sealed the valve to avoid leakage.
6. Keep the pot on sauté function and cook for 3 minutes.
7. Open the lid and serve warm!

Broccoli Breakfast Frittata

Prep Time: 8-10 min.
Cooking Time: 30 min.
Number of Servings: 3-4
Ingredients:
- 4 eggs
- 1 cup goats milk
- 1 cup shredded goat cheese
- 8 ounces ham cubed
- 2 cups frozen broccoli florets

- 1 teaspoon sea salt
- 2 teaspoons (finely ground) black pepper

Directions:
1. Spray a baking pan with some cooking spray. Arrange the broccoli and ham on the bottom.
2. In a bowl beat together the eggs, milk, pepper, and salt. Mix in the cheese.
3. Add the mix in over the ham and cover with a foil.
4. Take an Instant Pot; open the top lid.
5. Pour 2 cups water and place steamer basket/trivet inside the cooking pot.
6. Arrange the pan over the basket/trivet.
7. Close the top lid and make sure the valve is sealed.
8. Press "MANUAL" cooking function. Adjust cooking time to 20 minutes.
9. Allow pressure to build and cook the ingredients for the set time.
10. After the set cooking time ends, press "CANCEL" and then press "QPR". Instant Pot will quickly release pressure.
11. Open the top lid, add the cooked mixture in serving plates.
12. Serve warm.

Mushroom Oyster Frittata

Prep Time: 5 min.
Cooking Time: 13 min.
Number of Servings: 6
Ingredients:
- 2 cups mushrooms, sliced
- 10 oysters, well drained
- 1 cup coconut milk
- 1 tablespoon coconut oil (melted)
- 1/2 cup green onion, sliced
- 2 tablespoons cooked, crumbled bacon
- 6 eggs
- 1 cup water

Directions:
1. Take an Instant Pot; open the top lid.
2. Press "SAUTÉ" cooking function.
3. In the cooking pot area, add the oil, bacon, mushroom, oysters, and onions. Cook until turn translucent and softened for 4-5 minutes.
4. Beat the eggs, coconut milk, pepper and salt in a mixing bowl.
5. Pour mixture over oyster mixture.
6. Close the top lid and make sure the valve is sealed.
7. Press "MANUAL" cooking function. Adjust cooking time to 8 minutes.
8. Allow pressure to build and cook the ingredients for the set time.
9. After the set cooking time ends, press "CANCEL" and then press "QPR". Instant Pot will quickly release pressure.
10. Open the top lid, add the cooked mixture in serving plates.
11. Serve warm.

Sausage Cabbage Morning

Prep Time: 8-10 min.
Cooking Time: 20 min.
Number of Servings: 5-6
Ingredients:
- 1 head cabbage (make slices)
- 1 onion (diced)
- 1 pound Turkey Sausage (make slices)
- 2 tablespoons olive oil
- 4 cloves minced garlic
- 3 teaspoons wine vinegar

Directions:
1. Take an Instant Pot; open the top lid.
2. Press "SAUTÉ" cooking function.
3. In the cooking pot area, add the oil and sausage. Stir and cook until evenly brown for 10-12 minutes.
4. Add the cabbage, onion, and garlic and sauté for 8-10 minutes, stirring frequently.
5. Add the mixture to the serving plate. Sprinkle with the vinegar and serve.

Cauliflower Breakfast Pudding

Prep Time: 8-10 min.
Cooking Time: 20 min.
Number of Servings: 3-4
Ingredients:
- 1 cup cauliflower rice
- 2 teaspoons (finely ground) cinnamon powder
- 1 ½ cups unsweetened coconut or almond milk
- 1 cup water
- 1 teaspoon pure vanilla extract
- Pinch of salt

Directions:
1. Take an Instant Pot; open the top lid.
2. Add all the ingredients in the cooking pot. Using a spatula, gently stir to combine well.
3. Close the top lid and make sure the valve is sealed.
4. Press "MANUAL" cooking function. Adjust cooking time to 20 minutes.
5. Allow pressure to build and cook the ingredients for the set time.
6. After the set cooking time ends, press "CANCEL" and then press "NPR". Instant Pot will slowly and naturally release the pressure for 8-10 minutes.
7. Open the top lid, add the cooked mixture in serving plates.
8. Serve warm.

Sausage Egg Quiche

Prep Time: 15-20 min.
Cooking Time: 30 min.

Number of Servings: 3-4
Ingredients:
- 1 cup (finely ground) sausage, cooked
- ½ cup diced ham
- ½ cup goat milk
- 6 large eggs, well beaten
- 4 slices bacon, cooked and crumbled
- 1 cup shredded goat cheese
- 2 large green onions, chopped
- ½ teaspoon sea salt
- ½ teaspoon black pepper

Directions:
1. In a bowl, mix the eggs, goats milk, sea salt, and pepper.
2. In a soufflé dish, add and mix the sausage, bacon, ham, cheese, and green onions.
3. Pour the egg mixture over the meat, mix well.
4. Cover with aluminum foil.
5. Take an Instant Pot; open the top lid.
6. Pour 1 cup water and place steamer basket/trivet inside the cooking pot.
7. Arrange the dish over the basket/trivet.
8. Close the top lid and make sure the valve is sealed.
9. Press "MANUAL" cooking function. Adjust cooking time to 30 minutes.
10. Allow pressure to build and cook the ingredients for the set time.
11. After the set cooking time ends, press "CANCEL" and then press "QPR". Instant Pot will quickly release pressure.
12. Open the top lid, add the cooked mixture in serving plates.
13. Serve warm.

Wholesome Bacon Muffins

Prep Time: 10 min.
Cooking Time: 10 min.
Number of Servings: 5
Ingredients:
- 1 green onion, diced

- 1/4 tsp. lemon pepper seasoning

- 4 medium eggs

- 4 tablespoons cheddar cheese, shredded

- 4 slices turkey bacon (precooked), crumbled

Directions:
1. In a bowl of medium size, whisk the eggs; mix in the pepper and mix well.
2. Divide the green onion, bacon, and cheese into the muffin cups. Top with the egg mixture and stir gently.
3. Arrange your Instant Pot over a dry, clean platform. Plug it in power socket and turn it on.
4. Pour the water (1 ½ cups) in the pot. Arrange the trivet inside and add the cups over the trivet.

5. Close the lid and lock. Ensure that you have sealed the valve to avoid leakage.
6. Press "Manual" mode from available cooking settings and set cooking time to 8 minutes. Instant Pot will start cooking the ingredients after a few minutes.
7. After the timer reads zero, press "Cancel"; press "NPR" to naturally release pressure. It takes about 8-10 minutes to release pressure naturally.
8. Carefully remove the lid and serve the prepared keto dish warm!

Avocado Egg Morning

Prep Time: 5-8 min.
Cooking Time: 8 min.
Number of Servings: 4
Ingredients:
- 2 tablespoons green onions, finely chopped
- 1 teaspoon olive oil
- 1 medium-sized avocado, pitted and cubed
- 2 large eggs, beaten
- 1 tablespoon butter
- ½ teaspoon sea salt
- ¼ teaspoon red chili flakes
- ¼ teaspoon (ground) black pepper
- Milk (optional)

Directions:
1. Take your Instant Pot; open the top lid. Plug it and turn it on.
2. Press "SAUTÉ" setting and the pot will start heating up.
3. In the cooking pot area, add the butter and avocado cubes. Season with pepper and salt.
4. Cook until starts becoming softened for 3-4 minutes. Stir in between.
5. Add the eggs, green onions, and olive oil. Optionally, add 2 tablespoons of milk for a creamier texture.
6. Stir and cook for 3 minutes, or until the eggs are set.
7. Press "Cancel". Add in serving bowls and enjoy.

Baked Bacon Egg

Prep Time: 5-8 min.
Cooking Time: 10 min.
Number of Servings: 4
Ingredients:
- 8 eggs
- ½ cup milk
- 1 cup mozzarella cheese, shredded
- ¼ cup green onions, chopped
- ½ teaspoon salt
- 8 pieces bacon, chopped
- 2 cups cauliflower, chopped

Directions:
1. Take your Instant Pot; open the top lid. Plug it and turn it on.
2. Press "SAUTÉ" setting and the pot will start heating up.
3. In the cooking pot area, add the oil and bacon. Stir and cook until evenly brown from all sides.
4. Using a wooden spatula spread the bacon evenly over the bottom.
5. Add the cauliflower on top.
6. In another bowl, whisk the eggs and season with salt. Pour in the milk and whisk together until turn foamy.
7. Add the mixture over cauliflower and top with mozzarella cheese.
8. Close the top lid and seal its valve.
9. Press "MANUAL" setting. Adjust cooking time to 7 minutes.
10. Allow the recipe to cook for the set cooking time.
11. After the set cooking time ends, press "CANCEL" and then press "QPR (Quick Pressure Release)".
12. Instant Pot will quickly release the pressure.
13. Open the top lid, add the cooked recipe mix in serving plates.
14. Sprinkle with green onions and serve immediately.

Raisin Farro Breakfast

Prep Time: 5min.
Cooking Time: 5min.
Number of Servings: 3-4
Ingredients:
- 2 cups water
- ¼ cup brown sugar
- 1 cup farro
- 2 tablespoons vegetable oil
- 1 teaspoon vanilla extract
- ¼ teaspoon ground cinnamon
- ¼ cup raisins
- ¼ teaspoon salt
- chopped nuts of your choice

Directions:
1. Rinse the farro in a colander.
2. Take Instant Pot and carefully arrange it over a clean, dry kitchen platform. Turn on the appliance.
3. Find and press "Sauté" cooking function.
4. In the cooking pot area; add the oil and farro in the pot. Cook until turn fragrant. Add remainder of ingredients and stir again.
5. Close the pot lid and seal the valve to avoid any leakage. Find and press "Manual" cooking setting and set cooking time to 5 minutes.
6. Allow the recipe ingredients to cook for the set time, and after that, the timer reads "zero". Press "Cancel" and press "QPR" setting for quick pressure release.
7. Open the pot and arrange the cooked recipe in serving plates. Serve immediately topped with nuts and/or extra sugar.

Classic Apple Oats

Prep Time: 5min.
Cooking Time: 5 min.
Number of Servings: 2
Ingredients:

- ½ teaspoon cinnamon
- ¼ teaspoon ginger
- 2 apples, make half-inch chunks
- ½ cup oats, steel cut
- 1 ½ cups water
- Maple syrup, as needed
- Pinch of salt
- Pinch of clove
- Pinch of nutmeg

Directions:

1. Take Instant Pot and carefully arrange it over a clean, dry kitchen platform. Turn on the appliance.
2. In the cooking pot area, add the water, oats, cinnamon, ginger, clove, nutmeg, apple and salt. Stir the ingredients gently.
3. Close the pot lid and seal the valve to avoid any leakage. Find and press "Manual" cooking setting and set cooking time to 5 minutes.
4. Allow the recipe ingredients to cook for the set time, and after that, the timer reads "zero".
5. Press "Cancel" and press "NPR" setting for natural pressure release. It takes 8-10 times for all inside pressure to release.
6. Open the pot and arrange the cooked recipe in serving plates.
7. Sweeten as needed with maple or agave syrup and serve immediately. Top with some chopped nuts, optional.

Berry Chia Oats

Prep Time: 5 min.
Cooking Time: 6 min.
Number of Servings: 2
Ingredients:

- 1/2 cups old fashioned oats

- 1/2 cups almond milk, unsweetened

- 1/2 cups blueberries

- 1 teaspoon chia seeds

- Sweetener or sugar as needed

- Splash of vanilla

- Pinch of salt

- A pinch ground cinnamon

- 1 ½ cups water

Directions:
1. In a medium bowl, thoroughly mix all the ingredients. Add the bowl mixture to a pint size jar and cover with an aluminum foil.
2. In the pot, slowly pour the water. Take the trivet and arrange inside it; place the jar over it.
3. Close the lid and lock. Ensure that you have sealed the valve to avoid leakage.
4. Press "Manual" mode and set timer for 6 minutes. It will take a few minutes for the pot to build inside pressure and start cooking.
5. After the timer reads zero, press "Cancel" and naturally release pressure. It takes about 8-10 minutes to release pressure naturally.
6. Carefully remove the lid and take out the jar. Mix in the oatmeal; serve warm!

Cinnamon Spice Vegetable Oatmeal

Prep Time: 8-10 min.
Cooking Time: 3 hours
Number of Servings: 4
Ingredients:
- 2 teaspoons vanilla extract

- 1/8 teaspoon nutmeg, ground

- 1 small zucchini, peeled, grated

- ½ cup pecans, chopped

- 1/8 teaspoon cloves, ground

- 3/4 teaspoon cinnamon

- 1 large peeled carrot, grated

- 1 cup steel cut oats

- 3 cups almond milk or soy milk (vanilla flavored)

- 4 tablespoons maple syrup

Directions:
1. Take your Instant Pot and place it on a clean kitchen platform. Turn it on after plugging it into a power socket.
2. Open the lid from the top and put it aside; start adding the mentioned ingredients inside and gently stir them.
3. Close the lid and lock. Ensure that you have sealed the valve to avoid leakage.

4. Press "Slow Cook" mode and set the timer to 3 hours. It will take a few minutes for the pot to build inside pressure and start cooking.
5. After the timer reads zero, press "Cancel" and quick release pressure.
6. Carefully remove the lid and serve warm!

Chai Spiced Rice Pudding

Prep Time: 5 min.
Cooking Time: 15 min.
Number of Servings: 3-4
Ingredients:
- 6 Medjool dates, sliced
- 2 tablespoons brown sugar
- 1 teaspoon cinnamon powder
- 1 cup short grain rice
- 1 teaspoon ginger powder
- 1 cup almond milk, unsweetened
- 1 ½ cups water
- 1 cup coconut milk, unsweetened
- ¼ teaspoon nutmeg
- 5 cardamom pods
- 1 teaspoon vanilla extract
- Pinch of salt

To garnish: Chopped dates, nuts, pineapple, papaya or banana
Directions:
1. Take your Instant Pot and place it on a clean kitchen platform. Turn it on after plugging it into a power socket.
2. Open the lid from the top and put it aside; start adding the mentioned ingredients inside and gently stir them. Do not add the garnishes.
3. Close the lid and lock. Ensure that you have sealed the valve to avoid leakage.
4. Press "Manual" mode and set timer for 10 minutes. It will take a few minutes for the pot to build inside pressure and start cooking.
5. After the timer reads zero, press "Cancel" and naturally release pressure. It takes about 8-10 minutes to naturally release pressure.
6. Carefully remove the lid and mix the rice. Top with the garnishes and serve warm!

Instant Hot Chocolate

Prep Time: 5 min.
Cooking Time: 2 hours
Number of Servings: 8
Ingredients:
- 2/3 cup sugar or to taste

- 8 cups coconut or almond milk, unsweetened

- 1/8 teaspoon cinnamon, ground

- A pinch salt

- 2/3 cup cocoa powder

- For serving: coconut whipped cream (optional)

Directions:
1. Take your Instant Pot and place it on a clean kitchen platform. Turn it on after plugging it into a power socket.
2. Open the lid from the top and put it aside; start adding the mentioned ingredients inside and gently stir them.
3. Close the lid and lock. Ensure that you have sealed the valve to avoid leakage.
4. Press "Slow cook" mode and set the timer to 2 hours. It will take a few minutes for the pot to build inside pressure and start cooking.
5. After the timer reads zero, press "Cancel" and naturally release pressure. It takes about 8-10 minutes to naturally release pressure.
6. Carefully remove the lid.
7. Pour the hot chocolate into mugs. Add the coconut cream on top (optional).
8. Serve warm!

Buckwheat Walnut Porridge

Prep Time: 5 min.
Cooking Time: 6 min.
Number of Servings: 4-5
Ingredients:
- 2 tablespoons almonds

- 2 tablespoons walnuts

- 1 1/2 cups rice milk

- 2 tablespoons raisins

- 1/2 cup buckwheat groats, gently rinsed

- 1 banana, sliced

- 1/4 teaspoon vanilla

- 1/2 teaspoon cinnamon

Directions:
1. Take your Instant Pot and place it on a clean kitchen platform. Turn it on after plugging it into a power socket.
2. Open the lid from the top and put it aside; start adding the mentioned ingredients inside and gently stir them. Do not add the nuts.
3. Close the lid and lock. Ensure that you have sealed the valve to avoid leakage.

4. Press "Manual" mode and set timer for 6 minutes. It will take a few minutes for the pot to build inside pressure and start cooking.
5. After the timer reads zero, press "Cancel" and naturally release pressure. It takes about 8-10 minutes to naturally release pressure.
6. Carefully remove the lid.
7. Top with almonds and walnuts; serve warm!

Instant Spiced Pilaf

Prep Time: 5-10 min.
Cooking Time: 5 min.
Number of Servings: 3
Ingredients:
- 1 stick cinnamon

- 1 cup millet, decorticated

- 2 pods cardamom

- 1 large onion, sliced

- 2 teaspoons whole cumin

- 1 ½ cups water

- 1 tablespoon oil

- 1 bay leaf

- Salt as needed

Directions:
1. Take your Instant Pot and place it on a clean kitchen platform. Turn it on after plugging it into a power socket.
2. Put the pot on "Saute" mode. In the pot, add the oil and whole spices; cook until the cumin crackles.
3. Add the onions and cook for 2-3 minutes.
4. Turn off the pot and add the millet; cook for a few more minutes until the millet is well coated. Pour water and salt.
5. Close the lid and lock. Ensure that you have sealed the valve to avoid leakage.
6. Press "Manual" mode and set timer for 1 minutes. It will take a few minutes for the pot to build inside pressure and start cooking.
7. After the timer reads zero, press "Cancel" and naturally release pressure. It takes about 8-10 minutes to naturally release pressure.
8. Carefully remove the lid; fluff with the fork and serve warm!

Instant Fruit Cobbler

Prep Time: 5min.
Cooking Time: 15 min.
Number of Servings: 2
Ingredients:

- 3 tablespoons coconut oil
- ½ teaspoon cinnamon
- 1 apple, sliced
- 1 plum, sliced
- 1 pear, sliced
- ¼ cup shredded unsweetened coconut
- ½ cup pecans, chopped

Directions:

1. Take Instant Pot and carefully arrange it over a clean, dry kitchen platform. Turn on the appliance.
2. In the cooking pot area, add the mentioned ingredients except for coconut and pecans. Stir the ingredients gently.
3. Close the pot lid and seal the valve to avoid any leakage. Find and press "Steam" cooking setting and set cooking time to 10 minutes.
4. Allow the recipe ingredients to cook for the set time and after that, the timer reads "zero".
5. Press "Cancel" and press "NPR" setting for natural pressure release. It takes 8-10 times for all inside pressure to release.
6. Open the pot and take out the cooked ingredients in a bowl; keep the cooking liquid inside the pot.
7. Add the pecans and coconut with the cooking liquid; mix well. Using the sauté setting, cook for about five minutes while occasionally stirring until turn browned.
8. Add in serving plates and sprinkle the nut mixture over the fruit mixture. Enjoy!

Nutty Banana Oats

Prep Time: 5min.
Cooking Time: 3 min.
Number of Servings: 2
Ingredients:

- 2 sliced bananas
- 3 cups water
- 1 teaspoon ground cinnamon
- 1 cup oats, steel cut
- Pinch of ground nutmeg
- Maple syrup, as needed
- ½ cup chopped nuts (almonds, walnuts, pecans, etc.)

Directions:

1. Take Instant Pot and carefully arrange it over a clean, dry kitchen platform. Turn on the appliance.

2. In the cooking pot area, add the water, oats, cinnamon, ginger, and half of the sliced banana. Stir the ingredients gently.
3. Close the pot lid and seal the valve to avoid any leakage. Find and press "Manual" cooking setting and set cooking time to 3 minutes.
4. Allow the recipe ingredients to cook for the set time and after that, the timer reads "zero".
5. Press "Cancel" and press "NPR" setting for natural pressure release. It takes 8-10 times for all inside pressure to release.
6. Open the pot and arrange the cooked recipe in serving plates. Top with leftover banana and nuts, and enjoy the vegan recipe!

Black Bean Quinoa

Prep Time: 8-10min.
Cooking Time: 20 min.
Number of Servings: 4
Ingredients:
- 1/2 teaspoon salt
- 1 bell pepper, diced
- 1 teaspoon ground cumin
- 1 teaspoon olive oil, extra-virgin
- 1 cup water
- 1/2 red onion, diced
- 1 cup quinoa, rinse and drain
- 1 cup prepared salsa
- 1 1/2 cups black beans, cooked

Directions:
1. Take Instant Pot and carefully arrange it over a clean, dry kitchen platform. Turn on the appliance.
2. Find and press "Sauté" cooking function.
3. In the cooking pot area; add the oil, peppers, and onions in the pot. Cook for 6-8 minutes to cook well and soften.
4. Mix in the cumin and salt; cook for 1 more minute. Mix in the salsa, bean, quinoa, and water.
5. Close the pot lid and seal the valve to avoid any leakage. Find and press "Manual" cooking setting and set cooking time to 12 minutes.
6. Allow the recipe ingredients to cook for the set time and after that, the timer reads "zero".
7. Press "Cancel" and press "NPR" setting for natural pressure release. It takes 8-10 times for all inside pressure to release.
8. Open the pot; fluff the quinoa and arrange the cooked recipe in serving plates.
9. Top with some of your favorite toppings such as salsa, diced onions, lettuce, sliced avocado, etc. Enjoy the vegan recipe!

Pumpkin Spiced Espresso

Prep Time: 5 min.
Cooking Time: 3 hours min.
Number of Servings: 6
Ingredients:

- 4 cups almond milk

- 5 tablespoons maple syrup

- 2 teaspoons vanilla extract

- 4 cups espresso coffee

- 1/3 cup pumpkin puree

- 2 1/2 teaspoon pumpkin pie spice

Directions:
1. Take your Instant Pot and place it on a clean kitchen platform. Turn it on after plugging it into a power socket.
2. Open the lid from the top and put it aside; start adding the mentioned ingredients inside and gently stir them.
3. Close the lid and lock. Ensure that you have sealed the valve to avoid leakage.
4. Press "Slow cook" mode and set the timer to 2 hours 30 minutes to 3 hours. It will take a few minutes for the pot to build inside pressure and start cooking.
5. After the timer reads zero, press "Cancel" and naturally release pressure. It takes about 8-10 minutes to naturally release pressure.
6. Carefully remove the lid and serve warm!

Raisin Veggie Oats

Prep Time: 10-15 min.
Cooking Time: 10 min.
Number of Servings: 5-6
Ingredients:

- 1 tablespoon coconut butter
- 3 tablespoons maple syrup
- 1 teaspoon pumpkin pie spice
- 2 teaspoons cinnamon
- 1 cup grated carrots
- 1 cup steel cut oats
- 4 cups water
- A pinch of salt
- ¼ cup chia seeds
- ¾ cup raisins

Directions:

1. Take your Instant Pot and place into a clean kitchen platform. Turn it on after plugging it into a power socket.
2. Open the lid from the top and put it aside; start adding the coconut butter, water, cinnamon, carrots, maple syrup, salt and pie spice. Gently stir them.
3. Close the lid and lock. Ensure that you have sealed the valve to avoid leakage.
4. Press "Manual" mode and set timer for 10 minutes. It will take a few minutes for the pot to build inside pressure and start cooking.
5. After the timer reads zero, press "Cancel" and naturally release pressure. It takes about 8-10 minutes to naturally release pressure.
6. Carefully remove the lid and add the oats, chia seeds, and raisins.
7. Cover pot and place aside for 10 minutes. Serve warm!

Healthy Apple Butter

Prep Time: 8-10 min.
Cooking Time: 1 hour 15 min.
Number of Servings: As Needed
Ingredients:

- 2 ½ cups palm sugar
- ¼ teaspoon cloves, ground
- ½ cup cider vinegar
- 16 cored apples, sliced
- 3 teaspoons cinnamon

Directions:

1. Take your Instant Pot and place it on a clean kitchen platform. Turn it on after plugging it into a power socket.
2. Open the lid from the top and put it aside; add the apples in the pot.
3. Close the lid and lock. Ensure that you have sealed the valve to avoid leakage.
4. Press "Manual" mode and set timer for 55-60 minutes. It will take a few minutes for the pot to build inside pressure and start cooking.
5. After the timer reads zero, press "Cancel" and quick release pressure.
6. Carefully remove the lid and transfer the apples to your food processor. Blend to make a smooth puree.
7. Return apples to the pot, mix the palm sugar, vinegar, cinnamon, and cloves, stir well, cover the pot.
8. Cook on "Manual" setting for 15 minutes.
9. Transfer the mixture to jars and serve with some toasted bread.

Instant Quinoa Corn

Prep Time: 5 min.
Cooking Time: 8-10 min.
Number of Servings: 4
Ingredients:

- 15 ounces whole corn kernels, rinsed

- ¼ cup chives, minced

- 1 ½ cups mushroom

- 2 tablespoons olive oil

- 1 cup quinoa, un-rinsed

- 1 cup water

- 1 ½ cups vegetable broth

- A pinch white pepper and salt

Directions:
1. Take your Instant Pot and place it on a clean kitchen platform. Turn it on after plugging it into a power socket.
2. Put the pot on "Saute" mode. In the pot, add the oil and quinoa; cook until the quinoa starts releasing the aroma.
3. Add in remaining ingredients in the pot (except chives).
4. Close the lid and lock. Ensure that you have sealed the valve to avoid leakage.
5. Press "Manual" mode and set timer for 1 minutes. It will take a few minutes for the pot to build inside pressure and start cooking.
6. After the timer reads zero, press "Cancel" and naturally release pressure. It takes about 8-10 minutes to naturally release pressure.
7. Carefully remove the lid. Garnish with the chives and serve!

Wholesome Peach Oats

Prep Time: 5 min.
Cooking Time: 10 min.
Number of Servings: 2
Ingredients:
- 2 medium size peaches, diced

- 1 cup oats

- 2 cups water

- 1 cup coconut milk

Directions:
1. Take your Instant Pot and place it on a clean kitchen platform. Turn it on after plugging it into a power socket.
2. Open the lid from the top and put it aside; start adding the mentioned ingredients inside. Thoroughly mix them.
3. Close the lid and lock. Ensure that you have sealed the valve to avoid leakage.
4. Press "Manual" mode and set timer for 10 minutes. It will take a few minutes for the pot to build inside pressure and start cooking.

5. After the timer reads zero, press "Cancel" and naturally release pressure. It takes about 8-10 minutes to naturally release pressure.
6. Carefully remove the lid. Sweeten as desired and serve warm!

Vanilla Walnut Oats

Prep Time: 5 min.
Cooking Time: 3 min.
Number of Servings: 4
Ingredients:
- 1 cup steel-cut oats
- ½ vanilla bean
- 1 cinnamon stick
- 1 cup unsweetened, almond or soy milk
- 2 cup water
- Pinch of salt
- ¼ cup raisins or walnut
- 1 teaspoon ground cinnamon
- ½ tablespoon maple syrup
- ¼ cup toasted walnuts

Directions:
1. Take Instant Pot and carefully arrange it over a clean, dry kitchen platform. Turn on the appliance.
2. In the cooking pot area, add the oats, salt, milk, water, cinnamon stick, and ¼ cup of raisins. Stir the ingredients gently.
3. Close the pot lid and seal the valve to avoid any leakage. Find and press "Manual" cooking setting and set cooking time to 3 minutes.
4. Allow the recipe ingredients to cook for the set time and after that, the timer reads "zero".
5. Press "Cancel" and press "NPR" setting for natural pressure release. It takes 8-10 times for all inside pressure to release.
6. Open the pot and discard the cinnamon stick and vanilla bean. Set aside.
7. Stir well, and mix in the walnuts, cinnamon, and rest of the raisins.
8. Add sweetener and serve warm!

Potato Berry Breakfast

Prep Time: 10min.
Cooking Time: 20-30 min.
Number of Servings: 4
Ingredients:
- 2 medium potatoes, cubed
- 2 medium onions, sliced
- 2 cups white wheat berries, soaked overnight
- 5 stalks celery, sliced
- 3 smashed garlic cloves (optional)

- 1 tbs. vegan butter
- 1 tbs. salt
- 2 cups sliced carrots
- 6 1/2 cups water
- 1 teaspoon seasoning of your choice
- 1/8 teaspoon thyme

Directions:
1.Take Instant Pot and carefully arrange it over a clean, dry kitchen platform. Turn on the appliance.
2.Find and press "Sauté" cooking function.
3.In the cooking pot area; add the butter, garlic, celery, and onions in the pot. Cook for 2 minutes to cook well and soften.
4.Transfer the mixture in separate bowl; set aside.
5.In the cooking pot area, add the berries, potatoes, and carrots. Stir the ingredients gently.
6.Close the pot lid and seal the valve to avoid any leakage. Find and press "Multigrain" cooking setting. It will set cooking time automatically.
7.Allow the recipe ingredients to cook for the set time, and after that, the timer reads "zero".
8.Press "Cancel" and press "NPR" setting for natural pressure release. It takes 8-10 times for all inside pressure to release.
9.Open the pot and add the sautéed mixture.
10.Add the seasoning, thyme, and salt. Simmer the mixture for 25-30 minutes and serve warm!

Soy Milk Apple Quinoa

Prep Time: 10min.
Cooking Time: 1 min.
Number of Servings: 4
Ingredients:

- ¼ cup brown sugar

- ¼ teaspoon cinnamon powder

- ½ cup apple, peeled & make slices of ½-inch thick

- ½ cup apple, peeled &diced

- ½ cup soy milk

- 2 cups water

- 1 cup brown or red quinoa, rinsed & drained

- ¼ teaspoon squeezed lemon juice

Directions:
1. In a bowl of medium size, add the apples and top with the lemon juice. Set aside and drain the liquid.
2. Take Instant Pot and carefully arrange it over a clean, dry kitchen platform. Turn on the appliance.
3. In the cooking pot area, add the ingredients except for garnishes and milk. Stir the ingredients gently.

4. Close the pot lid and seal the valve to avoid any leakage. Find and press "Manual" cooking setting and set cooking time to 1 minutes.
5. Allow the recipe ingredients to cook for the set time and after that, the timer reads "zero".
6. Press "Cancel" and press "NPR" setting for natural pressure release. It takes 8-10 times for all inside pressure to release.
7. Open the pot and pour in the milk and season as needed.
8. Add equal portions of quinoa into serving bowls. Garnish with a few slices of apples. Serve warm!

Sausage Egg Pie

Prep Time: 10-15 min.
Cooking Time: 30 min.
Number of Servings: 7-8
Ingredients:

- ½ cup diced onion
- 3 teaspoons olive oil
- ¼ cup grated parmesan cheese
- 1 pound mild sausage
- 2 cups ricotta cheese
- 1 garlic clove, minced
- 1 cup shredded mozzarella cheese
- 3 eggs
- Pepper and salt, as needed
- 8 cups chopped Swiss chard
- 2 cups water

Directions:
1. Take your Instant Pot; open the top lid. Plug it and turn it on.
2. Press "SAUTÉ" setting and the pot will start heating up.
3. In the cooking pot area, add the oil, garlic, and onions. Cook until starts becoming translucent and softened for 3 minutes. Stir in between.
4. Add chard and cook for 2 minutes, or until it becomes wilted.
5. Season with some pepper and salt and transfer to a plate.
6. Beat the eggs in a mixing bowl and stir in the cheeses.
7. Roll out the sausage and press it firmly into the bottom of a greased baking dish. Top with the chard mix.
8. Add the cheesy egg mixture over it. Cover the dish with foil.
9. Pour the water and place steamer basket/trivet inside the pot; arrange the baking dish over the basket/trivet.
10. Close the top lid and seal its valve.
11. Press "MANUAL" setting. Adjust cooking time to 25 minutes.
12. Allow the recipe to cook for the set cooking time.
13. After the set cooking time ends, press "CANCEL" and then press "NPR (Natural Pressure Release)".
14. Instant Pot will slowly and naturally release the pressure.
15. Open the top lid, add the cooked recipe mix in serving plates.

16. Serve and enjoy!

Creamy Kale Eggs

Prep Time: 5-8 min.
Cooking Time: 5 min.
Number of Servings: 4
Ingredients:

- 3 tablespoons heavy cream
- 4 hardboiled eggs
- ¼ teaspoon pepper
- ¼ teaspoon salt
- 1 ½ cups water
- 4 kale leaves
- 4 prosciutto slices

Directions:
1. Peel the eggs and wrap them in kale. Wrap the eggs with prosciutto and sprinkle with pepper and salt.
2. Pour the water and place steamer basket/trivet inside the pot; arrange the eggs over the basket/trivet.
3. Press "MANUAL" setting. Adjust cooking time to 5 minutes.
4. Allow the recipe to cook for the set cooking time.
5. After the set cooking time ends, press "CANCEL" and then press "QPR (Quick Pressure Release)".
6. Instant Pot will quickly release the pressure.
7. Open the top lid.
8. Serve the eggs and enjoy!

Oats Apple Breakfast Cake

Prep Time: 8-10 min.
Cooking Time: 30 min.
Number of Servings: 7-8
Ingredients:
- 1 cup oats
- 2 cups flour, whole wheat or all purpose
- ½ cup stevia granular or raw honey
- ¼ tsp. salt
- 2 cups, diced apples
- ½ cup applesauce
- ½ cup almond milk
- 1 tsp. vanilla extract
- ¼ tsp. baking soda
- 2 tsps. cinnamon

Directions:

1. In a mixing bowl (heat-proof), mix all the mentioned ingredients.
2. Take an Instant Pot; open the top lid.
3. Pour 1 cup water and place steamer basket/trivet inside the cooking pot.
4. Arrange the bowl over the basket/trivet.
5. Close the top lid and make sure the valve is sealed.
6. Press "MANUAL" cooking function. Adjust cooking time to 20-25 minutes.
7. Allow pressure to build and cook the ingredients for the set time.
8. After the set cooking time ends, press "CANCEL" and then press "NPR". Instant Pot will slowly and naturally release the pressure for 8-10 minutes.
9. Open the top lid, add the cooked mixture in serving plates.
10. Serve warm.

Cheese Tomato Omelet

Prep Time: 8-10 min.
Cooking Time: 9 min.
Number of Servings: 5-6
Ingredients:

- 4 tablespoons tomato paste
- 1 teaspoon salt
- 5 eggs
- ½ cup milk
- 1 tablespoon turmeric
- ½ cup cilantro, minced
- 1 tablespoon butter
- 4 ounces Parmesan cheese, shredded

Directions:

1. Whisk the eggs with the milk and tomato paste in the mixing bowl. Mix in the salt and turmeric.
2. Mix in the cheese and cilantro.
3. Take an Instant Pot; open the top lid.
4. Press "SAUTÉ" cooking function.
5. In the cooking pot area, add the butter and melt it.
6. Add in the egg mixture and spread it to make a round shape.
7. Close the top lid and make sure the valve is sealed.
8. Press "STEAM" cooking function. Adjust cooking time to 8 minutes.
9. Allow pressure to build and cook the ingredients for the set time.
10. After the set cooking time ends, press "CANCEL" and then press "QPR". Instant Pot will quickly release pressure.
11. Open the top lid, add the cooked mixture in serving plates.
12. Serve warm.

Ham Egg Frittata

Prep Time: 8-10 min.
Cooking Time: 10 min.
Number of Servings: 4-6
Ingredients:

- 8 ounces ham, chopped
- 1 teaspoon white pepper
- 1 tablespoon lemon zest
- 1 teaspoon olive oil
- 1 teaspoon salt
- ½ teaspoon paprika
- ½ cup parsley, chopped
- 7 eggs
- ½ cup milk
- 1 tomato, chopped

Directions:

1. Beat the eggs in the mixing bowl. Mix in the milk, salt, paprika, white pepper, and lemon zest.
2. Blend the mix in a blender. Mix in the ham and tomatoes.
3. Take an Instant Pot; open the top lid.
4. Coat the pot using cooking oil. Add the ham mix in the cooking pot. Top with the parsley.
5. Close the top lid and make sure the valve is sealed.
6. Press "STEAM" cooking function. Adjust cooking time to 10 minutes.
7. Allow pressure to build and cook the ingredients for the set time.
8. After the set cooking time ends, press "CANCEL" and then press "QPR". Instant Pot will quickly release pressure.
9. Open the top lid, add the cooked mixture in serving plates.
10. Serve warm.

Spinach Omelet Morning

Prep Time: 8-10 min.
Cooking Time: 6 min.
Number of Servings: 4-5
Ingredients:

- ½ cup milk
- 1 teaspoon salt
- 1 tablespoon olive oil
- 2 cups spinach, chopped
- 8 eggs
- 1 teaspoon ground black pepper
- 4 ounces Parmesan cheese

Directions:

1. Add the eggs to a mixing bowl and whisk them. Mix in the spinach.
2. Mix in the milk, salt, olive oil, and black pepper. Stir the mixture well.
3. Take an Instant Pot; open the top lid.

4. Coat the pot using cooking oil. Add the mix in the cooking pot.
5. Close the top lid and make sure the valve is sealed.
6. Press "STEAM" cooking function. Adjust cooking time to 6 minutes.
7. Allow pressure to build and cook the ingredients for the set time.
8. After the set cooking time ends, press "CANCEL" and then press "QPR". Instant Pot will quickly release pressure.
9. Open the top lid, add the cooked mixture in serving plates.
10. Serve warm; top with the cheese.

Spiced Ham Eggs

Prep Time: 8-10 min.
Cooking Time: 4 min.
Number of Servings: 3
Ingredients:
- 1 teaspoon salt
- 3 eggs, beaten
- 6 ounces ham, cooked
- ½ teaspoon ground white pepper
- 1 teaspoon paprika
- ¼ teaspoon ground ginger
- 2 tablespoons chives

Directions:
1. Take three small ramekins; coat them with oil spray.
2. Add the eggs to the ramekins.
3. Sprinkle the salt, black pepper, and paprika.
4. Close the top lid and make sure the valve is sealed.
5. Press "STEAM" cooking function. Adjust cooking time to 4 minutes.
6. Allow pressure to build and cook the ingredients for the set time.
7. After the set cooking time ends, press "CANCEL" and then press "QPR". Instant Pot will quickly release pressure.
8. Open the top lid, add the ramekins in serving plates.
9. Chop the ham and chives; combine them.
10. Mix in the ground ginger.
11. Serve the ramekins with the ham mix on top.

Bacon Brussels Sprouts

Prep Time: 8-10 min.
Cooking Time: 12-15 min.
Number of Servings: 4
Ingredients:
- 4 bacon slices, center cut, make small pieces
- 3 shallots, finely diced
- 3 garlic cloves, minced

- 1 pound Brussels sprouts, make halves
- ½ cup water

Directions:
1. Take an Instant Pot; open the top lid.
2. Press "SAUTÉ" cooking function.
3. Coat the pot with some olive oil. In the cooking pot area, add the bacon. Cook until turn crisp for 5-6 minutes.
4. Add in the remaining ingredients; combine well.
5. Close the top lid and make sure the valve is sealed.
6. Press "MANUAL" cooking function. Adjust cooking time to 3-5 minutes.
7. Allow pressure to build and cook the ingredients for the set time.
8. After the set cooking time ends, press "CANCEL" and then press "QPR". Instant Pot will quickly release pressure.
9. Open the top lid, add the cooked mixture in serving plates.
10. Serve warm.

Breakfast Fruit Bowl

Prep Time: 8-10 min.
Cooking Time: 10 min.
Number of Servings: 2
Ingredients:
- 1 pear, cored and chopped
- 3 tablespoons coconut oil
- 2 tablespoons honey
- 1 plum, stone removed and chopped
- 1 apple, cored and chopped
- ½ teaspoon cinnamon
- 2 tablespoons sunflower seeds, roasted
- ¼ cup pecans, chopped
- ¼ cup coconut, shredded and unsweetened

Directions:
1. Take an Instant Pot; open the top lid.
2. Add the plum with apple, pear, oil, honey, and cinnamon in the cooking pot. Using a spatula, gently stir to combine well.
3. Close the top lid and make sure the valve is sealed.
4. Press "STEAM" cooking function. Adjust cooking time to 10 minutes.
5. Allow pressure to build and cook the ingredients for the set time.
6. After the set cooking time ends, press "CANCEL" and then press "QPR". Instant Pot will quickly release pressure.
7. Open the top lid, set aside the mix.
8. In the pot, mix in the pecans, sunflower seeds, and coconut. Cook on "SAUTE" mode for 4-5 minutes.
9. Add the mix over the fruit mix. Serve warm.

Bread Roll Egg Morning

Prep Time: 8-10 min.
Cooking Time: 10 min.
Number of Servings: 4-6
Ingredients:
- 7 ounces cheddar cheese, grated
- 1 teaspoon salt
- ½ teaspoon red chili flakes
- 3 large bread rolls
- 4 eggs
- ½ teaspoon sour cream
- 1 tablespoon butter

Directions:
1. Cut the rolls in half. Hollow out the center of each half partially.
2. In a mixing bowl, mix the salt, pepper flakes, and sour cream. Beat the eggs.
3. Add the eggs in bread halves.
4. Take an Instant Pot; open the top lid.
5. Grease the pot with butter and add the bread halves. Top with the spice mix and cheese.
6. Close the top lid and make sure the valve is sealed.
7. Press "STEAM" cooking function. Adjust cooking time to 10 minutes.
8. Allow pressure to build and cook the ingredients for the set time.
9. After the set cooking time ends, press "CANCEL" and then press "QPR". Instant Pot will quickly release pressure.
10. Open the top lid, add the cooked mixture in serving plates.
11. Serve warm.

Cinnamon Banana Smoothie

Prep Time: 8-10 min.
Cooking Time: 0 min.
Number of Servings: 2
Ingredients:
- 1 cup low-fat milk
- ½ cup non-fat Greek yogurt
- ¼ teaspoon cinnamon
- 2 dates, pitted, chopped
- 1 ripe banana, peeled, sliced
- 1 tablespoon honey
- Ice cubes as needed

Directions:
1. Add the ingredients one by one in your food processor or blender.
2. Close the lid and blend to make a smooth mix.
3. Add the prepare smoothie in tall serving glasses. Serve chilled.

Watermelon Chia Smoothie

Prep Time: 8-10 min.
Cooking Time: 0 min.
Number of Servings: 2
Ingredients:
- 2 slices lemon to garnish
- 1/3 cup water
- 3 cups watermelon cubes, deseeded
- 2 tablespoons chia seeds
- 2 sprigs mint
- Ice cubes as needed

Directions:
1. Add the ingredients one by one in your food processor or blender.
2. Close the lid and blend to make a smooth mix.
3. Add the prepare smoothie in tall serving glasses.
4. Serve chilled. Garnish with mint leaves and a lemon slice.

Cucumber Pineapple Smoothie

Prep Time: 8-10 min.
Cooking Time: 0 min.
Number of Servings: 2
Ingredients:
- 4 cups pineapple cubes, frozen
- 2 bunches flat leaf parsley
- 1 English cucumber, chopped
- 1 ½ cups coconut water
- Juice for 2-3 small lemons
- 8-10 drops stevia

Directions:
1. Add the ingredients one by one in your food processor or blender.
2. Close the lid and blend to make a smooth mix.
3. Add the prepare smoothie in tall serving glasses. Serve chilled.

Spinach Avocado Breakfast Chicken

Prep Time: 8-10 min.
Cooking Time: 20 min.
Number of Servings: 3
Ingredients:
- 1 large leek, finely chopped
- 1 cup avocado chunks
- 1 small onion, finely chopped
- 7 ounce boneless and skinless chicken breast, make bite-sized pieces
- 1 cup fresh spinach, chopped

- 3 tablespoons butter
- 1 teaspoon salt
- 1 garlic clove, crushed
- 1 cup cottage cheese
- ½ teaspoon dried rosemary

Directions:
1. Take your Instant Pot; open the top lid. Plug it and turn it on.
2. Press "SAUTÉ" setting and the pot will start heating up.
3. In the cooking pot area, add the butter, salt, and meat. Stir and cook for 12-15 minutes until evenly brown from all sides.
4. Add the avocado and continue to cook for 5 minutes. If needed, add more butter.
5. Add the onions, garlic, and chopped leeks. Give it a good stir and cook to soften.
6. Add the spinach and sprinkle with rosemary.
7. Press "Cancel" button. Let it sit for 10 minutes and add the cooked recipe mix in serving plates.
8. Stir in the cottage cheese and serve immediately.

Instant Pork & Eggs

Prep Time: 20-25 min.
Cooking Time: 8 hours
Number of Servings: 5-6
Ingredients:
- 1 yellow onion, diced
- 1 pound pork sausage, broken up
- 2 cups cauliflower, chopped finely
- 2 teaspoons dried basil
- 1 tablespoon garlic powder
- 8 eggs, whisked
- Pepper and salt as needed

Directions:
1. Arrange your Instant Pot over a dry, clean platform. Plug it in power socket and turn it on.
2. Open the lid from the top and put it aside. Grease the sides and the bottom with cooking spray. Evenly spread the pork sausage on bottom of the pot.
3. Spread chopped onions evenly on top of sausage.
4. Then top with the finely chopped cauliflower.
5. In a bowl of medium size, whisk the eggs. Mix in the pepper, garlic powder and salt. Pour the mixture into Instant Pot.
6. Close the lid and lock. Ensure that you have sealed the valve to avoid leakage.
7. Press "Slow cook" mode from available cooking settings and set cooking time to 8 hours. Instant Pot will start cooking the ingredients after a few minutes.
8. After the timer reads zero, press "Cancel" and quick release pressure.
9. Carefully remove the lid and serve the prepared keto dish warm!

Sausage Cheddar Breakfast

Prep Time: 10-15 min.
Cooking Time: 5 hours
Number of Servings: 5-6
Ingredients:
- ¾ cup whipping cream
- 10 medium eggs
- 1 medium head broccoli, chopped
- 1 cup Cheddar cheese, shredded
- ¼ teaspoon pepper
- ½ teaspoon salt
- 2 cloves garlic, minced
- 1 (12 ounces) pack sausage Links, cooked and sliced

Directions:
1. Arrange your Instant Pot over a dry, clean platform. Plug it in power socket and turn it on. Grease the sides and bottom of the inner pot with a cooking spray.
2. Add the broccoli, sausage, and cheese; combine well.
3. In a bowl, whisk the pepper, salt, garlic, whipping cream, and eggs. Pour the mixture into Instant Pot.
4. Close the lid and lock. Ensure that you have sealed the valve to avoid leakage.
5. Press "Slow cook" mode from available cooking settings and set cooking time to 5 hours. Instant Pot will start cooking the ingredients after a few minutes.
6. After the timer reads zero, press "Cancel" and quick release pressure.
7. Carefully remove the lid and serve the prepared keto dish warm! The casserole edges will become brown.

Creamy Eggs & Bacon

Prep Time: 5-8 min.
Cooking Time: 20 min.
Number of Servings: 6
Ingredients:
- 1 cup cheddar cheese
- 1 cup kale leaves, chopped
- 6 eggs
- ½ cup heavy cream
- 1 cup turkey bacon (cooked)
- 1 cup water
- ⅛ tsp. sea salt
- 1 onion chopped

- ⅛ tsp. pepper

- 1 tsp. Herbes de Provence

Directions:
1. In a bowl, thoroughly mix the heavy cream and the eggs. Add leftover ingredients and combine well.
2. Add the mixture to a heatproof dish.
3. Arrange your Instant Pot over a dry, clean platform. Plug it in power socket and turn it on.
4. Slowly pour the water into the pot order to avoid spilling out. Take the trivet and arrange in the pot; place dish over the trivet.
5. Close the lid and lock. Ensure that you have sealed the valve to avoid leakage.
6. Press "Manual" mode from available cooking settings and set cooking time to 20 minutes. Instant Pot will start cooking the ingredients after a few minutes.
7. After the timer reads zero, press "Cancel" and quick release pressure.
8. Carefully remove the lid and serve the prepared keto dish warm!

Chicken Herbal Breakfast

Prep Time: 8-10 min.
Cooking Time: 20 min.
Number of Servings: 5
Ingredients:
- 2 teaspoons basil

- ¼ cup heavy cream

- 13 ounce chicken fillet, strips

- 1 teaspoon salt

- 1 teaspoon cilantro

- 2 teaspoons oregano

- 1 teaspoon paprika

- 2 tablespoons melted butter

Directions:
1. In a bowl (medium or large size), thoroughly mix the salt, paprika, cilantro, oregano, and basil.
2. Top the chicken strips with the spices and cream; mix well.
3. Arrange your Instant Pot over a dry, clean platform. Plug it in power socket and turn it on.
4. Now press "Saute" mode from available options. In the cooking area, add the butter and strips; cook for 2-3 minutes to soften the added ingredients.
5. Close the lid and lock. Ensure that you have sealed the valve to avoid leakage.
6. Press "Manual" mode from available cooking settings and set cooking time to 20 minutes. Instant Pot will start cooking the ingredients after a few minutes.
7. After the timer reads zero, press "Cancel" and quick release pressure.

8. Carefully remove the lid and serve the prepared keto dish warm!

Spinach Egg Breakfast Ramekins

Prep Time: 5-8 min.
Cooking Time: 8 min.
Number of Servings: 4
Ingredients:
- 1 cup chopped baby spinach
- 1 1/4 cup crumbled feta cheese
- 6 eggs
- ½ cup shredded mozzarella cheese
- 1 teaspoon pepper
- ¼ teaspoon garlic powder
- 1 tomato, chopped
- ½ teaspoon salt
- 1 ½ cups water

Directions:
1. In a mixing bowl, beat the eggs along with the spices. Stir in the tomato and cheeses.
2. Grease 4 ramekins and add the spinach. Pour the egg mixture over.
3. Pour the water and place steamer basket/trivet inside the pot; arrange the ramekins over the basket/trivet.
4. Close the top lid and seal its valve.
5. Press "MANUAL" setting. Adjust cooking time to 8 minutes.
6. Allow the recipe to cook for the set cooking time.
7. After the set cooking time ends, press "CANCEL" and then press "QPR (Quick Pressure Release)".
8. Instant Pot will quickly release the pressure.
9. Open the top lid, add the cooked recipe mix in serving plates.
10. Serve and enjoy!

Classic Buckwheat Porridge

Prep Time: 8-10 min.
Cooking Time: 6 min.
Number of Servings: 2-3
Ingredients:
- 1/2 teaspoon vanilla extract
- 1 banana, peeled and sliced
- 1/4 cup raisins
- 3 cup rice milk
- 1 cup buckwheat groats, rinsed

Directions:
1. Take your 3-Quart Instant Pot; open the top lid. Plug it and turn it on.
2. In the cooking pot area, add the raisins, milk, buckwheat banana, and vanilla. Using a spatula, stir the ingredients.

3. Close the top lid and seal its valve.
4. Press "MANUAL" setting. Adjust cooking time to 6 minutes.
5. Allow the recipe to cook for the set cooking time.
6. After the set cooking time ends, press "CANCEL" and then press "QPR (Quick Pressure Release)".
7. Instant Pot will quickly release the pressure.
8. Open the top lid, add the cooked recipe mix in serving plates.
9. Serve and enjoy!

Classic Hash Brown Frittata

Prep Time: 8-10 min.
Cooking Time: 20 min.
Number of Servings: 2
Ingredients:
- 3 eggs
- 2 ounces hash browns
- 1/2 tablespoon butter, melted
- 2 tablespoons milk
- 2 tablespoons scallions, chopped
- A pinch of pepper and salt
- 1 small garlic clove, minced
- 2 ounces cheddar cheese, grated
- 1/2 teaspoon tomato paste
- 1 1/2 cup water

Directions:
1. In a bowl, mix the milk and tomato paste.
2. In another bowl, mix the eggs, garlic, scallions, salt, pepper and milk mix; combine everything.
3. Spread the browns into a greased baking dish; add the butter and pour eggs mix all over. Top with cheese.
4. Take your 3-Quart Instant Pot; open the top lid. Plug it and turn it on.
5. Pour the water and place steamer basket/trivet inside the pot; arrange the dish over the basket/trivet.
6. Press "MANUAL" setting. Adjust cooking time to 22 minutes.
7. Allow the recipe to cook for the set cooking time.
8. After the set cooking time ends, press "CANCEL" and then press "QPR (Quick Pressure Release)".
9. Instant Pot will quickly release the pressure.
10. Open the top lid, add the cooked recipe mix in serving plates.
11. Serve and enjoy!

Yogurt Oats Morning

Prep Time: 5 min.
Cooking Time: 6 min.

Number of Servings: 2
Ingredients:

- 2/3 cup Greek yogurt
- 2/3 cup blueberries
- 2 tablespoons chia seeds
- 2/3 cup almond milk
- 2/3 cup old-fashioned oats
- 1/2 teaspoon vanilla
- 1 1/2 cup water
- 1 teaspoon sugar
- A pinch of cinnamon powder

Directions:

1. In a heatproof bowl, mix the milk, yogurt, blueberries, oats, chia seeds, sugar, cinnamon, and vanilla.
2. Take your 3-Quart Instant Pot; open the top lid. Plug it and turn it on.
3. Pour the water and place steamer basket/trivet inside the pot; arrange the bowl over the basket/trivet.
4. Close the top lid and seal its valve.
5. Press "MANUAL" setting. Adjust cooking time to 6 minutes.
6. Allow the recipe to cook for the set cooking time.
7. After the set cooking time ends, press "CANCEL" and then press "QPR (Quick Pressure Release)".
8. Instant Pot will quickly release the pressure.
9. Open the top lid, add the cooked recipe mix in serving plates.
10. Serve and enjoy!

Berry Quinoa Morning

Prep Time: 5-8 min.
Cooking Time: 11 min.
Number of Servings: 2
Ingredients:

- 2 cups water
- A pinch of cinnamon powder
- 1 tablespoon maple syrup
- 1 cup quinoa
- 1/4 cup berries of your choice
- 1/4 teaspoon vanilla extract

Directions:

1. Take your 3-Quart Instant Pot; open the top lid. Plug it and turn it on.
2. In the cooking pot area, add the cinnamon, vanilla, quinoa, water and maple syrup. Using a spatula, stir the ingredients.
3. Close the top lid and seal its valve.
4. Press "MANUAL" setting. Adjust cooking time to 1 minutes.
5. Allow the recipe to cook for the set cooking time.

6. After the set cooking time ends, press "CANCEL" and then press "QPR (Quick Pressure Release)".
7. Instant Pot will quickly release the pressure.
8. Open the top lid, fluff the mix and add the cooked recipe mix in serving plates. Top with the berries.
9. Serve and enjoy!

Sweet Potato Hash Morning

Prep Time: 5 min.
Cooking Time: 15 min.
Number of Servings: 2
Ingredients:
- 1 cup bell pepper, chopped
- ¼ cup water
- 1 clove minced garlic
- 1 teaspoon paprika
- ½ teaspoon pepper
- 1 medium potato, diced
- 1 tablespoon oil
- 1 medium sweet potato, diced
- Pinch of cayenne
- ½ teaspoon salt
- 1 teaspoon cumin

Directions:
1. In a bowl, toss all the potatoes and pepper in the spices and oil.
2. Switch on your instant pot after placing it on a clean and dry kitchen platform. Add them to the bottom of the pot and add a half cup of water.
3. Close the pot by closing the top lid. Also, ensure to seal the valve.
4. Press "Manual" cooking function and set cooking time to 10 minutes. It will start cooking after a few minutes. Let the pot mix cook under pressure until the timer reads zero.
5. Turn off and press "Cancel" cooking function. Quick release pressure.
6. Open the pot and cook the mixture on sauté mode to brown the potatoes a little more. Serve warm!

Squash Cinnamon Porridge

Prep Time: 15-20 min.
Cooking Time: 8 min.
Number of Servings: 2
Ingredients:
- ½ cup chicken broth
- 2 tablespoons maple syrup
- 2 tablespoons gelatin
- ½ teaspoon ground cinnamon

- ⅛ teaspoon ground ginger
- ⅛ teaspoon ground cloves
- 1 (1¼-pound) whole squash
- 2 medium apples, cored and chopped roughly
- Pinch of salt

Directions:
1. Switch on the pot after placing it on a clean and dry platform.
2. Open the pot lid and place the squash, apples, broth, and spices in the cooking pot area. Give the ingredients a little stir.
3. Close the pot by closing the top lid. Also, ensure to seal the valve.
4. Press "Manual" cooking function and set cooking time to 8 minutes. It will start cooking after a few minutes. Let the pot mix cook under pressure until the timer reads zero.
5. Press "Cancel" cooking function and press "Natural release (NPR)" setting. It will take 8-10 minutes for natural pressure release.
6. Open the pot. Cool down the mixture and then transfer the squash onto a cutting board.
7. Cut the squash in half lengthwise and discard the seeds.
8. In a blender, add the squash, apple mixture from the pot, maple syrup, gelatin, and salt. Blend on a pulse mode until smooth.
9. Serve warm. Enjoy it with your loved one!

Cherry Apple Risotto

Prep Time: 5-8 min.
Cooking Time: 15 min.
Number of Servings: 2
Ingredients:
- ¾ cup risotto rice
- 1 large apple, peeled, cored, and diced
- 1 ½ cups milk
- ¼ cup brown sugar
- ½ cup apple juice
- ¾ teaspoon cinnamon
- ¼ cup dried cherries
- 1 tablespoon butter

Directions:
1. Switch on the pot after placing it on a clean and dry platform. Press "Saute" cooking function.
2. Open the pot lid; add the butter and rice in the pot; cook for 4 minutes to cook well and turn opaque.
3. Mix in the apples, spices, and brown sugar, stirring well to combine. Pour in the milk and juice and stir.
4. Close the pot by closing the top lid. Also, ensure to seal the valve.
5. Press "Manual" cooking function and set cooking time to 6 minutes. It will start cooking after a few minutes. Let the pot mix cook under pressure until the timer reads zero.
6. Press "Cancel" cooking function and press "Quick release" setting.
7. Open and add the dried cherries and stir well.

8. Transfer the mix into bowls and serve with a splash of milk, sliced almonds and a sprinkle of brown sugar.

Pistachio Quinoa Morning

Prep Time: 1 hour 8-10 min.
Cooking Time: 1 min.
Number of Servings: 2
Ingredients:
- ¾ cup white quinoa
- ⅛ cup raisins
- ½ cup apple juice
- ½ cup plain yogurt
- ½ cup apples, grated
- ½ tablespoon honey
- ¾ cup water
- 1 small cinnamon stick
- ⅛ cup pistachios, chopped
- 3 tablespoons blueberries

Directions:
1. Rinse the quinoa and strain gently using a fine mesh strainer.
2. Switch on the pot after placing it on a clean and dry platform.
3. Open the pot lid and place the water, quinoa and cinnamon stick in the cooking pot area.
4. Close the pot by closing the top lid. Also, ensure to seal the valve.
5. Press "Manual" cooking function and set cooking time to 1 minutes. It will start cooking after a few minutes. Let the pot mix cook under pressure until the timer reads zero.
6. Press "Cancel" cooking function and press "Natural release (NPR)" setting. It will take 8-10 minutes for natural pressure release.
7. Open the pot. Spoon the quinoa into a bowl and remove the cinnamon stick.
8. Mix in the apple, apple juice, raisins, and honey. Refrigerate for at least 1 hour or overnight. Add the yogurt and stir well.
9. Top with the pistachio and blueberries. Serve warm!

Bacon Egg Muffins

Prep Time: 5 min.
Cooking Time: 8 min.
Number of Servings: 2
Ingredients:
- 2 eggs
- ¼ teaspoon lemon pepper seasoning
- 2 crumbled bacon slices
- 1 medium diced onion
- Shredded cheese as needed

Directions:

1. In two silicon molds, separate the cheese, onion, and bacon.
2. Beat one of the eggs and pour it into one of the molds. Repeat the process with the other egg.
3. Switch on the pot after placing it on a clean and dry platform.
4. Pour 1 ½ cup water into the pot. Arrange the trivet inside it; arrange the molds over the trivet.
5. Close the pot by closing the top lid. Also, ensure to seal the valve.
6. Press "Manual" cooking function and set cooking time to 8 minutes. It will start cooking after a few minutes. Let the pot mix cook under pressure until the timer reads zero.
7. Press "Cancel" cooking function and press "Quick release" setting.
8. Open the pot and serve warm. Enjoy it with your loved one!

Cranberry Oats

Prep Time: 5 min.
Cooking Time: 15 min.
Number of Servings: 2
Ingredients:
- ½ cup steel cut oats
- ¼ cup orange juice
- 1 tablespoon butter
- 1 tablespoon orange zest
- 1 cup water
- ¼ cup dried cranberries
- ¼ teaspoon vanilla essence
- ¼ teaspoon cinnamon
- 1 ½ teaspoon maple syrup
- 1 cup whole milk

Directions:
1. Take a safe heat bowl and mix in all of the above ingredients.
2. Switch on the pot after placing it on a clean and dry platform.
3. Pour 1 cup water into the pot. Arrange the trivet inside it; arrange the bowl over the trivet.
4. Close the pot by closing the top lid. Also, ensure to seal the valve.
5. Press "Manual" cooking function and set cooking time to 6 minutes. It will start cooking after a few minutes. Let the pot mix cook under pressure until the timer reads zero.
6. Press "Cancel" cooking function and press "Natural release (NPR)" setting. It will take 8-10 minutes for natural pressure release.
7. Open the pot and mix in the berries; serve warm. Enjoy it with your loved one!

French Toast Bake

Prep Time: 15 minutes
Cooking Time: 25 minutes
Number of Servings: 4
Ingredients:
- 6 slices day-old bread, cubed
- 1/4 cup sugar
- 3 eggs

- 1/2 cup milk
- 1 teaspoon vanilla extract
- 1 teaspoon ground cinnamon
- 1 cup maple syrup for serving

Directions:

1. Beat the eggs, then whisk in milk, vanilla, and cinnamon. Stir the bread into the egg mixture until well coated.
2. Pour the bread and eggs into a baking dish that fits inside the Instant Pot. Place a trivet inside the pot and add enough water to reach the top of the trivet. Place the baking dish on top of the trivet.
3. Close the lid and set the cook time for 25 minutes on high pressure.
4. Serve French toast with maple syrup.

Spinach Eggs Morning

Prep Time: 8-10 min.
Cooking Time: 15 min.
Number of Servings: 2
Ingredients:
- 1 pound fresh spinach, chopped
- 1 teaspoon olive oil
- 8 ounce lean ground beef
- 1 medium onion, finely chopped
- 2 large eggs, beaten

Directions:
1. Take your Instant Pot and place over dry kitchen surface; open its top lid and switch it on.
2. Press "SAUTÉ".
3. In its cooking pot, add and heat the oil.
4. Add the beef; break into small pieces and cook for 4-5 minutes to evenly brown.
5. Set the meat aside.
6. In its cooking pot, add the onions; cook for 3-4 minutes until turn translucent and softened.
7. Add the spinach and 1 cup water.
8. Close its top lid and make sure that its valve it closed to avoid spillage.
9. Press "MANUAL". Adjust the timer to 3 minutes.
10. Pressure will slowly build up; let the added ingredients to cook until the timer indicates zero.
11. Press "CANCEL". Now press "QPR" to quickly release pressure.
12. Open the top lid, mix the cooked beef.
13. Press "SAUTÉ"; stir-fry the mix for 2 more minutes.
14. Add the eggs on top and season. Cook until the eggs are cooked well.
15. Transfer the cooked recipe in serving plates.
16. Serve the recipe warm.

Peas Tomato Eggs

Prep Time: 8-10 min.
Cooking Time: 10 min.
Number of Servings: 2
Ingredients:

- 1/2 cup green peas
- 1 large Roma tomato, chopped (finely)
- 2 teaspoons butter
- 6 large eggs
- 1 tablespoon fresh parsley, chopped (finely)
- ½ cup water
- Salt as needed

Directions:
1. In a mixing bowl, whisk the eggs. Set it aside.
2. Take your Instant Pot and place over dry kitchen surface; open its top lid and switch it on.
3. Add the tomato, beans, ½ cup water and salt in the cooking pot. Stir the ingredients to combine well.
4. Close its top lid and make sure that its valve it closed to avoid spillage.
5. Press "MANUAL". Adjust the timer to 7 minutes.
6. Pressure will slowly build up; let the added ingredients to cook until the timer indicates zero.
7. Press "CANCEL". Now press "QPR" to quickly release pressure.
8. Open the top lid, set aside the cooked mix.
9. Press "SAUTÉ"; add the butter and eggs.
10. Stir-cook the mix for 2-3 more minutes. Transfer the cooked recipe in serving plates; top with the tomato mix.
11. Serve the recipe warm.

Fresh Cheese & Tomato

Prep Time: 8-10 min.
Cooking Time: 4 min.
Number of Servings: 2
Ingredients:
- 1/4 teaspoon red wine vinegar
- 2 tomatoes, chopped
- 1 tablespoon olive oil
- 1/2 teaspoon sherry vinegar
- 1/4 cup cottage cheese
- Pepper and salt as needed

Directions:
1. Add the tomatoes in a blender or processor and puree until turns smooth.
2. Add the remaining ingredients except for the oil; blend again to make a smooth mix.
3. Take your Instant Pot and place over dry kitchen surface; open its top lid and switch it on.
4. Press "SAUTÉ".
5. In its cooking pot, add and heat the oil.
6. Add the tomato mix; cook for 3-4 minutes until turn translucent and softened.
7. Add the mix in the cooking pot; combine to mix well.
8. Transfer the cooked recipe in serving plates.
9. Serve the recipe warm.

Sweet Potato Bacon & Egg Breakfast

Prep Time: 8-10min.
Cooking Time: 7min.
Number of Servings: 4
Ingredients:

- 2 cups shredded sweet potatoes
- 5 slices of bacon, diced
- 8 eggs
- 1 cup shredded carrots
- ½ cup almond milk

Directions:

1. Switch on your instant pot after placing it on a clean and dry kitchen platform. Press "Saute" cooking function.
2. Open the pot lid; add and brown the bacon for about 2 minutes.
3. Arrange a layer of potato hash on top. Arrange the carrots on top.
4. Beat the eggs along with the milk in a mixing bowl. Add the mixture to the Instant Pot.
5. Close the pot by closing the top lid. Also, ensure to seal the valve.
6. Press "Manual" cooking function and set cooking time to 7 minutes. It will start cooking after a few minutes. Let the pot mix cook under pressure until the timer reads zero.
7. Turn off and press "Cancel" cooking function. Quick release pressure.
8. Open the pot and serve on a serving plate or bowl. Enjoy the Paleo dish!

Almond Honey Pancakes

Prep Time: 8-10min.
Cooking Time: 45 min.
Number of Servings: 4
Ingredients:

- 2 tablespoons honey
- 1 tablespoon lemon juice
- 2 eggs
- ½ teaspoon baking soda
- 1 cup coconut flour
- 1 cup ground almonds
- 1 ½ cups coconut milk

Directions:

1. Whisk the eggs and milk in a bowl. Add in the remaining ingredients until a batter consistency is formed.
2. Switch on your instant pot after placing it on a clean and dry kitchen platform.
3. Open the pot lid and grease the pot with cooking spray and pour the batter inside.
4. Close the pot by closing the top lid. Also, ensure to seal the valve.
5. Press "Manual" cooking function and set cooking time to 45 minutes. It will start cooking after a few minutes. Let the pot mix cook under pressure until the timer reads zero.
6. Turn off and press "Cancel" cooking function. Quick release pressure.
7. Open the pot and serve on a serving plate or bowl.
8. Divide into four parts and serve with favorite toppings and enjoy.

Pecan Banana Treat

Prep Time: 8min.
Cooking Time: 7 min.
Number of Servings: 2
Ingredients:

- 1 cup hot water
- 2 teaspoons honey
- 2 tablespoons coconut butter
- ½ teaspoon cinnamon
- ½ cup pecans, soaked overnight and drained
- ½ banana, mashed

Directions:

1. In a processor or blender, blend the pecans, with water, banana, coconut butter, cinnamon, and honey.
2. Switch on your instant pot after placing it on a clean and dry kitchen platform.
3. Open the pot lid and slowly start adding the mixture to the pot.
4. Close the pot by closing the top lid. Also, ensure to seal the valve.
5. Press "Manual" cooking function and set cooking time to 7 minutes. It will start cooking after a few minutes. Let the pot mix cook under pressure until the timer reads zero.
6. Turn off and press "Cancel" cooking function. Quick release pressure.
7. Open the pot and serve on a serving plate or bowl. Enjoy the Paleo dish!

Apple Cauliflower Breakfast

Prep Time: 8-10min.
Cooking Time: 12 min.
Number of Servings: 4
Ingredients:

- 1 and ½ cups cauliflower rice
- 1 and ½ teaspoons cinnamon powder
- 1 cup natural apple juice
- 3 cups almond milk
- 2 tablespoons ghee, melted
- 2 apples, peeled, cored and sliced
- 1/3 cup stevia
- A pinch of salt
- ½ cup cherries, dried

Directions:

1. Switch on your instant pot after placing it on a clean and dry kitchen platform. Press "Saute" cooking function.
2. Open the pot lid; add the ghee and rice in the pot; start cooking for 4-5 minutes to cook well and soften.
3. Combine them with stevia, apples, apple juice, milk, a pinch of salt and cinnamon; stir the mix.
4. Close the pot by closing the top lid. Also, ensure to seal the valve.

59

5. Press "Manual" cooking function and set cooking time to 6 minutes. It will start cooking after a few minutes. Let the pot mix cook under pressure until the timer reads zero.
6. Turn off and press "Cancel" cooking function. Quick release pressure.
7. Open the pot; add cherries, stir, cover, leave aside for 5 more minutes.
8. Divide into bowls and serve!

Cardamom Flax Morning

Prep Time: 8-10min.
Cooking Time: 6 min.
Number of Servings: 3
Ingredients:
- 1 cup carrots, chopped
- 1 teaspoon cardamom, ground
- A pinch of saffron
- 2 tablespoons agave nectar
- 2 cups coconut milk
- 3 tablespoons flax meal
- Some chopped pistachios for serving

Directions:
1. Switch on your instant pot after placing it on a clean and dry kitchen platform.
2. Open the pot lid and slowly start adding the milk, flax meal, carrots, agave nectar, saffron, and cardamom in the pot. Give the ingredients a little stir.
3. Close the pot by closing the top lid. Also, ensure to seal the valve.
4. Press "Manual" cooking function and set cooking time to 6 minutes. It will start cooking after a few minutes. Let the pot mix cook under pressure until the timer reads zero.
5. Turn off and press "Cancel" cooking function. Quick release pressure.
6. Open the pot and serve on a serving plate or bowl. Top with the chopped pistachios and serve!

Spinach Tomato Quiche

Prep Time: 8-10 min.
Cooking Time: 20 min.
Number of Servings: 4
Ingredients:
8 Eggs
⅓ cup Almond Milk
2 cups Baby Spinach, chopped
2 Green Onions, sliced
4 Tomato Slices, for topping
1 cup diced Tomato
1 teaspoon dried Basil
1 ½ cups Water
Directions:
1. Grease a baking dish with cooking spray. Beat the eggs along with the milk and basil in a mixing bowl.
2. Stir in the remaining ingredients. Pour the mixture into the dish.
3. Switch on your instant pot after placing it on a clean and dry kitchen platform.

4. Pour the water into the cooking pot area. Arrange the trivet inside it; arrange the dish over the trivet.
5. Close the pot by closing the top lid. Also, ensure to seal the valve.
6. Press "Manual" cooking function and set cooking time to 20 minutes. It will start cooking after a few minutes. Let the pot mix cook under pressure until the timer reads zero.
7. Turn off and press "Cancel" cooking function. Quick release pressure.
8. Open the pot and serve on a serving plate or bowl. Enjoy the Paleo dish!

Flax Meal Strawberry Breakfast

Prep Time: 10min.
Cooking Time: 10 min.
Number of Servings: 2
Ingredients:
- 3 tablespoons flax meal
- ½ teaspoon honey
- 2 cups water
- 2/3 cup almond milk
- 2 tablespoons strawberries, dried
- A pinch of salt

Directions:
1. Switch on your instant pot after placing it on a clean and dry kitchen platform.
2. Open the pot lid and slowly start adding the strawberries, water, flax meal, almond milk and honey in the pot. Give the ingredients a little stir.
3. Close the pot by closing the top lid. Also, ensure to seal the valve.
4. Press "Manual" cooking function and set cooking time to 10 minutes. It will start cooking after a few minutes. Let the pot mix cook under pressure until the timer reads zero.
5. Turn off and press "Cancel" cooking function. Quick release pressure.
6. Open the pot and serve on a serving plate or bowl. Enjoy the Paleo dish!

Pumpkin Oats Morning

Prep Time: 8-10 min.
Cooking Time: 10 min.
Number of Servings: 6
Ingredients:
- 1/4 cup oat flour
- 1 cup rolled oats
- 2 cups pumpkin puree
- 1 onion, chopped
- 3 garlic cloves, minced
- Cooking oil as needed

Directions:
1. In a bowl (medium-large size), combine all ingredients and mix well.
2. Make patties and gently press them.
3. Take your Instant Pot and place over dry kitchen surface; open its top lid and switch it on.
4. Press "SAUTÉ".

5. In its cooking pot, add and heat the oil.
6. Add the patties; cook for 3-4 minutes per side until cooks well.
7. Serve warm.

Broccoli with Eggs

Prep Time: 8-10 min.
Cooking Time: 30 min.
Number of Servings: 4
Ingredients:
- 1 onion chopped
- 6 eggs, beaten
- 1 pound broccoli, chopped
- Cooking spray as needed
- 1 tablespoon flour (all-purpose)

Directions:
1. Thoroughly mix the eggs, flour, and all spices in a mixing bowl. Mix in the broccoli. Set aside.
2. Line a pan with a parchment paper and grease with some cooking spray. Add in the mixture.
3. Take your Instant Pot and place over dry kitchen surface; open its top lid and switch it on.
4. Pour 1 cup water in the cooking pot area. Arrange the trivet or steamer basket inside it; arrange the pan over the trivet/basket.
5. Close its top lid and make sure that its valve it closed to avoid spillage.
6. Press "MANUAL". Adjust the timer to 30 minutes.
7. Pressure will slowly build up; let the added ingredients to cook until the timer indicates zero.
8. Press "CANCEL". Now press "QPR" to quickly release pressure.
9. Open the top lid, transfer in serving plates.
10. Serve the recipe warm.

Barley Pepper Breakfast

Prep Time: 8-10 min.
Cooking Time: 12 min.
Number of Servings: 6
Ingredients:
- 1 red bell pepper, chopped
- 1 onion, make slices
- 3 cups vegetable stock
- 1 cup pearl barley
- 3 tablespoons lemon juice

Directions:
1. Take your Instant Pot and place over dry kitchen surface; open its top lid and switch it on.
2. Add the barley and stock in the cooking pot. Stir the ingredients to combine well.
3. Close its top lid and make sure that its valve it closed to avoid spillage.
4. Press "MANUAL". Adjust the timer to 12 minutes.
5. Pressure will slowly build up; let the added ingredients to cook until the timer indicates zero.
6. Press "CANCEL". Now press "NPR" for natural release pressure. Instant Pot will gradually release pressure for about 8-10 minutes.
7. Open the top lid, transfer the cooked recipe in serving plates.

8. Mix in the veggies and lemon juice.
9. Serve the recipe warm.

Whole Grain Toast

Prep Time: 8-10 min.
Cooking Time: 6 min.
Number of Servings: 2
Ingredients:
- 1/2 zucchini, make slices
- 1/2 teaspoon salt
- 1 tablespoon olive oil
- 4 slices whole grain bread
- 1/4 teaspoon black pepper

Directions:
1. Mix the zucchini with salt. Set aside.
2. Take your Instant Pot and place over dry kitchen surface; open its top lid and switch it on.
3. Press "SAUTÉ".
4. In its cooking pot, add and heat the oil.
5. Add the zucchini; cook for 3-4 minutes per side until turn softened.
6. Add the mix between bread slices.
7. Season with more salt and pepper. Serve warm.

Peach Turkey Breakfast

Prep Time: 8-10 min.
Cooking Time: 20 min.
Number of Servings: 4
Ingredients:
- 1 tablespoon soy sauce
- 4 medium peaches, chopped
- 2 teaspoon olive oil
- 1 pound turkey fillets, thinly sliced
- 1 tablespoon Greek yogurt, fat-free

Directions:
1. Mix the turkey slices with soy sauce and set aside.
2. Take your Instant Pot and place over dry kitchen surface; open its top lid and switch it on.
3. Press "SAUTÉ".
4. In its cooking pot, add and heat the oil.
5. Add the slices; cook for 4-5 minutes to evenly brown and cooks completely. Set aside.
6. Add peaches and enough water to cover the peaches.
7. Close its top lid and make sure that its valve it closed to avoid spillage.
8. Press "MANUAL". Adjust the timer to 8 minutes.
9. Pressure will slowly build up; let the added ingredients to cook until the timer indicates zero.
10. Press "CANCEL". Now press "QPR" to quickly release pressure.
11. Open the top lid, mix the remaining ingredients.
12. Press "SAUTÉ"; stir-cook the mix for 2-3 more minutes.
13. Cool down and make a puree in a blender.

14. Transfer the cooked turkey in serving plates. Top with the puree.
15. Serve the recipe warm.

Apple Almond Rice Meal

Prep Time: 8-10min.
Cooking Time: 35 min.
Number of Servings:6
Ingredients:
- 1 chopped pear
- 3 ½ cups water
- 1 ½ cups wild rice
- 1 cup dried, mixed fruit
- 2 small apples, peeled and chopped
- ½ cup almonds, slivered
- 2 tablespoons apple juice
- 1 teaspoon cinnamon
- 1 tablespoon maple syrup
- 1 teaspoon veggie oil
- ½ teaspoon ground nutmeg
- Pepper and salt as needed

Directions:
1. Take Instant Pot and carefully arrange it over a clean, dry kitchen platform. Turn on the appliance.
2. In the cooking pot area, add the rice and water. Stir the ingredients gently.
3. Close the pot lid and seal the valve to avoid any leakage. Find and press "Manual" cooking setting and set cooking time to 30 minutes.
4. Allow the recipe ingredients to cook for the set time, and after that, the timer reads "zero".
5. Meanwhile, soak the dried fruit in just enough apple juice to cover everything in a bowl. Set aside for 30 minutes and then drain the fruit.
6. Press "Cancel" and press "NPR" setting for natural pressure release. It takes 8-10 times for all inside pressure to release.
7. Open the pot and transfer the mixture to serving bowl.
8. Find and press "Sauté" cooking function.
9. In the cooking pot area; add the oil, apples, pears, and almonds in the pot. Cook for 2 minutes to cook well and soften.
10. Mix in 2 tablespoon apple juice and keep cooking for a few minutes more. Mix in the syrup, cooked rice, soaked fruit, and seasonings.
11. Cook for 2-3 minutes and serve warm!

Multigrain Risotto

Prep Time: 5min.
Cooking Time: 20-22 min.
Number of Servings: 6
Ingredients:

- 1 cup mixture of quinoa, millet, bulgur, oats, and buckwheat, or any other grains of your choice, soaked in water overnight, drained
- 1 cup coconut milk
- 4 cups water
- Sweetener as needed (optional)

Directions:
1. Take Instant Pot and carefully arrange it over a clean, dry kitchen platform. Turn on the appliance.
2. In the cooking pot area, add the mentioned ingredients. Stir the ingredients gently.
3. Close the pot lid and seal the valve to avoid any leakage. Find and press "Porridge" cooking setting with default cooking time.
4. Allow the recipe ingredients to cook for the set time, and after that, the timer reads "zero".
5. Press "Cancel" and press "NPR" setting for natural pressure release. It takes 8-10 times for all inside pressure to release.
6. Open the pot and arrange the cooked recipe in serving plates. Enjoy the vegan recipe!

Garlic Bean Rice Meal

Prep Time: 10 min.
Cooking Time: 25 min.
Number of Servings:4
Ingredients:
- 2 tablespoons olive oil
- 2 cloves garlic, minced
- 1 cup brown rice, rinsed
- 1 cup black beans, rinsed
- 1 medium onion, chopped
- 4 ½ cups water
- ½ avocado, sliced to serve
- Salt as needed
- 2 teaspoons lime juice

Directions:
1. Take Instant Pot and carefully arrange it over a clean, dry kitchen platform. Turn on the appliance.
2. In the cooking pot area, add the mentioned ingredients except for lime juice and avocado. Stir the ingredients gently.
3. Close the pot lid and seal the valve to avoid any leakage. Find and press "Manual" cooking setting and set cooking time to 25 minutes.
4. Allow the recipe ingredients to cook for the set time, and after that, the timer reads "zero".
5. Press "Cancel" and press "NPR" setting for natural pressure release. It takes 8-10 times for all inside pressure to release.
6. Open the pot, fluff the mixture. Add lime juice and stir.
7. Spoon into bowls. Garnish with avocado slices and serve.

Avocado Rice Salad

Prep Time: 10min.
Cooking Time: 24 min.
Number of Servings: 6-8
Ingredients:
- 1 can (14 oz.) black beans, drained
- 1 ½ cups water
- ¼ cup cilantro, minced
- 1 cup brown rice
- 1 avocado, diced
- 12 grape tomatoes, make quarters
- ¼ teaspoon salt

For the dressing:
- 2 teaspoons Tabasco (optional)
- 2 garlic cloves, minced
- 3 tablespoons lime juice
- 3 tablespoons extra-virgin olive oil
- 1/ 8 teaspoon salt
- 1 teaspoon maple syrup

Directions:
1. Take Instant Pot and carefully arrange it over a clean, dry kitchen platform. Turn on the appliance.
2. In the cooking pot area, add the rice and water. Stir the ingredients gently.
3. Close the pot lid and seal the valve to avoid any leakage. Find and press "Manual" cooking setting and set cooking time to 24 minutes.
4. Allow the recipe ingredients to cook for the set time, and after that, the timer reads "zero".
5. Press "Cancel" and press "NPR" setting for natural pressure release. It takes 8-10 times for all inside pressure to release.
6. Open the pot and transfer the mixture to the serving container.
7. Mix the black beans, avocado, tomato, and cilantro.
8. In another mixing bowl, whisk the dressing ingredients together. Pour the dressing over the rice mix and combine; serve!

Spinach Chickpea Rice Meal

Prep Time: 8-10min.
Cooking Time: 25 min.
Number of Servings: 4
Ingredients:
- 1 teaspoon lime juice
- 2 small tomatoes, diced one
- Half inch piece ginger, grated
- ½ teaspoon salt
- 1 tablespoon curry powder
- 1 cup baby spinach

- ½ cup chopped yellow onion
- 2 cups water
- ¼ cup brown rice, cooked
- 1 teaspoon vegetable oil
- 4 garlic cloves, minced
- 1 small acorn squash
- 1 can chickpeas

Directions:
1. Slice squash in half and scrape seeds.
2. Take Instant Pot and carefully arrange it over a clean, dry kitchen platform. Turn on the appliance.
3. Find and press "Sauté" cooking function.
4. In the cooking pot area; add the oil and onions in the pot. Cook for 2-3 minutes to cook well and soften.
5. Add the garlic and cook 1 minute. Mix other ingredients besides squash and cook until spinach is wilted.
6. Place mixture inside each squash half.
7. Pour the water into the cooking pot area. Arrange the trivet inside it; arrange the squash halves over the trivet.
8. Close the pot lid and seal the valve to avoid any leakage. Find and press "Manual" cooking setting and set cooking time to 20 minutes.
9. Allow the recipe ingredients to cook for the set time, and after that, the timer reads "zero".
10. Press "Cancel" and press "NPR" setting for natural pressure release. It takes 8-10 times for all inside pressure to release.
11. Open the pot and arrange the cooked recipe in serving plates. Enjoy the vegan recipe!

Sorghum Pumpkin Meal

Prep Time: 5-8min.
Cooking Time: 25 min.
Number of Servings: 5-6
Ingredients:
- 1½ tablespoons pumpkin pie spice
- 1½ cups almond milk, unsweetened
- 1 ½ teaspoons vanilla extract
- 3 tablespoons maple syrup
- 1 ½ cups sorghum, rinsed
- 1 ¼ cups pumpkin puree
- 3 cups water

Directions:
1. Take Instant Pot and carefully arrange it over a clean, dry kitchen platform. Turn on the appliance.
2. In the cooking pot area, add the mentioned ingredients. Stir the ingredients gently.
3. Close the pot lid and seal the valve to avoid any leakage. Find and press "Manual" cooking setting and set cooking time to 25 minutes.
4. Allow the recipe ingredients to cook for the set time, and after that, the timer reads "zero".

5. Press "Cancel" and press "NPR" setting for natural pressure release. It takes 8-10 times for all inside pressure to release.
6. Open the pot and arrange the cooked recipe in serving plates. Serve with almond milk.

Spinach Mushroom Risotto

Prep Time: 5min.
Cooking Time: 8 min.
Number of Servings: 5
Ingredients:
- ½ cup white onion, minced
- 4-ounce mushrooms, chopped
- 1 cup Arborio rice
- 1 ½ tablespoon nutritional yeast
- 3 cups vegetable broth
- 2 cups spinach
- ¼ cup lemon juice
- ½ cup dry white wine
- 1 teaspoon salt
- 1 tablespoon vegan butter
- 1 tablespoon olive oil, optional
- 1 teaspoon thyme
- 3 cloves garlic, minced
- Black pepper as needed

Directions:
1. Take Instant Pot and carefully arrange it over a clean, dry kitchen platform. Turn on the appliance.
2. Find and press "Sauté" cooking function.
3. In the cooking pot area; add the oil, garlic, and onions in the pot. Cook for 2 minutes to cook well and soften.
4. Add the rice and stir well. Pour the broth, mushrooms, wine, thyme, and salt.
5. Close the pot lid and seal the valve to avoid any leakage. Find and press "Manual" cooking setting and set cooking time to 5 minutes.
6. Allow the recipe ingredients to cook for the set time, and after that, the timer reads "zero".
7. Press "Cancel" and press "NPR" setting for natural pressure release. It takes 8-10 times for all inside pressure to release.
8. Open the pot and arrange the cooked recipe in serving plates.
9. Mix the yeast, spinach, vegan butter, and pepper. Stir well and serve warm!

Green Tea Rice Risotto

Prep Time: 5min.
Cooking Time: 30 min.
Number of Servings: 5-6
Ingredients:
- 1 cup brown rice, rinsed
- ¼ cup lentils, rinsed

- 7 cups water
- 3 green tea bags
- Salt as needed

Directions:
1. Take Instant Pot and carefully arrange it over a clean, dry kitchen platform. Turn on the appliance.
2. In the cooking pot area, add the mentioned ingredients. Stir the ingredients gently.
3. Close the pot lid and seal the valve to avoid any leakage. Find and press "Manual" cooking setting and set cooking time to 30 minutes.
4. Allow the recipe ingredients to cook for the set time, and after that, the timer reads "zero".
5. Press "Cancel" and press "NPR" setting for natural pressure release. It takes 8-10 times for all inside pressure to release.
6. Open the pot, remove tea bags and arrange the cooked recipe in serving plates. Enjoy the vegan recipe!

Tomato Couscous

Prep Time: 8-10 min.
Cooking Time: 15 min.
Number of Servings: 4
Ingredients:
- 1 tomato, chopped
- 1 cucumber, make slices
- 1 tablespoon olive oil
- 2 cups water
- 1 cup couscous
- 1 tablespoon lemon juice
- Salt as needed

Directions:
1. Take your Instant Pot and place over dry kitchen surface; open its top lid and switch it on.
2. Add the couscous and 2 cups water in the cooking pot. Add the salt and oil; stir the ingredients to combine well.
3. Close its top lid and make sure that its valve it closed to avoid spillage.
4. Press "MANUAL". Adjust the timer to 15 minutes.
5. Pressure will slowly build up; let the added ingredients to cook until the timer indicates zero.
6. Press "CANCEL". Now press "QPR" to quickly release pressure.
7. Add the vegetables. Sprinkle with some more salt; serve warm.

Salmon Green Breakfast

Prep Time: 8-10 min.
Cooking Time: 20 min.
Number of Servings: 6
Ingredients:
- 6 ounce salmon fillets, make bite-sized pieces
- 1 pound fresh spinach, chopped
- 2 tablespoons flour (all-purpose)

- 6 large eggs
- 1 teaspoon baking powder

Directions:
1. In a mixing bowl, thoroughly mix all ingredients along with seasoning.
2. Add the mix into pre-greased muffin cups.
3. Take your Instant Pot and place over dry kitchen surface; open its top lid and switch it on.
4. Pour 1 cup water in the cooking pot area. Arrange the trivet or steamer basket inside it; arrange the muffin cups over the trivet/basket.
5. Close its top lid and make sure that its valve it closed to avoid spillage.
6. Press "MANUAL". Adjust the timer to 20 minutes.
7. Pressure will slowly build up; let the added ingredients to cook until the timer indicates zero.
8. Press "CANCEL". Now press "QPR" to quickly release pressure.
9. Open the top lid, transfer in serving plates.
10. Serve the recipe warm.

Banana Buckwheat Porridge

Prep Time: 2 minutes
Cooking Time: 6 minutes
Number of Servings: 2
Ingredients:
- 1 cup buckwheat groats, rinsed
- 3 cups milk, plus more for serving
- 1 ripe banana, sliced
- 1 teaspoon ground cinnamon
- 2 tablespoons brown sugar, plus more for serving

Directions:
1. Pour the groats, milk, banana, cinnamon, and sugar into the Instant Pot.
2. Close the lid and set to 6 minutes on high pressure.
3. Serve porridge with additional milk and brown sugar.

Carrot Cake Oatmeal

Prep Time: 10 minutes
Cooking Time: 10 minutes
Number of Servings: 2
Ingredients:
- 1 cup steel-cut oats
- 1 tablespoon butter
- 2 cups milk, plus more for serving
- 2 cups water
- 2 carrots, grated
- 1/4 cup brown sugar
- 1 teaspoon ground cinnamon
- 1/2 teaspoon nutmeg
- 1/2 cup raisins

Directions:

1. Set Instant Pot to Saute. Melt butter in the pot and add oats. Toast until oats are lightly browned and smell nutty.
2. Pour milk, water, carrots, sugar, cinnamon, nutmeg, and raisins into the pot.
3. Close lid and set cook time to 10 minutes on high pressure.
4. Serve with additional milk.

Nutritional Values (Per Serving):
Calories - 451
Fat - 17.4 g
Carbohydrates - 77.05 g
Fiber - 9.8 g
Protein - 16.57 g

Chapter 3: Beans & Grains

Southern Succotash

Prep Time: 10 minutes
Cooking Time: 30 minutes
Number of Servings: 4
Ingredients:
- 4 ounces bacon, diced
- 1 onion, diced
- 1 garlic clove, minced
- 1/2 cup crushed tomatoes
- 2 cups dried lima beans
- 3 cups fresh corn kernels
- 2 tablespoons fresh chives, chopped
- 1/4 teaspoon salt
- 1/2 teaspoon black pepper

Directions:
1. Set Instant Pot to Saute and add bacon. Cook until most of the fat renders.
2. Add onion and garlic to the pot and cook until garlic is translucent.
3. Add tomatoes, beans, and enough water to cover. Close lid and set cooking time for 20 minutes.
4. After steam releases, remove the lid and add corn, salt, pepper, and chives. Close and allow to sit until corn is heated through. Season to taste with salt and pepper.

Buttery Polenta

Prep Time: 5 min.
Cooking Time: 8 min.
Number of Servings: 2
Ingredients:
- ½ cup polenta
- ½ teaspoon salt
- 2 cup milk
- 3 tablespoons milk
- 3 tablespoons butter

Directions:
1. Switch on the pot after placing it on a clean and dry platform. Press "Sauté" cooking function.
2. Open the pot lid; add the milk and boil it. Mix in the polenta with the salt.
3. Close the pot by closing the top lid. Also, ensure to seal the valve.
4. Press "Manual" cooking function and set cooking time to 8 minutes. It will start cooking after a few minutes. Let the pot mix cook under pressure until the timer reads zero.
5. Press "Cancel" cooking function and press "Quick release" setting.
6. Open the pot; mix 3 tablespoons of milk and butter.
7. Serve warm. Enjoy it with your loved one!

Kidney Bean Sausage Risotto

Prep Time: 10-15 min.
Cooking Time: 44 min.
Number of Servings: 2
Ingredients:

- 1/3 pound red kidney beans
- 1/2 yellow onion, chopped
- 1 small red bell pepper, chopped
- A pinch of pepper and salt
- A pinch of white pepper
- 1 celery stalk, chopped
- 3 cup water
- 1 garlic clove, crushed or minced
- 1/2 teaspoon thyme, chopped
- 1/2 pound chicken sausage, sliced
- 3 cup rice, cooked
- 1/3 teaspoon hot sauce
- 1 bay leaf

Directions:

1. Take your 3-Quart Instant Pot; open the top lid. Plug it and turn it on.
2. In the cooking pot area, add the bell pepper, celery, onion, garlic, beans, salt, black pepper, white pepper, thyme, hot sauce, bay leaf, and water. Using a spatula, stir the ingredients.
3. Close the top lid and seal its valve.
4. Press "MANUAL" setting. Adjust cooking time to 28 minutes.
5. Allow the recipe to cook for the set cooking time.
6. After the set cooking time ends, press "CANCEL" and then press "QPR (Quick Pressure Release)".
7. Instant Pot will quickly release the pressure.
8. Add the sausage, stir gently.
9. Close the top lid and seal its valve.
10. Press "MANUAL" setting. Adjust cooking time to 15 minutes.
11. Allow the recipe to cook for the set cooking time.
12. After the set cooking time ends, press "CANCEL" and then press "QPR (Quick Pressure Release)".
13. Instant Pot will quickly release the pressure.
14. Divide rice on 2 plates, add the beans mix on top and serve.

Tangy Asparagus Risotto

Prep Time: 5 min.
Cooking Time: 10 min.
Number of Servings: 2-3
Ingredients:

- ¼ cup parmesan, grated
- 2 tablespoons orange juice
- ½ cup risotto rice

- 2 garlic cloves, chopped
- 1 small onion, chopped
- ½ pound diced asparagus
- 1 1/3 cup vegetable stock
- 1 tablespoon olive oil
- 1 tablespoon thyme

Directions:
1. Take your 3-Quart Instant Pot; open the top lid. Plug it and turn it on.
2. Press "SAUTÉ" setting and the pot will start heating up.
3. In the cooking pot area, add the oil and onions. Cook until starts becoming translucent and softened. Stir in between.
4. Mix the rice and the garlic, cook until the garlic becomes fragrant. Mix in the stock and the orange juice.
5. Close the top lid and seal its valve.
6. Press "MANUAL" setting. Adjust cooking time to 7 minutes.
7. Allow the recipe to cook for the set cooking time.
8. After the set cooking time ends, press "CANCEL" and then press "QPR (Quick Pressure Release)".
9. Instant Pot will quickly release the pressure.
10. Add the thyme and asparagus; combine gently. Do not cover, let it sit for 8 minutes for asparagus to soften.
11. Open the top lid, add the cooked recipe mix in serving plates.
12. Serve with the cheese on top and enjoy!

Spiced Chickpea Curry

Prep Time: 8-10 min.
Cooking Time: 18 min.
Number of Servings: 2
Ingredients:
- 1 cup chickpeas, soaked overnight or 7-8 hours and drained
- ½ cup spinach, chopped
- 1 cup water
- 1/2 cup tomatoes, chopped
- 1 tablespoon olive oil
- 4 tablespoons red onion, chopped
- 1 garlic clove, crushed or minced
- A pinch of turmeric powder
- 1 bay leaf
- 1/2 tablespoon curry powder
- A pinch of chili powder
- A pinch of garam masala
- 1/2 tablespoon lemon juice
- A pinch of pepper and salt
- 1 tablespoon cilantro, chopped

Directions:
1. Take your 3-Quart Instant Pot; open the top lid. Plug it and turn it on.
2. Press "SAUTÉ" setting and the pot will start heating up.
3. In the cooking pot area, add the oil, garlic, and onions. Cook until starts becoming translucent and softened for 2-3 minutes. Stir in between.
4. Add the tomatoes, stir and cook for 4 minutes more.
5. Add the chili powder, garam masala, turmeric, bay leaf and curry powder, stir and cook for 1 minute more.
6. Add chickpeas, spinach and water, stir gently.
7. Close the top lid and seal its valve.
8. Press "MANUAL" setting. Adjust cooking time to 10 minutes.
9. Allow the recipe to cook for the set cooking time.
10. After the set cooking time ends, press "CANCEL" and then press "QPR (Quick Pressure Release)".
11. Instant Pot will quickly release the pressure.
12. Open the top lid, add the cooked recipe mix in serving plates.
13. Discard the bay leaf, mix the lemon juice and cilantro, some salt and pepper.
14. Serve and enjoy!

Brown Rice Ham Treat

Prep Time: 5 min.
Cooking Time: 6 min.
Number of Servings: 2-3
Ingredients:
- ½ cup ham, diced
- 2 tablespoons scallions, sliced
- ½ cup carrots, make matchsticks
- 1 ½ cup brown rice
- 1 tablespoon butter
- 1 ½ cup water
- 1 tablespoon soy sauce

Directions:
1. Take your 3-Quart Instant Pot; open the top lid. Plug it and turn it on.
2. In the cooking pot area, add the ingredients. Using a spatula, stir the ingredients.
3. Close the top lid and seal its valve.
4. Press "MANUAL" setting. Adjust cooking time to 6 minutes.
5. Allow the recipe to cook for the set cooking time.
6. After the set cooking time ends, press "CANCEL" and then press "QPR (Quick Pressure Release)".
7. Instant Pot will quickly release the pressure.
8. Open the top lid, fluff the rice and add the cooked recipe mix in serving plates.
9. Serve and enjoy!
10. Ensure that the rice is tender and has there is no liquid left in the pot. If the rice is not tender, cook for a few more minutes.

BBQ Lentil Meal

Prep Time: 8-10 min.
Cooking Time: 15 min.
Number of Servings: 2
Ingredients:
- 1 tomato, make rounds
- Toasted bread to serve
- ½ cucumber, make rounds
- ¼ cup BBQ sauce

For lentils:
- 1 cup water
- ½ cup green lentils, soaked overnight and drained

Directions:
1. Take your 3-Quart Instant Pot; open the top lid. Plug it and turn it on.
2. In the cooking pot area, add the lentils and water. Using a spatula, stir the ingredients.
3. Close the top lid and seal its valve.
4. Press "MANUAL" setting. Adjust cooking time to 15 minutes.
5. Allow the recipe to cook for the set cooking time.
6. After the set cooking time ends, press "CANCEL" and then press "NPR (Natural Pressure Release)".
7. Instant Pot will slowly and naturally release the pressure.
8. Open the top lid, add the BBQ sauce and mix well.
9. Arrange the mix over toasted bread. On top of the breads, add sliced tomatoes and cucumber.
10. Serve and enjoy!

Mexican Bean Avocado Rice

Prep Time: 10-15 min.
Cooking Time: 28 min.
Number of Servings: 2-3
Ingredients:
- 2 garlic cloves, minced
- 1 lime, make wedges
- 1 avocado, pitted, peeled and sliced
- 1 cup black beans, washed
- 1/2 cup onion, chopped
- 1 cup brown rice
- 4 1/2 cup water
- A pinch of salt

Directions:
1. Take your 3-Quart Instant Pot; open the top lid. Plug it and turn it on.
2. In the cooking pot area, add the beans, water, rice, salt, garlic and onion. Using a spatula, stir the ingredients.
3. Close the top lid and seal its valve.
4. Press "MANUAL" setting. Adjust cooking time to 28 minutes.
5. Allow the recipe to cook for the set cooking time.

6. After the set cooking time ends, press "CANCEL" and then press "QPR (Quick Pressure Release)".
7. Instant Pot will quickly release the pressure.
8. Open the top lid, add the cooked recipe mix in serving plates.
9. Serve with lime wedges and avocado slices.

Ham & Rice Treat

Prep Time: 2 min.
Cooking Time: 6 min.
Number of Servings: 2
Ingredients:
- ½ cup ham, diced
- 1 ½ cup brown rice
- 1 tablespoon butter
- 2 tablespoons scallions, sliced
- ½ cup matchstick carrots
- 1 ½ cup water
- 1 tablespoon soy sauce

Directions:
1. Switch on the pot after placing it on a clean and dry platform.
2. Open the pot lid and put the above-mentioned ingredients in the cooking pot area. Give the ingredients a little stir.
3. Close the pot by closing the top lid. Also, ensure to seal the valve.
4. Press "Manual" cooking function and set cooking time to 6 minutes. It will start cooking after a few minutes. Let the pot mix cook under pressure until the timer reads zero.
5. Press "Cancel" cooking function and press "Quick release" setting.
6. Open the pot; fluff the mix and serve warm. Enjoy it with your loved one!

Potato Lentil Rice

Prep Time: 8-10 min.
Cooking Time: 10 min.
Number of Servings: 2
Ingredients:
- ½ tablespoon ginger paste
- 1 small potato, cut into small pieces
- ½ cup white rice, rinsed
- ½ cup split green lentils, rinsed
- 3 cups water
- 1 tomato, chopped finely
- ¼ teaspoon red chili powder
- ¼ teaspoon ground turmeric
- 1 tablespoon fresh cilantro, chopped
- ½ cup carrots, peeled and diced
- ½ cup fresh green peas, shelled
- 1 tablespoon olive oil

- ½ teaspoon cumin seeds
- ½ of a small onion, chopped
- Salt as per taste preference

Directions:
1. Switch on the pot after placing it on a clean and dry platform. Press "Sauté" cooking function.
2. Open the pot lid; add the oil and cumin seeds and cook for 30 seconds.
3. Add the onions and ginger and cook for about 2 minutes. Add the vegetables and spices and cook for 2 minutes.
4. Mix in other ingredients and stir well. Do not add the cilantro.
5. Close the pot by closing the top lid. Also, ensure to seal the valve.
6. Press "Manual" cooking function and set cooking time to 5 minutes. It will start cooking after a few minutes. Let the pot mix cook under pressure until the timer reads zero.
7. Press "Cancel" cooking function and press "Natural release (NPR)" setting. It will take 8-10 minutes for natural pressure release.
8. Open the pot; top with the cilantro and serve warm. Enjoy it with your loved one!

Oregano Polenta

Prep Time: 5 min.
Cooking Time: 8-10 min.
Number of Servings: 2
Ingredients:
- 1 bunch green onions
- 2 tablespoons cilantro
- 1 cup broth
- ½ teaspoon oregano
- 1 ½ teaspoon chili powder
- ¼ teaspoon paprika
- ½ teaspoon cumin
- 1 cup boiling water
- ½ cup cornmeal
- 1 teaspoon garlic, minced
- Pinch of cayenne

Directions:
1. Switch on the pot after placing it on a clean and dry platform. Press "Sauté" cooking function.
2. Open the pot lid; add some cooking oil, garlic, and onions in the pot; cook for 2-3 minutes to cook well and soften.
3. Mix in the broth, cilantro, cornmeal, spices and boiling water. Close the pot by closing the top lid. Also, ensure to seal the valve.
4. Press "Manual" cooking function and set cooking time to 5 minutes. It will start cooking after a few minutes. Let the pot mix cook under pressure until the timer reads zero.
5. Press "Cancel" cooking function and press "Natural release (NPR)" setting. It will take 8-10 minutes for natural pressure release.
6. Open the pot and serve warm. Enjoy it with your loved one!

Cheesy Asparagus Risotto

Prep Time: 5 min.
Cooking Time: 15 min.
Number of Servings: 2
Ingredients:
- 1 small onion, chopped
- 1 tablespoon olive oil
- 1 tablespoon thyme
- ½ cup risotto rice
- 2 garlic cloves, chopped
- ¼ cup parmesan, grated
- 2 tablespoons orange juice
- ½ pound asparagus, diced
- 1 1/3 cup vegetable stock

Directions:
1. Switch on the pot after placing it on a clean and dry platform. Press "Sauté" cooking function.
2. Open the pot lid; add the oil and onions in the pot; cook for 2 minutes to cook well and soften.
3. Mix the rice and the garlic; cook until the garlic becomes fragrant. Mix in the stock and the orange juice.
4. Close the pot by closing the top lid. Also, ensure to seal the valve.
5. Press "Manual" cooking function and set cooking time to 7 minutes. It will start cooking after a few minutes. Let the pot mix cook under pressure until the timer reads zero.
6. Press "Cancel" cooking function and press "Quick release" setting.
7. Open the pot and mix the thyme and asparagus. Do not cover, let it sit for 5-8 more minutes for asparagus to soften.
8. Place in a serving bowl and top with the cheese. Serve warm!

Chickpea Avocado Salad

Prep Time: 8-10 min.
Cooking Time: 12 min.
Number of Servings: 2
Ingredients:
- 1/4 cup avocado, chopped
- 2 tablespoons pomegranate seeds
- 1 cup chickpeas, soaked and rinsed
- 1/2 cup quinoa
- 1 teaspoon rice vinegar

Directions:
1. Take your Instant Pot and place over dry kitchen surface; open its top lid and switch it on.
2. Add the chickpea and 1 cup water in the cooking pot. Stir the ingredients to combine well.
3. Close its top lid and make sure that its valve it closed to avoid spillage.
4. Press "MANUAL". Adjust the timer to 10 minutes.
5. Pressure will slowly build up; let the added ingredients to cook until the timer indicates zero.
6. Press "CANCEL". Now press "QPR" to quickly release pressure.
7. Drain water and set aside chickpea.

8. Add the quinoa and 1/2 cup water in the cooking pot. Stir the ingredients to combine well.
9. Close its top lid and make sure that its valve it closed to avoid spillage.
10. Press "MANUAL". Adjust timer to 1 minutes.
11. Pressure will slowly build up; let the added ingredients to cook until the timer indicates zero.
12. Press "CANCEL". Now press "QPR" to quickly release pressure.
13. Drain and add quinoa with the chickpea.
14. Add the vinegar, pomegranate and avocado on top; serve.

Zucchini Bulgur Meal

Prep Time: 8-10 min.
Cooking Time: 30 min.
Number of Servings: 3
Ingredients:
- 3 medium zucchinis, make wedges
- 1 small onion, chopped
- 2 teaspoons olive oil
- 1 cup bulgur
- 1 tablespoon fresh parsley, chopped (finely)

Directions:
1. Take your Instant Pot and place over dry kitchen surface; open its top lid and switch it on.
2. Add the bulgur and 1 ½ cup water in the cooking pot. Stir the ingredients to combine well.
3. Close its top lid and make sure that its valve it closed to avoid spillage.
4. Press "MANUAL". Adjust the timer to 18 minutes.
5. Pressure will slowly build up; let the added ingredients to cook until the timer indicates zero.
6. Press "CANCEL". Now press "QPR" to quickly release pressure.
7. Drain water and set aside bulgur.
8. Press "SAUTÉ". Grease the pot with some cooking oil.
9. Add the onions; cook for 3-4 minutes until turn translucent and softened.
10. Add the zucchini. Cook for 4-5 minutes, stirring occasionally.
11. Add the bulgur to the pot and give it a good stir. Cook for 2 more minutes.
12. Serve warm with the parsley on top.

Broccoli Cream Pasta

Prep Time: 8-10 min.
Cooking Time: 15 min.
Number of Servings: 6-7
Ingredients:
- 8 ounce broccoli, chopped
- 1 cup cheddar cheese, grated
- 1 teaspoon butter
- 10 ounce rigatoni or your choice of pasta
- 1/2 cup heavy cream

Directions:
1. In the Instant Pot; add the pasta and water to cover.
2. Close its top lid and make sure that its valve it closed to avoid spillage.
3. Press "MANUAL". Adjust the timer to 7 minutes.

4. Pressure will slowly build up; let the added ingredients to cook until the timer indicates zero.
5. Press "CANCEL". Now press "QPR" to quickly release pressure.
6. Open the top lid, drain water and transfer the cooked pasta in a container.
7. Take your Instant Pot and place over dry kitchen surface; open its top lid and switch it on.
8. Press "SAUTÉ".
9. In its cooking pot, add and heat the butter.
10. Add the broccoli and cream; stir-cook for 3-4 minutes.
11. Add the cheese; cook for 6-7 minutes.
12. Mix in the pasta and serve.

Pure Basmati Rice Meal

Prep Time: 8-10 min.
Cooking Time: 10 min.
Number of Servings: 4
Ingredients:
- 1 small onion, make slices
- 1 cup basmati rice
- 1 teaspoon olive oil
- 1 cup cauliflower, chopped
- ¼ cup green onions, chopped

Directions:
1. Puree the cauliflower until smooth in a blender and set aside.
2. Take your Instant Pot and place over dry kitchen surface; open its top lid and switch it on.
3. Press "SAUTÉ". Grease the pot with some cooking oil.
4. Add the onions; cook for 2-3 minutes until turn translucent and softened.
5. Add the puree, rice and green onions.
6. Close its top lid and make sure that its valve it closed to avoid spillage.
7. Press "MANUAL". Adjust the timer to 4 minutes.
8. Pressure will slowly build up; let the added ingredients to cook until the timer indicates zero.
9. Press "CANCEL". Now press "QPR" to quickly release pressure.
10. Open the top lid, transfer the cooked recipe in serving plates.
11. Serve the recipe warm.

Mushroom Spinach Casserole

Prep Time: 8-10 min.
Cooking Time: 20 min.
Number of Servings: 3
Ingredients:
- 1 small onion, chopped
- ¼ cup Parmesan cheese, grated
- 7 ounce fresh spinach
- 2 cups button mushrooms, make slices
- 4 large eggs

Directions:
1. In a mixing bowl, thoroughly mix the eggs and cheese. Mix in the spinach, mushrooms, onion, and garlic.

2. Grease a baking pan and line with a parchment; add the bowl mix.
3. Take your Instant Pot and place over dry kitchen surface; open its top lid and switch it on.
4. Pour 1 cup water in the cooking pot area. Arrange the trivet or steamer basket inside it; arrange the pan over the trivet/basket.
5. Close its top lid and make sure that its valve it closed to avoid spillage.
6. Press "MANUAL". Adjust the timer to 20 minutes.
7. Pressure will slowly build up; let the added ingredients to cook until the timer indicates zero.
8. Press "CANCEL". Now press "QPR" to quickly release pressure.
9. Open the top lid, transfer the cooked recipe in serving plates.
10. Serve the recipe warm.

Cauliflower Pasta

Prep Time: 8-10 min.
Cooking Time: 20 min.
Number of Servings: 6
Ingredients:
- 12 ounce vermicelli pasta
- 1 small green chili pepper, chopped
- 1 teaspoon olive oil
- 1 cup cauliflower, chopped
- 2 tablespoons green onions, chopped

Directions:
1. In the Instant Pot; add the pasta and water to cover.
2. Close its top lid and make sure that its valve it closed to avoid spillage.
3. Press "MANUAL". Adjust timer to 7 minutes.
4. Pressure will slowly build up; let the added ingredients to cook until the timer indicates zero.
5. Press "CANCEL". Now press "QPR" to quickly release pressure.
6. Open the top lid, drain water and transfer the cooked pasta in a container.
7. Take your Instant Pot and place over dry kitchen surface; open its top lid and switch it on.
8. Press "SAUTÉ". Grease the pot with olive oil.
9. Add the cauliflower; cook for 7-8 minutes until turn softened.
10. Mix in the pasta and serve warm. Top with the green onions.

Tomato Onion Rice

Prep Time: 8-10 min.
Cooking Time: 12 min.
Number of Servings: 4
Ingredients:
- 1 small red onion, chopped
- 1 tablespoon tomato paste
- 1 teaspoon olive oil
- 1 cup rice, soaked for 1 hour and drained
- 2 tablespoons parsley, chopped (finely)

Directions:
1. Take your Instant Pot and place over dry kitchen surface; open its top lid and switch it on.
2. Press "SAUTÉ". Grease the pot with some cooking oil.

3. Add the onions; cook for 3-4 minutes until turn translucent and softened.
4. Add the rice and cook for another 3-4 minutes.
5. Stir 2 cups of water and tomato sauce.
6. Close its top lid and make sure that its valve it closed to avoid spillage.
7. Press "MANUAL". Adjust the timer to 4 minutes.
8. Pressure will slowly build up; let the added ingredients to cook until the timer indicates zero.
9. Press "CANCEL". Now press "QPR" to quickly release pressure.
10. Open the top lid, transfer the cooked recipe in serving plates.
11. Serve the recipe warm with some parsley on top.

Coconut Milk Rice

Prep Time: 8-10 min.
Cooking Time: 10 min.
Number of Servings: 5
Ingredients:
*   1 small onion, chopped
*   1 cup coconut milk, low-fat
*   1 teaspoon vegetable oil
*   1 cup jasmine rice
*   1 teaspoon fresh ginger, grated

Directions:
1. Take your Instant Pot and place over dry kitchen surface; open its top lid and switch it on.
2. Press "SAUTÉ". Grease the pot with some cooking oil.
3. Add the onions; cook for 2-3 minutes until turn translucent and softened.
4. Pour in the milk and stir the mix. Add 1 cup water and stir again; cook for 1-2 minutes.
5. Add the rice, ginger, and stir.
6. Close its top lid and make sure that its valve it closed to avoid spillage.
7. Press "MANUAL". Adjust the timer to 3 minutes.
8. Pressure will slowly build up; let the added ingredients to cook until the timer indicates zero.
9. Press "CANCEL". Now press "QPR" to quickly release pressure.
10. Open the top lid, transfer the cooked recipe in serving plates.
11. Serve the recipe warm.

Mushroom Rice Meal

Prep Time: 8-10 min.
Cooking Time: 35 min.
Number of Servings: 3
Ingredients:
*   1 small onion, chopped
*   1 cup button mushrooms, make slices
*   2 teaspoons olive oil
*   1 cup wild rice
*   1 tablespoon white wine vinegar

Directions:
1. Take your Instant Pot and place over dry kitchen surface; open its top lid and switch it on.
2. Press "SAUTÉ". Grease the pot with some cooking oil.

3. Add the onions; cook for 3-4 minutes until turn translucent and softened.
4. Add the mushrooms and cook for 8-10 minutes.
5. Pour in the vinegar; stir and cook for 1 minute more. Set aside the mix in a bowl.
6. Add 2 cups water and rice.
7. Close its top lid and make sure that its valve it closed to avoid spillage.
8. Press "MANUAL". Adjust the timer to 20 minutes.
9. Pressure will slowly build up; let the added ingredients to cook until the timer indicates zero.
10. Press "CANCEL". Now press "QPR" to quickly release pressure.
11. Open the top lid, transfer the cooked rice in a mushroom bowl.
12. Mix well and serve.

Onion Penne Pasta

Prep Time: 8-10 min.
Cooking Time: 10 min.
Number of Servings: 6
Ingredients:
- 1 cup skim milk
- 1 small onion, chopped
- 1 teaspoon olive oil
- Water as needed
- 12 ounce penne pasta

Directions:
1. In the Instant Pot; add 3 cup water and pasta.
2. Close its top lid and make sure that its valve it closed to avoid spillage.
3. Press "MANUAL". Adjust the timer to 6 minutes.
4. Pressure will slowly build up; let the added ingredients to cook until the timer indicates zero.
5. Press "CANCEL". Now press "QPR" to quickly release pressure.
6. Open the top lid, drain water and transfer the cooked pasta in a container.
7. Press "SAUTÉ". Grease the pot with some cooking oil.
8. Add the onions; cook for 2 minutes until turn translucent and softened.
9. Add the milk and cook for 2-3 minutes.
10. Mix in the pasta and serve.

Chickpea Egg Bowl

Prep Time: 8-10 min.
Cooking Time: 25 min.
Number of Servings: 3
Ingredients:
- 1 tablespoon lemon juice
- 1 green onion, chopped (finely)
- 1 cup chickpeas, rinsed and drained
- 2 tablespoons fresh parsley, chopped (finely)
- 2 large boiled eggs, chopped

Directions:
1. Take your Instant Pot and place over dry kitchen surface; open its top lid and switch it on.
2. Add the chickpea and 1 ½ cups in the cooking pot. Stir the ingredients to combine well.

3. Close its top lid and make sure that its valve it closed to avoid spillage.
4. Press "MANUAL". Adjust the timer to 12 minutes.
5. Pressure will slowly build up; let the added ingredients to cook until the timer indicates zero.
6. Press "CANCEL". Now press "QPR" to quickly release pressure.
7. Mix in the remaining ingredients and serve.

Tangy Spinach Pasta

Prep Time: 8-10 min.
Cooking Time: 16 min.
Number of Servings: 5
Ingredients:
- 12 ounce tomatoes, diced
- 12 ounce fusilli pasta
- 1 teaspoon olive oil
- 1 cup spinach, chopped
- 1 small onion, chopped

Directions:
1. In the Instant Pot; add 1 cup water and pasta.
2. Close its top lid and make sure that its valve it closed to avoid spillage.
3. Press "MANUAL". Adjust the timer to 7 minutes.
4. Pressure will slowly build up; let the added ingredients to cook until the timer indicates zero.
5. Press "CANCEL". Now press "QPR" to quickly release pressure.
6. Open the top lid, drain water and transfer the cooked pasta in a container.
7. Take your Instant Pot and place over dry kitchen surface; open its top lid and switch it on.
8. Press "SAUTÉ". Grease the pot with some cooking oil.
9. Add the onions; cook for 3-4 minutes until turn translucent and softened.
10. Mix in the spinach and tomatoes; cook for 4-5 minutes.
11. Mix in the pasta and serve warm.

Cajun Dirty Rice

Prep Time: 10 minutes
Cooking Time: 10 minutes
Number of Servings: 4
Ingredients:
- 1 tablespoon olive oil
- 6 ounces andouille sausage, diced
- 1 onion, diced
- 2 stalks celery, chopped
- 1 red bell pepper, chopped
- 2 garlic cloves, minced
- 1/2 teaspoon paprika
- 1/4 teaspoon black pepper
- 1/4 teaspoon cayenne
- 1/2 teaspoon dried oregano
- 1/2 teaspoon dried thyme
- 2 cups long-grain white rice

- 2 cups chicken stock

Directions:
1. Set Instant Pot to Saute and add oil. Add sausage and brown.
2. Add onion, celery, bell pepper, and garlic to the pot. Cook until onion is translucent.
3. Add paprika, pepper, cayenne, oregano, and thyme and toast 30 seconds.
4. Add rice and toast until grains begin to look opaque. Pour in stock and stir well.
5. Close the lid and set the cooking time to 4 minutes at high pressure.
6. When steam is released, open the lid and fluff the rice to a fork.

Escarole and Beans

Prep Time: 10 minutes
Cooking Time: 15 minutes
Number of Servings: 4
Ingredients:
- 2 tablespoons olive oil, plus more for serving
- 2 ounces soppressata, chopped
- 2 cloves garlic, minced
- 1 cup dried cannellini beans
- 4 cups homemade chicken or vegetable stock
- 1 bunch escarole, roughly chopped
- 1 cup grated Parmesan or Pecorino cheese
- 1/4 teaspoon salt
- 1/2 teaspoon black pepper

Directions:
1. Set Instant Pot to Saute and add oil. Brown soppressata in oil, then add garlic and cook until fragrant.
2. Add beans to the pot, followed by stock. Close the lid and set cooking time to 35 minutes on high pressure.
3. After steam releases, remove the lid and add escarole, cheese, salt, and pepper. Close the lid and allow to sit until escarole wilts.
4. Serve with additional olive oil and crusty Italian bread.

Cincinnati Chili

Prep Time: 20 minutes
Cooking Time: 45 minutes
Number of Servings: 6
Ingredients:
- 1 tablespoon olive oil
- 2 pounds ground beef
- 2 onions, diced
- 3 garlic cloves, minced
- 1/4 cup chili powder
- 1 tablespoon ground cumin
- 1 tablespoon ground coriander
- 1 tablespoon cocoa powder

- 1 teaspoon ground allspice
- 1 teaspoon ground cinnamon
- 1/2 teaspoon ground cloves
- 2 cups crushed tomatoes
- 4 cups water
- 2 tablespoons brown sugar
- 1 teaspoon salt
- 1 teaspoon black pepper
- 1 pound dried red kidney beans, rinsed
- 1 pound spaghetti, cooked
- 1/2 pound shredded Cheddar cheese

Directions:
1. Set Instant Pot to Saute mode. Pour in oil, followed by beef. Brown beef and drain excess fat from the pot.
2. Add onions, garlic, and spices. Cook until onion is translucent.
3. Pour in tomatoes, water, brown sugar, salt, pepper, and kidney beans. Close lid and set cooking time to 25 minutes on high pressure.
4. Serve chili over cooked spaghetti. Top with cheese.

Boston Baked Beans

Prep Time: 10 minutes
Cooking Time: 1 hour
Number of Servings: 4
Ingredients:

- 1 tablespoon olive oil
- 4 ounces ham or salt pork, diced
- 1 onion, diced
- 2 cloves garlic, minced
- 1/4 cup molasses
- 1/4 cup maple syrup
- 1 tablespoon mustard powder
- 1 tablespoon Worcestershire sauce
- 2 tablespoons ketchup
- 1 teaspoon salt
- 1/2 teaspoon black pepper
- 1 pound Navy beans
- 4 cups water

Directions:
1. Set Instant Pot to Saute and add oil, followed by ham or salt pork. Brown, then add onion and garlic. Cook until onion is translucent.
2. Add molasses, maple syrup, mustard powder, Worcestershire sauce, ketchup, salt, and pepper to the pot. Add beans and stir to combine. Pour in water.
3. Close lid and set cooking time for 30 minutes at high pressure.
4. When beans are cooked, season to taste with salt, pepper, Worcestershire, and sugar.

Superfood Quinoa Salad

Prep Time: 10 minutes
Cooking Time: 1 minute
Number of Servings: 2
Ingredients:
- 1 cup quinoa
- 1 cup water
- 2 tablespoons olive oil
- 2 tablespoons apple cider vinegar
- 1/2 teaspoon salt
- 1/2 teaspoon black pepper
- 1/2 avocado, diced
- 1 fresh tomato, diced
- 1/4 cup fresh cilantro, chopped

Directions:
1. Combine quinoa and water in a pot.
2. Close lid and set cooking time for 1 minute on high pressure.
3. While steam is releasing, make salad dressing. Whisk together oil, vinegar, salt, and pepper.
4. When quinoa is ready, toss with dressing, avocado, tomato, and cilantro. Serve warm or chilled.

Creamy Polenta

Prep Time: 5 minutes
Cooking Time: 15 minutes
Number of Servings: 2
Ingredients:
- 4 cups water
- 1 teaspoon salt
- 1 tablespoon butter
- 1 cup polenta
- 1/2 cup grated Pecorino or Parmesan cheese

Directions:

1. Set Instant Pot to Saute and add water, salt, and butter. When water boils, stir in polenta.
2. Close lid and press the Porridge setting.
3. Top with grated cheese and serve.

Chapter 4: Vegetables & Sides

Sweet Potato Casserole

Prep Time: 20 minutes
Cooking Time: 25 minutes
Number of Servings: 4
Ingredients:

- 2 pounds sweet potatoes, cut into chunks
- 1 cup water
- 2/3 cup brown sugar
- 3 tablespoons melted butter
- 1/2 teaspoon cinnamon
- 1/4 teaspoon nutmeg
- 1 egg
- 2 tablespoons cream
- 1 tablespoon flour
- 1/2 cup toasted pecans, chopped

Directions:
1. Pour water into the Instant Pot and place steamer basket over the water. Arrange sweet potatoes in the steamer basket.
2. Close lid and set cooking time to 8 minutes on high pressure.
3. When sweet potatoes are finished, place in a large bowl and mash well. Add 1/3 cup brown sugar, 2 tablespoons butter, cinnamon, and nutmeg. Beat well with an electric mixer, then beat in egg and cream. Pour into a baking dish that fits inside the Instant Pot.
4. In a small bowl, combine 1 tablespoon melted butter, 1/3 cup brown sugar, and flour. Stir well to combine. Scatter topping over sweet potato casserole.
5. Place trivet in Instant Pot and add enough water to reach the top of the trivet. Set baking dish over trivet. Close lid and set cooking time to 15 minutes on high pressure.
6. Remove baking dish from the pot. Sprinkle with toasted pecans and serve.

Sweet Brussels

Prep Time: 5 min.
Cooking Time: 4 min.
Number of Servings: 2
Ingredients:
- ½ pound Brussels sprouts, trimmed
- 1 tablespoon butter
- 1 ½ teaspoon maple syrup
- Pinch of salt
- 1 teaspoon orange zest
- Pinch of pepper
- 3 tablespoons orange juice

Directions:
1. Switch on the pot after placing it on a clean and dry platform.

2. Open the pot lid and place the above-mentioned ingredients in the cooking pot area. Give the ingredients a little stir.
3. Close the pot by closing the top lid. Also, ensure to seal the valve.
4. Press "Manual" cooking function and set cooking time to 4 minutes. It will start cooking after a few minutes. Let the pot mix cook under pressure until the timer reads zero.
5. Press "Cancel" cooking function and press "Quick release" setting.
6. Open the pot and serve warm. Enjoy it with your loved one!

Paprika Potato Appetizer

Prep Time: 8-10 min.
Cooking Time: 20 min.
Number of Servings: 2
Ingredients:
- 1 tablespoon dry mango powder
- 2 tablespoons vegetable oil
- 1 teaspoon paprika
- 3 large sweet potatoes, peeled and make wedges
- ½ teaspoon salt
- 1 cup water
- Cooking oil as needed.

Directions:
1. Switch on the pot after placing it on a clean and dry platform.
2. Pour 1 cup water into the pot. Arrange the trivet inside it; arrange the wedges over the trivet.
3. Close the pot by closing the top lid. Also, ensure to seal the valve.
4. Press "Manual" cooking function and set cooking time to 15 minutes. It will start cooking after a few minutes. Let the pot mix cook under pressure until the timer reads zero.
5. Press "Cancel" cooking function and press "Quick release" setting.
6. Open the lid and remove the water. Set aside the potato.
7. Press "Saute" cooking function.
8. Add the oil and potatoes in the pot; cook for 2 minutes to cook well and turn brown.
9. Combine the mango powder, salt, and paprika in a bowl and mix well. Coat the wedges with this mixture and serve warm!

Nutritional Values (Per Serving):
Calories - 164
Fat – 6.5g
Carbohydrates – 25.5g
Fiber – 3g
Protein – 1.5g

Eggplant Green Side

Prep Time: 5 min.
Cooking Time: 5 min.
Number of Servings: 2
Ingredients:
- 2 teaspoons minced garlic
- 1 tablespoon fish sauce

- ½ teaspoon olive oil
- 2 tablespoons soy sauce
- 1 tablespoon oyster sauce
- 1 cup chopped green beans
- 1 cup chopped eggplant
- ½ cup water

Directions:
1. Switch on the pot after placing it on a clean and dry platform. Press "Saute" cooking function.
2. Open the pot lid; add the oil and garlic in the pot; cook for 2 minutes to cook well and turn aromatic.
3. Add the green beans and eggplant to the pot, Mix in the soy sauce, oyster sauce, and fish sauce.
4. Add some water over the vegetables then stir well. Close the pot by closing the top lid. Also, ensure to seal the valve.
5. Press "Manual" cooking function and set cooking time to 3 minutes. It will start cooking after a few minutes. Let the pot mix cook under pressure until the timer reads zero.
6. Press "Cancel" cooking function and press "Quick release" setting.
7. Open the pot and serve warm. Enjoy it with your loved one!

Asparagus Lemon Side

Prep Time: 5 min.
Cooking Time: 2 min.
Number of Servings: 2
Ingredients:
- 2 tablespoons lemon juice
- ¼ pound Asparagus
- 1 cup water
- 1 teaspoon olive oil

Directions:
1. Trim the asparagus and remove the woody parts.
2. Add some lemon juice and olive oil over the asparagus then toss to combine.
3. Switch on the pot after placing it on a clean and dry platform.
4. Pour the water into the pot. Arrange the trivet inside it; arrange the asparagus over the trivet.
5. Close the pot by closing the top lid. Also, ensure to seal the valve.
6. Press "Manual" cooking function and set cooking time to 2 minutes. It will start cooking after a few minutes. Let the pot mix cook under pressure until the timer reads zero.
7. Press "Cancel" cooking function and press "Natural release (NPR)" setting. It will take 8-10 minutes for natural pressure release.
8. Open the pot and serve warm. Enjoy it with your loved one!

Bacon Green Appetizer

Prep Time: 8-10 min.
Cooking Time: 25 min.
Number of Servings: 6-7
Ingredients:

- 1 pound collard greens, stems trimmed, chopped
- 1/4 pound bacon, make cubes
- 1/2 tsp kosher salt
- Black pepper as needed
- 1/2 cup water

Directions:
1. Arrange your Instant Pot over a dry, clean platform. Plug it in power socket and turn it on.
2. Now press "Saute" mode from available options. In the cooking area, add the bacon; cook for 4-5 minutes to crisp it.
3. Add half of the collards and stir until wilted a little. Add remaining collards and stir until fully wilted.
4. Add the salt and water. Stir gently.
5. Close the lid and lock. Ensure that you have sealed the valve to avoid leakage.
6. Press "Manual" mode from available cooking settings and set cooking time to 20 minutes. Instant Pot will start cooking the ingredients after a few minutes.
7. After the timer reads zero, press "Cancel" and quick release pressure.
8. Carefully remove the lid and serve the prepared keto dish warm! Season with black pepper.

Cheesy Eggplant

Prep Time: 3-5 min.
Cooking Time: 5 min.
Number of Servings: 6-7
Ingredients:

- 1 tablespoon butter

- ½ cup cream cheese

- 1 teaspoon salt

- 1 garlic clove, sliced

- 2 eggplants, sliced

- 1 teaspoon black pepper

- 1 teaspoon paprika

Directions:
1. Season the eggplant with pepper and salt.
2. In medium-size bowl, mix the sliced garlic and paprika. Mix in the cheese and stir the mixture.
3. Arrange your Instant Pot over a dry, clean platform. Plug it in power socket and turn it on.
4. Now press "Saute" mode from available options. In the cooking area, add the butter and eggplant; cook for 2-3 minutes to soften the added ingredients.
5. Transfer to a serving bowl and spread with the cheese mixture.

Bacon Honey Sprouts

Prep Time: 5 min.
Cooking Time: 8-10 min.
Number of Servings: 4
Ingredients:
- 1 tablespoon honey
- 4 slices of bacon, chopped
- ½ cup water
- Sea salt as needed
- 4 cup Brussels sprouts, chopped

Directions:
1. Arrange your Instant Pot over a dry, clean platform. Plug it in power socket and turn it on.
2. Now press "Saute" mode from available options. In the cooking area, add the bacon; cook for 4-5 minutes to crisp it.
3. Add the sprouts and cook for 4-5 more minutes. Pour the water.
4. Close the lid and lock. Ensure that you have sealed the valve to avoid leakage.
5. Press "Manual" mode from available cooking settings and set cooking time to 2 minutes. Instant Pot will start cooking the ingredients after a few minutes.
6. After the timer reads zero, press "Cancel" and quick release pressure.
7. Carefully remove the lid and serve the prepared keto dish warm! Add some salt if needed.

Green Bean & Bacon

Prep Time: 8-10 min.
Cooking Time: 7 min.
Number of Servings: 5-6
Ingredients:
- 4 cups halved green beans
- 1 cup diced onion
- 1 teaspoon salt
- ¼ cup water
- 6 slices bacon, diced
- Coconut oil as needed
- 1 teaspoon (ground) black pepper

Directions:
1. Take your Instant Pot; open the top lid. Plug it and turn it on.
2. Press "SAUTÉ" setting and the pot will start heating up.
3. In the cooking pot area, add the oil, bacon, and onions. Cook until starts becoming translucent and softened for 3 minutes. Stir in between.
4. Add the green beans, water, salt, and pepper; stir gently.
5. Close the top lid and seal its valve.
6. Press "MANUAL" setting. Adjust cooking time to 8 minutes.
7. Allow the recipe to cook for the set cooking time.
8. After the set cooking time ends, press "CANCEL" and then press "QPR (Quick Pressure Release)".
9. Instant Pot will quickly release the pressure.

10. Open the top lid, add the cooked recipe mix in serving plates.
11. Serve and enjoy!

Cheesy Asparagus

Prep Time: 5-8 min.
Cooking Time: 2 min.
Number of Servings: 2-3
Ingredients:

- 1 tablespoon olive oil
- ½ cup water
- ½ teaspoon sea salt
- 9-ounce asparagus, make halves
- 1 tablespoon sesame seeds
- ½ garlic clove, chopped
- Cheddar, shredded as needed

Directions:
1. Take your Instant Pot; open the top lid. Plug it and turn it on.
2. In the cooking pot area, add the water, garlic, salt, oil, sesame seeds and asparagus. Using a spatula, stir the ingredients.
3. Close the top lid and seal its valve.
4. Press "STEAM" setting. Adjust cooking time to 2 minutes.
5. Allow the recipe to cook for the set cooking time.
6. After the set cooking time ends, press "CANCEL" and then press "QPR (Quick Pressure Release)".
7. Instant Pot will quickly release the pressure.
8. Open the top lid, add the cooked recipe mix in serving plates.
9. top with some shredded cheese.

Creamy Pepper & Corn

Prep Time: 5-8 min.
Cooking Time: 10 min.
Number of Servings: 5-6
Ingredients:

- 1 tablespoon coconut oil
- 2 poblano peppers, sliced lengthwise to make thick strips
- ¾ red onion, thinly sliced
- ½ cup fresh or frozen corn
- ¼ cup water
- 1-2 teaspoons salt
- 1 teaspoon ground cumin
- ½ cup heavy (whipping) cream
- Juice of ½ lemon
- 2 tablespoons sour cream

Directions:
1. In a mixing bowl, mix together the heavy cream, lemon juice, and sour cream.

2. Take your Instant Pot; open the top lid. Plug it and turn it on.
3. Press "SAUTÉ" setting and the pot will start heating up.
4. In the cooking pot area, add the oil and peppers. Cook for 5-7 minutes until turn softened.
5. Add the onion, corn, water, salt, and cumin to the pot. Stir gently.
6. Close the top lid and seal its valve.
7. Press "MANUAL" setting. Adjust cooking time to 1 minutes.
8. Allow the recipe to cook for the set cooking time.
9. After the set cooking time ends, press "CANCEL" and then press "QPR (Quick Pressure Release)".
10. Instant Pot will quickly release the pressure.
11. Open the top lid, add the cooked recipe mix in serving plates. Add the bowl mix on top.
12. Serve and enjoy!

Mashed Cauliflower

Prep Time: 8-10 min.
Cooking Time: 15 min.
Number of Servings: 8
Ingredients:

- 4 cups cauliflower, small florets

- 1 teaspoon salt

- 1 teaspoon turmeric

- 2 cups chicken stock

- 1 cup heavy cream

- 1 teaspoon onion powder

Directions:
1. Arrange your Instant Pot over a dry, clean platform. Plug it in power socket and turn it on.
2. Open the lid from the top and put it aside; add the stock, cauliflower, and salt. Gently stir them.
3. Close the lid and lock. Ensure that you have sealed the valve to avoid leakage.
4. Press "Manual" mode from available cooking settings and set cooking time to 15 minutes. Instant Pot will start cooking the ingredients after a few minutes.
5. After the timer reads zero, press "Cancel" and quick release pressure.
6. Carefully remove the lid and transfer the cauliflower to the blender.
7. Add the salt, cream, and onion powder. Blend to mash the mixture (ensure not to over blend) and serve!

Cream & Onion Mushroom

Prep Time: 10 min.
Cooking Time: 30 min.
Number of Servings: 6
Ingredients:

- 1 teaspoon white pepper, ground

- 1 teaspoon cilantro

- 1 tablespoon oregano

- 2 white onion, sliced

- 1 cup white mushrooms, sliced

- 1 cup heavy cream

- 2 tablespoons butter

Directions:
1. Top the onions with the cilantro and pepper.
2. Arrange your Instant Pot over a dry, clean platform. Plug it in power socket and turn it on.
3. Now press "Saute" mode from available options. In the cooking area, add the butter and mushrooms; cook for 8-10 minutes to soften the added ingredients.
4. Stir gently in between and then after, add the onion; continue to sauté for 5 minutes more. Mix the oregano and cream.
5. Close the lid and lock. Ensure that you have sealed the valve to avoid leakage.
6. Press "Manual" mode from available cooking settings and set cooking time to 15 minutes. Instant Pot will start cooking the ingredients after a few minutes.
7. After the timer reads zero, press "Cancel" and quick release pressure.
8. Carefully remove the lid and serve the prepared keto dish warm!

Wholesome Asparagus Appetizer

Prep Time: 2-3 min.
Cooking Time: 2 min.
Number of Servings: 4
Ingredients:
- 2 tablespoons olive oil

- 1 tablespoon onion

- Sea pepper and salt as needed

- 1 cup water

- 1 pound asparagus

Directions:
1. Arrange your Instant Pot over a dry, clean platform. Plug it in power socket and turn it on.
2. Slowly pour the water into the pot order to avoid spilling out. Take the trivet and arrange in the pot; place the asparagus over the trivet.
3. Drizzle them with the olive oil and onion.
4. Close the lid and lock. Ensure that you have sealed the valve to avoid leakage.
5. Press "Manual" mode from available cooking settings and set cooking time to 2 minutes. Instant Pot will start cooking the ingredients after a few minutes.
6. After the timer reads zero, press "Cancel" and quick release pressure.

7. Carefully remove the lid, season as needed and serve the prepared keto dish warm!

Sweet Spiced Ribs

Prep Time: 15-20 min.
Cooking Time: 25 min.
Number of Servings: 4
Ingredients:
- ½ teaspoon thyme
- ½ teaspoon ground nutmeg
- ½ teaspoon paprika
- 11-ounce pork ribs
- 1 tablespoon honey
- 1 teaspoon olive oil
- 1 tablespoon chicken stock

Directions:
1. Rub the ribs with the honey, thyme, ground nutmeg, paprika, and olive oil.
2. Let the pork ribs set aside for 5 minutes to marinate.
3. Pour the pork ribs with the chicken stock.
4. Pour the water and place steamer basket/trivet inside the pot; arrange the ribs over the basket/trivet.
5. Close the top lid and seal its valve.
6. Press "MEAT" setting. Adjust cooking time to 25 minutes.
7. Allow the recipe to cook for the set cooking time.
8. After the set cooking time ends, press "CANCEL" and then press "QPR (Quick Pressure Release)".
9. Instant Pot will quickly release the pressure.
10. Open the top lid, add the cooked recipe mix in serving plates.
11. Serve and enjoy!

Shrimp & Asparagus Sides

Prep Time: 5min.
Cooking Time: 3 min.
Number of Servings: 3-4
Ingredients:
- 1 pound shrimp, peeled and deveined
- ½ tablespoon Italian seasoning
- 1 bunch asparagus spears, trimmed
- 1 cup water
- 1 teaspoon olive oil

Directions:
1. Switch on your instant pot after placing it on a clean and dry kitchen platform.
2. Pour the water into the cooking pot area. Arrange the steamer basket inside it; arrange the shrimp and asparagus over the trivet.
3. Drizzle the oil, sprinkle Italian seasoning.
4. Close the pot by closing the top lid. Also, ensure to seal the valve.

5. Press "Manual" cooking function and set cooking time to 3 minutes. It will start cooking after a few minutes. Let the pot mix cook under pressure until the timer reads zero.
6. Turn off and press "Cancel" cooking function. Quick release pressure.
7. Open the pot and serve on a serving plate or bowl. Enjoy the Paleo dish!

Pine Spinach Appetizer

Prep Time: 8-10min.
Cooking Time: 5 min.
Number of Servings: 4
Ingredients:
- 3 tablespoons olive oil
- ¼ cup raisins
- ¼ cup pine nuts, toasted
- ¼ cup balsamic vinegar
- 1 apple, cored and sliced
- 1 yellow onion, sliced
- 6 garlic cloves, minced
- A pinch of sea salt and black pepper
- 5 cups mixed spinach and chard
- ½ cup water
- A pinch of nutmeg

Directions:
1. Switch on your instant pot after placing it on a clean and dry kitchen platform. Press "Saute" cooking function.
2. Open the pot lid; add the oil and onions in the pot; start cooking for 2 minutes to cook well and soften.
3. Add the garlic, apple, vinegar, and raisins stir and cook for 4 minutes more. Mix in the spinach, chard, and water.
4. Close the pot by closing the top lid. Also, ensure to seal the valve.
5. Press "Manual" cooking function and set cooking time to 4 minutes. It will start cooking after a few minutes. Let the pot mix cook under pressure until the timer reads zero.
6. Turn off and press "Cancel" cooking function. Quick release pressure.
7. Open the potting mix the nutmeg, pine nuts, a pinch of salt and pepper.
8. Combine and divide among small appetizer plates.

Minty Veggie Appetizer

Prep Time: 8-10min.
Cooking Time: 12 min.
Number of Servings: 5-6
Ingredients:
- 1 yellow onion, chopped
- 1 parsley bunch, chopped
- 2 mint bunches, chopped
- 4 garlic cloves, minced
- 1 celery bunch, roughly chopped

- 3 tablespoons olive oil
- 1 bunch green onion, chopped
- Black pepper to the taste
- 2 cups water

Directions:
1. Switch on your instant pot after placing it on a clean and dry kitchen platform. Press "Saute" cooking function.
2. Open the pot lid; add the oil, garlic, and onions in the pot; start cooking for 3-4 minutes to cook well and soften.
3. Add the celery, black pepper and water; stir gently.
4. Close the pot by closing the top lid. Also, ensure to seal the valve.
5. Press "Manual" cooking function and set cooking time to 6 minutes. It will start cooking after a few minutes. Let the pot mix cook under pressure until the timer reads zero.
6. Turn off and press "Cancel" cooking function. Quick release pressure.
7. Open the pot and add the parsley and mint, stir gently. Cover and cook for 2 minutes more.
8. Divide into bowls and serve warm!

Mushroom Risotto Sides

Prep Time: 8-10min.
Cooking Time: 14 min.
Number of Servings: 4
Ingredients:
- 2 garlic cloves, minced
- 2 ounces olive oil
- 2 cups cauliflower rice
- 4 ounces coconut cream
- 4 ounces white vinegar
- 4 cups chicken stock
- 1 yellow onion, chopped
- 8 ounces mushrooms, sliced
- 1-ounce basil, chopped

Directions:
1. Switch on your instant pot after placing it on a clean and dry kitchen platform. Press "Saute" cooking function.
2. Open the pot lid; add the oil, garlic, mushrooms, and onions in the pot; start cooking for 2 minutes to cook well and soften.
3. Close the pot by closing the top lid. Also, ensure to seal the valve.
4. Press "Manual" cooking function and set cooking time to 3 minutes. It will start cooking after a few minutes. Let the pot mix cook under pressure until the timer reads zero.
5. Turn off and press "Cancel" cooking function. Quick release pressure.
6. Open the pot and add the cauliflower rice, stock, and vinegar, stir gently. Cover and cook for 10 minutes.
7. Add the coconut cream and basil, stir gently. Divide among plates and serve warm!

Garlic Tuna Appetizing Patties

Prep Time: 8-10min.
Cooking Time: 10 min.
Number of Servings: 12 patties
Ingredients:
- 1 teaspoon dill, chopped
- 1 teaspoon garlic powder
- 1 tablespoon olive oil
- ½ cup water
- 15 ounces canned tuna, drain and flaked
- 1 teaspoon parsley, chopped
- ½ cup red onion, chopped
- A pinch of pepper and salt
- 3 eggs

Directions:
1. In a mixing bowl, mix the tuna, salt, pepper, dill, parsley, onion, garlic powder and eggs. Combine well and shape your patties; put them on a plate.
2. Switch on your instant pot after placing it on a clean and dry kitchen platform. Press "Saute" cooking function.
3. Open the pot lid; add the oil and patties in the pot; start cooking for 2 minutes to cook well and soften. Transfer them to a plate.
4. Clean your instant pot, add the water and add the steamer basket, and add tuna patties inside.
5. Close the pot by closing the top lid. Also, ensure to seal the valve.
6. Press "Manual" cooking function and set cooking time to 6 minutes. It will start cooking after a few minutes. Let the pot mix cook under pressure until the timer reads zero.
7. Turn off and press "Cancel" cooking function. Quick release pressure.
8. Open the pot and serve on a serving plate or bowl. Enjoy the Paleo dish!

Quick Corn on the Cob

Prep Time: 2 minutes
Cooking Time: 3 minutes
Number of Servings: 4
Ingredients:
- 2 cups water
- 4 ears fresh corn

Directions:
1. Pour water into Instant Pot. Place steamer basket over water and arrange corn in the basket.
2. Close lid and set cooking time to 3 minutes. Use the quick pressure release method to release steam. Serve corn hot with butter and salt.

Green Beans Almondine

Prep Time: 20 minutes
Cooking Time: 1 minute
Number of Servings: 4

Ingredients:
- 1 pound green beans, trimmed
- 1 cup water
- 2 tablespoons butter
- 1/4 teaspoon salt
- 1/4 teaspoon black pepper
- Juice of 1/2 lemon
- 1 cup slivered almonds, toasted

Directions:
1. Pour the water into the Instant Pot. Place the steamer basket over the water and arrange green beans in the basket.
2. Close the lid and set the cooking time to 1 minute on high pressure.
3. Toss beans with butter, salt, pepper, and lemon juice. Top with toasted almonds.

Southern Collard Greens

Prep Time: 10 minutes
Cooking Time: 25 minutes
Number of Servings: 4
Ingredients:
- 1 tablespoon olive oil
- 1/2 onion, diced
- 2 smoked turkey necks or 1 ham hock
- 1 pound collard greens, washed and trimmed
- 2 cups chicken stock
- 1/4 teaspoon salt
- 1/2 teaspoon black pepper

Directions:
1. Set Instant Pot to Saute mode and add olive oil. Cook onions in oil until translucent.
2. Add turkey or ham to pot and saute until some fat renders.
3. Add collard greens, chicken stock, and salt and pepper.
4. Close lid and set cooking time to 20 minutes on high. Serve greens warm, preferably with cornbread.

Scalloped Potatoes

Prep Time: 20 minutes
Cooking Time: 50 minutes
Number of Servings: 6
Ingredients:
- 3 large potatoes, peeled and sliced into 1/4 inch thick rounds
- 2 cups whole milk
- 1/4 cup butter
- 1/4 cup flour
- 1 cup + 1/4 cup grated Cheddar cheese
- 1/4 teaspoon salt
- 1/4 teaspoon black pepper

Directions:

1. Set the Instant Pot to Saute and add butter. When butter is melted, stir in flour. Cook until bubbling subsides and mixture has darkened slightly.
2. Pour in milk, stirring constantly, and cook until thickened. Add 1 cup cheese and stir until melted. Turn off heat.
3. Arrange a layer of potato slices on the bottom of a baking dish that fits into the Instant Pot. Top with a layer of cheese sauce, followed by another layer of potato slices. Continue this sequence until all the sauce and potatoes are used up. Sprinkle with remaining cheese. Wash out the inner pot.
4. Place trivet in the pot and add enough water to reach the top of the trivet. Place baking dish over trivet. Close lid and set cooking time to 35 minutes on high pressure.
5. If desired, place casserole under the broiler for 2-5 minutes to the brown top after cooking is complete.

Potato Salad with Eggs

Prep Time: 20 minutes
Cooking Time: 4 minutes
Number of Servings: 6
Ingredients:
- 6 large potatoes, peeled and cubed
- 2 cups water
- 3 eggs
- 2 shallots, finely chopped
- 1 cup mayonnaise
- 1 tablespoon vinegar
- 1 tablespoon fresh dill, minced
- 1/4 teaspoon salt
- 1/2 teaspoon black pepper

Directions:
1. Pour water into the Instant Pot. Place the steamer basket over the water and add potatoes and eggs.
2. Close lid and set the timer to 4 minutes on high pressure. When steam releases, place eggs in a bowl of cold water while you prepare the dressing.
3. Combine mayonnaise, vinegar, dill, salt, and pepper in a large bowl. Add potatoes to bowl. Peel and chop eggs and add alongside the potatoes. Toss contents of the bowl until potatoes and eggs are well coated.
4. Chill before serving.

Zucchini Potato Appetizer

Prep Time: 5min.
Cooking Time: 10 min.
Number of Servings: 6-7
Ingredients:
- 1 bell pepper, cubed
- 6 cherry tomatoes, halved
- 1 large potato, cubed
- 1 zucchini, make thick rounds
- 1 onion, make small wedges

- A handful pine nuts
- 1/2 tablespoon raisins, soaked in water
- 1 cup basil, chopped
- 1 large eggplant, cubed
- 1/4 cup olive oil
- 1/2 tablespoon capers
- 2 tablespoons green olives, pitted
- Pepper and salt as needed

Directions:
1. Add the salt over eggplant cubes and arrange in a strainer for 25-30 minutes.
2. Take Instant Pot and carefully arrange it over a clean, dry kitchen platform. Turn on the appliance.
3. Find and press "Sauté" cooking function.
4. In the cooking pot area; add the oil and eggplant cubes in the pot. Cook for 2-3 minutes to cook well and soften.
5. Add the onion and some pepper; sauté until translucent.
6. Add rest the ingredients and cook for 2-3 more minutes. Add 1/2 cup water, salt, and some pepper.
7. Close the pot lid and seal the valve to avoid any leakage. Find and press "Manual" cooking setting and set cooking time to 4 minutes.
8. Allow the recipe ingredients to cook for the set time and after that, the timer reads "zero".
9. Press "Cancel" and press "NPR" setting for natural pressure release. It takes 8-10 times for all inside pressure to release.
10. Open the pot and arrange the cooked recipe in serving plates. Enjoy the vegan recipe!

Eggplant Tomatino

Prep Time: 5min.
Cooking Time: 4 min.
Number of Servings: 6-7
Ingredients:
- 2 ½ pounds eggplant, make 1-inch cubes
- 7 ½ ounces canned tomato sauce
- 2 cans (16 ounces each) diced tomatoes with its juice
- 4 celery stalks, make 1-inch pieces
- 2 large onions, thinly sliced
- 2 tablespoons olive oil, divided
- 2 tablespoons capers, drained
- 1 tablespoon maple syrup
- 1 cup olives, pitted and halved
- 4 tablespoons balsamic vinegar
- 2 teaspoons dried basil
- Pepper and salt as needed
- Basil leaves to garnish

Directions:
1. Take Instant Pot and carefully arrange it over a clean, dry kitchen platform. Turn on the appliance.
2. In the cooking pot area, add the mentioned ingredients. Stir the ingredients gently.
3. Close the pot lid and seal the valve to avoid any leakage. Find and press "Manual" cooking setting and set cooking time to 4 minutes.
4. Allow the recipe ingredients to cook for the set time, and after that, the timer reads "zero". Press "Cancel" and press "QPR" setting for quick pressure release.
5. Open the pot and arrange the cooked recipe in serving plates. Garnish with fresh basil and serve.

Spinach Tomato Appetizer

Prep Time: 5min.
Cooking Time: 10-12 min.
Number of Servings: 4
Ingredients:
- 2 teaspoons garlic, minced
- 10 cups fresh spinach, chopped
- 1 ½ cups vegetable broth
- 1 tablespoon lemon juice
- 1 cup tomatoes, chopped
- ½ cup tomato puree
- 2 tablespoons olive oil
- 2 small onions, chopped
- ½ teaspoon red pepper flakes, crushed
- Pepper and salt as needed

Directions:
1. Take Instant Pot and carefully arrange it over a clean, dry kitchen platform. Turn on the appliance.
2. Find and press "Sauté" cooking function.
3. In the cooking pot area; add the oil and onions in the pot. Cook for 2-3 minutes to cook well and soften.
4. Add the garlic and red pepper flakes and cook for 1 minute. Add spinach and cook for 2 minutes.
5. In the cooking pot area, add the remaining ingredients. Stir the ingredients gently.
6. Close the pot lid and seal the valve to avoid any leakage. Find and press "Manual" cooking setting and set cooking time to 6 minutes.
7. Allow the recipe ingredients to cook for the set time, and after that, the timer reads "zero". Press "Cancel" and press "QPR" setting for quick pressure release.
8. Open the pot and arrange the cooked recipe in serving plates. Enjoy the vegan recipe!

Chili Garlic Okra

Prep Time: 8-10min.
Cooking Time: 7-8 min.
Number of Servings: 4
Ingredients:
- 1 teaspoon cumin seeds
- 2 medium onions, sliced
- 2 medium tomatoes, chopped

- 2-pound okra, cut into 1-inch pieces
- ½ cup vegetable broth
- 1 teaspoon ground coriander
- ½ teaspoon red chili powder
- ½ teaspoon ground turmeric
- 2 tablespoons olive oil
- 6 garlic cloves, chopped
- Pepper and salt as needed

Directions:
1. Take Instant Pot and carefully arrange it over a clean, dry kitchen platform. Turn on the appliance.
2. Find and press "Sauté" cooking function.
3. In the cooking pot area; add the oil, cumin seeds, and garlic in the pot. Cook for 1 minutes to cook well and soften.
4. Add the onion and cook for 4 minutes. Add the remaining ingredients and cook for 1 more minute.
5. Close the pot lid and seal the valve to avoid any leakage. Find and press "Manual" cooking setting and set cooking time to 2 minutes.
6. Allow the recipe ingredients to cook for the set time, and after that, the timer reads "zero". Press "Cancel" and press "QPR" setting for quick pressure release.
7. Open the pot and arrange the cooked recipe in serving plates. Enjoy the vegan recipe!

Tomato Eggplant Spread

Prep Time: 5-8 min.
Cooking Time: 10 min.
Number of Servings: 4
Ingredients:
- 3 tablespoons olive oil
- 1 cup yellow onion, chopped
- 2 minced garlic cloves
- 2 cups eggplant, chopped
- 1 cup sweet bell pepper, chopped
- ¼ cup sun-dried tomatoes, minced
- 2 tablespoons tomato paste
- ¼ cup vegetable stock
- Black pepper and salt as needed

Directions:
1. Take your Instant Pot and place it on a clean kitchen platform. Turn it on after plugging it into a power socket.
2. Put the pot on "Saute" mode. In the pot, add the oil and onion; cook for 2-3 minutes until the ingredients become soft.
3. Mix in the garlic, bell pepper, and eggplant; stir and cook for 2 minutes more.
4. Add the tomatoes, stock, salt, pepper and tomato paste; stir gently.
5. Close the lid and lock. Ensure that you have sealed the valve to avoid leakage.
6. Press "Manual" mode and set timer for 5 minutes. It will take a few minutes for the pot to build inside pressure and start cooking.

7. After the timer reads zero, press "Cancel" and quick release pressure.
8. Carefully remove the lid. Serve on toasted bread as an appetizer.

Polenta Snacky Bites

Prep Time: 8-10 min.
Cooking Time: 25 min.
Number of Servings: 7-8
Ingredients:
- 4 cups vegetable stock
- 1 cup polenta
- ¼ cup cilantro, chopped
- 2 teaspoons Cajun seasoning
- ¼ teaspoon salt
- Olive oil spray

Directions:
1. Take your Instant Pot and place it on a clean kitchen platform. Turn it on after plugging it into a power socket.
2. Open the lid from the top and put it aside; add the stock, cilantro, salt, Cajun seasoning, and polenta. Gently stir them.
3. Close the lid and lock. Ensure that you have sealed the valve to avoid leakage.
4. Press "Manual" mode and set timer for 5 minutes. It will take a few minutes for the pot to build inside pressure and start cooking.
5. After the timer reads zero, press "Cancel" and quick release pressure.
6. Carefully remove the lid and set aside to cool down.
7. Make small balls from the mixture and place on a baking sheet (sprayed with cooking oil).
8. Bake at 450 degrees F for 20 minutes. Enjoy them with your favorite vegan dip!

Cinnamon Peanut Snack

Prep Time: 8-10 min.
Cooking Time: 25 min.
Number of Servings: 7-8
Ingredients:
- 2 pounds raw peanuts, with shell

- 2 chunks rock sugar

- 4-star anise

- 6 medium-size cloves garlic

- 4 sticks cinnamon

- 8 pieced dried red chili peppers (optional)

Directions:
1. Take your Instant Pot and place it on a clean kitchen platform. Turn it on after plugging it into a power socket.

2. Open the lid from the top and put it aside; start adding the mentioned ingredients inside and pour enough water to cover the peanuts.
3. Close the lid and lock. Ensure that you have sealed the valve to avoid leakage.
4. Press "Manual" mode and set timer for 25 minutes. It will take a few minutes for the pot to build inside pressure and start cooking.
5. After the timer reads zero, press "Cancel" and naturally release pressure. It takes about 8-10 minutes to naturally release pressure.
6. Carefully remove the lid, shell the peanuts and serve warm!

Cashew Snack Dip

Prep Time: 8-10 min.
Cooking Time: 5 min.
Number of Servings: 4-5
Ingredients:
- 10 ounces canned tomatoes and green chilies, chopped
- 1 teaspoon smoked paprika
- ½ teaspoon jalapeno powder
- ½ cup chopped cilantro
- 2 cups water
- ½ cup cashews
- ½ cup nutritional yeast
- 4 cups cauliflower florets
- 1 ½ cups carrot, chopped
- Black pepper and salt as needed
- ½ teaspoon chili powder
- ¼ teaspoon mustard powder

Directions:
1. Take your Instant Pot and place it on a clean kitchen platform. Turn it on after plugging it into a power socket.
2. Open the lid from the top and put it aside; start adding the cauliflower, carrots, water, and cashews. Gently stir them.
3. Close the lid and lock. Ensure that you have sealed the valve to avoid leakage.
4. Press "Manual" mode and set timer for 5 minutes. It will take a few minutes for the pot to build inside pressure and start cooking.
5. After the timer reads zero, press "Cancel" and quick release pressure.
6. Carefully remove the lid and transfer the mixture in a blender; add the salt, pepper, tomatoes and chilies, paprika, chili powder, mustard powder, jalapeno powder, cilantro, and yeast.
7. Blend to make it smooth over pulse mode.
8. Serve with veggie sticks or your favorite snack!

Artichoke Coconut Dip

Prep Time: 8-10 min.
Cooking Time: 20 min.
Number of Servings: 6
Ingredients:

- 1 cup water
- 1 pound baby artichokes, trimmed and discard stems
- ½ cup cannellini beans (soak for 12 hours and drain liquid)
- 2 garlic cloves, minced
- Juice of ½ lemon
- 1 cup coconut cream
- Pepper and salt as needed

Directions:
1. Take your Instant Pot and place it on a clean kitchen platform. Turn it on after plugging it into a power socket.
2. Open the lid from the top and put it aside; start adding the beans, artichokes, water, salt, and pepper. Gently stir them.
3. Close the lid and lock. Ensure that you have sealed the valve to avoid leakage.
4. Press "Manual" mode and set timer for 20 minutes. It will take a few minutes for the pot to build inside pressure and start cooking.
5. After the timer reads zero, press "Cancel" and quick release pressure.
6. Carefully remove the lid and transfer the mixture in a blender; add the cream and garlic.
7. Blend to make it smooth over pulse mode.
8. Serve as an appetizer.

Orange Brussels Sprouts

Prep Time: 5 min.
Cooking Time: 5 min.
Number of Servings: 7-8
Ingredients:
- 1 teaspoon orange zest, grated
- ¼ cup orange juice
- 2 pounds Brussels sprouts, trimmed
- 1 tablespoon olive oil
- 2 tablespoons stevia or sugar
- Black pepper and salt as needed

Directions:
1. Take your Instant Pot and place it on a clean kitchen platform. Turn it on after plugging it into a power socket.
2. Put the pot on "Saute" mode. In the pot, add the oil and sprouts; cook for 1-2 minutes until the ingredients become soft.
3. Add the zest, orange juice, stevia/sugar, salt, and pepper; stir well.
4. Close the lid and lock. Ensure that you have sealed the valve to avoid leakage.
5. Press "Manual" mode and set timer for 4 minutes. It will take a few minutes for the pot to build inside pressure and start cooking.
6. After the timer reads zero, press "Cancel" and quick release pressure.
7. Carefully remove the lid and serve as a side dish!

Instant Mustard Cabbage

Prep Time: 8-10 min.
Cooking Time: 6 min.
Number of Servings: 4
Ingredients:
- 2 teaspoons stevia or sugar
- 1 tablespoon olive oil
- 2 teaspoons balsamic vinegar
- 1 cabbage head, sliced
- 1 yellow onion, chopped
- 3 garlic cloves, minced
- Black pepper and salt as needed
- 2 teaspoons mustard

Directions:
1. Take your Instant Pot and place it on a clean kitchen platform. Turn it on after plugging it into a power socket.
2. Put the pot on "Saute" mode. In the pot, add the oil, onion, and garlic; cook for 2-3 minutes until the ingredients become soft.
3. Mix in the cabbage, stevia/sugar, vinegar, mustard, salt, and pepper; mix well.
4. Close the lid and lock. Ensure that you have sealed the valve to avoid leakage.
5. Press "Manual" mode and set timer for 4 minutes. It will take a few minutes for the pot to build inside pressure and start cooking.
6. After the timer reads zero, press "Cancel" and quick release pressure.
7. Carefully remove the lid and serve as a side dish!

Classic Bean & Pepper

Prep Time: 5-8 min.
Cooking Time: 30 min.
Number of Servings: 5-6
Ingredients:
- 12 ounces green bell pepper, chopped
- 12 ounces sweet onion, chopped
- 1 teaspoon olive oil
- 16 ounces black beans, soaked overnight and drained
- 2 tablespoons tomato paste
- 1 teaspoons stevia or sugar
- 4 garlic cloves, minced
- 2 ½ teaspoons cumin, ground
- 2 quarts water
- A pinch of salt

Directions:
1. Take your Instant Pot and place it on a clean kitchen platform. Turn it on after plugging it into a power socket.
2. Put the pot on "Saute" mode. In the pot, add the oil, green pepper, and onion; cook for 4-5 minutes until the ingredients become soft.

3. Mix in the stevia/sugar, garlic, cumin, and tomato paste; stir the mixture and cook for 1 minute.
4. Add the beans and water; stir again.
5. Close the lid and lock. Ensure that you have sealed the valve to avoid leakage.
6. Press "Manual" mode and set timer for 25 minutes. It will take a few minutes for the pot to build inside pressure and start cooking.
7. After the timer reads zero, press "Cancel" and quick release pressure.
8. Carefully remove the lid.
9. Mash beans a bit, add the salt; stir and serve as a side dish.

Just Jalapeno Beans

Prep Time: 8-10 min.
Cooking Time: 35 min.
Number of Servings: 4
Ingredients:
- 4 garlic cloves, chopped
- 2 teaspoons dried oregano
- 1 ½ teaspoons cumin, ground
- 3 tablespoons olive oil
- 1 ½ cups yellow onion, chopped
- 2 pounds soaked pinto beans
- 1 jalapeno, chopped
- Black pepper and salt as needed
- 4 cups vegetable stock
- 4 cups water

Directions:
1. Take your Instant Pot and place it on a clean kitchen platform. Turn it on after plugging it into a power socket.
2. Put the pot on "Saute" mode. In the pot, add the oil and onion; cook for 2-3 minutes until the ingredients become soft.
3. Add the garlic, and cook for 1 minute more.
4. Mix in the beans, oregano, jalapeno, salt, pepper, cumin, stock, and water; stir the ingredients.
5. Close the lid and lock. Ensure that you have sealed the valve to avoid leakage.
6. Press "Manual" mode and set timer for 30 minutes. It will take a few minutes for the pot to build inside pressure and start cooking.
7. After the timer reads zero, press "Cancel" and quick release pressure.
8. Carefully remove the lid and transfer the mixture in a blender to make it smooth.
9. Serve warm!

Cauliflower Potatoes

Prep Time: 5-8 min.
Cooking Time: 5 min.
Number of Servings: 4
Ingredients:
- 8 ounces cauliflower florets
- 2 pounds peeled potatoes, sliced

- 1 ½ cups water
- 1 garlic clove, minced
- A pinch of salt

Directions:
1. Take your Instant Pot and place it on a clean kitchen platform. Turn it on after plugging it into a power socket.
2. Open the lid from the top and put it aside; start adding the potatoes, water, salt and cauliflower; gently stir them.
3. Close the lid and lock. Ensure that you have sealed the valve to avoid leakage.
4. Press "Manual" mode and set timer for 5 minutes. It will take a few minutes for the pot to build inside pressure and start cooking.
5. After the timer reads zero, press "Cancel" and quick release pressure.
6. Carefully remove the lid. Add the garlic, stir and mash well.
7. Serve as a side dish.

Maple Bacon Brussels Sprouts

Prep Time: 10 minutes
Cooking Time: 10 minutes
Number of Servings: 4
Ingredients:
- 1 pound Brussels sprouts, trimmed and halved
- 1 cup water
- 4 ounces bacon, diced
- 2 shallots, finely chopped
- 1 garlic clove, minced
- 2 tablespoons maple syrup

Directions:
1. Pour water into Instant Pot. Place steamer basket above water and add Brussels sprouts.
2. Close lid and set cooking time for 3 minutes on high pressure.
3. Remove sprouts to a plate. Pour out water and dry inner pot.
4. Set Instant Pot to Saute mode and brown bacon. Add shallots and garlic and cook until shallots are translucent. Add maple syrup and bring to a boil.
5. Pour Brussels sprouts into the pot and toss to combine. Pour back into the bowl with sauce, shallots, and garlic and serve hot.

Beet Salad

Prep Time: 20 minutes
Cooking Time: 15 minutes
Number of Servings: 4
Ingredients:
- 6 beets, trimmed and peeled
- 1 cup water
- 1/4 cup balsamic vinegar
- 1/2 cup olive oil
- 1/4 teaspoon salt
- 1/4 teaspoon black pepper

- 1/4 cup goat cheese
- 1/4 cup toasted walnuts
- 3 cups baby spinach

Directions:
1. Pour water into the Instant Pot. Place the steamer basket over the water and add beets.
2. Close lid and set cooking time to 15 minutes on high pressure.
3. When steam releases, remove beets from the pot and chop into 1-inch pieces. Place in a bowl with cheese and nuts.
4. Whisk together vinegar, oil, salt, and pepper. Pour over beets, cheese, and nuts. Toss to combine.
5. Serve beet mixture over baby spinach.

Chapter 5: Sauces & Spreads

Apple Mango Spread/Chutney

Prep Time: 5min.
Cooking Time: 7 min.
Number of Servings: Makes 2 cups
Ingredients:

- 1 apple, core removed and chopped
- 2 mangoes, diced
- 1 tablespoon ginger, grated
- 1 shallot, sliced thinly
- ½ teaspoon red pepper flakes
- 1 tablespoon vegetable oil
- 1 ¼ cups apple cider vinegar
- 1 ¼ cups sugar
- 2 teaspoons salt
- Pinch of cinnamon
- Pinch of cardamom powder

Directions:

1. Take Instant Pot and carefully arrange it over a clean, dry kitchen platform. Turn on the appliance.
2. Find and press "Sauté" cooking function.
3. In the cooking pot area; add the oil, shallots, and ginger in the pot. Cook for 2 minutes to cook well and soften.
4. Add spices and stir, cooking for 10 seconds. Add everything else and stir until sugar dissolves.
5. Close the pot lid and seal the valve to avoid any leakage. Find and press "Manual" cooking setting and set cooking time to 7 minutes.
6. Allow the recipe ingredients to cook for the set time, and after that, the timer reads "zero".
7. Press "Cancel" and press "NPR" setting for natural pressure release. It takes 8-10 times for all inside pressure to release.
8. Open lid, and using sauté setting, continue cooking until the mix turns thick. Transfer to the jar, cool down and then refrigerate until use.

BBQ Sauce

Prep Time: 5-8min.
Cooking Time: 13-15 min.
Number of Servings: Makes 2 ½ cups
Ingredients:

- 1 teaspoon hot sauce of choice
- 1 teaspoon liquid smoke
- ¾ cup dried prunes
- ¼ teaspoon cumin
- ¼ cup agave or maple syrup
- ¼ teaspoon garlic powder

- ½ cup water
- ¼ cup apple cider vinegar
- 1 teaspoon salt
- 1 medium onion, chopped
- 1 tablespoon vegetable oil
- ½ cup tomato puree

Directions:
1. Take Instant Pot and carefully arrange it over a clean, dry kitchen platform. Turn on the appliance.
2. Find and press "Sauté" cooking function.
3. In the cooking pot area; add the oil and onions in the pot. Cook for 2 minutes to cook well and soften.
4. Mix the vinegar, syrup, tomato puree and water and mix well until syrup is dissolved.
5. Add hot sauce and spices, then add the prunes.
6. Close the pot lid and seal the valve to avoid any leakage. Find and press "Manual" cooking setting and set cooking time to 10 minutes.
7. Allow the recipe ingredients to cook for the set time, and after that, the timer reads "zero". Press "Cancel" and press "QPR" setting for quick pressure release.
8. Open the pot and puree the mixture, then pour into glass bottles and seal.
9. Once cooled, store in the refrigerator, and use later as needed!

Oregano Tomato Sauce

Prep Time: 10 min.
Cooking Time: 50 min.
Number of Servings: 7-8
Ingredients:
- ½ teaspoon red pepper flakes
- 4 garlic cloves, minced
- 1 yellow onion, make halves
- 1 carrot, cut into chunks
- 1 stem basil
- ½ tablespoon oregano, dried
- 54 ounces crushed tomatoes
- 2 tablespoon olive oil
- 2 tablespoons vegan butter
- ¼ cup basil leaves, chopped
- Salt and black pepper to the taste

Directions:
1. Take your Instant Pot and place it on a clean kitchen platform. Turn it on after plugging it into a power socket.
2. Put the pot on "Saute" mode. In the pot, add the butter, garlic, and oil; stir and cook for 2-3 minutes until the ingredients become soft.
3. Add oregano and flakes, stir and cook for 1 minute more. Add the carrots, onion, all tomatoes (reserve 1 cup), basil stem, salt, and pepper.

4. Gently stir the added ingredients; close the lid and lock. Ensure that you have sealed the valve to avoid leakage.
5. Press "Manual" mode and set timer for 45 minutes. It will take a few minutes for the pot to build inside pressure and start cooking.
6. After the timer reads zero, press "Cancel" and quick release pressure.
7. Carefully remove the lid. Remove the basil stem, carrot chunks and onion halves.
8. Add the reserved tomatoes, chopped basil, pepper, and salt; stir and transfer to airtight containers.
9. Use it later with your favorite recipes!

Zucchini Spiced Sauce

Prep Time: 5 min.
Cooking Time: 8-10 min.
Number of Servings: 5-6
Ingredients:
- 1 ½ pounds chopped zucchinis
- 1 yellow onion, chopped
- 1 tablespoon olive oil
- ½ cup water
- 2 garlic cloves, minced
- 1 bunch basil leaves
- Black pepper and salt as needed

Directions:
1. Take your Instant Pot and place it on a clean kitchen platform. Turn it on after plugging it into a power socket.
2. Put the pot on "Saute" mode. In the pot, add the onion and 1 tablespoon oil; cook for 2-3 minutes until the ingredients become soft.
3. Add the zucchini, water, and salt.
4. Gently stir the added ingredients; close the lid and lock. Ensure that you have sealed the valve to avoid leakage.
5. Press "Manual" mode and set timer for 3 minutes. It will take a few minutes for the pot to build inside pressure and start cooking.
6. After the timer reads zero, press "Cancel" and naturally release pressure. It takes about 8-10 minutes to naturally release pressure.
7. Carefully remove the lid; add the basil and garlic and stir well.
8. Pour the mixture into your blender and blend well. Serve warm!

Tangy Cranberry Sauce

Prep Time: 5 min.
Cooking Time: 5 min.
Number of Servings: 4-6
Ingredients:
- 1 teaspoon lemon juice
- ¾ cup cranberry juice
- 1 cup cranberries, dried

- ¾ cup water

Directions:
1. Take your Instant Pot and place it on a clean kitchen platform. Turn it on after plugging it into a power socket.
2. Open the lid from the top and put it aside; start adding the cranberries, water, lemon juice and cranberry juice inside.
3. Gently stir the added ingredients; close the lid and lock. Ensure that you have sealed the valve to avoid leakage.
4. Press "Manual" mode and set timer for 5 minutes. It will take a few minutes for the pot to build inside pressure and start cooking.
5. After the timer reads zero, press "Cancel" and naturally release pressure. It takes about 8-10 minutes to naturally release pressure.
6. Carefully remove the lid. Transfer the sauce to your blender; in pulse mode, blend the ingredients well.
7. Serve warm or refrigerate and serve chilled!

Garlic Tomato Sauce

Prep Time: 5min.
Cooking Time: 45 min.
Number of Servings: Makes 6-7 cups
Ingredients:
- 1 medium onion, chopped
- 2 tablespoons vegetable oil
- 7 cups can diced tomatoes
- 2 carrots, diced cayenne
- 6 garlic cloves, minced
- Pepper and salt
- ¼ cup chopped fresh herbs

Directions:
1. Take Instant Pot and carefully arrange it over a clean, dry kitchen platform. Turn on the appliance.
2. Find and press "Sauté" cooking function.
3. In the cooking pot area; add the oil and onions in the pot. Cook for 3-4 minutes to cook well and soften.
4. Add the garlic and cook 1 minute. Add everything else.
5. Close the pot lid and seal the valve to avoid any leakage. Find and press "Manual" cooking setting and set cooking time to 45 minutes.
6. Allow the recipe ingredients to cook for the set time, and after that, the timer reads "zero". Press "Cancel" and press "QPR" setting for quick pressure release.
7. Open the pot. Add Pepper and salt and cayenne, if necessary and serve.

Pumpkin Butter

Prep Time: 5min.
Cooking Time: 3 min.
Number of Servings: Makes 3 cups

Ingredients:

- 1 teaspoon cinnamon
- Pinch of clove
- ½ cup sugar
- Pinch allspice
- Pinch nutmeg
- 1 cup apple juice
- 1 teaspoon ground ginger
- 2 can pumpkin puree

Directions:

1. Take Instant Pot and carefully arrange it over a clean, dry kitchen platform. Turn on the appliance.
2. In the cooking pot area, add the mentioned ingredients. Stir the ingredients gently.
3. Close the pot lid and seal the valve to avoid any leakage. Find and press "Manual" cooking setting and set cooking time to 3 minutes.
4. Allow the recipe ingredients to cook for the set time, and after that, the timer reads "zero".
5. Press "Cancel" and press "NPR" setting for natural pressure release. It takes 8-10 times for all inside pressure to release.
6. Open the pot. Pour into jars, seal and let cool. You can store in the fridge one week.

Chapter 6: Fish & Seafood

Foil-Steamed Tilapia

Prep Time: 10 minutes
Cooking Time: 3 minutes
Number of Servings: 2
Ingredients:
- 4 tilapia fillets
- Juice of 1 lemon
- 1/2 tablespoon olive oil
- 1/2 teaspoon salt
- 1/2 teaspoon black pepper
- 4 garlic cloves
- 3 sprigs fresh dill

Directions:
1. Place the fillets on top of a sheet of aluminum foil. Season on both sides with lemon, olive oil, salt, and pepper. Place garlic and dill on top of the fish. Add another sheet of aluminum foil on top and fold in the edges to seal.
2. Pour 2 cups of water into the Instant Pot and add the foil package. Close the lid and set the cooking time for 3 minutes at high pressure.
3. Use quick release to remove the steam.

Cheddar Creamy Haddock

Prep Time: 8-10 min.
Cooking Time: 10 min.
Number of Servings: 4
Ingredients:
- ½ cup heavy cream
- 5-ounces cheddar cheese, grated
- 3 tablespoons diced onions
- 12-ounces haddock fillets
- 1 tablespoon butter
- ¼ teaspoon garlic salt
- ¼ teaspoon pepper

Directions:
1. Take your Instant Pot; open the top lid. Plug it and turn it on.
2. Press "SAUTÉ" setting and the pot will start heating up.
3. In the cooking pot area, add the butter and onions. Cook until starts becoming translucent and softened for 3 minutes. Stir in between.
4. Season the fish with pepper and salt. Add the fish in the pot and cook for 2 minutes per side. Pour the cream over and top with the cheese.
5. Close the top lid and seal its valve.
6. Press "MANUAL" setting. Adjust cooking time to 5 minutes.
7. Allow the recipe to cook for the set cooking time.

8. After the set cooking time ends, press "CANCEL" and then press "NPR (Natural Pressure Release)".
9. Instant Pot will slowly and naturally release the pressure.
10. Open the top lid, add the cooked recipe mix in serving plates.
11. Serve and enjoy!

Banana Mackerel

Prep Time: 8-10 min.
Cooking Time: 28 min.
Number of Servings: 5
Ingredients:
- 2 tablespoons water
- ¼ cup cream
- 3 peeled bananas, ripe and chopped
- 1 teaspoon brown sugar
- 3 tablespoons oregano
- 1 teaspoon olive oil
- 1-pound mackerel
- 1 teaspoon ground white pepper
- ¼ cup water
- ¼ teaspoon cinnamon

Directions:
1. Sprinkle the bananas with the brown sugar and cream; stir well.
2. Take an Instant Pot; open the top lid.
3. Press "SAUTÉ" cooking function.
4. In the cooking pot area, add the banana mix and sauté for 8 minutes. Stir the bananas frequently.
5. Chop the fish roughly and mix it with the water, ground white pepper, olive oil, and cinnamon.
6. Add in the fish mix and water; combine well.
7. Close the top lid and make sure the valve is sealed.
8. Press "MEAT/STEW" cooking function. Adjust cooking time to 20 minutes.
9. Allow pressure to build and cook the ingredients for the set time.
10. After the set cooking time ends, press "CANCEL" and then press "QPR". Instant Pot will quickly release pressure.
11. Open the top lid, add the cooked mixture in serving plates.
12. Serve warm.

Basil Herbed Salmon

Prep Time: 8-10 min.
Cooking Time: 10 min.
Number of Servings: 4
Ingredients:
- ¼ teaspoon rosemary
- ½ teaspoon dried basil
- 2 tomatoes, chopped
- ½ teaspoon oregano
- 24-ounces wild salmon

- ¼ teaspoon pepper flakes
- 2 tablespoons balsamic vinegar
- ¼ cup basil, chopped
- Pepper and salt as per taste
- 2 teaspoons olive oil
- 1 cup water

Directions:
1. Mix the oregano, basil, pepper flakes, pepper, salt and rosemary in a mixing bowl.
2. Use the mix to season the salmon. Wrap and seal the salmon in a baking sheet.
3. Take an Instant Pot; open the top lid.
4. Pour the water and place steamer basket/trivet inside the cooking pot.
5. Arrange the wrapped salmon over the basket/trivet.
6. Close the top lid and make sure the valve is sealed.
7. Press "MANUAL" cooking function. Adjust cooking time to 8-10 minutes.
8. Allow pressure to build and cook the ingredients for the set time.
9. After the set cooking time ends, press "CANCEL" and then press "QPR". Instant Pot will quickly release pressure.
10. Open the top lid, add the cooked mixture in serving plates.
11. Mix the basil, vinegar, tomatoes, pepper, salt, and olive oil in a bowl. Set aside.
12. Serve warm with the tomato mix.

Rosemary Buttery Fish Meal

Prep Time: 8-10 min.
Cooking Time: 8 min.
Number of Servings: 3-4
Ingredients:
- 4 tablespoons butter
- 1 teaspoon sea salt
- 1 red chili pepper, seeded and sliced
- 10-ounces anchovies
- ½ teaspoon paprika
- 1 teaspoon dried dill
- 1 teaspoon rosemary
- 1 teaspoon red chili flakes
- 1 tablespoon basil
- ⅓ cup breadcrumbs

Directions:
1. Mix the chili flakes, paprika, sea salt, basil, dry dill, and rosemary together in a bowl.
2. Coat the anchovies with the spice mix.
3. Mix in the chili pepper and let the mixture rest for 10 minutes.
4. Take an Instant Pot; open the top lid.
5. Press "SAUTÉ" cooking function.
6. In the cooking pot area, melt the butter.
7. Dip the spiced anchovies in the breadcrumbs and put in the pot.
8. Cook the anchovies for 4 minutes on each side.

9. Drain on paper towel and serve warm.

Vegetable Salmon Delight

Prep Time: 8-10 min.
Cooking Time: 10 min.
Number of Servings: 4
Ingredients:
- 1-pound salmon fillet, skin on
- 1 carrot, julienned
- 1 bell pepper, julienned
- 1 zucchini, julienned
- 1/2 lemon, make slices
- 2 teaspoons olive oil
- 31/2 teaspoon black pepper
- 3/4 cup water
- 1/4 teaspoon salt

Direction:
1. Coat the salmon with the oil and season with pepper and salt.
2. Take an Instant Pot; open the top lid.
3. Pour the water and place steamer basket/trivet inside the cooking pot.
4. Arrange the salmon over the basket/trivet.
5. Close the top lid and make sure the valve is sealed.
6. Press "MANUAL" cooking function. Adjust cooking time to 3 minutes.
7. Allow pressure to build and cook the ingredients for the set time.
8. After the set cooking time ends, press "CANCEL" and then press "QPR". Instant Pot will quickly release pressure.
9. Open the top lid, take out the steamer rack and set aside the cooked salmon.
10. Press "SAUTÉ" cooking function.
11. In the cooking pot area, add the oil and vegetables. Cook until turn softened for 2 minutes.
12. Serve the salmon with sautéed vegetables.

Wine Marinates Shrimps

Prep Time: 8-10 min.
Cooking Time: 7 min.
Number of Servings: 3
Ingredients:
- 1 tablespoon lemon juice
- ½ teaspoon lemon zest
- 2 tablespoons cilantro
- 2 tablespoons apple cider vinegar
- ½ tablespoon salt
- ½ teaspoon ground ginger
- 1 tablespoon olive oil
- ¼ cup white wine
- 1 teaspoon brown sugar

- ½ tablespoon minced garlic
- 1 teaspoon nutmeg
- 1 cup water
- 5 ½ pound peeled shrimps, deveined
- 1 cup parsley

Directions:
1. Chop the cilantro and parsley. Mix the lemon juice, vinegar, lemon zest, salt, white wine, and sugar together in a mixing bowl.
2. Stir the mixture until sugar and salt dissolve completely.
3. Mix the shrimps in the lemon juice mixture. Add the cilantro and parsley and stir well.
4. Mix in the ginger, olive oil, nutmeg, and water. Allow marinating for 15 minutes.
5. Take an Instant Pot; open the top lid.
6. Add the shrimp mix in the cooking pot. Using a spatula, gently stir to combine well.
7. Close the top lid and make sure the valve is sealed.
8. Press "MANUAL" cooking function. Adjust cooking time to 8 minutes.
9. Allow pressure to build and cook the ingredients for the set time.
10. After the set cooking time ends, press "CANCEL" and then press "QPR". Instant Pot will quickly release pressure.
11. Open the top lid, add the cooked mixture in serving plates.
12. Serve warm.

Bean Shrimp Rice Meal

Prep Time: 8-10 min.
Cooking Time: 25 min.
Number of Servings: 4
Ingredients:
- 1 ½ cups, low sodium vegetable broth
- 2 tablespoon minced garlic
- 1 cup rice
- ¼ cup butter
- 1 pound, cooked shrimp
- 1 can black beans, rinsed and drained
- Dried cilantro as required

Directions:
1. Take an Instant Pot; open the top lid.
2. Press "SAUTÉ" cooking function.
3. In the cooking pot area, add the butter and rice.
4. Cook for about 2-3 minutes or until it gets a brown texture.
5. Mix in the pepper, garlic, and salt and stir cook for further 2 minutes.
6. Mix in the shrimps, black beans, and broth.
7. Close the top lid and make sure the valve is sealed.
8. Press "MANUAL" cooking function. Adjust cooking time to 4-5 minutes.
9. Allow pressure to build and cook the ingredients for the set time.
10. After the set cooking time ends, press "CANCEL" and then press "NPR". Instant Pot will slowly and naturally release the pressure for 8-10 minutes.
11. Open the top lid, add the cooked mixture in serving plates.

12. Serve warm with cilantro on top.

Tangy Orange Trout

Prep Time: 10-15 min.
Cooking Time: 5 min.
Number of Servings: 4
Ingredients:

- 2-ounce lemon, juiced
- 1 teaspoon lemon zest
- ¼ orange, juiced
- 1 tablespoon smoked paprika
- 14-ounce trout
- 1 teaspoon sea salt
- ½ teaspoon oregano
- 1 teaspoon honey
- 1 tablespoon olive oil

Directions:
1. Chop the trout into 4 medium pieces.
2. Mix the lemon, orange, sea salt, oregano, honey, and olive oil in a mixing bowl.
3. Coat the trout with the lemon mixture from each side.
4. Take your Instant Pot; open the top lid. Plug it and turn it on.
5. Pour the water and place steamer basket/trivet inside the pot; arrange the trout over the basket/trivet.
6. Close the top lid and seal its valve.
7. Press "STEAM" setting. Adjust cooking time to 5 minutes.
8. Allow the recipe to cook for the set cooking time.
9. After the set cooking time ends, press "CANCEL" and then press "QPR (Quick Pressure Release)".
10. Instant Pot will quickly release the pressure.
11. Open the top lid, add the cooked recipe mix in serving plates.
12. Serve and enjoy!

Shrimp Zoodles Meal

Prep Time: 5-8 min.
Cooking Time: 5 min.
Number of Servings: 4
Ingredients:

- 1 cup veggie stock
- 2 tablespoons olive oil
- 3 teaspoons minced garlic
- 4 cups zucchini noodles
- 2 tablespoon ghee
- Juice of ½ lemon
- 1 tablespoon chopped basil

- 1-pound shrimp, peeled and deveined
- ½ teaspoon paprika

Directions:
1. Take your Instant Pot; open the top lid. Plug it and turn it on.
2. Press "SAUTÉ" setting and the pot will start heating up.
3. In the cooking pot area, add the oil, ghee, and garlic.
4. Cook for 1 minute and add the shrimp and lemon juice.
5. Cook for 1 more minute. Add the zoodles, paprika, and stock.
6. Close the top lid and seal its valve.
7. Press "MANUAL" setting. Adjust cooking time to 3 minutes.
8. Allow the recipe to cook for the set cooking time.
9. After the set cooking time ends, press "CANCEL" and then press "QPR (Quick Pressure Release)".
10. Instant Pot will quickly release the pressure.
11. Open the top lid, add the cooked recipe mix in serving plates. Top with basil.
12. Serve and enjoy!

Shrimp Sausage Meal

Prep Time: 8-10 min.
Cooking Time: 5 min.
Number of Servings: 4
Ingredients:
- 1 tablespoon old bay
- 4 ears of corn, chopped
- 2 yellow onions, chopped
- 1 teaspoon red pepper flakes, crushed
- 16 ounces beer
- 12 ounces sliced and cooked sausage
- 1½ pounds deveined shrimp
- Black pepper and salt as needed
- 8 minced garlic cloves

Directions:
1. Arrange your Instant Pot over a dry, clean platform. Plug it in power socket and turn it on.
2. Open the lid from the top and put it aside; add the ingredients and gently stir them.
3. Close the lid and lock. Ensure that you have sealed the valve to avoid leakage.
4. Press "Manual" mode from available cooking settings and set cooking time to 5 minutes. Instant Pot will start cooking the ingredients after a few minutes.
5. After the timer reads zero, press "Cancel" and quick release pressure.
6. Carefully remove the lid and serve the prepared keto dish warm!

Herbed Trout Fillet

Prep Time: 5-8 min.
Cooking Time: 25 min.
Number of Servings: 4
Ingredients:

- 1 teaspoon stevia

- 1/2 cup basil, chopped

- 1 teaspoon black pepper

- 1 teaspoon dried dill

- 1 pound trout fillet, divide into pieces

- 1 teaspoon fresh ginger, crushed

Directions:
1. Season the fish with the pepper and dill. Add the sugar and stir gently.
2. Top with the basil and ginger; set aside for 8-10 minutes.
3. Arrange your Instant Pot over a dry, clean platform. Plug it in power socket and turn it on.
4. Open the lid from the top and put it aside; add the fish and marinade. Gently stir them.
5. Close the lid and lock. Ensure that you have sealed the valve to avoid leakage.
6. Press "Manual" mode from available cooking settings and set cooking time to 15 minutes. Instant Pot will start cooking the ingredients after a few minutes.
7. After the timer reads zero, press "Cancel" and quick release pressure.
8. Carefully remove the lid and serve the prepared keto dish warm!

Garlic Shrimp with Rice

Prep Time: 5 min.
Cooking Time: 5 min.
Number of Servings: 4-5
Ingredients:

- 1½ cup water
- Juice of 1 lemon
- Crushed red pepper
- ¼ cup chopped parsley
- Black pepper and sea salt as needed
- 1 cup jasmine rice
- 20 large deveined shrimp
- ¼ cup ghee
- A pinch of saffron
- 4 minced garlic cloves
- Grated cheddar cheese as needed

Directions:
1. Arrange your Instant Pot over a dry, clean platform. Plug it in power socket and turn it on.
2. Now press "Saute" mode from available options. In the cooking area, add some water and rice; cook for 1 minutes.
3. Add the shrimps, ghee, parsley, salt, pepper, red pepper, lemon juice, saffron, garlic, and water. Stir well.

4. Close the lid and lock. Ensure that you have sealed the valve to avoid leakage.
5. Press "Manual" mode from available cooking settings and set cooking time to 5 minutes. Instant Pot will start cooking the ingredients after a few minutes.
6. After the timer reads zero, press "Cancel" and quick release pressure.
7. Carefully remove the lid. Peel the shrimps and divide them between on plates.
8. Add the parsley, cheese and rice mix on top. Serve the prepared keto dish warm!

Raspberry Salmon

Prep Time: 10 min.
Cooking Time: 8 min.
Number of Servings: 5-6
Ingredients:

- 2 garlic cloves, minced
- 1 cup clam juice
- 2 tablespoons parsley, chopped
- 2 tablespoons lemon juice
- 4 leeks, chopped
- 2 tablespoons olive oil
- 6 salmon steaks
- Sea salt black pepper and salt as needed
- 2 pints red raspberries
- 1/3 cup dill, chopped
- 1 teaspoon sherry
- 1-pint cider vinegar

Directions:
1. Mix the berries and vinegar in a bowl and stir well. Mix in the salmon, stir, cover and keep in the fridge for 2 hours.
2. Arrange your Instant Pot over a dry, clean platform. Plug it in power socket and turn it on.
3. Now press "Saute" mode from available options. In the cooking area, add the garlic, parsley, and leeks; cook for 2-3 minutes to soften.
4. Add the lemon juice, clam juice, salt, pepper, cherry, and dill; stir well and cook for 2 minutes. Add the salmon and stir well.
5. Close the lid and lock. Ensure that you have sealed the valve to avoid leakage.
6. Press "Manual" mode from available cooking settings and set cooking time to 4 minutes. Instant Pot will start cooking the ingredients after a few minutes.
7. After the timer reads zero, press "Cancel"; press "NPR" to naturally release pressure. It takes about 8-10 minutes to release pressure naturally.
8. Carefully remove the lid and serve the prepared keto dish warm!

Zesty Salmon Burger

Prep Time: 10-15 min.
Cooking Time: 12 min.
Number of Servings: 4
Ingredients:

- 1 pound salmon, ground
- 2 tablespoons lemon zest
- 1 teaspoon olive oil
- ½ cup almond meal
- Black pepper and salt as needed

For serving:
- Mustard, tomato slices, cheese slice, and arugula leaves

Directions:
1. In a blender, mix the salmon with almond meal, salt, pepper and lemon zest.
2. Stir the mix well; make 4 burger patties.
3. Arrange your Instant Pot over a dry, clean platform. Plug it in power socket and turn it on.
4. Now press "Saute" mode from available options. In the cooking area, add the oil and patties.
5. Close the lid and lock. Ensure that you have sealed the valve to avoid leakage.
6. Set cooking time to 10 minutes. Instant Pot will start cooking the ingredients after a few minutes.
7. After the timer reads zero, press "Cancel"; press "NPR" to naturally release pressure. It takes about 8-10 minutes to release pressure naturally.
8. Carefully remove the lid.
9. Press "Saute" button again and cook patties for 2 minutes more.
10. Make burgers with the patties along with tomato slices, arugula, and mustard.

Seasoned Mayo Fish Meal

Prep Time: 5-8 min.
Cooking Time: 7 min.
Number of Servings: 4
Ingredients:
- ½ cup vegetable stock
- 2 tablespoon lemon juice
- 1-pound haddock
- 2 tablespoon mayonnaise
- 1 teaspoon chopped dill
- 1 teaspoon olive oil
- ¼ teaspoon old bay seasoning

Directions:
1. Take your Instant Pot; open the top lid. Plug it and turn it on.
2. In the cooking pot area, add the stock, lemon juice, dill, oil, seasoning, and mayonnaise. Using a spatula, stir the ingredients.
3. Add the fish and stir again.
4. Close the top lid and seal its valve.
5. Press "MANUAL" setting. Adjust cooking time to 7 minutes.
6. Allow the recipe to cook for the set cooking time.
7. After the set cooking time ends, press "CANCEL" and then press "QPR (Quick Pressure Release)".
8. Instant Pot will quickly release the pressure.
9. Open the top lid, add the cooked recipe mix in serving plates.

10. Serve and enjoy!

Almond Cheddar Tuna

Prep Time: 5-8 min.
Cooking Time: 3 min.
Number of Servings: 4
Ingredients:
- 2 tablespoon butter
- 1 teaspoon garlic powder
- 2 cans of tuna, drained
- 1 cup shaved almonds
- 1 cup grated cheddar cheese

Directions:
1. Take your Instant Pot; open the top lid. Plug it and turn it on.
2. Press "SAUTÉ" setting and the pot will start heating up.
3. Melt the butter and add the tuna, almonds, and cheddar.
4. Cook for 3-4 minutes.
5. add the cooked recipe mix in serving plates.
6. Serve alone or with cauliflower rice and enjoy!

Mahi Mahi Chili

Prep Time: 5-8 min.
Cooking Time: 8 min.
Number of Servings: 4
Ingredients:
- 2 tablespoons butter, melted
- ¼ teaspoon salt
- 1/3 cup chopped green chilies
- 4 Mahi Mahi fillets
- ¼ teaspoon pepper
- 1 ½ cups water

Directions:
1. Sprinkle the fish with pepper and salt.
2. Take your Instant Pot; open the top lid. Plug it and turn it on.
3. Press "SAUTÉ" setting and the pot will start heating up.
4. In the cooking pot area, add the butter and fish. Cook for a minute per side.
5. Pour the water and place steamer basket/trivet inside the pot; arrange the fish over the basket/trivet. Top with chilies.
6. Close the top lid and seal its valve.
7. Press "MANUAL" setting. Adjust cooking time to 5 minutes.
8. Allow the recipe to cook for the set cooking time.
9. After the set cooking time ends, press "CANCEL" and then press "QPR (Quick Pressure Release)".
10. Instant Pot will quickly release the pressure.

11. Open the top lid, add the cooked recipe mix in serving plates.
12. Serve and enjoy!

Poached Salmon with Relish

Prep Time: 8-10 min.
Cooking Time: 3-5 min.
Number of Servings: 4
Ingredients:
- 2 tablespoons capers, rinsed and minced
- 2 tablespoons tarragon, minced and stems reserved
- 2 tablespoons parsley, minced and stems reserved
- 1 shallot, minced
- Pepper and salt to taste
- 1 tablespoon extra-virgin olive oil
- 1 tablespoon cider vinegar
- 4 (6-ounce) fillets of salmon
- 1 lemon, make ¼-inch thick circles

Directions:
1. Arrange the lemon slices on bottom of Instant Pot; place the herb stems on top of the lemon.
2. Season salmon with pepper and salt. Arrange the salmon on top of lemon slices with skin side down.
3. Pour water to the pot until it barely touches the salmon.
4. Close the lid and lock. Ensure that you have sealed the valve to avoid leakage.
5. Press "Steam" mode from available cooking settings and set cooking time to 3 minutes. Instant Pot will start cooking the ingredients after a few minutes.
6. After the timer reads zero, press "Cancel" and quick release pressure.
7. Carefully remove the lid.
8. In a bowl of medium size, thoroughly mix the olive oil, vinegar, capers, shallot, tarragon, and parsley. Season with pepper and salt.
9. Arrange the salmon over a serving plate and top with the relish.

Milky White Fish Curry

Prep Time: 10 min.
Cooking Time: 20-22 min.
Number of Servings: 6
Ingredients:
- 1 yellow onion, chopped
- 1 cauliflower head, separated into florets
- 13 ounces milk
- 14 ounces chicken stock
- 14 ounces half and half
- 6 white fish fillets, make chunks
- Black pepper and salt as needed
- 14 ounces water

Directions:

1. Arrange your Instant Pot over a dry, clean platform. Plug it in power socket and turn it on.
2. Open the lid from the top and put it aside; add the cauliflower, fish, onion, milk, stock, and water. Gently stir them.
3. Close the lid and lock. Ensure that you have sealed the valve to avoid leakage.
4. Press "Manual" mode from available cooking settings and set cooking time to 10 minutes. Instant Pot will start cooking the ingredients after a few minutes.
5. After the timer reads zero, press "Cancel" and quick release pressure.
6. Carefully remove the lid.
7. Press "Simmer" button, mix in the half and half, pepper and salt; stir the mix and cook for 10 minutes. Serve the prepared keto dish warm!

Coconut Milk Salmon

Prep Time: 8-10 min.
Cooking Time: 5 min.
Number of Servings: 3-4
Ingredients:
3 tablespoons almond milk
- 1 teaspoon coconut milk
- 1-pound salmon fillet
- ½ teaspoon cayenne pepper
- 1 tablespoon almond flour
- 1 teaspoon dried dill
- 1 teaspoon kosher salt

Directions:

1. Chop the salmon roughly and add in a mixing bowl. Add the almond milk and cayenne pepper. Combine well and add the coconut milk, salt, and dill.
2. In the cooking pot area, add the salmon mix and almond flour. Using a spatula, stir the ingredients.
3. Close the top lid and seal its valve.
4. Press "MANUAL" setting. Adjust cooking time to 5 minutes.
5. Allow the recipe to cook for the set cooking time.
6. After the set cooking time ends, press "CANCEL" and then press "NPR (Natural Pressure Release)".
7. Instant Pot will slowly and naturally release the pressure.
8. Open the top lid, add the cooked recipe mix in serving plates.
9. Serve and enjoy!

Classic Shrimps

Prep Time: 5-8 min.
Cooking Time: 7 min.
Number of Servings: 4
Ingredients:
- ½ teaspoon (ground) black pepper
- 2 teaspoons olive oil
- ½ teaspoon minced garlic clove

- 9-ounce shrimps, peeled
- ½ teaspoon paprika
- 2 tablespoons fish stock
- 1 tablespoon cilantro, chopped

Directions:
1. Combine the paprika, (ground) black pepper, olive oil, minced garlic, and chopped cilantro in the mixing bowl.
2. Add fish stock and stir well. Add the shrimps in the cilantro mixture and coat well.
3. Pour the water and place steamer basket/trivet inside the pot; arrange the shrimp over the basket/trivet.
4. Close the top lid and seal its valve.
5. Press "MANUAL" setting. Adjust cooking time to 7 minutes.
6. Allow the recipe to cook for the set cooking time.
7. After the set cooking time ends, press "CANCEL" and then press "QPR (Quick Pressure Release)".
8. Instant Pot will quickly release the pressure.
9. Open the top lid, add the cooked recipe mix in serving plates.
10. Serve and enjoy!
11. Optionally, you can serve with steamed asparagus and lemon slices.

Southern Shrimp and Grits

Prep Time: 5 minutes
Cooking Time: 15 minutes
Number of Servings: 6
Ingredients:
- 2 tablespoons butter
- 1 cup grits
- 4 cups chicken stock
- 1 cup shredded Cheddar cheese
- 1/4 teaspoon salt
- 1/2 teaspoon black pepper
- 1/4 pound bacon
- 1 shallot, chopped
- 1 garlic clove, minced
- 1 pound shrimp
- Juice of 1 lemon

Directions:
1. Set the Instant Pot to Saute mode. Melt butter in the pan. Add grits and toast about 30 seconds. Pour stock over grits, add cheese, salt, and pepper, and stir.
2. Close the lid and set cooking time to 10 minutes. After cooking time, use the quick release to remove steam. Pour grits into a bowl and cover to keep warm.
3. Wipe out the pot. Set to Saute and add bacon and cook until most of the fat renders. Add shallot and garlic cook until shallot is translucent. Add shrimp and cook through about 3 minutes. Squeeze lemon juice over shrimp. Pour contents of pot over grits.

Sweet Soy Salmon

Prep Time: 8-10 min.
Cooking Time: 7 min.
Number of Servings: 2
Ingredients:
- 2 tablespoons soy sauce
- ¾ pound salmon fillets
- 1 teaspoon vegetable oil
- 1 tablespoon lemon juice
- ¼ teaspoon pepper
- 2 tablespoons brown sugar
- 1 tablespoon fish sauce
- ¼ teaspoon lemon zest
- ½ teaspoon ginger

Directions:
1. Season the salmon with pepper and salt. Set aside.
2. In a bowl, mix the oil, sugar, fish sauce, soy sauce, ginger, lemon zest, and lemon juice.
3. Take your 3-Quart Instant Pot; open the top lid. Plug it and turn it on.
4. Press "SAUTÉ" setting and the pot will start heating up.
5. In the cooking pot area, add the bowl mix and cook for 2 minutes to caramelize. Add the salmon.
6. Close the top lid and seal its valve.
7. Press "MANUAL" setting. Adjust cooking time to 5 minutes.
8. Allow the recipe to cook for the set cooking time.
9. After the set cooking time ends, press "CANCEL" and then press "NPR (Natural Pressure Release)".
10. Instant Pot will slowly and naturally release the pressure.
11. Open the top lid, add the cooked recipe mix in serving plates.
12. Serve with some green vegetables of your choice and enjoy!

Orangy Cod Dinner

Prep Time: 5-8 min.
Cooking Time: 7 min.
Number of Servings: 2
Ingredients:
- 1/2 cup fish stock
- A pinch of pepper and salt
- 2 cod fillets, boneless
- A drizzle of olive oil
- 1-inch ginger, grated
- Zest and juice from 1/2 orange
- 2 sprigs onions, chopped
- More orange juice to drizzle

Directions:
1. Season the cod with salt and pepper, drizzle oil and rub well.

132

2. Take your 3-Quart Instant Pot; open the top lid. Plug it and turn it on.
3. Add the stock with orange zest, juice, ginger and sprigs onions and place steamer basket/trivet inside the pot; arrange the seasoned cod over the basket/trivet.
4. Close the top lid and seal its valve.
5. Press "MANUAL" setting. Adjust cooking time to 7 minutes.
6. Allow the recipe to cook for the set cooking time.
7. After the set cooking time ends, press "CANCEL" and then press "QPR (Quick Pressure Release)".
8. Instant Pot will quickly release the pressure.
9. Open the top lid, add the cooked recipe mix in serving plates.
10. Serve with some more orange juice on top and enjoy!

Broccoli Salmon Meal

Prep Time: 8-10 min.
Cooking Time: 6 min.
Number of Servings: 2
Ingredients:
- 1 cinnamon stick
- 2 salmon fillets, boneless and skin on
- 2 cups broccoli florets
- 1 bay leaf
- 1 tablespoon olive oil
- 1 cup water
- 3 cloves
- Some lime wedges for serving
- 1 cup baby carrots
- 1 pinch of pepper and salt

Directions:
1. In a bowl, season the salmon with salt and pepper, brush it with the oil and mix with carrots and broccoli.
2. Take your 3-Quart Instant Pot; open the top lid. Plug it and turn it on.
3. Pour the cinnamon, cloves, bay leaf and water and place steamer basket/trivet inside the pot; arrange the salmon mix over the basket/trivet.
4. Close the top lid and seal its valve.
5. Press "MANUAL" setting. Adjust cooking time to 6 minutes.
6. Allow the recipe to cook for the set cooking time.
7. After the set cooking time ends, press "CANCEL" and then press "QPR (Quick Pressure Release)".
8. Instant Pot will quickly release the pressure.
9. Open the top lid, add the cooked recipe mix in serving plates.
10. Discard bay leaf, cloves and cinnamon.
11. Serve with some lime wedges and enjoy!

Shrimp Pasta Meal

Prep Time: 8-10 min.

Cooking Time: 3 min.
Number of Servings: 2-3
Ingredients:
- 1 pound shrimp
- 1 tablespoon olive oil
- 1 tablespoon butter
- 1/2 tablespoon garlic, minced
- 1/4 cup chicken broth
- A pinch of pepper and salt
- Your favorite pasta, cooked
- 1/4 cup chicken stock
- 1/2 tablespoon lemon juice
- 1 tablespoon parsley, chopped

Directions:
1. Take your 3-Quart Instant Pot; open the top lid. Plug it and turn it on.
2. Press "SAUTÉ" setting and the pot will start heating up.
3. In the cooking pot area, add the oil and butter; heat it.
4. Add the garlic; cook until starts becoming translucent and softened for 1 minutes. Stir in between.
5. Add the stock and chicken broth; add the shrimp and parsley.
6. Close the top lid and seal its valve.
7. Press "MANUAL" setting. Adjust cooking time to 2 minutes.
8. Allow the recipe to cook for the set cooking time.
9. After the set cooking time ends, press "CANCEL" and then press "QPR (Quick Pressure Release)".
10. Instant Pot will quickly release the pressure.
11. Open the top lid, add the cooked recipe mix in serving plates.
12. Serve with cooked pasta and enjoy!

Fish Coconut Curry

Prep Time: 5-8 min.
Cooking Time: 7-8 min.
Number of Servings: 2
Ingredients:
- 1 pound fish fillets, make small chunks
- 1 tablespoon oil
- ¼ teaspoon turmeric powder
- ¼ teaspoon ground fenugreek
- 1 tomato, chopped
- 1 bell pepper, thinly sliced
- 2 cloves garlic, crushed
- ¼ teaspoon chili powder
- 1 teaspoon ground cumin
- 1 teaspoon ginger, grated
- 1 teaspoon ground coriander
- 1 cup coconut milk

- 1 tablespoon lemon juice
- A handful curry leaves
- Salt as needed

Directions:
1. Take your 3-Quart Instant Pot; open the top lid. Plug it and turn it on.
2. Press "SAUTÉ" setting and the pot will start heating up.
3. In the cooking pot area, add the oil and curry leaves.
4. Mix in the onion, ginger, and garlic, cook to soften and translucent.
5. Add all the spices and sauté for a few seconds until the mixture becomes fragrant.
6. Add remaining ingredients except for lemon juice; gently stir the mix.
7. Close the top lid and seal its valve.
8. Press "MANUAL" setting. Adjust cooking time to 5 minutes.
9. Allow the recipe to cook for the set cooking time.
10. After the set cooking time ends, press "CANCEL" and then press "QPR (Quick Pressure Release)".
11. Instant Pot will quickly release the pressure.
12. Open the top lid, add the cooked recipe mix in serving plates.
13. Mix in the lemon juice and enjoy!

Garlic Chili Salmon

Prep Time: 5-8 min.
Cooking Time: 5 min.
Number of Servings: 2
Ingredients:
- 2 salmon fillets
- 1 cup water
- Juice from 1 lime
- 1/2 teaspoon cumin, ground
- A pinch of pepper and salt
- 1 jalapeno, chopped
- 2 garlic cloves, minced
- 1 tablespoon honey
- 1 tablespoon hot water
- 1/2 teaspoon sweet paprika
- 1 tablespoon olive oil
- 1 tablespoon parsley, chopped
- Chili sauce as needed

Directions:
1. In a bowl, mix the jalapeno with lime juice, garlic, honey, oil, 1 tablespoon water, parsley, paprika and cumin. Whisk the mix.
2. Take your 3-Quart Instant Pot; open the top lid. Plug it and turn it on.
3. Pour 1 cup water and place steamer basket/trivet inside the pot; arrange the salmon over the basket/trivet. Season the salmon with pepper and salt.
4. Close the top lid and seal its valve.
5. Press "STEAM" setting. Adjust cooking time to 5 minutes.

6. Allow the recipe to cook for the set cooking time.
7. After the set cooking time ends, press "CANCEL" and then press "QPR (Quick Pressure Release)".
8. Instant Pot will quickly release the pressure.
9. Open the top lid, add the cooked recipe mix in serving plates.
10. Add the sauce on top. Serve and enjoy!

Wine Braised Cod

Prep Time: 5 min.
Cooking Time: 5 min.
Number of Servings: 2
Ingredients:
- 1 cup white wine
- 1 teaspoon oregano
- 1 sprig fresh rosemary
- 2 garlic cloves, smashed
- 1 teaspoon paprika
- 1 pound cod, cut into 4 filets
- 1 bag (10 ounces) frozen peas
- 1 cup fresh parsley

Directions:
1. In a bowl, mix the wine, herbs, salt, and spices together.
2. Add the liquid into the Instant Pot and add the peas.
3. Arrange the fish into a steamer basket and lower it to the liquid.
4. Close the pot by closing the top lid. Also, ensure to seal the valve.
5. Press "Manual" cooking function and set cooking time to 5 minutes. It will start cooking after a few minutes. Let the pot mix cook under pressure until the timer reads zero.
6. Press "Cancel" cooking function and press "Quick release" setting.
7. Open the pot and serve warm. Enjoy it with your loved one!

Jalapeno Pepper Shrimp

Prep Time: 8-10 min.
Cooking Time: 5 min.
Number of Servings: 2
Ingredients:
- 1 teaspoon white pepper
- 1 teaspoon cayenne pepper
- 2 cloves garlic, minced
- 1 sweet onion, minced
- 1 can diced tomatoes (15 ounces)
- 1 jalapeno pepper, minced
- 1 pound frozen shrimp, peeled and deveined
- 1 lemon, juiced
- 1 teaspoon black pepper

Directions:
1. Allow the frozen shrimp to rest at room temperature for 15 minutes. Switch on the pot after placing it on a clean and dry platform.
2. Open the pot lid and place the above-mentioned ingredients in the cooking pot area. Give the ingredients a little stir.
3. Close the pot by closing the top lid. Also, ensure to seal the valve.
4. Press "Manual" cooking function and set cooking time to 5 minutes. It will start cooking after a few minutes. Let the pot mix cook under pressure until the timer reads zero.
5. Press "Cancel" cooking function and press "Quick release" setting.
6. Open the pot and serve warm. Enjoy it with your loved one!

White Wine Haddock

Prep Time: 5-8 min.
Cooking Time: 8 min.
Number of Servings: 2
Ingredients:
- 4 green onions
- 1 cup white wine
- 4 fillets of haddock
- 2 lemons
- Pepper and salt as per taste preference
- 2 tablespoons olive oil
- 1-inch fresh ginger, chopped

Directions:
1. Rub the olive oil into the fish fillets and sprinkle them with pepper and salt.
2. Juice your lemons and zest one lemon.
3. Switch on the pot after placing it on a clean and dry platform.
4. Open the pot lid and place everything except fish in the cooking pot area. Give the ingredients a little stir.
5. Place the fish in a steamer basket and lower it to the liquid. Close the pot by closing the top lid. Also, ensure to seal the valve.
6. Press "Manual" cooking function and set cooking time to 8 minutes. It will start cooking after a few minutes. Let the pot mix cook under pressure until the timer reads zero.
7. Press "Cancel" cooking function and press "Quick release" setting.
8. Open the pot and serve warm with the veggie salad or rice. Enjoy it with your loved one!

Tangy Crabs

Prep Time: 5 min.
Cooking Time: 3 min.
Number of Servings: 2
Ingredients:
- 2 tablespoons fish sauce
- ¼ cup butter, melted
- ½ cup water
- 1 tablespoon lemon juice
- ¼ teaspoon salt

- 1-½ pounds. crabs
- ¼ cup minced garlic

Directions:
1. Switch on the pot after placing it on a clean and dry platform.
2. Place crabs in an Instant Pot then season with salt and garlic. Mix the fish sauce and add butter over the crabs then pour water. Give the ingredients a little stir.
3. Close the pot by closing the top lid. Also, ensure to seal the valve.
4. Press "Manual" cooking function and set cooking time to 3 minutes. It will start cooking after a few minutes. Let the pot mix cook under pressure until the timer reads zero.
5. Press "Cancel" cooking function and press "Quick release" setting.
6. Open the pot; top with lemon juice and serve warm. Enjoy it with your loved one!

Mussels Tomatino

Prep Time: 8-10 min.
Cooking Time: 3 min.
Number of Servings: 2
Ingredients:
- ½ cup white wine
- ½ tablespoon dried parsley
- ½ tablespoon pepper
- 2 pounds fresh mussels, cleaned and rinsed
- 1 cup diced tomatoes
- Salt as per taste preference

Directions:
1. Switch on the pot after placing it on a clean and dry platform.
2. Pour the tomatoes into the Instant Pot with the juices and add the wine. Add the pepper, salt, and parsley.
3. Place the mussels in a steamer basket and lower it to the liquid.
4. Close the pot by closing the top lid. Also, ensure to seal the valve.
5. Press "Manual" cooking function and set cooking time to 3 minutes. It will start cooking after a few minutes. Let the pot mix cook under pressure until the timer reads zero.
6. Press "Cancel" cooking function and press "Quick release" setting.
7. Open the pot and serve warm with garlic bread. Enjoy it with your loved one!

Sweet Caramel Salmon

Prep Time: 8-10 min.
Cooking Time: 10 min.
Number of Servings: 2
Ingredients:
- 2 tablespoons brown sugar
- 1-tablespoon fish sauce
- 2 tablespoons soy sauce
- ¾ pound. salmon fillets
- 1-teaspoon vegetable oil
- 1 tablespoon lemon juice

- ¼ teaspoon pepper
- ½ teaspoon ginger
- ¼ teaspoon lemon zest

Directions:
1. Season the salmon with pepper and salt. Set aside. In a bowl mix the vegetable oil with brown sugar, fish sauce, soy sauce, ginger, lemon zest, and lemon juice.
2. Switch on the pot after placing it on a clean and dry platform. Press "Sauté" cooking function.
3. Open the pot lid; add the oil mix in the pot; cook for 2 minutes to caramelize. Add the salmon.
4. Close the pot by closing the top lid. Also, ensure to seal the valve.
5. Press "Manual" cooking function and set cooking time to 5 minutes. It will start cooking after a few minutes. Let the pot mix cook under pressure until the timer reads zero.
6. Press "Cancel" cooking function and press "Natural release (NPR)" setting. It will take 8-10 minutes for natural pressure release.
7. Open the pot and serve warm with the liquid. Enjoy it with your loved one!

Rosemary Salmon

Prep Time: 8-10 min.
Cooking Time: 10 min.
Number of Servings: 2-3
Ingredients:
- 4 Roma tomatoes
- 2 lemons
- ½ cup chopped shallots
- 4 salmon filets
- 2 cups water
- 4 sprigs rosemary
- Pepper and salt as per taste preference

Directions:
1. Slice the tomatoes and the lemons. Make two foil pouches by adding two pieces of salmon over each.
2. Arrange the salmon down on the foil and mix with pepper and salt. Add other remaining ingredients equally.
3. Fold up the foil, so it creates a secure package. Switch on the pot after placing it on a clean and dry platform.
4. Pour the water into the pot. Arrange the trivet inside it; arrange the pockets over the trivet.
5. Close the pot by closing the top lid. Also, ensure to seal the valve.
6. Press "Manual" cooking function and set cooking time to 10 minutes. It will start cooking after a few minutes. Let the pot mix cook under pressure until the timer reads zero.
7. Press "Cancel" cooking function and press "Quick release" setting.
8. Open the pot and serve warm. Enjoy it with your loved one!

Tangy Lime Salmon

Prep Time: 5min.
Cooking Time: 5 min.
Number of Servings: 4

Ingredients:
- 1 tablespoon olive oil
- 1 tablespoon honey
- 4 salmon fillets
- Juice of 2 limes
- 1 tablespoon chopped parsley
- 1 tablespoon hot water
- 1 teaspoon paprika
- ½ teaspoon cumin
- 1 cup water

Directions:
1. Switch on your instant pot after placing it on a clean and dry kitchen platform.
2. Pour the water into the cooking pot area. Arrange the trivet inside it; arrange the salmon over the trivet.
3. Close the pot by closing the top lid. Also, ensure to seal the valve.
4. Press "Manual" cooking function and set cooking time to 5 minutes. It will start cooking after a few minutes. Let the pot mix cook under pressure until the timer reads zero.
5. Turn off and press "Cancel" cooking function. Quick release pressure.
6. Open the pot and transfer to a serving plate or bowl.
7. Whisk all of the remaining ingredients in a bowl. Drizzle the sauce over the fillets. Serve warm!

Olive Cod Mystery

Prep Time: 5-8min.
Cooking Time: 10 min.
Number of Servings: 4
Ingredients:
- 1 cup water
- 2 tablespoons capers, chopped
- 1 cup black olives, pitted and chopped
- 17 ounces cherry tomatoes, halved
- 4 cod fillets, boneless and skinless
- 1 garlic clove, minced
- 1 tablespoon olive oil
- A pinch of pepper and salt
- 1 tablespoon parsley, finely chopped

Directions:
1. In a heatproof dish, mix the tomatoes, salt, pepper, parsley, oil, fish, olives, capers, and garlic. Toss to combine well.
2. Switch on your instant pot after placing it on a clean and dry kitchen platform.
3. Pour the water into the cooking pot area. Arrange the trivet inside it; arrange the dish over the trivet.
4. Close the pot by closing the top lid. Also, ensure to seal the valve.
5. Press "Manual" cooking function and set cooking time to 8 minutes. It will start cooking after a few minutes. Let the pot mix cook under pressure until the timer reads zero.
6. Turn off and press "Cancel" cooking function. Quick release pressure.

7. Open the pot and serve on a serving plate or bowl. Enjoy the Paleo dish!

Classic Garlic Shrimp

Prep Time: 8-10min.
Cooking Time: 5 min.
Number of Servings: 4
Ingredients:
- 2 tablespoons coconut oil
- 3 tablespoons chopped parsley
- Juice of 1 lemon
- 1 ½ pounds shrimp, peeled and deveined
- ¾ cup chicken broth
- 3 garlic cloves, minced

Directions:
1. Switch on your instant pot after placing it on a clean and dry kitchen platform. Press "Saute" cooking function.
2. Open the pot lid; add the oil and garlic in the pot; start cooking for 1-2 minutes to cook well and soften.
3. Add the shrimp and chicken broth.
4. Close the pot by closing the top lid. Also, ensure to seal the valve.
5. Press "Manual" cooking function and set cooking time to 2 minutes. It will start cooking after a few minutes. Let the pot mix cook under pressure until the timer reads zero.
6. Turn off and press "Cancel" cooking function. Quick release pressure.
7. Open the pot and mix in the parsley and lemon juice. Serve warm and enjoy.

Orange Gingery Fillets

Prep Time: 8-10min.
Cooking Time: 8 min.
Number of Servings: 4
Ingredients:
- 4 pieces of your favorite fillets
- 4 tablespoons honey
- 2 garlic cloves, minced
- Juice of 1 lime
- 1-inch ginger piece, grated
- 4 tablespoons sriracha
- 2 tablespoons orange juice
- 1 cup of water

Directions:
1. Switch on your instant pot after placing it on a clean and dry kitchen platform.
2. Pour the water into the cooking pot area. Arrange the steamer basket inside it; arrange the fish over the trivet.
3. Whisk all of the remaining ingredients in a bowl and pour the sauce over the fillets.
4. Close the pot by closing the top lid. Also, ensure to seal the valve.

5. Press "Manual" cooking function and set cooking time to 5 minutes. It will start cooking after a few minutes. Let the pot mix cook under pressure until the timer reads zero.
6. Turn off and press "Cancel" cooking function. Quick release pressure.
7. Open the pot and serve on a serving plate or bowl. Enjoy the Paleo dish!

Asparagus Tomato Clams

Prep Time: 8-10min.
Cooking Time: 20 min.
Number of Servings: 4
Ingredients:
- 1 cup cherry tomatoes, halved
- 2 tbs. olive oil
- 4 frozen salmon fillets
- 1 rosemary sprig
- 1 cup water
- 15 oz. asparagus

Directions:
1. Switch on your instant pot after placing it on a clean and dry kitchen platform.
2. Pour the water into the cooking pot area. Arrange the trivet inside it; arrange the salmon over the trivet.
3. Add the rosemary sprig and top with the asparagus.
4. Close the pot by closing the top lid. Also, ensure to seal the valve.
5. Press "Manual" cooking function and set cooking time to 3 minutes. It will start cooking after a few minutes. Let the pot mix cook under pressure until the timer reads zero.
6. Turn off and press "Cancel" cooking function. Allow the inside pressure to release naturally; it will take 8-10 minutes to release all inside pressure.
7. Open the pot. Discard the rosemary and arrange the salmon and asparagus on a plate.
8. Add the tomatoes and drizzle with olive oil. Serve warm!

Broccoli Salmon Veggies

Prep Time: 8min.
Cooking Time: 10 min.
Number of Servings: 2
Ingredients:
- 1 cup water
- 2 salmon fillets, boneless and skin on
- 2 cups broccoli florets
- 1 cup baby carrots
- 1 cinnamon stick
- 1 tablespoon olive oil
- 1 bay leaf
- 3 cloves
- A pinch of pepper and salt
- Some lime wedges for serving

Directions:
1. Switch on your instant pot after placing it on a clean and dry kitchen platform.
2. Pour the water into the cooking pot area and add the cinnamon, cloves and bay leaf. Arrange the trivet inside it; arrange the salmon over the trivet.
3. Season the salmon with salt and pepper, brush it with the oil and mix with carrots and broccoli.
4. Close the pot by closing the top lid. Also, ensure to seal the valve.
5. Press "Manual" cooking function and set cooking time to 6 minutes. It will start cooking after a few minutes. Let the pot mix cook under pressure until the timer reads zero.
6. Turn off and press "Cancel" cooking function. Quick release pressure.
7. Open the pot and serve on a serving plate or bowl. Enjoy the Paleo dish!
8. Divide salmon and veggies between plates, remove bay leaf, cloves and cinnamon.
9. On top add the sauce from the pot and serve with lime wedges.

Wonder Wine Clams

Prep Time: 8-10min.
Cooking Time: 8 min.
Number of Servings: 4
Ingredients:
- 2 ½ pounds clams, scrubbed
- 2 tbs. lemon juice
- 2 cups vegetable broth
- ¼ cup white wine
- ¼ cup olive oil
- 2 garlic cloves, minced
- ¼ cup chopped basil

Directions:
1. Switch on your instant pot after placing it on a clean and dry kitchen platform. Press "Saute" cooking function.
2. Open the pot lid; add the oil and garlic in the pot; start cooking for 2 minutes to cook well and soften.
3. Mix in the basil, broth, lemon juice, and wine. Bring to a boil and boil for one minute.
4. Arrange the trivet inside it; arrange the clams over the trivet. Close the pot by closing the top lid. Also, ensure to seal the valve.
5. Press "Manual" cooking function and set cooking time to 4 minutes. It will start cooking after a few minutes. Let the pot mix cook under pressure until the timer reads zero.
6. Turn off and press "Cancel" cooking function. Quick release pressure.
7. Open the pot and remove the clams that haven't opened.
8. Place the clams on a serving plate. Pour the liquid over. Serve warm!

Mayonnaise Lemon Fish

Prep Time: 8-10 min.
Cooking Time: 6 min.
Number of Servings: 7-8
Ingredients:
- 3 teaspoons olive oil
- 1 tablespoon mayonnaise, fat-free

- 2 pounds mackerel fillets, thinly make slices
- 2 tablespoons fresh lemon juice
- 1 teaspoon onion powder
- Salt as needed

Directions:
1. In a mixing bowl, thoroughly mix the mayonnaise, and onion powder.
2. Add and coat the fish pieces. Mix in the oil, salt and lemon juice.
3. Refrigerate for 20 minutes.
4. Take your Instant Pot and place over dry kitchen surface; open its top lid and switch it on.
5. Press "SAUTÉ". Grease the pot with some cooking oil.
6. Add the fish mix and cook 2-3 minutes on each side.
7. Add 1 cup water and stir the mix.
8. Close its top lid and make sure that its valve it closed to avoid spillage.
9. Press "MANUAL". Adjust the timer to 3 minutes.
10. Pressure will slowly build up; let the added ingredients to cook until the timer indicates zero.
11. Press "CANCEL". Now press "QPR" to quickly release pressure.
12. Open the top lid, transfer the cooked recipe in serving plates.
13. Serve the recipe warm.

Crab Onion Patties

Prep Time: 8-10 min.
Cooking Time: 12 min.
Number of Servings: 6
Ingredients:
- 1 small red onion, chopped (finely)
- 3 large eggs, lightly beaten
- 1 pound crab meat
- Breadcrumbs and butter as needed

Directions:
1. Take your Instant Pot and place over dry kitchen surface; open its top lid and switch it on.
2. Press "SAUTÉ". Grease the pot with some cooking oil.
3. Add the onions; cook for 4-5 minutes until turn translucent and softened. Set aside in a mixing bowl.
4. Add the crab meat, and eggs in a bowl and mix well. Prepare medium size patties from the mix and refrigerate for 20 minutes.
5. Press "SAUTÉ". Grease the pot with some cooking oil.
6. Cook the patties 3-4 minutes on each side to evenly brown.
7. Serve warm.

Creamy Shrimp Pasta

Prep Time: 8-10 min.
Cooking Time: 15 min.
Number of Servings: 8
Ingredients:
- 1 small red onion, diced
- 1/3 cup heavy cream

- 1 teaspoon butter
- 12 ounce shrimps, peeled and deveined
- 12 ounce linguine pasta

Directions:
1. In the Instant Pot; add 4 cup water and pasta.
2. Close its top lid and make sure that its valve it closed to avoid spillage.
3. Press "MANUAL". Adjust the timer to 7 minutes.
4. Pressure will slowly build up; let the added ingredients to cook until the timer indicates zero.
5. Press "CANCEL". Now press "QPR" to quickly release pressure.
6. Open the top lid, drain water and transfer the cooked pasta in a container.
7. Press "SAUTÉ".
8. In its cooking pot, add and heat the butter.
9. Add the shrimp; stir-cook for 2 minutes per side. Add the mix with the pasta.
10. Add the onions; cook for 4-5 minutes until turn translucent and softened.
11. Stir in the cream; cook for 2-3 minutes more.
12. Serve the pasta with the cream sauce.

Salmon Peas Meal

Prep Time: 8-10 min.
Cooking Time: 10 min.
Number of Servings: 3
Ingredients:
- 7 ounce salmon fillets
- 1/4 cup green peas
- 2 teaspoons olive oil
- 1 cup cauliflower florets, chopped (finely)
- 2 medium celery stalk, chopped
- Salt as needed

Directions:
1. Take your Instant Pot and place over dry kitchen surface; open its top lid and switch it on.
2. Press "SAUTÉ".
3. In its cooking pot, add and heat the oil.
4. Add the celery, salmon, and peas; stir-cook for 3-4 minutes.
5. Add 1 cup of water and cauliflower.
6. Cook for 4-5 more minutes, stirring occasionally.
7. Season with salt and serve warm.

Shrimp Green Curry

Prep Time: 8-10 min.
Cooking Time: 60 min.
Number of Servings: 5
Ingredients:
- 2 tablespoons green curry paste
- 4 teaspoons fish sauce
- 1 teaspoon coconut oil

- 7 ounce shrimps, cleaned and deveined
- 4 tablespoons Thai basil leaves

Directions:
1. Take your Instant Pot and place over dry kitchen surface; open its top lid and switch it on.
2. Press "SAUTÉ".
3. In its cooking pot, add and heat the oil.
4. Add the chili and shrimp; stir-cook for 2 minutes.
5. Add the fish sauce, paste, and basil; cook for 1 minute more.
6. Close its top lid and make sure that its valve it closed to avoid spillage.
7. Press "SLOW COOK". Adjust the timer to 60 minutes.
8. Pressure will slowly build up; let the added ingredients to cook until the timer indicates zero.
9. Press "CANCEL". Now press "NPR" for natural release pressure. Instant Pot will gradually release pressure for about 8-10 minutes.
10. Open the top lid, transfer the cooked recipe in serving plates.
11. Serve the recipe warm.

Black Bean Shrimp Meal

Prep Time: 8-10 min.
Cooking Time: 25 min.
Number of Servings: 4
Ingredients:
- 1 ½ cups vegetable broth
- ¼ cup butter
- 1 pound shrimp, cooked
- 2 tablespoons garlic, minced
- 1 cup rice
- 1 can black beans, rinsed and drained
- Salt as needed

Directions:
1. Take your Instant Pot and place over dry kitchen surface; open its top lid and switch it on.
2. Press "SAUTÉ".
3. In its cooking pot, add and heat the butter.
4. Add the rice; cook for 2-3 minutes to soften and turn light brown.
5. Mix in the pepper, garlic, and salt; cook for 2-3 minutes.
6. Mix in the remaining ingredients.
7. Close its top lid and make sure that its valve it closed to avoid spillage.
8. Press "MANUAL". Adjust the timer to 5 minutes.
9. Pressure will slowly build up; let the added ingredients to cook until the timer indicates zero.
10. Press "CANCEL". Now press "NPR" for natural release pressure. Instant Pot will gradually release pressure for about 8-10 minutes.
11. Open the top lid, transfer the cooked recipe in serving plates.
12. Serve the recipe warm.

Yogurt Fish Patties

Prep Time: 8-10 min.
Cooking Time: 8 min.
Number of Servings: 4
Ingredients:
- 1 small onion, chopped (finely)
- 3 tablespoons flour (all-purpose)
- 1 pound fish fillets, chopped (finely)
- 1/4 cup Greek yogurt, fat-free
- 1 teaspoon baking soda

Directions:
1. In a mixing bowl, thoroughly mix fish, yogurt, onion, flour, and baking soda.
2. Make 6 balls and press them to make patties.
3. Take your Instant Pot and place over dry kitchen surface; open its top lid and switch it on.
4. Press "SAUTÉ". Grease the pot with some cooking oil.
5. Add the patties and cook for 3-4 minutes on each side. Serve warm.

Swordfish Fra Diavolo

Prep Time: 10 minutes
Cooking Time: 5 minutes
Number of Servings: 2
Ingredients:
- 2 tablespoons olive oil
- 4 garlic cloves, minced
- 1/2 teaspoon red pepper flakes
- 1 can whole peeled tomatoes, crushed
- 1/2 teaspoon salt
- 1/2 teaspoon black pepper
- 1 pound swordfish steaks

Directions:
1. Set the Instant Pot to Saute mode. Add garlic and red pepper flakes and cook until fragrant. Add tomatoes, salt, and pepper.
2. Place swordfish in the sauce. Flip once to coat.
3. Close lid and set cooking time to 3 minutes. After cooking time, use the quick release to remove steam. Serve with pasta.

Cajun Crab Etouffee

Prep Time: 10 minutes
Cooking Time: 35 minutes
Number of Servings: 4
Ingredients:
- 1 cup uncooked white rice
- 1 1/4 cups water
- 1/4 cup butter
- 1/4 cup flour

- 1 tablespoon olive oil
- 1 onion, chopped
- 1 celery stalk, chopped
- 1 bell pepper, chopped
- 2 garlic cloves, minced
- 1 teaspoon Creole seasoning
- 1/2 cup white wine
- 1 cup chicken stock
- 1 tablespoon tomato paste
- 2 cups fresh cooked crabmeat
- 1/4 cup fresh parsley, chopped

Directions:
1. Combine water and rice in the pot. Close lid and cook on Rice Cooker mode. Transfer rice to a covered dish and set aside. Wipe out the pot.
2. Set Instant Pot to Saute mode and melt butter in the pot. Add flour and cook until roux is brown. Transfer to a bowl. Wipe out the pot.
3. Add olive oil to the pan, followed by onion, celery, bell pepper, garlic, and Creole seasoning. Cook until onion is translucent, then deglaze the pan with white wine.
4. Add chicken stock, tomato paste, and crabmeat. Bring to a boil. Add roux and cook, stirring constantly, until thickened. Close lid and set cooking time for 5 minutes on high pressure.
5. Serve etouffee over rice. Top with fresh parsley.

Chinese Takeout Shrimp Fried Rice

Prep Time: 10 minutes
Cooking Time: 35 minutes
Number of Servings: 4
Ingredients:
- 1 cup white rice
- 1 1/4 cup water
- 1 pound shrimp
- 1 cup water
- 2 tablespoons olive oil
- 1 egg, beaten
- 2 garlic cloves, minced
- 2 tablespoons soy sauce
- 1/4 cup green onions, sliced

Directions:
1. Combine rice and 1 1/4 cups water in the Instant Pot. Cook on Rice Cooker mode. Transfer to a bowl and set aside. Wipe out the pot.
2. Pour the water into the Instant Pot and place a steamer basket over the water. Arrange shrimp in the basket. Close lid and set cooking time for 1 minute on high pressure. After cooking time, use the quick release to remove the steam. Transfer shrimp to a bowl of cold water. When cool enough to handle, peel and chop the shrimp. Wipe out the pot.
3. Set the Instant Pot to Saute and add oil. Pour the egg into the pan and scramble into small grains. Add garlic and cook until fragrant. Pour in rice, chopped shrimp, and soy sauce and toss until well combined. Serve.

Seafood Paella

Prep Time: 10 minutes
Cooking Time: 10 minutes
Number of Servings: 4
Ingredients:
- 1 tablespoon olive oil
- 1/2 pound chorizo
- 1 onion, chopped
- 1 red bell pepper, chopped
- 2 garlic cloves, minced
- 1 pinch saffron
- 2 teaspoons dried thyme
- 2/3 cup bomba or arborio rice
- 1 pound whole shrimp
- 2 tablespoons tomato paste
- 1/3 cup stock or water
- 1/2 teaspoon salt
- 1/2 teaspoon black pepper

Directions:
1. Set Instant Pot to Saute mode. Add oil, then brown chorizo.
2. Add onion and bell pepper and cook until onion is translucent, then add garlic, saffron, and thyme. Cook until fragrant.
3. Add rice and toast until grains become opaque.
4. Add tomato paste and shrimp and toss until shrimp are well-coated with seasonings. Pour in stock or water, salt, and pepper.
5. Close lid. Set cooking time to 6 minutes on high pressure.

Cape Cod Lobster Bake

Prep Time: 10 minutes
Cooking Time: 10 minutes
Number of Servings: 4
Ingredients:
- 6 cups water
- 2 tablespoons Old Bay
- 1 tablespoon paprika
- 1 teaspoon salt
- 1 onion, quartered
- 3 cloves garlic, peeled
- 3 sprigs thyme
- 2 bay leaves
- 1 pound small red potatoes, halved
- 1/2 pound chorizo, sliced
- 2 cobs of corn, halved
- 1 1-pound lobster
- 1 pound crab legs
- 1 pound shrimp
- 1 lemon, cut into wedges

Directions:
1. Set Instant Pot to Saute mode. Add water, Old Bay, paprika, salt, onion, garlic, thyme, and bay leaves. Bring to a boil. Add potatoes and cook 5 minutes.
2. Stack the remaining ingredients of the lobster bake in this order: chorizo, corn, lobster, crab, shrimp.
3. Close the lid and set the cooking time for 5 minutes on high pressure. Use quick release to remove the steam after cooking.
4. Transfer potatoes, chorizo, corn, lobster, crab, and shrimp to a bowl. Discard bay leaf and thyme sprigs. Serve with lemon.

New Orleans Gumbo

Prep Time: 10 minutes
Cooking Time: 15 minutes
Number of Servings: 4
Ingredients:
- 1/2 pound bacon
- 1/4 cup flour
- 1 tablespoon olive oil
- 1/2 pound andouille sausage
- 1 onion, chopped
- 1 stalk celery
- 1 red bell pepper, chopped
- 2 cloves garlic, minced
- 1/2 teaspoon dried thyme
- 1 pound shrimp
- 1 pound okra, sliced
- 1 can whole plum tomatoes
- 1 cup chicken stock
- 2 bay leaves
- 1/2 teaspoon salt
- 1/2 teaspoon black pepper
- 1/4 cup fresh parsley

Directions:
1. Set Instant Pot to Saute and add bacon. Cook until most of the fat is rendered. Use a slotted spoon to remove the bacon to a paper towel, leaving the grease in the pan.
2. Add the flour to the pan and stir to combine with the grease. Cook until the flour browns slightly. Remove the roux to a bowl.
3. Wipe out the pot. Add 1 tablespoon olive oil, then add onion, celery, and red pepper. Cook until onion is translucent. Add garlic and thyme and cook until fragrant.
4. Add shrimp and okra and stir until well coated with seasonings. Pour in tomatoes, stock, bay leaves, and salt and pepper.
5. Close lid and set cooking time to 5 minutes. When cooking time ends, use the quick release to remove the steam.
6. Open the lid and set Instant Pot to Saute. Bring to a boil and add roux, stirring continuously. Cook until liquid thickens.
7. Top with parsley and serve.

Chapter 7: Meatless Mains

Black Bean Burgers

Prep Time: 10 minutes
Cooking Time: 30 minutes
Number of Servings:
Ingredients:
- 1 cup dry black beans
- 1 cup farro
- 6 cups water
- 1 onion, finely chopped
- 2 cloves garlic, minced
- 1 egg
- 1 cup breadcrumbs
- 1 teaspoon salt
- 1/2 teaspoon black pepper
- 2 tablespoons olive oil
- 6 hamburger buns

Directions:
1. Combine beans, farro, and water in the Instant Pot. Close lid and set cooking time for 25 minutes.
2. Place drained beans and farro in a bowl with onion, garlic, egg, breadcrumbs, salt, and pepper. Mash together all ingredients until well-combined. Shape bean mixture into patties.
3. Wipe out the Instant Pot and set to Saute mode. Add oil. Cook the patties in batches until well-browned on both sides. Serve on hamburger buns with your favorite condiments.

Masala Kidney Beans

Prep Time: 5min.
Cooking Time: 40 min.
Number of Servings: 5-6
Ingredients:
- 1 teaspoon ginger paste
- 1 ½ teaspoons ground cumin
- Chili powder as needed
- 1 teaspoon garlic paste
- 1 teaspoon garam masala
- 2 teaspoons ground coriander
- ½ teaspoon turmeric
- 2 cups dry kidney beans, soaked overnight and drained
- 2 tablespoons vegetable oil
- 2 large onions, chopped
- 3 large tomatoes, chopped
- Water and salt as needed
- Cilantro to garnish

Directions:

151

1. Take Instant Pot and carefully arrange it over a clean, dry kitchen platform. Turn on the appliance.
2. Find and press "Sauté" cooking function.
3. In the cooking pot area; add the oil and onions in the pot. Cook for 2 minutes to cook well and soften.
4. Add the ginger and garlic pastes and sauté for 2–3 minutes. Add the turmeric, cumin, coriander, garam masala and chili powder and sauté for a few seconds.
5. Add tomatoes and sauté for 2 minutes. Add the kidney beans, stir, and add enough water (2 inches above the ingredients) and salt.
6. Close the pot lid and seal the valve to avoid any leakage. Find and press "Bean/Chili" cooking setting and set cooking time to 30 minutes.
7. Allow the recipe ingredients to cook for the set time, and after that, the timer reads "zero".
8. Press "Cancel" and press "NPR" setting for natural pressure release. It takes 8-10 times for all inside pressure to release.
9. Open the pot. Garnish with cilantro. Serve over rice.

Spinach Jalapeno Lentil Curry

Prep Time: 8-10 min.
Cooking Time: 15 min.
Number of Servings: 3
Ingredients:
- 2 medium yellow potatoes, cubed
- 1 jalapeño, diced and seeds removed
- 3 medium tomatoes, diced
- 1 tablespoon curry powder
- 2 teaspoons vegetable oil
- 1 cup baby spinach
- 1 cup water
- ¾ teaspoons salt
- 1/3 cup dry brown lentils
- 4 garlic cloves, minced
- 1-inch piece of ginger, grated

Directions:
1. Soak lentils for one hour.
2. Take Instant Pot and carefully arrange it over a clean, dry kitchen platform. Turn on the appliance.
3. Find and press "Sauté" cooking function.
4. In the cooking pot area; add the oil and onions in the pot. Cook for 3-4 minutes to cook well and soften.
5. Add the ginger, garlic, and pepper. Cook for 2 minutes. Add the tomato, curry powder, water, lentils, and salt.
6. Add the spinach and cook until wilted.
7. Close the pot lid and seal the valve to avoid any leakage. Find and press "Manual" cooking setting and set cooking time to 8 minutes.
8. Allow the recipe ingredients to cook for the set time, and after that, the timer reads "zero".

9. Press "Cancel" and press "NPR" setting for natural pressure release. It takes 8-10 times for all inside pressure to release.
10. Open the pot and arrange the cooked recipe in serving plates. Enjoy the vegan recipe!

Creamy Lima Beans

Prep Time: 8-10min.
Cooking Time: 15 min.
Number of Servings: 4
Ingredients:
- 1 pound lima beans
- 1 cup sour cream, vegan
- 1 tablespoon dark syrup or your choice such as Karo
- ¾ cup vegan butter
- ¾ brown sugar
- 1 tablespoon dry mustard
- 2 teaspoon salt

Directions:
1. Soak the beans in 10 cups water; add the salt and set aside.
2. In the cooking pot area, add the water and beans. Stir the ingredients gently.
3. Close the pot lid and seal the valve to avoid any leakage. Find and press "Manual" cooking setting and set cooking time to 4 minutes.
4. Allow the recipe ingredients to cook for the set time, and after that, the timer reads "zero".
5. Press "Cancel" and press "NPR" setting for natural pressure release. It takes 8-10 times for all inside pressure to release.
6. Open the pot and drain the beans.
7. Add back in the pot. Add other ingredients and mix gently together.
8. Close the pot lid and seal the valve to avoid any leakage. Find and press "Manual" cooking setting and set cooking time to 10 minutes.
9. Allow the recipe ingredients to cook for the set time, and after that, the timer reads "zero".
10. Press "Cancel" and press "NPR" setting for natural pressure release. It takes 8-10 times for all inside pressure to release.
11. Open the pot and transfer the mixture to serving bowl.

Instant Peas Risotto

Prep Time: 10 min.
Cooking Time: 10 min.
Number of Servings: 3
Ingredients:
- 1 cup baby green peas
- 1 cup Arborio rice
- 2 cloves garlic, diced
- 3 tablespoons olive oil
- 1 brown onion, diced
- ½ teaspoon salt
- 2 celery sticks, make small cubes

- ½ teaspoon pepper
- 2 tablespoons lemon juice
- 2 cups vegetable stock

Directions:
1. Take your Instant Pot and place it on a clean kitchen platform. Turn it on after plugging it into a power socket.
2. Put the pot on "Saute" mode. In the pot, add the oil, celery, onions, pepper, and salt; cook for 4-5 minutes until the ingredients become soft.
3. Mix in the zest, stock, garlic, peas, and rice. Stir the ingredients.
4. Close the lid and lock. Ensure that you have sealed the valve to avoid leakage.
5. Press "Manual" mode and set timer for 5 minutes. It will take a few minutes for the pot to build inside pressure and start cooking.
6. After the timer reads zero, press "Cancel" and quick release pressure.
7. Carefully remove the lid, add the lemon juice and serve warm!

Tofu Veggie Treat

Prep Time: 5-8 min.
Cooking Time: 5 min.
Number of Servings: 4
Ingredients:
- 3 teaspoons tamari
- 8 ounces soft tofu, make small cubes
- ½ cup red bell pepper
- 1 yellow onion, thinly sliced
- 6 large mushrooms, sliced
- ½ cup green beans
- ¼ cup vegetable stock
- Cooking oil as needed
- Salt and white pepper to the taste

Directions:
1. Take your Instant Pot and place it on a clean kitchen platform. Turn it on after plugging it into a power socket.
2. Put the pot on "Saute" mode. In the pot, add the oil, mushrooms, and onions; cook for 2-3 minutes until the ingredients become soft.
3. Add the tamari and tofu; cook for 2 more minutes. Mix in the stock and stir gently.
4. Close the lid and lock. Ensure that you have sealed the valve to avoid leakage.
5. Press "Manual" mode and set timer for 3 minutes. It will take a few minutes for the pot to build inside pressure and start cooking.
6. After the timer reads zero, press "Cancel" and quick release pressure.
7. Add the green beans and bell pepper. Press "Manual" mode and set timer to 1 minutes. After the timer reads zero, press "Cancel" and quick release pressure.
8. Carefully remove the lid; add the pepper and salt. Serve warm!

Mushroom Zucchini Pasta

Prep Time: 8 min.

Cooking Time: 20 min.
Number of Servings: 5-6
Ingredients:

- 12 mushrooms, thinly sliced
- 1 zucchini, thinly sliced
- A few drops of sherry wine
- 1 shallot, finely chopped
- 15 ounces penne pasta
- 5 ounces tomato paste
- 2 tablespoons soy sauce
- 1 yellow onion, thinly sliced
- 2 garlic cloves, minced
- 1 tablespoon olive oil
- 1 cup vegetable stock
- 2 cups water
- A pinch of basil, dried
- A pinch of oregano, dried
- Black pepper and salt as needed

Directions:
1. Take your Instant Pot and place it on a clean kitchen platform. Turn it on after plugging it into a power socket.
2. Put the pot on "Saute" mode. In the pot, add the oil, onion, shallot, pepper and salt; cook for 2-3 minutes until the ingredients become soft.
3. Add the garlic, stir and cook for 1 minute more. Mix in the mushrooms, zucchini, basil, and oregano, stir and cook 1 more minute.
4. Mix in the wine, stock, water and soy sauce; stir well and then add the pasta and tomato sauce. Add more pepper and salt, if needed.
5. Close the lid and lock. Ensure that you have sealed the valve to avoid leakage.
6. Press "Manual" mode and set timer for 5 minutes. It will take a few minutes for the pot to build inside pressure and start cooking.
7. After the timer reads zero, press "Cancel" and quick release pressure.
8. Carefully remove the lid and serve warm!

Potato Mustard Salad

Prep Time: 8-10 min.
Cooking Time: 10 min.
Number of Servings: 6
Ingredients:

- 1 celery stalk, chopped
- 1 cup water
- 3 teaspoons dill, finely chopped
- 1 small yellow onion, chopped
- 1 teaspoon cider vinegar
- 3 ounces vegan mayo
- 6 red potatoes
- 1 teaspoon mustard

- Black pepper and salt as needed

Directions:
1. Take your Instant Pot and place it on a clean kitchen platform. Turn it on after plugging it into a power socket.
2. Open the lid from the top and put it aside; add the potatoes and water.
3. Close the lid and lock. Ensure that you have sealed the valve to avoid leakage.
4. Press "Manual" mode and set timer for 3 minutes. It will take a few minutes for the pot to build inside pressure and start cooking.
5. After the timer reads zero, press "Cancel" and quick release pressure.
6. Carefully remove the lid and chop the potatoes.
7. In a bowl of medium size, thoroughly mix the onion, potatoes, celery, salt, pepper, and dill.
8. Add the vegan mayo, vinegar, and mustard; stir well. Serve warm!

Chickpea Burger

Prep Time: 8-10 min.
Cooking Time: 20 min.
Number of Servings: 5-6
Ingredients:
- 1 teaspoon cumin
- 2 bay leaves
- 1 cup chickpeas (dried), soaked for 4 hours
- 1 teaspoon thyme, dried
- 3 tablespoons tomato paste
- ½ cup whole wheat flour
- 1 teaspoon salt
- 1 teaspoon garlic powder
- Pepper as needed

Directions:
1. Take your Instant Pot and place it on a clean kitchen platform. Turn it on after plugging it into a power socket.
2. Open the lid from the top and put it aside; add the chickpeas and enough water to cover them.
3. Add the cumin powder, bay leaves, garlic powder, thyme, onion salt and pepper. Gently stir them.
4. Close the lid and lock. Ensure that you have sealed the valve to avoid leakage.
5. Press "Manual" mode and set timer for 15 minutes. It will take a few minutes for the pot to build inside pressure and start cooking.
6. After the timer reads zero, press "Cancel" and quick release pressure.
7. Carefully remove the lid. Discard bay leaves and drain water.
8. Transfer the mixture in a blender; blend to make it smooth. Add the flour and tomato paste; blend again.
9. Make 5 burger patties from the mix and grill them until turn golden on both sides.
10. Add them to the burger buns and add your favorite veggies and vegan mayo. Enjoy!

Spinach Pasta Treat

Prep Time: 5 min.

156

Cooking Time: 15 min.
Number of Servings: 4
Ingredients:
- 2 garlic cloves, crushed
- 2 garlic cloves, chopped
- 1 pound spinach
- 1 pound fusilli pasta
- A drizzle of olive oil
- ¼ cup pine nuts, chopped
- Black pepper and salt to taste

Directions:
1. Take your Instant Pot and place it on a clean kitchen platform. Turn it on after plugging it into a power socket.
2. Put the pot on "Saute" mode. In the pot, add the oil, garlic, and spinach; cook for 6-7 minutes until the ingredients become soft.
3. Add the pasta, salt, and pepper; add water to cover the pasta.
4. Close the lid and lock. Ensure that you have sealed the valve to avoid leakage.
5. Press "Manual" mode and set timer for 6 minutes. It will take a few minutes for the pot to build inside pressure and start cooking.
6. After the timer reads zero, press "Cancel" and quick release pressure.
7. Carefully remove the lid; mix the chopped garlic and pine nuts.
8. Serve warm!

Mexican Style Vegan Rice

Prep Time: 5 min.
Cooking Time: 8-10 min.
Number of Servings: 5-6
Ingredients:
- ½ piece chopped white onion

- 2 cups water

- 2 cups white rice, long-grain

- 3 cloves minced garlic

- 1 jalapeño, optional

- ½ cup tomato paste

- 2 teaspoon salt

Directions:
1. Take your Instant Pot and place it on a clean kitchen platform. Turn it on after plugging it into a power socket.
2. Put the pot on "Saute" mode. In the pot, add the oil, garlic, onion, rice, and salt; cook for 3-4 minutes until the ingredients become soft.
3. Mix the tomato paste, pepper and water; stir well.

4. Close the lid and lock. Ensure that you have sealed the valve to avoid leakage.
5. Press "Manual" mode and set timer for 4 minutes. It will take a few minutes for the pot to build inside pressure and start cooking.
6. After the timer reads zero, press "Cancel" and naturally release pressure. It takes about 8-10 minutes to naturally release pressure.
7. Carefully remove the lid, fluff the mix and serve warm!

Wholesome Lentil Tacos

Prep Time: 5 min.
Cooking Time: 15 min.
Number of Servings: 6-8
Ingredients:
- 1 teaspoon onion powder

- 2 cups lentils, dry

- 1 teaspoon chili powder

- 4 cups water

- 4-ounce tomato sauce

- 1 teaspoon garlic powder

- ½ teaspoon cumin

- 1 teaspoon salt

Directions:
1. Take your Instant Pot and place it on a clean kitchen platform. Turn it on after plugging it into a power socket.
2. Open the lid from the top and put it aside; start adding the mentioned ingredients inside and gently stir them.
3. Close the lid and lock. Ensure that you have sealed the valve to avoid leakage.
4. Press "Manual" mode and set timer for 15 minutes. It will take a few minutes for the pot to build inside pressure and start cooking.
5. After the timer reads zero, press "Cancel" and naturally release pressure. It takes about 8-10 minutes to naturally release pressure.
6. Carefully remove the lid.
7. Take your choice of tacos and add the cooked mixture; enjoy the vegan tacos!

Pumpkin Bean Stew

Prep Time: 8-10 min.
Cooking Time: 20-22 min.
Number of Servings: 4
Ingredients:
- 2 cloves garlic, minced

- 3 cups water

- 2 medium tomatoes, chopped

- 1/2 cup dried chickpeas (soaked for 12 hours and drained)

- 3 small onions, chopped

- 1 cup raw pumpkin, peeled, cubed

- 1/2 cup dried navy beans (soaked for 12 hours and drained)

- Pepper and salt as needed

- 2 teaspoon harissa

- 2 tablespoons parsley, chopped

Directions:
1. Take your Instant Pot and place it on a clean kitchen platform. Turn it on after plugging it into a power socket.
2. Put the pot on "Saute" mode. In the pot, add the oil, garlic, and onions; cook for 2-3 minutes until the ingredients become soft.
3. Add other ingredients to the pot. Stir gently.
4. Close the lid and lock. Ensure that you have sealed the valve to avoid leakage.
5. Press "Bean/Chili" mode and set the timer for 6 minutes. It will take a few minutes for the pot to build inside pressure and start cooking.
6. After the timer reads zero, press "Cancel" and naturally release pressure. It takes about 8-10 minutes to naturally release pressure.
7. Carefully remove the lid.
8. Check if the beans are tender, if not add some more water; cook on "Manual" mode for 8-10 minutes.
9. Top with parsley and serve.

Mushroom Bean Farro

Prep Time: 8-10 min.
Cooking Time: 30 min.
Number of Servings: 3-4
Ingredients:
- 3 cups mushrooms, chopped
- 1 seeded jalapeno pepper, chopped
- 1 tablespoon shallot powder
- 2 tablespoons barley
- 1 tablespoon red curry paste
- ½ cup farro
- 1 cup navy beans, dried
- 2 tablespoons onion powder
- 9 garlic cloves, minced
- 2 tomatoes, diced
- Pepper and salt as needed

Directions:
1. Take your Instant Pot and place it on a clean kitchen platform. Turn it on after plugging it into a power socket.
2. Open the lid from the top and put it aside; start adding the beans, faro, barley, mushrooms, garlic, jalapeno, curry paste, shallot and onion powder, pepper and salt.
3. Add water to cover all the ingredients; gently stir them.
4. Close the lid and lock. Ensure that you have sealed the valve to avoid leakage.
5. Press "Manual" mode and set timer for 30 minutes. It will take a few minutes for the pot to build inside pressure and start cooking.
6. After the timer reads zero, press "Cancel" and naturally release pressure. It takes about 8-10 minutes to naturally release pressure.
7. Carefully remove the lid and add the tomatoes.
8. Sprinkle cilantro and scallions; serve warm!

Sorghum Raisin Meal

Prep Time: 8-10 min.
Cooking Time: 60 min.
Number of Servings: 4
Ingredients:
- 3 cups water
- 1 cup coconut milk
- 3 tablespoons rice wine vinegar
- 1 cup sorghum
- ½ teaspoon chili powder
- 1 tablespoon curry powder
- 2 cups chopped carrots
- ½ cup raisins, golden
- ¼ cup green onion, finely chopped
- 2 teaspoons palm sugar
- Salt as needed

Directions:
1. Take your Instant Pot and place it on a clean kitchen platform. Turn it on after plugging it into a power socket.
2. Open the lid from the top and put it aside; start adding the sorghum, salt and water. Gently stir them.
3. Close the lid and lock. Ensure that you have sealed the valve to avoid leakage.
4. Press "Manual" mode and set timer for 55-60 minutes. It will take a few minutes for the pot to build inside pressure and start cooking.
5. After the timer reads zero, press "Cancel" and naturally release pressure. It takes about 8-10 minutes to naturally release pressure.
6. Carefully remove the lid; drain the sorghum.
7. In a medium-size bowl, mix the palm sugar, coconut milk, vinegar, salt, curry powder and chili powder.
8. In the bowl, add the sorghum, carrots, and onions. Serve!

Squash Eggplant Mania

Prep Time: 8-10 min.
Cooking Time: 20 min.
Number of Servings: 4
Ingredients:

- 14 ounces eggplant, chopped
- 2 yellow onions, chopped
- 14 ounces squash, chopped
- 4 tomatoes, chopped
- 1 tablespoon olive oil, extra virgin
- 3 garlic cloves, finely minced
- ½ teaspoon thyme, dried
- 1 red capsicum, chopped
- 1 green capsicum, chopped
- 2 teaspoons dried basil
- Black pepper and salt as needed

Directions:
1. Take your Instant Pot and place it on a clean kitchen platform. Turn it on after plugging it into a power socket.
2. Put the pot on "Saute" mode. In the pot, add the oil, garlic, and onion; cook for 3-4 minutes until the ingredients become soft.
3. Add the squash, eggplant, both capsicum, tomatoes, thyme, salt, pepper and basil; stir well.
4. Close the lid and lock. Ensure that you have sealed the valve to avoid leakage.
5. Press "Manual" mode and set timer for 10 minutes. It will take a few minutes for the pot to build inside pressure and start cooking.
6. After the timer reads zero, press "Cancel" and naturally release pressure. It takes about 8-10 minutes to naturally release pressure.
7. Carefully remove the lid and serve warm!

Zucchini Eggplant Meal

Prep Time: 5min.
Cooking Time: 8 min.
Number of Servings: 6-8
Ingredients:

- 2 cloves minced garlic
- 12 ounces roasted red peppers, make slices
- 1 onion, make thin slices
- 4 zucchini, sliced thin
- 1 can (28 oz.) tomatoes, crushed
- 2 eggplants, peeled and make thin slices
- ½ cup water
- 1 tablespoon olive oil
- 1 teaspoon salt

Directions:

161

1. Take Instant Pot and carefully arrange it over a clean, dry kitchen platform. Turn on the appliance.
2. Find and press "Sauté" cooking function.
3. Add the zucchini, eggplant, oil, and onion; heat for 2-3 minutes to cook well and soften.
4. Season with the salt and then add the tomatoes and water; stir to combine.
5. Close the pot lid and seal the valve to avoid any leakage. Find and press "Manual" cooking set with 4 minutes cooking time.
6. Allow the recipe ingredients to cook for the set time, and after that, the timer reads "zero".
7. Press "Cancel" and press "NPR" setting for natural pressure release. It takes 8-10 times for all inside pressure to release.
8. Open the pot and arrange the cooked recipe in serving plates. Enjoy the vegan recipe!

Jalapeno Bean Meal

Prep Time: 8-10min.
Cooking Time: 40 min.
Number of Servings: 4
Ingredients:
- ½ pound pinto beans, rinsed
- 2 cloves garlic, minced
- 3 cups water
- ½ teaspoon cumin powder
- 1 small onion, chopped
- ½ tablespoon olive oil
- 1 small jalapeño, chopped
- Salt as needed
- A handful of cilantro, chopped

Directions:
1. Take Instant Pot and carefully arrange it over a clean, dry kitchen platform. Turn on the appliance.
2. Find and press "Sauté" cooking function.
3. In the cooking pot area; add the oil, jalapeno, garlic, and onions in the pot. Cook until turn translucent and soften.
4. Add the beans, cumin, and water. Mix well.
5. Close the pot lid and seal the valve to avoid any leakage. Find and press "Bean/Chili" cooking setting and set cooking time to 30 minutes.
6. Allow the recipe ingredients to cook for the set time, and after that, the timer reads "zero".
7. Press "Cancel" and press "NPR" setting for natural pressure release. It takes 8-10 times for all inside pressure to release.
8. Open the pot, add salt and arrange the cooked recipe in serving plates. Garnish with cilantro and serve.

Wholesome Cauliflower Meal

Prep Time: 8-10min.
Cooking Time: 1 min.
Number of Servings:4

Ingredients:
- 1 cauliflower head, medium-sized
- 2 tablespoons olive oil
- 2 tablespoons cilantro, chopped
- 1 cup water
- ½ teaspoon dried parsley
- ½ teaspoon salt
- ¼ teaspoon paprika
- ¼ teaspoon ground cumin
- ¼ teaspoon turmeric powder

Directions:
1. Make large pieces of the cauliflower.
2. Take Instant Pot and carefully arrange it over a clean, dry kitchen platform. Turn on the appliance.
3. Pour the water into the cooking pot area. Arrange the trivet inside it; arrange the cauliflower over the trivet.
4. Close the pot lid and seal the valve to avoid any leakage. Find and press "Steam" cooking setting and set cooking time to 1 minutes.
5. Allow the recipe ingredients to cook for the set time, and after that, the timer reads "zero".
6. Press "Cancel" and press "NPR" setting for natural pressure release. It takes 8-10 times for all inside pressure to release.
7. Open the pot and arrange the cooked recipe in serving plates.
8. Empty the pot. Select "Saute". Add the oil and cooked cauliflower; heat for 2 minutes to cook well and soften.
9. Mash it well and mix all the spices; combine and cook for a few minutes. Serve warm!

Faro Peas Collard Wraps

Prep Time: 5 min.
Cooking Time: 13 min.
Number of Servings: 8
Ingredients:
- 3 tablespoons olive oil
- 1 onion, chopped
- 1 ¼ cups dry black-eyed peas, rinsed
- 6 cloves garlic, minced
- 8 collard green leaves
- 1 teaspoon thyme, dried
- 4 teaspoons soy sauce
- 1 teaspoon dried basil
- 1 1/3 cups faro (semi-pearled), soaked for 30-45 minutes
- 1 teaspoon hot sauce
- Salt as needed
- 2 cups water
- 2 cups broth
- 2 tablespoons oil

Directions:

1. Take Instant Pot and carefully arrange it over a clean, dry kitchen platform. Turn on the appliance.
2. Find and press "Sauté" cooking function.
3. Add the oil and farro; heat for 2-3 minutes to cook well and soften. Add other ingredients except for broth and collard; cook for a few more minutes.
4. Add the broth and stir.
5. Close the pot lid and seal the valve to avoid any leakage. Find and press "Manual" cooking setting and set cooking time to 10 minutes.
6. Allow the recipe ingredients to cook for the set time, and after that, the timer reads "zero".
7. Press "Cancel" and press "NPR" setting for natural pressure release. It takes 8-10 times for all inside pressure to release.
8. Place the collard on a platform. Spread the mixture over them, roll and serve.

Chili Bean Tacos

Prep Time: 8-10min.
Cooking Time: 40 min.
Number of Servings:5-6
Ingredients:

- 1 teaspoon salt
- 2 tablespoons tomato paste
- ½ teaspoon cumin
- 2 teaspoons chili powder
- 2 teaspoons oregano
- 1 small onion, chopped
- 3 cups water
- 1 pound dried chili beans, plus extra water
- 6 taco shells or tortillas
- 1 bell pepper, minced
- 2 garlic cloves, chopped

Directions:

1. Take Instant Pot and carefully arrange it over a clean, dry kitchen platform. Turn on the appliance.
2. Find and press "Sauté" cooking function. Fill the pot with water to come above the surface of the beans and boil.
3. Boil the mix 5 minutes. Drain.
4. Put the beans back in the pot. Add the chili powder, oregano, cumin, garlic, and onion.
5. Close the pot lid and seal the valve to avoid any leakage. Find and press "Manual" cooking setting and set cooking time to 5 minutes.
6. Allow the recipe ingredients to cook for the set time, and after that, the timer reads "zero".
7. Press "Cancel" and press "NPR" setting for natural pressure release. It takes 8-10 times for all inside pressure to release.
8. Open and add remaining ingredients. Cook uncovered 30 minutes.
9. Serve the mix on taco shells.

Chickpea Curry

Prep Time: 10 minutes
Cooking Time: 40 minutes
Number of Servings: 4
Ingredients:
- 1 cup dried chickpeas
- 2 cups water
- 1 tablespoon olive oil
- 1 onion, finely chopped
- 2 garlic cloves, minced
- 1 inch ginger, minced
- 1/2 teaspoon turmeric
- 1 teaspoon coriander
- 1 teaspoon cumin
- 1 teaspoon garam masala
- 1 cup canned tomatoes, crushed
- 1 cup water
- 1/4 cup fresh cilantro, chopped

Directions:
1. Combine chickpeas and 2 cups water in the Instant Pot. Close lid and set cooking time for 35 minutes. When cooked, drain and set aside.
2. Wipeout Instant Pot and set to Saute. Add olive oil, followed by onion, garlic, and ginger. When the onion is translucent, add turmeric, coriander, cumin, and garam masala. Toast for about 30 seconds, then add tomatoes, water, and cooked chickpeas. Simmer until slightly thickened and heated through.
3. Top with fresh cilantro. Serve with naan or rice.

Refried Bean Enchiladas

Prep Time: 10 minutes
Cooking Time: 1 hour
Number of Servings: 4
Ingredients:

- 1 cup dry pinto beans
- 2 cups water
- 2 tablespoons olive oil
- 1 onion, finely chopped
- 2 garlic cloves, minced
- 2 cups shredded Mexican cheese blend
- 12 small corn tortillas
- 2 cans enchilada sauce

Directions:
1. Combine beans and water in the Instant Pot. Close the lid and set the cooking time for 45 minutes.
2. When beans are cooked, drain away all but 1/2 cup of the cooking liquid. Mash or blend to a smooth consistency.

165

3. Wipe out the Instant Pot and set to Saute mode. Add olive oil, followed by onion and garlic. Cook until onion is translucent. Add bean paste and cook about 5 minutes or until light and fluffy.
4. Preheat the oven to 400℉. Lightly grease a large casserole dish. Coat both sides of a tortilla in enchilada sauce. Lay about 2 tablespoons of the refried beans in a line along the center of the tortilla and top with an equal amount of cheese. Roll the tortilla into a tube and place it seam-side down in the casserole dish. Repeat with the remaining tortillas.
5. Pour the remaining enchilada sauce over the tortillas, followed by the remaining cheese. Place the dish in the oven and cook 15 minutes or until sauce is bubbling and cheese is browned.

Brown Rice Stuffed Peppers

Prep Time: 10 minutes
Cooking Time: 45 minutes
Number of Servings:
Ingredients:
- 1/2 cup brown rice
- 1/2 cup wild rice
- 1 cup vegetable stock
- 6 bell peppers
- 1 onion, finely chopped
- 2 cloves garlic, minced
- 1 large tomato, diced
- 2 scallions, sliced
- 1/2 teaspoon salt
- 1/2 teaspoon black pepper
- 1/2 teaspoon dried oregano
- 1/2 teaspoon dried basil
- 1/2 teaspoon dried parsley
- 1/4 teaspoon garlic powder
- 2 cups tomato sauce
- 1/2 cup shredded Cheddar cheese

Directions:
1. Combine water and stock in the Instant Pot. Cook on Rice Cooker mode. Transfer rice to a large bowl.
2. Mix onions, garlic, tomato, scallions, salt, pepper, oregano, basil, parsley, garlic powder, and 1/2 cup the tomato sauce into the rice.
3. Cut the tops off the peppers and scoop out the seeds and ribs. Stuff the rice mixture into the peppers. Stand the peppers in the Instant Pot. Top each pepper with 2 tablespoons tomato sauce, followed by the cheese.
4. Pour the remaining tomato sauce and 1 cup water around the peppers. Close the lid and set the cooking time for 15 minutes on high pressure.

"Baked" Ziti

Prep Time: 10 minutes
Cooking Time: 10 minutes
Number of Servings: 4
Ingredients:

- 1 tablespoon olive oil
- 1 onion, chopped
- 2 cloves garlic, minced
- 2 cups whole peeled tomatoes with juice, crushed
- 1 pound uncooked ziti pasta
- 2 cups shredded mozzarella cheese

Directions:
1. Set the Instant Pot to Saute and add the olive oil, followed by the onion and garlic. Cook until onion is translucent.
2. Add tomatoes and pasta. Add enough water to cover the pasta and stir. Close the lid and set cooking time for 5 minutes at low pressure.
3. Use quick release to remove the steam, then open the lid. Arrange cheese over the pasta. Close the lid and allow to sit on Keep Warm setting 5 minutes or until cheese melts.

Quick Mac & Cheese

Prep Time: 5 minutes
Cooking Time: 15 minutes
Number of Servings: 4
Ingredients:
- 1 pound uncooked macaroni
- 4 cups water
- 2 tablespoons butter
- 2 tablespoons flour
- 3 cups whole milk
- 1 cup shredded Cheddar cheese
- 1/2 teaspoon salt
- 1/2 teaspoon black pepper

Directions:
1. Combine the macaroni and water in the instant pot. Close the lid and set cooking time for 4 minutes on high pressure. After cooking time, use the quick release to remove the steam. Drain the pasta and wipe out the pot.
2. With pot set to Saute mode, melt butter. Add flour and cook until bubbling subsides and the mixture is slightly browned. Gradually add milk, stirring constantly, and cook until thickened slightly. Stir in cheese until melted. Season to taste with salt and pepper.
3. Stir in pasta. Heat through and serve.

Pasta Primavera

Prep Time: 10 minutes
Cooking Time: 4 minutes
Number of Servings: 4
Ingredients:
- 1 pound penne pasta
- 4 cups water
- 2 zucchini, julienned
- 1 red bell pepper, julienned
- 1 onion, sliced thin
- 2 cloves garlic, minced
- 1 large tomato, diced

- 1/4 cup fresh basil, chopped
- 2 tablespoons olive oil
- 1/2 cup grated Parmesan
- 1/2 teaspoon salt
- 1/2 teaspoon black pepper

Directions:
1. Combine pasta and water in the Instant Pot. Place the steamer basket over the water and arrange zucchini, pepper, onion, garlic, and tomato in the basket. Close lid and set cooking time for 4 minutes on high pressure.
2. Use quick release to remove the steam. Drain the pasta. Pour the contents of the steamer basket into the pasta and toss with olive oil, basil, and Parmesan. Season to taste with salt and pepper.

Eggplant Parmesan

Prep Time: 30 minutes
Cooking Time: 4 hours 30 minutes
Number of Servings: 4
Ingredients:
- 1 large eggplant, thinly sliced
- 1/4 cup flour
- 1/2 teaspoon salt
- 1 egg, beaten
- 1 cup Italian seasoned breadcrumbs
- 1/2 cup olive oil
- 1 onion, finely chopped
- 2 cloves garlic, minced
- 1/2 teaspoon salt
- 1/2 teaspoon black pepper
- 2 cups canned tomato sauce
- 1/2 cup grated Parmesan cheese
- 1 cup sliced mozzarella cheese

Directions:
1. Mix the salt into the flour. Dip an eggplant slice into the flour, followed by the egg. Press the breadcrumbs onto the slice. Continue with the rest of the eggplant slices.
2. Heat the oil in the Instant Pot on Saute mode. Fry the breaded eggplant in batches until brown on both sides. Remove to a paper towel. Pour excess olive oil out of the pot, leaving about 1 tablespoon.
3. Add the onions and garlic to the pot and cook until onions are translucent. Add salt, pepper, and tomato sauce. Transfer the sauce to a bowl, leaving about 1/4 cup in the pot. Turn off heat.
4. Lay a single layer of eggplant slices over the tomato sauce. Cover the slices with another thin layer of sauce, followed by about 1 tablespoon of Parmesan and enough mozzarella to cover. Continue this pattern until all ingredients are exhausted, making sure to reserve some mozzarella to put on top.
5. Close lid and set cooking time for 4 hours on Slow Cooker mode. Serve with pasta or bread.

Vegetarian Shepherd's Pie

Prep Time: 20 minutes
Cooking Time: 20 minutes

Number of Servings: 4
Ingredients:
- 1 cup dry lentils
- 2 cups water
- 2 small sweet potatoes
- 1 teaspoon salt
- 1 teaspoon black pepper
- 1 tablespoon butter
- 1/4 cup shredded Cheddar cheese
- 1 onion, chopped
- 2 cloves garlic, minced
- 1 teaspoon thyme
- 1 tablespoon tomato paste
- 1 teaspoon Worcestershire sauce

Directions:
1. Pour lentils and water into the Instant Pot. Place a steamer basket over the pot and arrange sweet potatoes in the steamer. Close lid and set cooking time for 20 minutes on high pressure.
2. Transfer sweet potatoes to a bowl of cold water. When cool enough to handle, remove the skins and transfer to a clean bowl. Mash with 1/4 teaspoon salt, 1/2 teaspoon pepper, butter, and Cheddar cheese. Set aside.
3. Drain water from lentils and wipe out the pot. Set to Saute mode and add olive oil. Add onion, garlic, and thyme and cook until onions are translucent. Pour lentils back into the pot. Add tomato paste, Worcestershire sauce, and season with salt and pepper. Transfer to a baking dish.
4. Layer the mashed potatoes on top of the lentils. Serve, or first set under the broiler 5 minutes or until the top browns.

Nutritional Values (Per Serving):
Calories - 236
Fat - 5.62 g
Carbohydrates - 41.2 g
Fiber - 5.2 g
Protein - 7.84 g

Chapter 8: Poultry

Creamy Chicken and Rice Casserole

Prep Time: 5 minutes
Cooking Time: 10 minutes
Number of Servings: 4
Ingredients:
- 1 pound boneless chicken, cubed
- 1/2 teaspoon salt
- 1/2 teaspoon black pepper
- 1 can cream of chicken soup
- 1 cup water
- 1 onion, finely chopped
- 1 teaspoon dried thyme
- 3/4 cup uncooked rice
- 2 cups broccoli florets, chopped small
- 1/2 cup shredded Cheddar cheese

Directions:
1. Season the chicken with salt and pepper. Place in instant pot with soup, water, onion, thyme, rice, broccoli, and cheese.
2. Close lid and set cooking time for 10 minutes. Allow steam to release naturally. Serve.

Rosemary Chicken

Prep Time: 5-8 min.
Cooking Time: 10 min.
Number of Servings: 2
Ingredients:
- 2 tablespoons minced garlic
- 1-cup low sodium chicken broth
- 1 ½ teaspoons olive oil
- ¾ pound chopped boneless chicken
- ½ cup chopped onion
- ¼ teaspoon thyme
- ½ teaspoon salt
- ½ teaspoon pepper
- 1 bay leaf
- 1 tablespoon chopped rosemary
- 2 tablespoons chopped celery

Directions:
1. Switch on the pot after placing it on a clean and dry platform. Press "Sauté" cooking function.
2. Open the pot lid; add the oil, garlic, and onions in the pot; cook for 2 minutes to cook well and turn lightly golden.
3. Add chicken cubes to the pot. Mix the salt, pepper, bay leaf, chopped rosemary, and thyme.
4. Close the pot by closing the top lid. Also, ensure to seal the valve.

5. Press "Manual" cooking function and set cooking time to 10 minutes. It will start cooking after a few minutes. Let the pot mix cook under pressure until the timer reads zero.
6. Press "Cancel" cooking function and press "Natural release (NPR)" setting. It will take 8-10 minutes for natural pressure release.
7. Open the pot; topped with some celery and serve warm. Enjoy it with your loved one!

Tangy Potato Chicken

Prep Time: 8-10 min.
Cooking Time: 20 min.
Number of Servings: 2
Ingredients:
- ½ cup low sodium chicken broth
- 1-½ tablespoons Dijon mustard
- 1 tablespoon Italian seasoning
- 2 tablespoons lemon juice
- 1 teaspoon lemon zest
- 1 pound. chopped chicken
- 1 pound potatoes, peeled and make wedges
- ½ teaspoon salt
- ½ teaspoon pepper

Directions:
1. Season the chicken with pepper and salt. Switch on the pot after placing it on a clean and dry platform.
2. Open the pot lid and place the above-mentioned ingredients in the cooking pot area. Give the ingredients a little stir.
3. Close the pot by closing the top lid. Also, ensure to seal the valve.
4. Press "Manual" cooking function and set cooking time to 15 minutes. It will start cooking after a few minutes. Let the pot mix cook under pressure until the timer reads zero.
5. Press "Cancel" cooking function and press "Natural release (NPR)" setting. It will take 8-10 minutes for natural pressure release.
6. Open the pot and serve warm. Enjoy it with your loved one!

Oregano Pasta Chicken

Prep Time: 8-10 min.
Cooking Time: 12 min.
Number of Servings: 2
Ingredients:
- ½ teaspoon olive oil
- ½ cup diced tomatoes
- ¼ teaspoon salt
- 1 bay leaf
- 2 tablespoons chopped parsley
- ½ teaspoon pepper
- ½ cup chopped onion
- 1 ½ cup diced chicken

- ½ cup diced red bell pepper
- ½ teaspoon oregano

Directions:
1. Take your 3-Quart Instant Pot; open the top lid. Plug it and turn it on.
2. Press "SAUTÉ" setting and the pot will start heating up.
3. In the cooking pot area, add the oil and onions. Cook until starts becoming translucent and softened. Stir in between.
4. Add the diced chicken, bell pepper and tomatoes. Season with salt, pepper, oregano, and bay leaf then stir well.
5. Close the top lid and seal its valve.
6. Press "MANUAL" setting. Adjust cooking time to 10 minutes.
7. Allow the recipe to cook for the set cooking time.
8. After the set cooking time ends, press "CANCEL" and then press "NPR (Natural Pressure Release)".
9. Instant Pot will slowly and naturally release the pressure.
10. Open the top lid, add the cooked recipe mix in serving plates.
11. Serve with some pasta and parsley on top and enjoy!

Chicken Soy Tortilla

Prep Time: 8-10 min.
Cooking Time: 10 min.
Number of Servings: 2
Ingredients:
- 1/2 pound chicken, ground
- 2 tablespoons soy sauce
- 2 teaspoons garlic, minced
- A pinch of ginger, grated
- 2 tortillas for serving
- 1 small yellow onion, chopped
- 2 tablespoons chicken stock
- 2 tablespoons balsamic vinegar
- A pinch of allspice, ground
- 4 tablespoons water chestnuts

Directions:
1. Take your 3-Quart Instant Pot; open the top lid. Plug it and turn it on.
2. In the cooking pot area, add the onion, garlic, ginger, allspice, chicken, chestnuts, soy sauce, stock, and vinegar. Using a spatula, stir the ingredients.
3. Close the top lid and seal its valve.
4. Press "MANUAL" setting. Adjust cooking time to 10 minutes.
5. Allow the recipe to cook for the set cooking time.
6. After the set cooking time ends, press "CANCEL" and then press "QPR (Quick Pressure Release)".
7. Instant Pot will quickly release the pressure.
8. Open the top lid, add the cooked recipe mix in serving plates.
9. Fill the tortillas, make wraps and enjoy!

Nut & Date Chicken

Prep Time: 10 min.
Cooking Time: 30 min.
Number of Servings: 2
Ingredients:

- 1 teaspoon coriander, ground
- 4 chicken thighs, skinless and boneless
- A pinch of pepper and salt
- 1 teaspoon cumin, ground
- 1 teaspoon smoked paprika
- 1/2 tablespoon olive oil
- 1 garlic clove, crushed or minced
- Chopped mint for serving
- 1/2 yellow onion, chopped
- 1 carrot, chopped
- 4 tablespoons green olives, pitted
- 2 tablespoons pine nuts
- 14 ounces tomatoes, chopped
- 4 tablespoons chicken stock
- 4 Medjool dates, chopped
- 1/2 lemon, cut into wedges

Directions:

1. In a bowl, mix the chicken, salt, pepper, oil, cumin, paprika and coriander and toss.
2. Take your 3-Quart Instant Pot; open the top lid. Plug it and turn it on.
3. Press "SAUTÉ" setting and the pot will start heating up.
4. In the cooking pot area, add the meat. Stir and cook until evenly brown from all sides for 4-5 minutes.
5. Add the garlic, onion, carrot, tomatoes, stock, dates and olives; stir gently.
6. Close the top lid and seal its valve.
7. Press "MANUAL" setting. Adjust cooking time to 20 minutes.
8. Allow the recipe to cook for the set cooking time.
9. After the set cooking time ends, press "CANCEL" and then press "QPR (Quick Pressure Release)".
10. Instant Pot will quickly release the pressure.
11. Open the top lid, add the cooked recipe mix in serving plates.
12. Serve with mint and pine nuts on top and enjoy!

Maple Tomato Chicken

Prep Time: 5-8 min.
Cooking Time: 10 min.
Number of Servings: 2
Ingredients:

- 2 red onions, chopped

- 2 garlic cloves, minced
- 2 chicken breasts, boneless and skinless
- 2 tomatoes, chopped
- 1 tablespoon maple syrup
- 1 teaspoon chili powder
- 1 cup water
- 1 teaspoon cloves
- 1 teaspoon basil, dried

Directions:
1. Take your 3-Quart Instant Pot; open the top lid. Plug it and turn it on.
2. In the cooking pot area, add the tomatoes, onions, chicken, garlic, maple syrup, chili powder, basil, water, and cloves. Using a spatula, stir the ingredients.
3. Close the top lid and seal its valve.
4. Press "MANUAL" setting. Adjust cooking time to 10 minutes.
5. Allow the recipe to cook for the set cooking time.
6. After the set cooking time ends, press "CANCEL" and then press "QPR (Quick Pressure Release)".
7. Instant Pot will quickly release the pressure.
8. Open the top lid, take out the meat and shred it.
9. Add back to the mix and combine; add the cooked recipe mix in serving plates.
10. Serve and enjoy!

Couple's BBQ Chicken

Prep Time: 8-10 min.
Cooking Time: 10 min.
Number of Servings: 2
Ingredients:
- 1 cup water
- ½ cup chopped onion
- 2-½ tablespoons raw honey
- ½ cup barbecue sauce
- ¼ teaspoon salt
- ½ teaspoon pepper
- 2 pounds chicken wings

Directions:
1. Take your 3-Quart Instant Pot; open the top lid. Plug it and turn it on.
2. In the cooking pot area, add the ingredients. Using a spatula, stir the ingredients.
3. Close the top lid and seal its valve.
4. Press "MANUAL" setting. Adjust cooking time to 10 minutes.
5. Allow the recipe to cook for the set cooking time.
6. After the set cooking time ends, press "CANCEL" and then press "QPR (Quick Pressure Release)".
7. Instant Pot will quickly release the pressure.
8. Open the pot and add the mixture in a saucepan.
9. Cook for a few minutes to thicken the sauce.

10. Serve and enjoy!

Mexican Style Pepper Turkey

Prep Time: 5-8 min.
Cooking Time: 20 min.
Number of Servings: 3
Ingredients:
- 1/2 cup chicken stock
- 1 clove garlic, chopped
- 1 pound turkey breast, ground
- ½ tablespoon butter
- 1/2 red onion, sliced
- 1 cup canned diced tomatoes
- 1/2 red bell pepper, chopped
- 1/2 green bell pepper, chopped

Directions:
1. Take your 3-Quart Instant Pot; open the top lid. Plug it and turn it on.
2. Press "SAUTÉ" setting and the pot will start heating up.
3. In the cooking pot area, add the butter and meat. Stir and cook for 5 minutes to soften.
4. Mix in the tomatoes with their juices, garlic, onion, peppers, and stock.
5. Close the top lid and seal its valve.
6. Press "MANUAL" setting. Adjust cooking time to 8 minutes.
7. Allow the recipe to cook for the set cooking time.
8. After the set cooking time ends, press "CANCEL" and then press "QPR (Quick Pressure Release)".
9. Instant Pot will quickly release the pressure.
10. Open the top lid, add the cooked recipe mix in serving plates.
11. Serve and enjoy!

Tangy Olive Chicken

Prep Time: 8-10 min.
Cooking Time: 13 min.
Number of Servings: 2
Ingredients:
- 3 tablespoons butter
- Juice from 1/2 lemon
- A pinch of cumin, ground
- 2 chicken breasts, skinless and boneless
- 1/2 cup green olives, pitted
- 3 tablespoons red onion, chopped
- A pinch of pepper and salt
- 2 lemon slices
- 1/2 cup chicken stock

Directions:

1. Take your 3-Quart Instant Pot; open the top lid. Plug it and turn it on.
2. Press "SAUTÉ" setting and the pot will start heating up.
3. In the cooking pot area, add the chicken breasts, season with salt, pepper, and cumin.
4. Cook and brown for 3 minutes on each side.
5. Add the butter, lemon juice, lemon slices, stock, olives, and onion; gently stir.
6. Close the top lid and seal its valve.
7. Press "MANUAL" setting. Adjust cooking time to 10 minutes.
8. Allow the recipe to cook for the set cooking time.
9. After the set cooking time ends, press "CANCEL" and then press "QPR (Quick Pressure Release)".
10. Instant Pot will quickly release the pressure.
11. Open the top lid, add the cooked recipe mix in serving plates.
12. Serve and enjoy!

Lemongrass Coconut Chicken

Prep Time: 5 min.
Cooking Time: 15 min.
Number of Servings: 2
Ingredients:
- 2 teaspoons minced garlic
- 3 teaspoons fish sauce
- ¼ teaspoon pepper
- 1 tablespoon lemon juice
- ¼ cup chopped onion
- 1 lemongrass
- 1-teaspoon ginger
- 4 chicken drumsticks
- ½ teaspoon coconut oil
- ¾ cup coconut milk

Directions:
1. Chop the lemongrass and add in a blender. Add the garlic, ginger, fish sauce, pepper, and lemon juice; combine well.
2. Add the coconut milk. Blend until smooth and incorporated.
3. Switch on the pot after placing it on a clean and dry platform. Press "Sauté" cooking function.
4. Open the pot lid; add the oil and onions in the pot; cook for 2 minutes to cook well and soften.
5. Add the drumsticks to the pot; top with the coconut mixture over the chicken.
6. Close the pot by closing the top lid. Also, ensure to seal the valve.
7. Press "Manual" cooking function and set cooking time to 10 minutes. It will start cooking after a few minutes. Let the pot mix cook under pressure until the timer reads zero.
8. Press "Cancel" cooking function and press "Natural release (NPR)" setting. It will take 8-10 minutes for natural pressure release.
9. Open the pot and serve warm. Enjoy it with your loved one!

Cola Chicken Wings

Prep Time: 8-10 min.

Cooking Time: 20 min.
Number of Servings: 2
Ingredients:

- 2 tablespoons chopped onion
- 1-½ tablespoons low sodium soy sauce
- ½ tablespoon rice wine
- ½ tablespoon sesame oil
- ½ teaspoon ginger
- 1 cup your choice of cola
- 1 pound. chicken wings
- 2 teaspoons minced garlic

Directions:

1. Switch on the pot after placing it on a clean and dry platform. Press "Sauté" cooking function.
2. Open the pot lid; add the oil, garlic, and onions in the pot; cook for 2 minutes to cook well and soften.
3. Add the chicken wings and sauté until brown. Mix in the cola, soy sauce, and rice wine then stir well.
4. Close the pot by closing the top lid. Also, ensure to seal the valve.
5. Press "Manual" cooking function and set cooking time to 20 minutes. It will start cooking after a few minutes. Let the pot mix cook under pressure until the timer reads zero.
6. Press "Cancel" cooking function and press "Natural release (NPR)" setting. It will take 8-10 minutes for natural pressure release.
7. Open the pot and serve warm. Enjoy it with your loved one!

BBQ Chicken

Prep Time: 5 min.
Cooking Time: 15 min.
Number of Servings: 2
Ingredients:

- 1-cup water
- ½ cup chopped onion
- 2-½ tablespoons raw honey
- 2 pounds. chicken wings
- ½ cup barbecue sauce
- ¼ teaspoon salt
- ½ teaspoon pepper

Directions:

1. In a bowl, mix the barbecue sauce with water, raw honey, salt, and pepper. Switch on the pot after placing it on a clean and dry platform.
2. Open the pot lid and place the chicken and sauce in the cooking pot area. Give the ingredients a little stir.
3. Close the pot by closing the top lid. Also, ensure to seal the valve.
4. Press "Manual" cooking function and set cooking time to 10 minutes. It will start cooking after a few minutes. Let the pot mix cook under pressure until the timer reads zero.
5. Press "Cancel" cooking function and press "Quick release" setting.

6. Open the pot.
7. Preheat a pan over medium heat; add the chicken mix to the pan. Bring to simmer and stir until the barbecue sauce is thickened.
8. Serve warm!

Turkey Tomato Meal

Prep Time: 8-10 min.
Cooking Time: 20 min.
Number of Servings: 2
Ingredients:
- 1 red onion, sliced
- 1 cup chicken stock
- 1 tablespoon butter
- 1 red bell pepper, chopped
- 1 green bell pepper, chopped
- 2 pounds ground turkey breast
- 1 15-ounce can of diced tomatoes
- 2 cloves garlic, chopped

Directions:
1. Switch on the pot after placing it on a clean and dry platform. Press "Sauté" cooking function.
2. Open the pot lid; add the butter and meat in the pot; cook for 5 minutes to cook well and soften.
3. Add the tomatoes with their juices, garlic, onion, peppers, and stock.
4. Close the pot by closing the top lid. Also, ensure to seal the valve.
5. Press "Manual" cooking function and set cooking time to 15 minutes. It will start cooking after a few minutes. Let the pot mix cook under pressure until the timer reads zero.
6. Press "Cancel" cooking function and press "Quick release" setting.
7. Open the pot and serve warm. Enjoy it with your loved one!

Oregano Pasta Chicken

Prep Time: 5 min.
Cooking Time: 15 min.
Number of Servings: 2
Ingredients:
- ½ teaspoon olive oil
- ½ cup diced tomatoes
- ½ cup diced red bell pepper
- ½ teaspoon oregano
- 1 bay leaf
- ½ cup chopped onion
- 1 ½ cup diced chicken
- ¼ teaspoon salt
- ½ teaspoon pepper
- 2 tablespoons chopped parsley
- Cooked pasta of your choice

178

Directions:
1. Switch on the pot after placing it on a clean and dry platform. Press "Sauté" cooking function.
2. Open the pot lid; add the oil and onions in the pot; cook for 2 minutes to cook well and soften.
3. Add the chicken, bell pepper, and diced tomatoes. Mix the salt, pepper, oregano, and bay leaf.
4. Close the pot by closing the top lid. Also, ensure to seal the valve.
5. Press "Manual" cooking function and set cooking time to 10 minutes. It will start cooking after a few minutes. Let the pot mix cook under pressure until the timer reads zero.
6. Press "Cancel" cooking function and press "Natural release (NPR)" setting. It will take 8-10 minutes for natural pressure release.
7. Open the pot; top with some parsley and serve with cooked pasta!

Tangy Cranberry Turkey

Prep Time: 8-10 min.
Cooking Time: 20 min.
Number of Servings: 4
Ingredients:
- 2 tablespoons olive oil
- 1½ cups cranberries, dried
- 1 yellow onion, roughly chopped
- 1 cup orange juice
- 1 cup walnuts
- 4 turkey wings
- 2 tablespoons ghee, melted
- A pinch of pepper and salt
- 1 bunch thyme, chopped

Directions:
1. Switch on your instant pot after placing it on a clean and dry kitchen platform. Press "Saute" cooking function.
2. Open the pot lid; add the oil, ghee, turkey, pepper, and salt in the pot; start cooking to brown evenly. Transfer to a plate.
3. Add the onion, walnuts, berries, and thyme to the pot; stir and cook for 2-3 minutes.
4. Mix the orange juice, return turkey wings to pot, stir gently.
5. Close the pot by closing the top lid. Also, ensure to seal the valve.
6. Press "Manual" cooking function and set cooking time to 20 minutes. It will start cooking after a few minutes. Let the pot mix cook under pressure until the timer reads zero.
7. Turn off and press "Cancel" cooking function. Quick release pressure.
8. Open the pot. Divide turkey wings between plates and keep warm.
9. Set instant pot on Simmer mode, cook cranberry mix for 4-5 minutes more. Drizzle the mix over turkey wings and serve warm!

Rosemary Garlic Chicken

Prep Time: 5-8 min.
Cooking Time: 10 min.
Number of Servings: 2
Ingredients:
- 2 tablespoons minced garlic

- 1-cup low sodium chicken broth
- 1 ½ teaspoons olive oil
- ¾ pound chopped boneless chicken
- ½ cup chopped onion
- ¼ teaspoon thyme
- ½ teaspoon salt
- ½ teaspoon pepper
- 1 bay leaf
- 1 tablespoon chopped rosemary
- 2 tablespoons chopped celery

Directions:
8. Switch on the pot after placing it on a clean and dry platform. Press "Sauté" cooking function.
9. Open the pot lid; add the oil, garlic, and onions in the pot; cook for 2 minutes to cook well and turn lightly golden.
10. Add chicken cubes to the pot. Mix the salt, pepper, bay leaf, chopped rosemary, and thyme.
11. Close the pot by closing the top lid. Also, ensure to seal the valve.
12. Press "Manual" cooking function and set cooking time to 10 minutes. It will start cooking after a few minutes. Let the pot mix cook under pressure until the timer reads zero.
13. Press "Cancel" cooking function and press "Natural release (NPR)" setting. It will take 8-10 minutes for natural pressure release.
14. Open the pot; topped with some celery and serve warm. Enjoy it with your loved one!

Tangy Potato Chicken

Prep Time: 8-10 min.
Cooking Time: 20 min.
Number of Servings: 2
Ingredients:
- ½ cup low sodium chicken broth
- 1-½ tablespoons Dijon mustard
- 1 tablespoon Italian seasoning
- 2 tablespoons lemon juice
- 1 teaspoon lemon zest
- 1 pound. chopped chicken
- 1 pound potatoes, peeled and make wedges
- ½ teaspoon salt
- ½ teaspoon pepper

Directions:
7. Season the chicken with pepper and salt. Switch on the pot after placing it on a clean and dry platform.
8. Open the pot lid and place the above-mentioned ingredients in the cooking pot area. Give the ingredients a little stir.
9. Close the pot by closing the top lid. Also, ensure to seal the valve.
10. Press "Manual" cooking function and set cooking time to 15 minutes. It will start cooking after a few minutes. Let the pot mix cook under pressure until the timer reads zero.

11. Press "Cancel" cooking function and press "Natural release (NPR)" setting. It will take 8-10 minutes for natural pressure release.
12. Open the pot and serve warm. Enjoy it with your loved one!

Lemongrass Coconut Chicken

Prep Time: 5 min.
Cooking Time: 15 min.
Number of Servings: 2
Ingredients:
- 2 teaspoons minced garlic
- 3 teaspoons fish sauce
- ¼ teaspoon pepper
- 1 tablespoon lemon juice
- ¼ cup chopped onion
- 1 lemongrass
- 1-teaspoon ginger
- 4 chicken drumsticks
- ½ teaspoon coconut oil
- ¾ cup coconut milk

Directions:
10. Chop the lemongrass and add in a blender. Add the garlic, ginger, fish sauce, pepper, and lemon juice; combine well.
11. Add the coconut milk. Blend until smooth and incorporated.
12. Switch on the pot after placing it on a clean and dry platform. Press "Sauté" cooking function.
13. Open the pot lid; add the oil and onions in the pot; cook for 2 minutes to cook well and soften.
14. Add the drumsticks to the pot; top with the coconut mixture over the chicken.
15. Close the pot by closing the top lid. Also, ensure to seal the valve.
16. Press "Manual" cooking function and set cooking time to 10 minutes. It will start cooking after a few minutes. Let the pot mix cook under pressure until the timer reads zero.
17. Press "Cancel" cooking function and press "Natural release (NPR)" setting. It will take 8-10 minutes for natural pressure release.
18. Open the pot and serve warm. Enjoy it with your loved one!

Cola Chicken Wings

Prep Time: 8-10 min.
Cooking Time: 20 min.
Number of Servings: 2
Ingredients:
- 2 tablespoons chopped onion
- 1-½ tablespoons low sodium soy sauce
- ½ tablespoon rice wine
- ½ tablespoon sesame oil
- ½ teaspoon ginger
- 1 cup your choice of cola
- 1 pound. chicken wings

181

- 2 teaspoons minced garlic

Directions:

8. Switch on the pot after placing it on a clean and dry platform. Press "Sauté" cooking function.
9. Open the pot lid; add the oil, garlic, and onions in the pot; cook for 2 minutes to cook well and soften.
10. Add the chicken wings and sauté until brown. Mix in the cola, soy sauce, and rice wine then stir well.
11. Close the pot by closing the top lid. Also, ensure to seal the valve.
12. Press "Manual" cooking function and set cooking time to 20 minutes. It will start cooking after a few minutes. Let the pot mix cook under pressure until the timer reads zero.
13. Press "Cancel" cooking function and press "Natural release (NPR)" setting. It will take 8-10 minutes for natural pressure release.
14. Open the pot and serve warm. Enjoy it with your loved one!

Potato Chicken Roast

Prep Time: 8-10 min.
Cooking Time: 20 min.
Number of Servings: 5-6
Ingredients:

- 2 cloves garlic, minced
- 2 teaspoons fresh thyme
- 1 teaspoon black pepper
- 1 large roasting chicken
- 2 teaspoons extra-virgin olive oil
- 1 teaspoon paprika
- 1 cup baby carrots
- 1 ½ cup water
- 1 teaspoon sea salt
- 2 stalks celery, chopped
- 2 medium potatoes, cubed

Directions:

1. Coat the chicken with the olive oil, garlic, thyme, black pepper, paprika, and salt. Add the celery and carrots inside the chicken cavity.
2. Take an Instant Pot; open the top lid.
3. Add the chicken and water in the cooking pot. Add the potatoes.
4. Close the top lid and make sure the valve is sealed.
5. Press "MANUAL" cooking function. Adjust cooking time to 20 minutes.
6. Allow pressure to build and cook the ingredients for the set time.
7. After the set cooking time ends, press "CANCEL" and then press "NPR". Instant Pot will slowly and naturally release the pressure for 8-10 minutes.
8. Open the top lid, add the cooked mixture in serving plates. Cook on sauté for a few minutes, if you want to thicken the sauce.
9. Serve warm.

Coconut Curry Chicken

Prep Time: 8-10 min.
Cooking Time: 10 min.
Number of Servings: 5-6
Ingredients:

- 1 tablespoon curry powder
- 1 teaspoon turmeric
- 1/4 cup lemon juice
- 1 can full-fat coconut milk
- 1/2 teaspoon lemon zest
- 1/2 teaspoon salt
- 4-pounds chicken breast, skin removed

Directions:

1. In a mixing bowl, mix the lemon juice, coconut milk, curry powder, turmeric, lemon zest, and salt.
2. Take an Instant Pot; open the top lid.
3. Add the chicken and bowl mix in the cooking pot. Using a spatula, gently stir to combine well.
4. Close the top lid and make sure the valve is sealed.
5. Press "POULTRY" cooking function with default cooking time.
6. Allow pressure to build and cook the ingredients for the set time.
7. After the set cooking time ends, press "CANCEL" and then press "NPR". Instant Pot will slowly and naturally release the pressure for 8-10 minutes.
8. Open the top lid, add the cooked mixture in serving plates.
9. Serve warm.

Garlic Salsa Chicken

Prep Time: 8-10 min.
Cooking Time: 25 min.
Number of Servings: 5-6
Ingredients:

- 1/8 teaspoon oregano
- Salt as needed
- ¼ teaspoon garlic powder
- 1 ½ pound skinless chicken tenders
- 1/8 teaspoon ground cumin
- 16 ounces roasted salsa verde

Directions:

1. Mix the oregano, garlic powder, salt, and cumin in a mixing bowl.
2. Coat the chicken with the prepared mix and set aside for 30 minutes to season.
3. Take an Instant Pot; open the top lid.
4. Add the seasoned chicken and salsa in the cooking pot. Using a spatula, gently stir to combine well.
5. Close the top lid and make sure the valve is sealed.
6. Press "MANUAL" cooking function. Adjust cooking time to 18-20 minutes.
7. Allow pressure to build and cook the ingredients for the set time.
8. After the set cooking time ends, press "CANCEL" and then press "QPR". Instant Pot will quickly release pressure.
9. Open the top lid, shred the chicken; add the cooked mixture in serving plates.

10. Serve warm.

Chicken Yogurt Salsa

Prep Time: 8-10 min.
Cooking Time: 15 min.
Number of Servings: 3-4
Ingredients:
- ½ cup water or chicken broth
- 4 chicken breasts
- 1 jar salsa
- 1 cup plain, fat-free Greek yogurt

Directions:
1. Take an Instant Pot; open the top lid.
2. Add all the ingredients in the cooking pot. Using a spatula, gently stir to combine well.
3. Close the top lid and make sure the valve is sealed.
4. Press "MANUAL" cooking function. Adjust cooking time to 15 minutes.
5. Allow pressure to build and cook the ingredients for the set time.
6. After the set cooking time ends, press "CANCEL" and then press "NPR". Instant Pot will slowly and naturally release the pressure for 8-10 minutes.
7. Open the top lid, add the cooked mixture in serving plates.
8. Serve warm.

Chicken Rosemary Congee

Prep Time: 8-10 min.
Cooking Time: 40 min.
Number of Servings: 5-6
Ingredients:
- ½ teaspoon ground ginger
- 1 tablespoon butter
- 5 cups water
- 1 teaspoon rosemary
- 1 pound chicken fillet, chopped
- 2 cups rice
- 1 teaspoon salt
- 1 tablespoon oregano
- 1 teaspoon turmeric
- ½ cup dill

Directions:
1. Take an Instant Pot; open the top lid.
2. Add the rice, chicken, and water in the cooking pot. Add the oregano and ginger. Using a spatula, gently stir to combine well.
3. Close the top lid and make sure the valve is sealed.
4. Press "MANUAL" cooking function. Adjust cooking time to 30 minutes.
5. Allow pressure to build and cook the ingredients for the set time.

6. After the set cooking time ends, press "CANCEL" and then press "QPR". Instant Pot will quickly release pressure.
7. Open the top lid; add the butter, turmeric, dill, and rosemary. Stir the mixture gently. Sauté the mixture in the pot for 10 minutes.
8. Add the cooked mixture in serving plates.
9. Serve warm.

Creamy Cheese Chicken

Prep Time: 8-10 min.
Cooking Time: 40 min.
Number of Servings: 3-4
Ingredients:
- 1 1/3 pound boneless chicken breasts, make cubes
- 5 1/2 ounce low-fat cream cheese
- 7 1/2 ounce low-fat sour cream
- 2 cups water

Directions:
1. Take an Instant Pot; open the top lid.
2. Add the ingredients to the cooking pot. Using a spatula, gently stir to combine well.
3. Close the top lid and make sure the valve is sealed.
4. Press "MANUAL" cooking function. Adjust cooking time to 12-15 minutes.
5. Allow pressure to build and cook the ingredients for the set time.
6. After the set cooking time ends, press "CANCEL" and then press "NPR". Instant Pot will slowly and naturally release the pressure for 8-10 minutes.
7. Open the top lid, add the cooked mixture in serving plates.
8. Serve warm.

Spaghetti Turkey Meal

Prep Time: 8-10 min.
Cooking Time: 35 min.
Number of Servings: 4-5
Ingredients:
- 1 clove minced garlic
- ¼ cup diced onion
- 2 cups water
- ¾ teaspoon kosher salt
- 1-pound ground turkey
- 1 can (25 oz.) tomato basil sauce
- 1 cup spaghetti, whole wheat

Directions:
1. Take an Instant Pot; open the top lid.
2. Press "SAUTÉ" cooking function.
3. Grease the pot with some cooking oil.
4. In the cooking pot area, add the turkey and salt; stir cook for about 2–4 minutes.
5. Add the garlic and onion and cook for 4–5 minutes more.
6. Mix in the tomato basil sauce along with water and spaghetti.

7. Close the top lid and make sure the valve is sealed.
8. Press "MANUAL" cooking function. Adjust cooking time to 8-10 minutes.
9. Allow pressure to build and cook the ingredients for the set time.
10. After the set cooking time ends, press "CANCEL" and then press "QPR". Instant Pot will quickly release pressure.
11. Open the top lid, add the cooked mixture in serving plates.
12. Serve warm.

Sesame Sherry Chicken

Prep Time: 8-10 min.
Cooking Time: 13 min.
Number of Servings: 3-4
Ingredients:
- 1 tablespoon low-sodium soy sauce
- 1-pound boneless chicken breast, skin less
- 1 tablespoon maple syrup
- 2 tablespoons raw sesame seeds
- 1 tablespoon water
- ½ teaspoon five-spice powder
- 1 teaspoon ginger root, grated
- 1 tablespoon dry sherry
- Pepper and salt as per taste
- 1 cup water
- 2 tablespoons peanut oil

Directions:
1. Take an Instant Pot; open the top lid.
2. Press "SAUTÉ" cooking function.
3. In the cooking pot area, add and toast the sesame seeds for 3 minutes.
4. In a mixing bowl, combine the water, soy sauce, and maple syrup. Add the ginger, five-spice powder and sherry.
5. In a mixing dish, mix the flour, pepper, and salt. Coat the chicken with the flour mixture.
6. Add the chicken in the pot. Sauté until the sides have browned. Add the soy sauce mixture and add 1 cup water.
7. Close the top lid and make sure the valve is sealed.
8. Press "MANUAL" cooking function. Adjust cooking time to 10 minutes.
9. Allow pressure to build and cook the ingredients for the set time.
10. After the set cooking time ends, press "CANCEL" and then press "NPR". Instant Pot will slowly and naturally release the pressure for 8-10 minutes.
11. Open the top lid, add the cooked mixture in serving plates.
12. Serve warm with peanut oil on top.

Coconut Chicken Delight

Prep Time: 8-10 min.
Cooking TIme: 10 min.
Number of Servings: 2
Ingredients:

- 1 teaspoon fish sauce
- 1 tbs. olive oil
- 2 cups chicken thighs (skinless and boneless)
- 1 tbs. lime juice
- 1 tbs. coconut milk
- 7-8 fresh mint leaves
- ½ tbs. grated fresh ginger
- Fresh cilantro as needed

Directions:
1. In a mixing bowl (heat-proof), mix all the mentioned ingredients except the chicken.
2. Take an Instant Pot; open the top lid.
3. Add the chicken and bowl mix in the cooking pot. Using a spatula, gently stir to combine well.
4. Close the top lid and make sure the valve is sealed.
5. Press "POULTRY" cooking function. Adjust cooking time to 10 minutes.
6. Allow pressure to build and cook the ingredients for the set time.
7. After the set cooking time ends, press "CANCEL" and then press "QPR". Instant Pot will quickly release pressure.
8. Open the top lid, add the cooked mixture in serving plates.
9. Serve warm.

Classic Spiced Chicken

Prep Time: 8-10 min.
Cooking Time: 30 min.
Number of Servings: 5-6
Ingredients:
- ½ teaspoon dried parsley
- 1 teaspoon onion powder
- 1 teaspoon garlic powder
- 1 ½ pound, raw chicken breast, skinless and boneless
- ½ teaspoon dried oregano
- ½ teaspoon dried basil
- 2 cups chicken broth
- ¼ teaspoon black pepper
- ¼ teaspoon salt

Directions:
1. Add all the spices to season the chicken.
2. Take an Instant Pot; open the top lid.
3. Add the chicken and broth in the cooking pot. Using a spatula, gently stir to combine well.
4. Close the top lid and make sure the valve is sealed.
5. Press "MANUAL" cooking function. Adjust cooking time to 8 minutes.
6. Allow pressure to build and cook the ingredients for the set time.
7. After the set cooking time ends, press "CANCEL" and then press "NPR". Instant Pot will slowly and naturally release the pressure for 8-10 minutes.
8. Open the top lid, shred the chicken and add the cooked mixture in serving plates.
9. Serve warm.

Oregano Chicken Strips

Prep Time: 8-10 min.
Cooking Time: 8 min.
Number of Servings: 6-7
Ingredients:
- 1 teaspoon cayenne pepper
- 1/2 teaspoon cilantro
- 1 cup flour
- 1 teaspoon kosher salt
- 1/2 teaspoon oregano
- 1-pound chicken filet, make strips
- 3 tablespoons sesame oil
- 1/2 teaspoon paprika
- 1/2 cup milk
- 1 teaspoon turmeric

Directions:
1. Add the flour in a mixing bowl. Mix in the salt, cayenne pepper, cilantro, oregano, paprika, and turmeric.
2. Pour the milk in a separate bowl.
3. Dip the chicken strips in the milk; dip them in the flour mixture to coat well.
4. Take an Instant Pot; open the top lid.
5. Press "SAUTÉ" cooking function.
6. In the cooking pot area, add the oil and chicken strips.
7. Cook the chicken strips for 3 minutes on each side.
8. Add the chicken to paper towel; serve warm.

Soy Turkey Meatballs

Prep Time: 8-10 min.
Cooking Time: 10 min.
Number of Servings: 2-3
Ingredients:
- 2 saltine crackers, crushed
- 1 ½ tablespoons buttermilk
- ½ pound turkey meat, ground
- ½ tablespoon canola oil
- 2 tablespoons green onion, chopped
- A pinch of salt and black pepper
- ½ tablespoon sesame seeds

For the sauce:
- 2 tablespoon rice vinegar
- 1 teaspoon ginger, grated
- 1 garlic clove, minced
- 4 tablespoons soy sauce

- 1 ½ tablespoon brown sugar
- 1 tablespoon canola oil
- A pinch of black pepper
- ½ tablespoon cornstarch

Directions:

1. In a bowl, mix the turkey, crackers, green onions, salt, pepper, and buttermilk.
2. Prepare 8 meatballs and leave them aside.
3. In another mixing bowl, mix the soy sauce, vinegar, garlic, ginger, canola oil (1 tbs.), brown sugar, black pepper and, cornstarch and stir well.
4. Take an Instant Pot; open the top lid.
5. Press "SAUTÉ" cooking function.
6. In the cooking pot area, add the ½ tbs. oil and heat it.
7. Add the meatballs and brown them for 2 minutes on each side.
8. Add the sauce and stir.
9. Close the top lid and make sure the valve is sealed.
10. Press "MANUAL" cooking function. Adjust cooking time to 10 minutes.
11. Allow pressure to build and cook the ingredients for the set time.
12. After the set cooking time ends, press "CANCEL" and then press "QPR". Instant Pot will quickly release pressure.
13. Open the top lid, add the cooked mixture in serving plates.
14. Serve warm with sesame seeds on top.

Classic BBQ Chicken

Prep Time: 5 min.
Cooking Time: 15 min.
Number of Servings: 2
Ingredients:

- 1-cup water
- ½ cup chopped onion
- 2-½ tablespoons raw honey
- 2 pounds. chicken wings
- ½ cup barbecue sauce
- ¼ teaspoon salt
- ½ teaspoon pepper

Directions:

9. In a bowl, mix the barbecue sauce with water, raw honey, salt, and pepper. Switch on the pot after placing it on a clean and dry platform.
10. Open the pot lid and place the chicken and sauce in the cooking pot area. Give the ingredients a little stir.
11. Close the pot by closing the top lid. Also, ensure to seal the valve.
12. Press "Manual" cooking function and set cooking time to 10 minutes. It will start cooking after a few minutes. Let the pot mix cook under pressure until the timer reads zero.
13. Press "Cancel" cooking function and press "Quick release" setting.
14. Open the pot.
15. Preheat a pan over medium heat; add the chicken mix to the pan. Bring to simmer and stir until the barbecue sauce is thickened.

16. Serve warm!

Turkey Tomato Meal

Prep Time: 8-10 min.
Cooking Time: 20 min.
Number of Servings: 2
Ingredients:
- 1 red onion, sliced
- 1 cup chicken stock
- 1 tablespoon butter
- 1 red bell pepper, chopped
- 1 green bell pepper, chopped
- 2 pounds ground turkey breast
- 1 15-ounce can of diced tomatoes
- 2 cloves garlic, chopped

Directions:
8. Switch on the pot after placing it on a clean and dry platform. Press "Sauté" cooking function.
9. Open the pot lid; add the butter and meat in the pot; cook for 5 minutes to cook well and soften.
10. Add the tomatoes with their juices, garlic, onion, peppers, and stock.
11. Close the pot by closing the top lid. Also, ensure to seal the valve.
12. Press "Manual" cooking function and set cooking time to 15 minutes. It will start cooking after a few minutes. Let the pot mix cook under pressure until the timer reads zero.
13. Press "Cancel" cooking function and press "Quick release" setting.
14. Open the pot and serve warm. Enjoy it with your loved one!

Oregano Pasta Chicken

Prep Time: 5 min.
Cooking Time: 15 min.
Number of Servings: 2
Ingredients:
- ½ teaspoon olive oil
- ½ cup diced tomatoes
- ½ cup diced red bell pepper
- ½ teaspoon oregano
- 1 bay leaf
- ½ cup chopped onion
- 1 ½ cup diced chicken
- ¼ teaspoon salt
- ½ teaspoon pepper
- 2 tablespoons chopped parsley
- Cooked pasta of your choice

Directions:
8. Switch on the pot after placing it on a clean and dry platform. Press "Sauté" cooking function.
9. Open the pot lid; add the oil and onions in the pot; cook for 2 minutes to cook well and soften.

10. Add the chicken, bell pepper, and diced tomatoes. Mix the salt, pepper, oregano, and bay leaf.
11. Close the pot by closing the top lid. Also, ensure to seal the valve.
12. Press "Manual" cooking function and set cooking time to 10 minutes. It will start cooking after a few minutes. Let the pot mix cook under pressure until the timer reads zero.
13. Press "Cancel" cooking function and press "Natural release (NPR)" setting. It will take 8-10 minutes for natural pressure release.
14. Open the pot; top with some parsley and serve with cooked pasta!

Fresh Veggie Turkey

Prep Time: 10min.
Cooking Time: 50 min.
Number of Servings: 7-8
Ingredients:
- 1 bay leaf
- 2 garlic cloves cut in half
- 1 celery stalk, quartered
- 1 medium onion, quartered
- 1 medium carrot, quartered
- 8 pounds fresh turkey
- 1/2 cup water
- Black pepper and salt as needed

Directions:
1. Season the meat with pepper and salt. Add half onion and garlic into the turkey cavity.
2. Switch on your instant pot after placing it on a clean and dry kitchen platform.
3. Open the pot lid and slowly start adding other ingredients to the pot. Give the ingredients a little stir.
4. Arrange the trivet inside it; arrange the meat over the trivet.
5. Close the pot by closing the top lid. Also, ensure to seal the valve.
6. Press "Manual" cooking function and set cooking time to 48 minutes. It will start cooking after a few minutes. Let the pot mix cook under pressure until the timer reads zero.
7. Turn off and press "Cancel" cooking function. Quick release pressure.
8. Open the pot and serve on a serving plate or bowl. Enjoy the Paleo dish!

Classic Honey Turkey

Prep Time: 5-8min.
Cooking Time: 20 min.
Number of Servings: 6
Ingredients:
- 1/2 cup water
- 1 teaspoon ground black pepper
- 2 teaspoons honey
- 1/2 teaspoon garlic powder
- 6 turkey drumsticks
- 1/2 cup chicken broth
- 1 tablespoon kosher salt

Directions:

1. Season the meat with the garlic powder, pepper, salt, and honey.
2. Switch on your instant pot after placing it on a clean and dry kitchen platform.
3. Pour the water into the cooking pot area. Arrange the trivet inside it; arrange the meat over the trivet.
4. Close the pot by closing the top lid. Also, ensure to seal the valve.
5. Press "Manual" cooking function and set cooking time to 20 minutes. It will start cooking after a few minutes. Let the pot mix cook under pressure until the timer reads zero.
6. Turn off and press "Cancel" cooking function. Allow the inside pressure to release naturally; it will take 8-10 minutes to release all inside pressure.
7. Open the pot and serve on a serving plate or bowl. Enjoy the Paleo dish!

Cashew Chicken Chili

Prep Time: 8-10min.
Cooking Time: 30 min.
Number of Servings: 4-5
Ingredients:

- 2 teaspoons coriander
- 2 teaspoons green chilies
- 1 teaspoon garlic, minced
- 5 large (boneless and skinless) chicken thighs
- 1 onion, chopped
- 1/2 teaspoon spice mix
- 1/ 4 teaspoon turmeric
- 2 teaspoons olive oil
- 1/2 teaspoon cumin
- 1 1/2 cup coconut milk
- 1/2 teaspoon ginger
- 1/2 cup cashews
- Cilantro for garnish

Directions:

1. Switch on your instant pot after placing it on a clean and dry kitchen platform.
2. Open the pot lid and slowly start adding the above-mentioned ingredients in the pot. Give the ingredients a little stir. Do not add the cashew and cilantro.
3. Close the pot by closing the top lid. Also, ensure to seal the valve.
4. Press "Manual" cooking function and set cooking time to 30 minutes. It will start cooking after a few minutes. Let the pot mix cook under pressure until the timer reads zero.
5. Turn off and press "Cancel" cooking function. Allow the inside pressure to release naturally; it will take 8-10 minutes to release all inside pressure.
6. Open the pot and shred the meat. Add the cashews and cilantro. Serve warm!

Sweet Potato Turkey Meal

Prep Time: 8-10min.
Cooking Time: 20 min.
Number of Servings: 4

Ingredients:
- 4 tablespoons dairy-free buffalo sauce
- 1 onion, diced
- 3 tablespoons ghee
- ½ teaspoon garlic powder
- 1 ½ pounds turkey breast, cut into cubes
- 1 pound sweet potatoes, cut into cubes

Directions:
1. Switch on your instant pot after placing it on a clean and dry kitchen platform. Press "Saute" cooking function.
2. Open the pot lid; add the 1 tablespoon ghee and onions in the pot; start cooking for 2-3 minutes to cook well and soften.
3. Stir in the remaining ingredients.
4. Close the pot by closing the top lid. Also, ensure to seal the valve.
5. Press "Poultry" cooking function and set cooking time to 18 minutes. It will start cooking after a few minutes. Let the pot mix cook under pressure until the timer reads zero.
6. Turn off and press "Cancel" cooking function. Quick release pressure.
7. Open the pot and serve on a serving plate or bowl. Enjoy the Paleo dish!

Classic Lemon Coconut Chicken

Prep Time: 8-10 min.
Cooking Time: 25 min.
Number of Servings: 6-8
Ingredients:
- 1 can full-fat coconut milk
- ¼ cup lemon juice
- ½ teaspoon salt
- 1 teaspoon turmeric
- 4 pounds chicken breasts (or chicken thighs)
- 1 tablespoon curry powder
- 1 teaspoon lemon zest (optional)

Directions:
1. Mix the lemon juice, coconut milk, curry powder, and turmeric in a bowl.
2. Switch on your instant pot after placing it on a clean and dry kitchen platform.
3. Sprinkle the bottom of your instant pot with a small amount of this mixture. Add the chicken breasts.
4. Top with the remaining mixture.
5. Close the pot by closing the top lid. Also, ensure to seal the valve.
6. Press "Poultry" cooking function and set cooking time to 15 minutes. It will start cooking after a few minutes. Let the pot mix cook under pressure until the timer reads zero.
7. Turn off and press "Cancel" cooking function. Quick release pressure.
8. Open the pot and if the chicken is not pink enough then cook for 10 more minutes on manual mode.
9. Shred the chicken and add the zest. Serve on a serving plate or bowl. Enjoy the Paleo dish!

Lemongrass Chicken Treat

Prep Time: 12-15min.
Cooking Time: 18 min.
Number of Servings:4
Ingredients:
- 1 stalk lemongrass, trimmed and smashed
- 1 teaspoon grated ginger
- 1 teaspoon ghee
- 4 garlic cloves, crushed
- 3 tablespoons coconut aminos
- 8 chicken drumsticks, skin removed
- 1 onion, sliced
- 1 cup coconut milk
- 1 teaspoon five spice powder
- 2 tablespoons fish sauce

Directions:
1. Nicely blend the lemongrass, fish sauce, ginger, garlic, five-spice powder, and coconut aminos in a blender.
2. Pour in the coconut milk and blend until becomes smooth.
3. Switch on your instant pot after placing it on a clean and dry kitchen platform. Press "Saute" cooking function.
4. Open the pot lid; add the ghee and onions in the pot; start cooking for 3 minutes to cook well and soften.
5. Add the drumsticks and pour the coconut mixture over.
6. Close the pot by closing the top lid. Also, ensure to seal the valve.
7. Press "Manual" cooking function and set cooking time to 15 minutes. It will start cooking after a few minutes. Let the pot mix cook under pressure until the timer reads zero.
8. Turn off and press "Cancel" cooking function. Allow the inside pressure to release naturally; it will take 8-10 minutes to release all inside pressure.
9. Open the pot and serve on a serving plate or bowl. Enjoy the Paleo dish!

Chicken Marsala

Prep Time: 5 minutes
Cooking Time: 15 minutes
Number of Servings: 4
Ingredients:
- 4 chicken thighs
- 1/2 teaspoon salt
- 1/2 teaspoon black pepper
- 1 tablespoon olive oil
- 1 tablespoon butter
- 1 onion, finely chopped
- 1 garlic clove, minced
- 1 cup mushrooms, sliced
- 1 teaspoon thyme
- 1/2 teaspoon rosemary

- 2 tablespoons flour
- 2 cups chicken stock
- 1/2 cup marsala wine

Directions:
1. Season chicken thighs with salt and pepper. Set Instant Pot to Saute and add olive oil. Brown chicken on both sides, then removes to a plate.
2. Add butter to pot. When melted, add onion and garlic. When the onion is translucent, add mushrooms and cook until tender. Add thyme and rosemary and cook 30 seconds.
3. Stir flour into the pot and cook about 1 minute or until the flour begins to take on color. Add wine, stirring constantly, and deglaze the pot. Stir in chicken stock and wine. Replace chicken in the pot.
4. Close the lid and set cooking time for 10 minutes on high.
5. Serve with pasta or crusty bread.

Cajun Chicken Meal

Prep Time: 8-10 min.
Cooking Time: 14 min.
Number of Servings: 6
Ingredients:
- 1 small red bell pepper, make strips
- 1 small zucchini, thinly make slices
- 1 1/2 teaspoon olive oil
- 1 pound chicken drumsticks, skinless
- ½ teaspoon Cajun seasoning

Directions:
1. Take your Instant Pot and place over dry kitchen surface; open its top lid and switch it on.
2. Press "SAUTÉ".
3. In its cooking pot, add and heat 1 teaspoon oil.
4. Add the meat and bell pepper; stir-cook for 4-5 minutes to evenly brown. Set aside.
5. In its cooking pot, add and heat the remaining oil.
6. Add the zucchini slices and Cajun; stir-cook for 2-3 minutes to turn crisp and light brown.
7. Serve the chicken with grilled zucchini.

Broccoli Chicken Pasta

Prep Time: 8-10 min.
Cooking Time: 13 min.
Number of Servings: 5
Ingredients:
- 1 cup broccoli, make florets
- 2 teaspoon chicken broth, reduced sodium
- Smoked paprika
- 1 pound chicken fillets, make bite-sized pieces
- 8 ounce linguine pasta

Directions:
1. Thoroughly mix the broth, and smoked paprika in a mixing bowl.

195

2. Take your Instant Pot and place over dry kitchen surface; open its top lid and switch it on.
3. Press "SAUTÉ". Grease the pot with some cooking oil.
4. In its cooking pot, add and heat the oil.
5. Add the chicken and broccoli; cook for 4-5 minutes.
6. Add the broth mix and stir-cook for 2 minutes. Add the mix to a bowl (medium-large size) and cover with a lid.
7. In the Instant Pot; add ½ cup water and pasta.
8. Close its top lid and make sure that its valve it closed to avoid spillage.
9. Press "MANUAL". Adjust the timer to 4 minutes.
10. Pressure will slowly build up; let the added ingredients to cook until the timer indicates zero.
11. Press "CANCEL". Now press "QPR" to quickly release pressure.
12. Open the top lid, drain water and transfer the cooked pasta in a container.
13. Press "SAUTÉ".
14. In its cooking pot, add and heat the butter.
15. Add the pasta; cook for 2 minutes.
16. Serve the pasta with the chicken.

Turkey Cauliflower Meal

Prep Time: 8-10 min.
Cooking Time: 13 min.
Number of Servings: 4
Ingredients:
- 1 cup cauliflower, chopped
- 1 teaspoon dried thyme, ground
- 1 pound turkey breasts
- 1 tablespoon fresh parsley, chopped (finely)
- 1/2 teaspoon garlic powder

Directions:
1. Make cauliflower puree in a blender.
2. Take your Instant Pot and place over dry kitchen surface; open its top lid and switch it on.
3. Add the 1 cup water, puree, garlic powder, and thyme in the cooking pot. Stir the ingredients to combine well.
4. Close its top lid and make sure that its valve it closed to avoid spillage.
5. Press "MANUAL". Adjust the timer to 2 minutes.
6. Pressure will slowly build up; let the added ingredients to cook until the timer indicates zero.
7. Press "CANCEL". Now press "QPR" to quickly release pressure.
8. Drain the cauliflower and add to a bowl. Cover and set aside.
9. Empty the pot. Press "SAUTÉ". Grease the pot with some cooking oil.
10. Add the turkey. Cook for 3-4 on each side.
11. Add the cauliflower puree on top of the turkey cutlets. Serve.

Chicken Peas Rice

Prep Time: 8-10 min.
Cooking Time: 12 min.
Number of Servings: 4
Ingredients:

- 4 ounce chicken breasts, make small pieces
- 1/2 cup green peas
- 1 teaspoon olive oil
- 2 cups white rice
- 1 small onion, chopped

Directions:
1. Take your Instant Pot and place over dry kitchen surface; open its top lid and switch it on.
2. Press "SAUTÉ".
3. In its cooking pot, add and heat the oil.
4. Add the meat; stir-cook for 4-5 minutes to evenly brown. Set aside.
5. Add the onions. Stir-cook for 3-4 minutes, or until turn softened.
6. Add the rice, 2 cups water, and green peas.
7. Close its top lid and make sure that its valve it closed to avoid spillage.
8. Press "MANUAL". Adjust the timer to 4 minutes.
9. Pressure will slowly build up; let the added ingredients to cook until the timer indicates zero.
10. Press "CANCEL". Now press "QPR" to quickly release pressure.
11. Open the top lid, transfer the cooked recipe in serving plates.
12. Serve with cooked chicken.

Chicken Meatballs with Sauce

Prep Time: 8-10 min.
Cooking Time: 6 min.
Number of Servings: 6
Ingredients:
- 2 tablespoons flour (all-purpose)
- 4 large eggs
- 1 pound ground chicken breasts
- 1 small onion, chopped (finely)
- 2 large yellow bell pepper, chopped

Directions:
1. In a mixing bowl, thoroughly mix the chicken, onions, flour, and eggs. Form into meatballs.
2. Take your Instant Pot and place over dry kitchen surface; open its top lid and switch it on.
3. Press "SAUTÉ". Grease the pot with some cooking oil.
4. Add the meatballs; stir-cook for 4-5 minutes to evenly brown. Set aside.
5. Add ½ cup water and bell pepper.
6. Close its top lid and make sure that its valve it closed to avoid spillage.
7. Press "MANUAL". Adjust the timer to 1 minute.
8. Pressure will slowly build up; let the added ingredients to cook until the timer indicates zero.
9. Press "CANCEL". Now press "QPR" to quickly release pressure.
10. Open the top lid, cool down the mix, drain liquid, and transfer into a blender and make the puree.
11. Serve the meatballs with the puree.

Cherry Tomato Chicken

Prep Time: 8-10 min.
Cooking Time: 15 min.

197

Number of Servings: 4
Ingredients:
- 1 whole lime, freshly juiced
- 1/2 cup cherry tomatoes, thinly make slices
- Water as needed
- 12 ounce chicken breasts, make large pieces
- 1 small onion, chopped

Directions:
1. Take your Instant Pot and place over dry kitchen surface; open its top lid and switch it on.
2. Add the chicken and water to cover them in the cooking pot. Stir the ingredients to combine well.
3. Close its top lid and make sure that its valve it closed to avoid spillage.
4. Press "MANUAL". Adjust the timer to 5 minutes.
5. Pressure will slowly build up; let the added ingredients to cook until the timer indicates zero.
6. Press "CANCEL". Now press "QPR" to quickly release pressure.
7. Drain and add to a greased baking sheet. Add the tomatoes and onions.
8. Preheat an oven to 450 F.
9. Bake for 10 minutes; serve warm.

Broccoli Chicken Treat

Prep Time: 5-8 min.
Cooking Time: 5 min.
Number of Servings: 4
Ingredients:

- 3 cups cooked and shredded chicken
- 2 cups broccoli florets
- 1/3 cup grated parmesan cheese
- ½ cup heavy cream
- 1 cup chicken broth
- Pepper and salt, as needed

Directions:
1. Take your Instant Pot; open the top lid. Plug it and turn it on.
2. In the cooking pot area, add the broth, broccoli, and chicken. Using a spatula, stir the ingredients.
3. Close the top lid and seal its valve.
4. Press "MANUAL" setting. Adjust cooking time to 2 minutes.
5. Allow the recipe to cook for the set cooking time.
6. After the set cooking time ends, press "CANCEL" and then press "QPR (Quick Pressure Release)".
7. Instant Pot will quickly release the pressure.
8. Open the top lid, stir in the remaining ingredients. Cook on sauté for 2 more minutes.
9. Serve and enjoy!

Cheesy Bacon Chicken

Prep Time: 5-8 min.
Cooking Time: 30 min.

Number of Servings: 4
Ingredients:

- 8-ounces cream cheese
- 8 bacon slices, cooked and crumbled
- 2 tablespoons arrowroot
- 1 cup water
- 2 pounds chicken breasts
- 1 packet ranch seasoning
- 4-ounces cheddar cheese, shredded

Directions:
1. Take your Instant Pot; open the top lid. Plug it and turn it on.
2. In the cooking pot area, add the cream cheese, water, chicken, and seasoning. Using a spatula, stir the ingredients.
3. Close the top lid and seal its valve.
4. Press "MANUAL" setting. Adjust cooking time to 25 minutes.
5. Allow the recipe to cook for the set cooking time.
6. After the set cooking time ends, press "CANCEL" and then press "QPR (Quick Pressure Release)".
7. Instant Pot will quickly release the pressure.
8. Open the top lid, take out the meat and shred it.
9. Add back to the mix and combine; add the remaining ingredients.
10. Cook on sauté for 3-4 minutes, add the cooked recipe mix in serving plates.
11. Serve and enjoy!

Garlic Spiced Turkey

Prep Time: 10 min.
Cooking Time: 15 min.
Number of Servings: 2-3
Ingredients:
- 14-ounce turkey fillet, roughly chopped
- 1 teaspoon chili pepper
- 1 teaspoon (ground) black pepper
- 3 tablespoons chicken stock
- 1 garlic clove, chopped
- 1 teaspoon ghee
- 1 tomato, chopped
- 1 teaspoon olive oil
- 1 teaspoon cilantro
- ½ teaspoon chopped parsley

Directions:
1. Combine the chili pepper, (ground) black pepper, chopped tomato, olive oil, cilantro, chopped parsley, and chopped garlic clove in a mixing bowl.
2. Add the turkey fillet and chicken stock; stir it. Leave the mixture for 10 minutes to marinate.
3. Take your Instant Pot; open the top lid. Plug it and turn it on.

4. Press "SAUTÉ" setting, add the ghee and the pot will start heating up.
5. Add the chicken mix. Close the top lid and seal its valve.
6. Press "POULTRY" setting. Adjust cooking time to 15 minutes.
7. Allow the recipe to cook for the set cooking time.
8. After the set cooking time ends, press "CANCEL" and then press "QPR (Quick Pressure Release)".
9. Instant Pot will quickly release the pressure.
10. Open the top lid, add the cooked recipe mix in serving plates.
11. Serve and enjoy!

Chicken Drumsticks

Prep Time: 15-20 min.
Cooking Time: 10 min.
Number of Servings: 4
Ingredients:
- 1-pound chicken drumsticks
- 2 tablespoons coconut, shredded
- 2 tablespoons almond flour
- ½ teaspoon cayenne pepper
- 1 teaspoon olive oil
- 1 egg
- ¼ cup almond milk
- 1 teaspoon salt

Directions:
1. Combine the coconut and almond flour together in the mixing bowl. Mix in the almond milk and salt.
2. Add the cayenne pepper and olive oil. Stir the mixture.
3. Add the mixture into a large mixing bowl and add the chicken drumsticks.
4. Coat the chicken drumsticks in the coconut mixture.
5. Pour 1 cup water and place steamer basket/trivet inside the pot; arrange the drumsticks over the basket/trivet.
6. Close the top lid and seal its valve.
7. Press "POULTRY" setting. Adjust cooking time to 10 minutes.
8. Allow the recipe to cook for the set cooking time.
9. After the set cooking time ends, press "CANCEL" and then press "QPR (Quick Pressure Release)".
10. Instant Pot will quickly release the pressure.
11. Open the top lid, add the cooked recipe mix in serving plates.
12. Serve and enjoy!

White Wine Mushroom Turkey

Prep Time: 5-8 min.
Cooking Time: 20 min.
Number of Servings: 8-10
Ingredients:
- 1 ¼ pounds turkey breast

- 1/3 cup white wine
- 6-ounces white button mushrooms, sliced
- 1 tablespoon arrowroot
- 2/3 cup chicken stock
- 3 tablespoons heavy cream
- 1 garlic clove, minced
- 3 tablespoon minced shallots
- 2 tablespoons olive oil
- ½ teaspoon parsley

Directions:
1. Take your Instant Pot; open the top lid. Plug it and turn it on.
2. Press "SAUTÉ" setting and the pot will start heating up.
3. In the cooking pot area, add the turkey and oil. Stir and cook until evenly brown from all sides. Set aside the cooked turkey.
4. Add the shallots, mushrooms, garlic, and parsley, and cook for a few more minutes.
5. Add back the turkey to the pot. Add the broth and stir gently.
6. Close the top lid and seal its valve.
7. Press "MANUAL" setting. Adjust cooking time to 8 minutes.
8. Allow the recipe to cook for the set cooking time.
9. After the set cooking time ends, press "CANCEL" and then press "QPR (Quick Pressure Release)".
10. Instant Pot will quickly release the pressure.
11. Open the top lid, slice the turkey and mix with the pot mix.
12. Mix in the cream and arrowroot; serve warm.

Pumpkin Hot Chili

Prep Time: 8-10 min.
Cooking Time: 20 min.
Number of Servings: 5-6
Ingredients:
- 1 pound turkey, ground
- 1 (14.5 ounces) can diced tomatoes
- 1/2 cup Cheddar cheese, shredded
- 1/2 cup sour cream
- 2 cups pumpkin puree
- 1 1/2 tablespoons chili powder
- ¼ teaspoon oregano
- 1 tablespoon coconut oil
- 1 garlic clove, minced
- ¼ teaspoon cumin
- 1/2 teaspoon ground black pepper
- 1 dash salt
- 1 cup water

Directions:

1. Arrange your Instant Pot over a dry, clean platform. Plug it in power socket and turn it on.
2. Now press "Saute" mode from available options. In the cooking area, add the oil and turkey; cook to make it brown.
3. Add the garlic, onion, and pumpkin, mix well. Mix in the chili powder, salt, oregano, cumin; combine well.
4. Pour water into the pot.
5. Close the lid and lock. Ensure that you have sealed the valve to avoid leakage.
6. Press "Manual" mode from available cooking settings and set cooking time to 20 minutes. Instant Pot will start cooking the ingredients after a few minutes.
7. After the timer reads zero, press "Cancel" and quick release pressure.
8. Carefully remove the lid and serve the prepared keto dish warm topped with Cheddar cheese.

Cheese Jalapeno Chicken

Prep Time: 10-15 min.
Cooking Time: 12 min.
Number of Servings: 4
Ingredients:
- 8 ounces cream cheese
- 8 ounces cheddar cheese
- ¾ cup sour cream
- 1 pound chicken breast, boneless
- 3 jalapenos, make slices
- ½ cup water

Directions:
1. Arrange your Instant Pot over a dry, clean platform. Plug it in power socket and turn it on.
2. Open the lid from the top and put it aside; add the water, cream cheese, jalapenos and chicken breast. Gently stir them.
3. Close the lid and lock. Ensure that you have sealed the valve to avoid leakage.
4. Press "Manual" mode from available cooking settings and set cooking time to 12 minutes. Instant Pot will start cooking the ingredients after a few minutes.
5. After the timer reads zero, press "Cancel" and quick release pressure.
6. Carefully remove the lid. Mix the sour cream and cheddar; serve warm!

Instant Lemon Chicken

Prep Time: 8-10 min.
Cooking Time: 35 min.
Number of Servings: 8-10
Ingredients:
- 2 tablespoons lemon juice
- ¼ teaspoon pepper
- 1 tablespoon coconut oil
- 6 garlic cloves, peeled
- 1 teaspoon paprika
- 4-pound chicken (whole)
- ½ teaspoon sea salt

- 1 ½ cup bone broth
- 1 teaspoon thyme

Directions:
1. In a bowl of medium size, thoroughly mix the pepper, salt, thyme, and paprika. Rub this mixture all over the chicken.
2. Arrange your Instant Pot over a dry, clean platform. Plug it in power socket and turn it on.
3. Now press "Saute" mode from available options. In the cooking area, add the coconut oil and chicken; cook for 6-7 minutes to soften.
4. Flip the chicken and add the garlic cloves, broth, and lemon juice. Stir gently.
5. Close the lid and lock. Ensure that you have sealed the valve to avoid leakage.
6. Press "Manual" mode from available cooking settings and set cooking time to 25 minutes. Instant Pot will start cooking the ingredients after a few minutes.
7. After the timer reads zero, press "Cancel" and quick release pressure.
8. Carefully remove the lid and serve the prepared keto dish warm!

Creamy Turkey Chicken

Prep Time: 10 min.
Cooking Time: 30 min.
Number of Servings: 8
Ingredients:
- 4 ounce light cream cheese, cubed

- 2-pound chicken breasts

- ¼ cup raw turkey bacon, chopped

- 1-ounce packet ranch seasoning

- 1 cup chicken broth

- Green onions chopped as required

Directions:
1. Arrange your Instant Pot over a dry, clean platform. Plug it in power socket and turn it on.
2. Now press "Saute" mode from available options. In the cooking area, add the oil and turkey; cook for 3-4 minutes to soften.
3. Add the chicken, seasoning, and broth.
4. Close the lid and lock. Ensure that you have sealed the valve to avoid leakage.
5. Press "Manual" mode from available cooking settings and set cooking time to 20 minutes. Instant Pot will start cooking the ingredients after a few minutes.
6. After the timer reads zero, press "Cancel" and quick release pressure.
7. Carefully remove the lid; take out the chicken and shred.
8. Remove half of the liquid from the pot, mix the cheese and add back to the pot.
9. Sauté for 2-3 minutes to fully melt the cheese. Add the chicken to the pot and mix well.
10. Serve warm with the onions topped over!

Mexican Style Creamy Chicken

Prep Time: 5-8 min.
Cooking Time: 12 min.
Number of Servings: 4
Ingredients:
- ¾ cup sour cream
- 3 jalapenos, seeded and sliced
- 1 pound chicken breasts
- 8-ounces cheddar cheese, grated
- ½ cup water
- 8-ounces cream cheese
- Pepper and salt, as needed

Directions:
1. Take your Instant Pot; open the top lid. Plug it and turn it on.
2. In the cooking pot area, add the water, sour cream, and cheeses. Using a spatula, stir the ingredients.
3. Stir in the jalapenos and place the chicken inside. Season with some pepper and salt.
4. Close the top lid and seal its valve.
5. Press "MANUAL" setting. Adjust cooking time to 12 minutes.
6. Allow the recipe to cook for the set cooking time.
7. After the set cooking time ends, press "CANCEL" and then press "QPR (Quick Pressure Release)".
8. Instant Pot will quickly release the pressure.
9. Open the top lid, add the cooked recipe mix in serving plates.
10. Serve and enjoy!

Bacon Chicken

Prep Time: 10 min.
Cooking Time: 30 min.
Number of Servings: 7-8
Ingredients:
- 4 ounce light cream cheese, cut into small cubes
- 2 pound chicken breasts
- ¼ cup raw turkey bacon, chopped
- Green onions chopped as required
- 1 ounce packet ranch seasoning
- 1 cup chicken broth

Directions:
1. Take your Instant Pot; open the top lid. Plug it and turn it on.
2. Press "SAUTÉ" setting and the pot will start heating up.
3. In the cooking pot area, add the turkey bacon. Stir and cook until evenly brown from all sides.
4. Add the chicken, seasoning, and broth. Close the top lid and seal its valve.
5. Press "MANUAL" setting. Adjust cooking time to 20 minutes.
6. Allow the recipe to cook for the set cooking time.
7. After the set cooking time ends, press "CANCEL" and then press "QPR (Quick Pressure Release)".

8. Instant Pot will quickly release the pressure.
9. Open the top lid, take out the meat and shred it.
10. Add the cheese to the pot. Sauté for 2-3 minutes to fully melt the cheese.
11. Add the chicken to the pot and mix well.
12. Top with the onions and serve.

Rosemary Turkey

Prep Time: 5-8 min.
Cooking Time: 20 min.
Number of Servings: 4
Ingredients:
- 3 tablespoons soy sauce
- 1 tablespoon Dijon-style mustard
- 1 pound turkey tenderloin
- 2 teaspoons rosemary, dried and crushed
- 1/3 cup chicken broth

Directions:
1. In a bowl of medium size, thoroughly mix the soy sauce, mustard, and rosemary.
2. Arrange your Instant Pot over a dry, clean platform. Plug it in power socket and turn it on.
3. Open the lid from the top and put it aside; add the turkey, bowl mix and stock; gently stir them.
4. Close the lid and lock. Ensure that you have sealed the valve to avoid leakage.
5. Press "Poultry" mode from available cooking settings and set cooking time to 18 minutes. Instant Pot will start cooking the ingredients after a few minutes.
6. After the timer reads zero, press "Cancel"; press "NPR" to naturally release pressure. It takes about 8-10 minutes to release pressure naturally.
7. Carefully remove the lid and serve the prepared keto dish warm!

Turkey Apple Curry

Prep Time: 8-10 min.
Cooking Time: 20 min.
Number of Servings: 3-4
Ingredients:
- 2 tablespoons lemon juice
- 1/2 cup full fat yogurt
- 1 teaspoon curry powder
- 1/2 pound turkey breasts, cooked and chopped
- 1 apple, cored and sliced
- 2 tablespoons olive oil
- 1 cup onion, sliced
- 1 cup water

Directions:
1. Arrange your Instant Pot over a dry, clean platform. Plug it in power socket and turn it on.
2. Now press "Saute" mode from available options. In the cooking area, add the oil and onion; cook for 2-3 minutes to soften.

3. Add the garlic, sauté for 20 more seconds. Add the curry powder, apple, turkey, water, pepper, and salt. Mix well.
4. Close the lid and lock. Ensure that you have sealed the valve to avoid leakage.
5. Press "Manual" mode from available cooking settings and set cooking time to 12 minutes. Instant Pot will start cooking the ingredients after a few minutes.
6. After the timer reads zero, press "Cancel" and quick release pressure.
7. Carefully remove the lid. Add the yogurt, sprinkle with lemon juice and mix well.
8. Press "Sauté" button and cook for 5 minutes stirring well. Serve the prepared keto dish warm!

Bacon Cream Chicken

Prep Time: 10 min.
Cooking Time: 25 min.
Number of Servings: 7-8
Ingredients:
- 2 pounds chicken breast, boneless
- 1 cup water
- 8 bacon slices
- 1 teaspoon ranch seasoning
- 4 ounces cheddar cheese
- 8 ounces cream cheese
- 3 tablespoons cornstarch

Directions:
1. Arrange your Instant Pot over a dry, clean platform. Plug it in power socket and turn it on.
2. Open the lid from the top and put it aside; add the cream cheese and chicken breast. Add the ranch and water; gently stir.
3. Close the lid and lock. Ensure that you have sealed the valve to avoid leakage.
4. Press "Manual" mode from available cooking settings and set cooking time to 25 minutes. Instant Pot will start cooking the ingredients after a few minutes.
5. After the timer reads zero, press "Cancel" and quick release pressure.
6. Carefully remove the lid. Take out the chicken and shred it with a fork.
7. Set "Saute" and add the cornstarch to the pot. Whisk and add the shredded chicken and cheddar cheese.
8. Combine well and add the bacon slices. Serve warm!

Turkey Asparagus Meal

Prep Time: 8-10 min.
Cooking Time: 15 min.
Number of Servings: 4
Ingredients:
- 4 tablespoons chicken broth, reduced sodium
- 1 cup asparagus, trimmed and make bite-sized pieces
- 1 pound turkey breasts, skinless and boneless
- 1 tablespoon flour (all-purpose)
- 2 teaspoons fresh lime juice
- Oil as needed

Directions:

1. In a bowl (medium-large size), thoroughly mix lime juice and chicken broth.
2. Mix in the breasts; refrigerate for at least 30 minutes. Drain the marinade and reserve it for later use.
3. Take your Instant Pot and place over dry kitchen surface; open its top lid and switch it on.
4. Press "SAUTÉ". Grease the pot with some cooking oil.
5. Add the breasts; stir-cook for 3-4 minutes each side to evenly brown.
6. Add the oil and asparagus.
7. Cook for 2-3 minutes and add 1 cup of water.
8. Close its top lid and make sure that its valve it closed to avoid spillage.
9. Press "MANUAL". Adjust the timer to 2 minutes.
10. Pressure will slowly build up; let the added ingredients to cook until the timer indicates zero.
11. Press "CANCEL". Now press "QPR" to quickly release pressure.
12. Open the top lid, add the marinade and mix well. Mix in the flour.
13. Press "SAUTÉ"; cook for 4-5 minutes.
14. Serve the recipe warm.

Broccoli Chicken Meal

Prep Time: 8-10 min.
Cooking Time: 8 min.
Number of Servings: 6
Ingredients:

*   2 tablespoons flour (all-purpose)
*   1 tablespoon fresh parsley, chopped (finely)
*   1 pound chicken breasts
*   2 large eggs
*   1 cup broccoli, make florets
*   Cooling oil as needed

Directions:

1. In a mixing bowl, thoroughly mix eggs and parsley.
2. Coat the chicken and then coat with the flour. Set aside.
3. Take your Instant Pot and place over dry kitchen surface; open its top lid and switch it on.
4. Press "SAUTÉ".
5. In its cooking pot, add and heat the oil.
6. Add the coated chicken; stir-cook for 3-4 minutes each side to evenly brown. Set aside.
7. Add the broccoli and ½ cup water; mix well.
8. Close its top lid and make sure that its valve it closed to avoid spillage.
9. Press "MANUAL". Adjust the timer to 2 minutes.
10. Pressure will slowly build up; let the added ingredients to cook until the timer indicates zero.
11. Press "CANCEL". Now press "QPR" to quickly release pressure.
12. Open the top lid, drain transfer the cooked recipe in serving plates.
13. Serve with cooked chicken.

Mushroom Turkey Meal

Prep Time: 8-10 min.
Cooking Time: 18 min.

Number of Servings: 6
Ingredients:
- 1 pound turkey breasts
- 1 cup button mushrooms, make slices
- 1 tablespoon flour (all-purpose)
- 1 small red onion, make slices
- Garlic as needed

Directions:
1. Take your Instant Pot and place over dry kitchen surface; open its top lid and switch it on.
2. Press "SAUTÉ". Grease the pot with some cooking oil.
3. Add the onions and garlic; cook for 3-4 minutes until turn translucent and softened. Set aside.
4. Add the turkey; stir-cook for 3-4 minutes per side to evenly brown.
5. Add 1 cup water and mushrooms.
6. Close its top lid and make sure that its valve it closed to avoid spillage.
7. Press "MANUAL". Adjust the timer to 4 minutes.
8. Pressure will slowly build up; let the added ingredients to cook until the timer indicates zero.
9. Press "CANCEL". Now press "QPR" to quickly release pressure.
10. Mix in the flour. Cook for 2-3 minutes on Sauté mode.
11. Serve the turkey with the onion mix and gravy.

Cream Chicken Quiche

Prep Time: 8-10 min.
Cooking Time: 20 min.
Number of Servings: 3
Ingredients:
- 1/2 cup heavy cream
- 1 cup cottage cheese
- 3 ½ ounce chicken breast
- 5 large eggs
- 3 tablespoons fresh parsley, chopped (finely)

Directions:
1. In a mixing bowl, whisk the eggs, cream, and cheese. Mix in the parsley.
2. Add the chicken and coat well.
3. Take 2-3 small tart pans; grease them with cooking oil.
4. Add the quiche mixture and set aside.
5. Take your Instant Pot and place over dry kitchen surface; open its top lid and switch it on.
6. Pour 1 cup water in the cooking pot area. Arrange the trivet or steamer basket inside it; arrange the pans over the trivet/basket.
7. Close its top lid and make sure that its valve it closed to avoid spillage.
8. Press "MANUAL". Adjust the timer to 20 minutes.
9. Pressure will slowly build up; let the added ingredients to cook until the timer indicates zero.
10. Press "CANCEL". Now press "QPR" to quickly release pressure.
11. Open the top lid, transfer in serving plates.
12. Serve warm.

Turkey Rice Bowl

Prep Time: 8-10 min.
Cooking Time: 10 min.
Number of Servings: 6
Ingredients:
- 3 large egg whites
- ¼ cup spring onions, chopped (finely)
- 8 ounce turkey breasts
- 1 ½ cup brown rice
- 1 small carrot, make small cubes

Directions:
1. Take your Instant Pot and place over dry kitchen surface; open its top lid and switch it on.
2. Press "SAUTÉ". Grease the pot with some cooking oil.
3. Add the turkey; stir-cook for 4-5 minutes to evenly brown. Set aside.
4. Add the egg whites.
5. Cook for 2 minutes and add to the turkey bowl.
6. Add 2 cups water and rice.
7. Close its top lid and make sure that its valve it closed to avoid spillage.
8. Press "RICE". Adjust the timer to 7 minutes.
9. Pressure will slowly build up; let the added ingredients to cook until the timer indicates zero.
10. Press "CANCEL". Now press "QPR" to quickly release pressure.
11. Stir in the onions. Press "SAUTÉ" and cook for another 2 minutes.
12. Mix it with the turkey mix and serve.

Chicken Coconut Curry

Prep Time: 8-10 min.
Cooking Time: 25 min.
Number of Servings: 6
Ingredients:
- 2 tablespoons green curry paste
- 3/4 cup coconut milk, reduced fat
- 1 tablespoon oil
- 7 ounce chicken breast
- 2 large onions, chopped (finely)

Directions:
1. Take your Instant Pot and place over dry kitchen surface; open its top lid and switch it on.
2. Press "SAUTÉ".
3. Grease the pot with some cooking oil.
4. Add the meat; stir-cook for 2-3 minutes to evenly brown.
5. Add the onion. Cook for another 3-4 minutes to soften.
6. Mix in the milk and 2 cups water. Add the curry paste and mix.
7. Close its top lid and make sure that its valve it closed to avoid spillage.
8. Press "MANUAL". Adjust the timer to 20 minutes.
9. Pressure will slowly build up; let the added ingredients to cook until the timer indicates zero.
10. Press "CANCEL". Now press "QPR" to quickly release pressure.

11. Open the top lid, transfer the cooked recipe in serving plates.
12. Serve the recipe warm.

Classic Lemon Chicken

Prep Time: 8-10 min.
Cooking Time: 30 min.
Number of Servings: 4
Ingredients:
- 1 medium purple onion, make slices
- 1 garlic clove, crushed
- 2 teaspoons olive oil
- 4 chicken thighs
- 2 tablespoons fresh lemon juice

Directions:
1. Line a baking pan with a parchment paper and set aside.
2. In a mixing bowl, thoroughly mix olive oil and lemon juice.
3. Coat the chicken and add to the baking pan; top with the garlic and onion.
4. Take your Instant Pot and place over dry kitchen surface; open its top lid and switch it on.
5. Pour 1 cup water in the cooking pot area. Arrange the trivet or steamer basket inside it; arrange the pan over the trivet/basket.
6. Close its top lid and make sure that its valve it closed to avoid spillage.
7. Press "MANUAL". Adjust the timer to 30 minutes.
8. Pressure will slowly build up; let the added ingredients to cook until the timer indicates zero.
9. Press "CANCEL". Now press "QPR" to quickly release pressure.
10. Open the top lid, transfer the cooked recipe in serving plates.
11. Serve the recipe warm.

Chicken and Dumplings

Prep Time: 15 minutes
Cooking Time: 25 minutes
Number of Servings: 4
Ingredients:
- 4 boneless, skinless chicken thighs, cubed
- 1/2 teaspoon salt
- 1/2 teaspoon black pepper
- 1 tablespoon olive oil
- 1 tablespoon butter
- 2 stalks celery, sliced
- 2 carrots, sliced
- 1 onion, chopped
- 1 garlic clove, minced
- 1 teaspoon thyme
- 1/2 teaspoon rosemary
- 2 tablespoons flour
- 4 cups chicken stock
- 2 cups Bisquick mix
- 1 cup milk

- 1/4 cup cream

Directions:
1. Season chicken with salt and pepper. Set Instant Pot to Saute and add olive oil. Brown the chicken in the oil and remove to a plate.
2. Melt butter in the pot. Add celery, carrots, onion, garlic, rosemary, and thyme and brown the vegetables. Add flour and cook until the flour begins to take on color. Pour in the stock, stirring constantly to avoid lumps.
3. Replace chicken in the pot. Close lid and set cooking time to 8 minutes on high. After cooking time, use the quick release to remove the steam. Meanwhile, whisk together Bisquick and milk.
4. Open the lid and set to Saute mode. Drop the Bisquick mix into the sauce in heaping tablespoons. Cook the dumplings for about 10 minutes.
5. Stir in cream and serve.

Tender Cornish Hens with Gravy

Prep Time: 5 minutes
Cooking Time: 25 minutes
Number of Servings: 2
Ingredients:

- 2 small Cornish hens
- 1 teaspoon salt
- 1/2 teaspoon black pepper
- 1 teaspoon thyme
- 1/2 teaspoon rosemary
- 1 cup chicken stock
- 2 tablespoons flour
- 2 tablespoons water

Directions:
1. Rub the Cornish hens with salt, pepper, thyme, and rosemary. Place into Instant Pot and add a stock.
2. Close lid and set cooking time for 20 minutes. Use quick release to remove steam. Open the lid and transfer hen to a serving dish.
3. Set Instant Pot to Saute and bring a stock to a boil. Stir together flour and water in a small bowl. Pour into boiling stock, stirring constantly, and cook until thickened.
4. Serve gravy with the hen.

Midwestern Barbecue Pulled Chicken

Prep Time: 5 minutes
Cooking Time: 15 minutes
Number of Servings: 4
Ingredients:
- 2 pounds bone-in chicken breasts
- 1 onion, diced
- 1 can cola
- 1 teaspoon chili powder
- 1/2 teaspoon garlic powder

- 1/2 teaspoon salt
- 1/2 teaspoon black pepper
- 1 cup barbecue sauce

Directions:
1. Place chicken, onion, cola, chili powder, garlic powder, salt, and pepper in the Instant Pot.
2. Close lid and set cooking time to 15 minutes on high pressure. Use quick release to remove the steam. Open the lid and transfer chicken to a dish, leaving the liquid in the pot.
3. Remove the bones from the chicken. Use 2 forks to shred the flesh into strands.
4. Pour barbecue sauce over chicken and toss to coat. Serve on bread.

Game Day Buffalo Wings

Prep Time: 5 minutes
Cooking Time: 5 minutes
Number of Servings: 4
Ingredients:
- 2 pounds chicken wings
- 1 teaspoon salt
- 1 teaspoon black pepper
- 2/3 cup hot sauce (preferably Frank's Red Hot)
- 1/2 cup butter
- 1 tablespoon apple cider vinegar
- 1/4 teaspoon Worcestershire sauce
- 1 garlic clove, minced
- 1/2 cup water

Directions:
1. Season the chicken wings with salt and pepper.
2. Combine hot sauce, butter, vinegar, Worcestershire sauce, garlic, and water in the Instant Pot. Put the steamer basket in place and arrange the wings in it.
3. Close the lid and set cooking time for 5 minutes. Use quick release to remove the steam.
4. Remove the steamer basket with the wings. Set the pot to Saute mode and reduce the sauce to your desired consistency.
5. Toss the wings with the sauce and serve with blue cheese dressing.

Texas Chicken Tamales

Prep Time: 30 minutes
Cooking Time: 25 minutes
Number of Servings: 6
Ingredients:

- 3 cups masa flour
- 1 teaspoon salt
- 1 teaspoon baking powder
- 1 cup olive oil
- 2 cups chicken stock
- 1/2 teaspoon black pepper
- 1 pack corn husks, rinsed and soaked

- 2 cups cooked, shredded chicken
- 1 can chipotle sauce
- 1 cup shredded Mexican cheese

Directions:
1. In a bowl, mix together flour, salt, and baking powder, then stir in oil and stock.
2. In a separate bowl, mix together chicken and chipotle sauce.
3. Place about 1/4 cup of masa mixture on a corn husk and shape into a log. Layer 2 tablespoons of chicken over the masa, followed by an equal amount of cheese. Roll the husk into a tube and fold down the ends. Repeat with the remaining corn husks.
4. Pour 1 cup of water into the Instant Pot and set the steamer basket in place. Arrange the tamales in the basket. Close the lid and set the cooking time for 25 minutes on high.

Chicken Ragout

Prep Time: 10 minutes
Cooking Time: 15 minutes
Number of Servings: 4
Ingredients:
- 2 tablespoons olive oil
- 4 chicken thighs
- 1 onion, diced
- 1 clove garlic, minced
- 1 teaspoon thyme
- 1/2 teaspoon rosemary
- 1 tablespoon tomato paste
- 1 cup red wine
- 2 cups chicken stock
- 1 bay leaf
- 1/2 teaspoon salt
- 1/2 teaspoon black pepper

Directions:
1. Set Instant Pot to Saute and oil. Brown chicken thighs in hot oil; remove to a plate.
2. Add onion and garlic and cook until onion is translucent, then add thyme and rosemary and cook 30 seconds. Add tomato sauce and cook an additional 30 seconds. Pour in the wine and deglaze the pan, then add chicken stock, bay leaf, salt, and pepper. Place chicken back in the pot.
3. Close the lid and set cooking time for 10 minutes on high pressure. Serve with crusty bread.

Chapter 9: Beef & Pork

Soy Sauce Pork Belly

Prep Time: 5 minutes
Cooking Time: 35 minutes
Number of Servings: 6
Ingredients:
- 2 pounds pork belly, cut into 2-inch cubes
- 2 cups water
- 1 tablespoon sugar
- 1/4 cup rice wine or dry sherry
- 1/4 cup soy sauce
- 1 star anise
- 2 garlic cloves, peeled,
- 2 slices ginger, peeled

Directions:
1. Combine all ingredients in the Instant Pot. Close lid and set cooking time for 35 minutes.
2. Discard anise and ginger and serve with white rice.

Beef Stroganoff

Prep Time: 10 minutes
Cooking Time: 25 minutes
Number of Servings: 4
Ingredients:
- 2 pounds steak tips, cubed
- 1 teaspoon salt
- 1/2 teaspoon black pepper
- 1 tablespoon butter
- 1 onion, finely chopped
- 1 cup mushrooms, sliced
- 1/2 teaspoon thyme
- 1/2 teaspoon tarragon
- 1/2 cup white wine
- 1 cup beef broth
- 1/2 cup sour cream

Directions:
1. Season steak tips with salt and pepper. Melt butter in Instant Pot set to Saute mode and add beef. Brown on all sides, then remove to a plate.
2. Add onion and cook until translucent. Add mushrooms and cook until tender. Add thyme and tarragon and coast 30 seconds.
3. Deglaze the pot with white wine, then add broth. Replace meat in the pot. Close lid and set cooking time for 20 minutes.
4. Use quick release to remove the steam. Stir in sour cream. Serve over egg noodles or with boiled potatoes.

Garlic Roast

Prep Time: 5 min.
Cooking Time: 40-45 min.
Number of Servings: 8-10
Ingredients:
- ½ cup onion, chopped
- 2 cups water
- ¼ teaspoon xanthan gum
- 1 teaspoon garlic powder
- 3-pound chuck roast, boneless
- ¼ cup balsamic vinegar
- Parsley, chopped to garnish
- 1 teaspoon pepper
- 1 tablespoon kosher salt

Directions:
1. Slice your roast in half and season with the garlic, pepper, and salt.
2. Arrange your Instant Pot over a dry, clean platform. Plug it in power socket and turn it on.
3. Now press "Saute" mode from available options. In the cooking area, add the meat; cook to brown.
4. Add the onion, water, and vinegar. Stir gently.
5. Close the lid and lock. Ensure that you have sealed the valve to avoid leakage.
6. Press "Manual" mode from available cooking settings and set cooking time to 35 minutes. Instant Pot will start cooking the ingredients after a few minutes.
7. After the timer reads zero, press "Cancel" and quick release pressure.
8. Carefully remove the lid. Carefully take the meat and make chunks.
9. Set the pot back on sauté; boil the mix for around 10 minutes.
10. Mix the gum and mix the shredded meat. Serve the prepared keto dish warm!

Spicy Vinegar Lamb

Prep Time: 5-8 min.
Cooking Time: 25 min.
Number of Servings: 6
Ingredients:

- 1 tablespoon paprika

- 1 chili pepper, chopped

- 1 medium-size white onion, diced

- 1 tablespoon apple cider vinegar

- 1 pound lamb rack

- 1 teaspoon black pepper

- 1 teaspoon chili flakes

- 1 teaspoon olive oil

Directions:
1. Season the meat with the pepper and chili flakes. Sprinkle the lamb the vinegar and olive oil. Rub the meat with the paprika.
2. Arrange your Instant Pot over a dry, clean platform. Plug it in power socket and turn it on.
3. Open the lid from the top and put it aside; add the lamb, pepper, and onion.
4. Close the lid and lock. Ensure that you have sealed the valve to avoid leakage.
5. Press "Manual" mode from available cooking settings and set cooking time to 25 minutes. Instant Pot will start cooking the ingredients after a few minutes.
6. After the timer reads zero, press "Cancel" and quick release pressure.
7. Carefully remove the lid and serve the prepared keto dish warm!

Sweet Potato Steak

Prep Time: 10 min.
Cooking Time: 32-35 min.
Number of Servings: 5
Ingredients:

- 2 teaspoons black pepper

- 1 tablespoon maple syrup

- 2 large sweet potatoes, peeled & cubed

- 1/2 cup beef broth

- 1 cup water

- 1/2 pound turkey bacon, sliced

- 2 tablespoons parsley

- 2 tablespoons thyme

- 1 tablespoon olive oil

- 5 carrots. make sticks

- 1 large red onion, sliced

- 1 pound flank steak

- 2 teaspoons rock salt

- 2 cloves garlic minced

Directions:
1. Pat dry the beef and season it.
2. Arrange your Instant Pot over a dry, clean platform. Plug it in power socket and turn it on.

3. Now press "Saute" mode from available options. In the cooking area, add the oil and beef; cook to brown evenly.
4. Add the onion, turkey bacon and other ingredients.
5. Close the lid and lock. Ensure that you have sealed the valve to avoid leakage.
6. Press "Manual" mode from available cooking settings and set cooking time to 25 minutes. Instant Pot will start cooking the ingredients after a few minutes.
7. After the timer reads zero, press "Cancel" and quick release pressure.
8. Carefully remove the lid and serve the prepared keto dish warm!

Pork & Bacon Dinner Meal

Prep Time: 15-20 min.
Cooking Time: 30 min.
Number of Servings: 7-8
Ingredients:
- 3-ounce bacon, sliced
- 2-pound pork shoulder
- 9-ounce cabbage, chopped
- ½ cup water
- 2 garlic cloves, peeled, chopped

Directions:
1. Season the pork with the chopped garlic.
2. Take your Instant Pot; open the top lid. Plug it and turn it on.
3. In the cooking pot area, add the water and cabbage.
4. Top with the bacon and pork shoulder. Close the top lid and seal its valve.
5. Press "MANUAL" setting. Adjust cooking time to 30 minutes.
6. Allow the recipe to cook for the set cooking time.
7. After the set cooking time ends, press "CANCEL" and then press "NPR (Natural Pressure Release)".
8. Instant Pot will slowly and naturally release the pressure.
9. Open the top lid, add the cooked recipe mix in serving plates.
10. Serve and enjoy!

Oregano Spiced Beef Chops

Prep Time: 5-8 min.
Cooking Time: 25 min.
Number of Servings: 2-3
Ingredients:
- 1 teaspoon dried dill
- 1-pound beef chops
- 1 teaspoon dried parsley
- ½ teaspoon coriander
- 1 teaspoon thyme
- 1 teaspoon oregano
- 1 tablespoon olive oil
- ¼ cup water

217

- ½ teaspoon salt

Directions:
1. Combine the thyme, oregano, dill, parsley, coriander, salt, and olive oil in a mixing bowl. Stir the mixture and mix the chops with the spice mix.
2. Close the top lid and seal its valve.
3. Press "MANUAL" setting. Adjust cooking time to 25 minutes.
4. Allow the recipe to cook for the set cooking time.
5. After the set cooking time ends, press "CANCEL" and then press "NPR (Natural Pressure Release)".
6. Instant Pot will slowly and naturally release the pressure.
7. Open the top lid, add the cooked recipe mix in serving plates.
8. Serve and enjoy!

Milky Beef Roast

Prep Time: 10 min.
Cooking Time: 30 min.
Number of Servings: 7-8
Ingredients:
- 1 tablespoon paprika
- 2-pounds beef roast
- 1 cup almond milk
- 1 teaspoon salt
- 1 teaspoon raw honey

Directions:
1. Combine the almond milk and salt in a mixing bowl. Add the paprika and raw honey. Stir the mixture well; add the beef roast in the almond milk mixture and leave for 15 minutes.
2. Take your Instant Pot; open the top lid. Plug it and turn it on.
3. In the cooking pot area, add the bowl mix. Using a spatula, stir the ingredients.
4. Close the top lid and seal its valve.
5. Press "MANUAL" setting. Adjust cooking time to 30 minutes.
6. Allow the recipe to cook for the set cooking time.
7. After the set cooking time ends, press "CANCEL" and then press "QPR (Quick Pressure Release)".
8. Instant Pot will quickly release the pressure.
9. Open the top lid, add the cooked recipe mix in serving plates.
10. Serve and enjoy!

Beef Avocado Bowl

Prep Time: 10 min.
Cooking Time: 10-12 min.
Number of Servings: 4
Ingredients:
- 2 teaspoons lime juice
- 1 tablespoon olive oil, extra virgin
- 1/2 teaspoon cracked pepper

- 1/2 teaspoon sea salt
- 1/2 teaspoon chili powder
- 2 pounds beef steak strips
- 1 garlic clove, minced
- 1 tablespoon water
- 3 avocado, diced

Directions:
1. Arrange your Instant Pot over a dry, clean platform. Plug it in power socket and turn it on.
2. Now press "Saute" mode from available options. In the cooking area, add the oil and garlic; cook for 1-2 minutes to soften.
3. Add water, lime juice, sea salt, chili powder, and pepper; stir gently.
4. Close the lid and lock. Ensure that you have sealed the valve to avoid leakage.
5. Press "Manual" mode from available cooking settings and set cooking time to 10 minutes. Instant Pot will start cooking the ingredients after a few minutes.
6. After the timer reads zero, press "Cancel" and quick release pressure.
7. Carefully remove the lid.
8. Press "Sauté" button, add the steak strips and stir and cook for 2 minutes.
9. Continue sautéing until chili becomes thicker and reduced by half size. Top with diced avocados.

Broccoli Beef with Garlic Twist

Prep Time: 5-8 min.
Cooking Time: 20 min.
Number of Servings: 5
Ingredients:
- 1/2 cup poultry broth

- 1/8 teaspoon salt

- 1 pound cooked beef

- 2 teaspoons garlic, crushed

- 1 tablespoon animal fat

- 6 cups broccoli, cut to prepare small florets

- 1 onion, chopped

- 1 turnip, chopped

Directions:
1. Arrange your Instant Pot over a dry, clean platform. Plug it in power socket and turn it on.
2. Open the lid from the top and put it aside; add the mentioned ingredients and gently stir them.
3. Close the lid and lock. Ensure that you have sealed the valve to avoid leakage.
4. Press "Manual" mode from available cooking settings and set cooking time to 20 minutes. Instant Pot will start cooking the ingredients after a few minutes.
5. After the timer reads zero, press "Cancel" and quick release pressure.
6. Carefully remove the lid and serve the prepared keto dish warm!

Beef Broccoli Curry

Prep Time: 8-10 min.
Cooking Time: 45 min.
Number of Servings: 6
Ingredients:

- 1/2 pound broccoli florets
- 2 tablespoons curry powder
- 14 ounces coconut milk
- Salt as needed
- 2 1/2 pound beef stew chunks, small cubes
- 2 medium zucchinis, chopped
- ½ cup water or chicken broth
- 1 tablespoon garlic powder

Directions:

1. Arrange your Instant Pot over a dry, clean platform. Plug it in power socket and turn it on.
2. Open the lid from the top and put it aside; add the ingredients and gently stir them.
3. Close the lid and lock. Ensure that you have sealed the valve to avoid leakage.
4. Press "Manual" mode from available cooking settings and set cooking time to 45 minutes. Instant Pot will start cooking the ingredients after a few minutes.
5. After the timer reads zero, press "Cancel" and quick release pressure.
6. Carefully remove the lid. Add the milk and stir.
7. Add salt as needed and serve the prepared keto dish warm!

Parmesan Beef Meatballs

Prep Time: 8-10 min.
Cooking Time: 10 min.
Number of Servings: 5
Ingredients:

- 2 tablespoons parsley, chopped
- 2 medium eggs
- ½ cup almond flour
- 1 1/2 pound lean ground beef
- 3 ounces parmesan cheese, grated
- ¼ teaspoons oregano, dried
- 1 cup marinara sauce
- 1 teaspoon onion flakes, dried
- ¼ teaspoon garlic powder
- ¼ teaspoon black pepper
- 1 teaspoon kosher salt
- 1/3 cup warm water
- 1 teaspoon olive oil

Directions:

1. In a bowl of medium size, thoroughly mix the ingredients except for sauce and olive oil. Prepare around 15 balls from it.

2. Arrange your Instant Pot over a dry, clean platform. Plug it in power socket and turn it on.
3. Now press "Saute" mode from available options. In the cooking area, add the oil and meatballs; cook to brown evenly.
4. Add the marinara sauce to Instant Pot.
5. Close the lid and lock. Ensure that you have sealed the valve to avoid leakage.
6. Press "Manual" mode from available cooking settings and set cooking time to 10 minutes. Instant Pot will start cooking the ingredients after a few minutes.
7. After the timer reads zero, press "Cancel" and quick release pressure.
8. Carefully remove the lid and serve the prepared keto dish warm!
9. Serve with spaghetti squash or zucchini noodles topped with meatballs and sauce!

Pork Chops Tomatino

Prep Time: 10-15 min.
Cooking Time: 34 min.
Number of Servings: 5
Ingredients:
- 16-ounce pork chops, chopped
- ½ cup cherry tomatoes, chopped
- 1 teaspoon grated onion
- 1 tablespoon dill, chopped
- 1 teaspoon olive oil
- ¼ teaspoon minced garlic
- ¼ teaspoon paprika
- 2 cup water

Directions:
1. Take your Instant Pot; open the top lid. Plug it and turn it on.
2. Press "SAUTÉ" setting and the pot will start heating up.
3. In the cooking pot area, add the oil and chopped meat. Stir and cook until evenly brown from all sides.
4. Add the cherry tomatoes, grated onion, minced garlic, paprika, and dill. Stir the mixture and add water.
5. Close the top lid and seal its valve.
6. Press "MEAT/STEW" setting. Adjust cooking time to 30 minutes.
7. Allow the recipe to cook for the set cooking time.
8. After the set cooking time ends, press "CANCEL" and then press "QPR (Quick Pressure Release)".
9. Instant Pot will quickly release the pressure.
10. Open the top lid, take out the meat and shred it.
11. Add back to the mix and combine; add the cooked recipe mix in serving plates.
12. Serve and enjoy!

Wine Braised Beef Roast

Prep Time: 10 min.
Cooking Time: 48 min.
Number of Servings: 5-6

Ingredients:
- 2 celery stalks, chopped
- 1 bell pepper, chopped
- 2 tablespoons olive oil
- 2 tablespoons Italian seasoning
- 2 ½ pounds beef roast
- 1 onion, sliced
- 2 garlic cloves, sliced
- 1 cup red wine
- 1 cup beef broth
- 2 tablespoons steak sauce, sugar-free

Directions:
1. Take your Instant Pot; open the top lid. Plug it and turn it on.
2. Press "SAUTÉ" setting and the pot will start heating up.
3. In the cooking pot area, add the meat and half of the oil. Stir and cook for 4-5 minutes until evenly brown from all sides.
4. Set aside in a plate.
5. Heat the remaining olive oil and add the onions, celery, and peppers. Cook for 3 minutes to soften.
6. Stir in the garlic and seasonings and cook for 1 minute. Return the beef to the pot.
7. Add the broth, sauce, and red wine; whisk the mixture.
8. Close the top lid and seal its valve.
9. Press "MANUAL" setting. Adjust cooking time to 40 minutes.
10. Allow the recipe to cook for the set cooking time.
11. After the set cooking time ends, press "CANCEL" and then press "NPR (Natural Pressure Release)".
12. Instant Pot will slowly and naturally release the pressure.
13. Open the top lid, add the cooked recipe mix in serving plates.
14. Serve and enjoy!

Creamy Pork Treat

Prep Time: 5-8 min.
Cooking Time: 10 min.
Number of Servings: 4
Ingredients:
- 4 garlic cloves, minced
- 2 cups milk
- 1 teaspoon thyme
- 1-pound pork sausage
- ¼ cup arrowroot
- ¼ teaspoon pepper
- ½ tablespoon olive oil
- ½ teaspoon salt

Directions:
1. Take your Instant Pot; open the top lid. Plug it and turn it on.

2. Press "SAUTÉ" setting and the pot will start heating up.
3. In the cooking pot area, add the oil, garlic, and thyme. Cook until starts becoming translucent and softened for 1 minutes. Stir in between.
4. Add sausage and cook it until it becomes brown. Make sure to break the sausage.
5. Pour 1 ½ cups the milk over it.
6. In a bowl, whisk together the arrowroot, remaining milk, salt, and pepper.
7. Close the top lid and seal its valve.
8. Press "MANUAL" setting. Adjust cooking time to 5 minutes.
9. Allow the recipe to cook for the set cooking time.
10. After the set cooking time ends, press "CANCEL" and then press "QPR (Quick Pressure Release)".
11. Instant Pot will quickly release the pressure.
12. Add the bowl mix and cook on "SAUTE" for 5 minutes.
13. Serve and enjoy!

Buttery Garlic Lamb Shanks

Prep Time: 5-8 min.
Cooking Time: 25 min.
Number of Servings: 4
Ingredients:
- ½ cup port wine
- ½ cup chicken broth
- 1 tablespoon olive oil
- 2-pounds lamb shanks
- 1 tablespoon butter
- ½ teaspoon thyme
- 10 garlic cloves, peeled
- 1 tablespoon tomato paste
- 1 teaspoon balsamic vinegar

Directions:
1. Take your Instant Pot; open the top lid. Plug it and turn it on.
2. Press "SAUTÉ" setting and the pot will start heating up.
3. In the cooking pot area, add the oil and garlic. Cook until starts becoming translucent and softened. Stir in between.
4. Add the tomato paste, broth, thyme, and port wine. Stir to combine and add the lamb shanks.
5. Close the top lid and seal its valve.
6. Press "MANUAL" setting. Adjust cooking time to 20 minutes.
7. Allow the recipe to cook for the set cooking time.
8. After the set cooking time ends, press "CANCEL" and then press "NPR (Natural Pressure Release)".
9. Instant Pot will slowly and naturally release the pressure.
10. Open the top lid, add the cooked recipe mix in serving plates. Stir in the butter and vinegar.
11. Serve and enjoy!

Spiced Cream Lamb

Prep Time: 10-15 min.
Cooking Time: 30 min.
Number of Servings: 5-6
Ingredients:

- 2 tablespoons ghee
- 2 cups cherry tomatoes, chopped
- 2-pound boneless leg lamb, make bite-sized pieces
- ¼ cup heavy cream
- 3 cups vegetable stock
- 1 teaspoon ginger powder
- 1 teaspoon cumin powder
- 1 teaspoon salt
- 1 tablespoon coriander powder
- 2 tablespoons chili powder
- 1 teaspoon garam masala
- ½ teaspoon garlic powder
- 1 cinnamon stick
- 3 bay leaves
- 1 ½ teaspoon cumin seeds
- 3 cloves, whole

Directions:

1. In a mixing bowl, mix the heavy cream and garam masala. Tightly wrap with aluminum foil. Refrigerate overnight.
2. Rinse the meat under cold running water and pat dry with a kitchen paper; chop into bite-sized pieces.
3. Take your Instant Pot; open the top lid. Plug it and turn it on.
4. Press "SAUTÉ" setting and the pot will start heating up.
5. In the cooking pot area, add the ghee, bay leaves, cardamom, cinnamon, cloves, and cumin seeds
6. Briefly cook for 1-2 minutes; add the remaining spices and stir well.
7. Continue to cook for 1 minute. Add the meat along with the cream mix.
8. Mix in the stock and cherry tomatoes. Stir well and seal the lid.
9. Close the top lid and seal its valve.
10. Press "MANUAL" setting. Adjust cooking time to 25 minutes.
11. Allow the recipe to cook for the set cooking time.
12. After the set cooking time ends, press "CANCEL" and then press "NPR (Natural Pressure Release)".
13. Instant Pot will slowly and naturally release the pressure.
14. Open the top lid, add the cooked recipe mix in serving plates.
15. Serve and enjoy!

Pineapple Pork

Prep Time: 8-10 min.
Cooking Time: 25 min.
Number of Servings: 2
Ingredients:

- 1 cup unsweetened pineapple juice
- ½ cup pineapple chunks
- ½ teaspoon nutmeg
- ½ teaspoon cinnamon
- 2 cloves
- ¼ cup chopped onion
- ½ teaspoon rosemary
- ½ pounds. pork tenderloin, sliced
- ½ cup tomato puree

Directions:

1. Switch on the pot after placing it on a clean and dry platform.
2. Open the pot lid and place the above-mentioned ingredients in the cooking pot area. Give the ingredients a little stir. Do not add the chunks.
3. Close the pot by closing the top lid. Also, ensure to seal the valve.
4. Press "Manual" cooking function and set cooking time to 25 minutes. It will start cooking after a few minutes. Let the pot mix cook under pressure until the timer reads zero.
5. Press "Cancel" cooking function and press "Quick release" setting.
6. Open the pot; add the chunks and serve warm. Enjoy it with your loved one!

Green Chili Beef

Prep Time: 8-10 min.
Cooking Time: 60 min.
Number of Servings: 2
Ingredients:

- 1 pound beef roast, make medium size cubes
- 2 garlic cloves, minced
- 1 tablespoon coconut vinegar
- 2 ounces green chilies, chopped
- 1 teaspoon oregano, dried
- A pinch of pepper and salt
- 2 teaspoons cumin, ground
- 1/2 cup water
- 1 small yellow onion, chopped
- 1 chipotle pepper, chopped
- Juice from 1 lime

Directions:

1. Take your 3-Quart Instant Pot; open the top lid. Plug it and turn it on.
2. In the cooking pot area, add the garlic, onion, green chilies, beef, oregano, salt, pepper, chipotle pepper, lime juice, vinegar, cumin and water. Using a spatula, stir the ingredients.

3. Close the top lid and seal its valve.
4. Press "MANUAL" setting. Adjust cooking time to 60 minutes.
5. Allow the recipe to cook for the set cooking time.
6. After the set cooking time ends, press "CANCEL" and then press "QPR (Quick Pressure Release)".
7. Instant Pot will quickly release the pressure.
8. Open the top lid, add the cooked recipe mix in serving plates.
9. Serve and enjoy!

Beef Red Potato Stew

Prep Time: 8-10 min.
Cooking Time: 25 min.
Number of Servings: 2
Ingredients:
- 1 pound beef meat, make medium size cubes
- 1 tablespoon olive oil
- 2 tablespoons parsley, chopped
- 3 tablespoons beef broth
- 1 tablespoon flour
- 1/2 tablespoon tomato paste
- A pinch of pepper and salt
- 1 small yellow onion, chopped
- 1 garlic clove, crushed or minced
- 1 cup beef stock
- 1 celery stalk, chopped
- 2 small carrots, chopped
- 1/2 pound red potatoes, chopped

Directions:
1. In a bowl, mix the beef meat, salt, pepper and flour and toss.
2. Take your 3-Quart Instant Pot; open the top lid. Plug it and turn it on.
3. Press "SAUTÉ" setting and the pot will start heating up.
4. In the cooking pot area, add the oil and meat. Stir and cook until evenly brown from all sides.
5. Add the beef broth and cook for 2 minutes.
6. Add the carrots, garlic, onions, potatoes, celery, stock and tomato paste, stir gently.
7. Close the top lid and seal its valve.
8. Press "MANUAL" setting. Adjust cooking time to 20 minutes.
9. Allow the recipe to cook for the set cooking time.
10. After the set cooking time ends, press "CANCEL" and then press "QPR (Quick Pressure Release)".
11. Instant Pot will quickly release the pressure.
12. Open the top lid, add the cooked recipe mix in serving plates.
13. Serve top with some parsley and enjoy!

Spiced Potato Lamb Dinner

Prep Time: 10 min.
Cooking Time: 35 min.
Number of Servings: 2-3
Ingredients:
- 1 tomato, chopped
- 1/2 pound rack of lamb
- 1/2 pound baby potatoes
- 1 carrot, chopped
- 1 cup chicken stock
- 1/2 onion, chopped
- 1 celery stalk, chopped
- A pinch of rosemary, dried
- 1 tablespoon ketchup
- 1 tablespoon beef broth
- 2 garlic cloves, minced
- A pinch of pepper and salt
- 1 teaspoon sweet paprika
- 1 teaspoon cumin, ground
- A pinch of oregano, dried

Directions:
1. Take your 3-Quart Instant Pot; open the top lid. Plug it and turn it on.
2. In the cooking pot area, add the baby potatoes, carrot, onion, celery, tomato, stock, garlic, salt, pepper, paprika, cumin, oregano, rosemary, ketchup, lamb, and beef broth. Using a spatula, stir the ingredients.
3. Close the top lid and seal its valve.
4. Press "MANUAL" setting. Adjust cooking time to 35 minutes.
5. Allow the recipe to cook for the set cooking time.
6. After the set cooking time ends, press "CANCEL" and then press "QPR (Quick Pressure Release)".
7. Instant Pot will quickly release the pressure.
8. Open the top lid, add the cooked recipe mix in serving plates.
9. Serve and enjoy!

Pork Meatball Curry

Prep Time: 10-15 min.
Cooking Time: 25 min.
Number of Servings: 2-3
Ingredients:
- ¼ cup coconut milk
- ¾ teaspoon brown sugar
- 1 tablespoon breadcrumb
- ¾ pounds pork, ground
- ¼ cup chopped onion
- 1 egg, medium size

Directions:

1. Mix the pork with egg and breadcrumbs. Shape the mixture into balls.
2. Take your 3-Quart Instant Pot; open the top lid. Plug it and turn it on.
3. Press "SAUTÉ" setting and the pot will start heating up.
4. In the cooking pot area, add the milk, meatballs, onions and sugar; stir gently.
5. Close the top lid and seal its valve.
6. Press "MANUAL" setting. Adjust cooking time to 25 minutes.
7. Allow the recipe to cook for the set cooking time.
8. After the set cooking time ends, press "CANCEL" and then press "NPR (Natural Pressure Release)".
9. Instant Pot will slowly and naturally release the pressure.
10. Open the top lid, add the cooked recipe mix in serving plates.
11. Serve and enjoy!

Squash Wine Lamb Meal

Prep Time: 10 min.
Cooking Time: 50 min.
Number of Servings: 2-3
Ingredients:

- ½ butternut squash, make medium size cubes
- 1 small onion, chopped
- 2 parsnips, make medium size cubes
- 2 cloves garlic crushed
- ¼ cup white wine
- ¼ cup stock
- Olive oil as needed
- Pepper and salt as needed
- ¾ pound lamb
- 2 carrots, make medium size cubes

Directions:

1. Take your 3-Quart Instant Pot; open the top lid. Plug it and turn it on.
2. Press "SAUTÉ" setting and the pot will start heating up.
3. In the cooking pot area, add the meat. Stir and cook until evenly brown from all sides.
4. Add rest the ingredients and stir gently.
5. Close the top lid and seal its valve.
6. Press "MEAT/STEW" setting. Adjust cooking time to 45 minutes.
7. Allow the recipe to cook for the set cooking time.
8. After the set cooking time ends, press "CANCEL" and then press "QPR (Quick Pressure Release)".
9. Instant Pot will quickly release the pressure.
10. Open the top lid, take out the meat and shred it.
11. Add back to the mix and combine; add the cooked recipe mix in serving plates.
12. Serve and enjoy!

Artichoke Mayo Beef

Prep Time: 10 min.
Cooking Time: 15 min.
Number of Servings: 2
Ingredients:
- 1 pound beef, ground
- 1 small yellow onion, chopped
- 1/2 teaspoon dill, dried
- 1/2 teaspoon apple cider vinegar
- 3 tablespoons mayonnaise
- 1/2 teaspoon garlic powder
- 1/2 teaspoon oregano, dried
- 1/2 tablespoon olive oil
- 1/3 cup water
- 1/2 teaspoon onion powder
- A pinch of pepper and salt
- 1 ¼ cup artichoke hearts

Directions:
1. Take your 3-Quart Instant Pot; open the top lid. Plug it and turn it on.
2. Press "SAUTÉ" setting and the pot will start heating up.
3. In the cooking pot area, add the oil and onions. Cook until starts becoming translucent and softened for 3 minutes. Stir in between.
4. Add the beef, salt, pepper, oregano, dill, garlic and onion powder, stir and cook for 3 minutes.
5. Add water and artichokes; stir gently.
6. Close the top lid and seal its valve.
7. Press "MANUAL" setting. Adjust cooking time to 7 minutes.
8. Allow the recipe to cook for the set cooking time.
9. After the set cooking time ends, press "CANCEL" and then press "QPR (Quick Pressure Release)".
10. Instant Pot will quickly release the pressure.
11. Open the top lid, add the cooked recipe mix in serving plates.
12. Drain excess water, mix the vinegar and mayo.
13. Serve and enjoy!

Apple Pork Roast

Prep Time: 5-8 min.
Cooking Time: 30 min.
Number of Servings: 2
Ingredients:
- 1/2 tablespoon olive oil
- A pinch of onion powder
- 1-pound pork roast
- A pinch of pepper and salt
- 1 cup water
- A pinch of chili powder

- A pinch of garlic powder
- 3 tablespoons apple juice

Directions:
1. In a bowl, mix the chili powder, onion powder, roast, garlic powder, salt, and pepper.
2. Take your 3-Quart Instant Pot; open the top lid. Plug it and turn it on.
3. Press "SAUTÉ" setting and the pot will start heating up.
4. In the cooking pot area, add the oil and meat mix. Stir and cook until evenly brown from all sides for 4-5 minutes.
5. Add the apple juice and water.
6. Close the top lid and seal its valve.
7. Press "MANUAL" setting. Adjust cooking time to 25 minutes.
8. Allow the recipe to cook for the set cooking time.
9. After the set cooking time ends, press "CANCEL" and then press "QPR (Quick Pressure Release)".
10. Instant Pot will quickly release the pressure.
11. Open the top lid, take out the meat and slice it.
12. Add back to the mix and combine; add the cooked recipe mix in serving plates.
13. Serve and enjoy!

Garlic Pulled Pork

Prep Time: 8-10 min.
Cooking Time: 40 min.
Number of Servings: 2
Ingredients:
- ¼ teaspoon salt
- 1-tablespoon cornstarch
- 3 tablespoons water
- ½ cup beef broth
- ½ cup chopped onion
- 1 pound pork belly, make cubes
- 1 ½ teaspoons black pepper
- 1-teaspoon thyme

Directions:
1. Switch on the pot after placing it on a clean and dry platform.
2. Open the pot lid and place the above-mentioned ingredients in the cooking pot area. Give the ingredients a little stir. Do not add the water and cornstarch.
3. Close the pot by closing the top lid. Also, ensure to seal the valve.
4. Press "Manual" cooking function and set cooking time to 35 minutes. It will start cooking after a few minutes. Let the pot mix cook under pressure until the timer reads zero.
5. Press "Cancel" cooking function and press "Quick release" setting.
6. Open the pot. Combine cornstarch with water then stir into the Instant Pot.
7. Add the liquid over the pork then serve warm!

Saucy Pork Meatballs

Prep Time: 8-10 min.
Cooking Time: 25 min.
Number of Servings: 2
Ingredients:
- 1 tablespoon breadcrumb
- ¼ cup coconut milk
- ¾ teaspoon brown sugar
- ¾ pounds. ground pork
- ¼ cup chopped onion
- 1 organic egg

Directions:
1. Combine the meat with egg and breadcrumbs. Shape the mixture into balls.
2. Switch on the pot after placing it on a clean and dry platform.
3. Open the pot lid and place the balls and milk in the cooking pot area. Add the brown sugar and chopped onion. Give the ingredients a little stir.
4. Close the pot by closing the top lid. Also, ensure to seal the valve.
5. Press "Manual" cooking function and set cooking time to 25 minutes. It will start cooking after a few minutes. Let the pot mix cook under pressure until the timer reads zero.
6. Press "Cancel" cooking function and press "Natural release (NPR)" setting. It will take 8-10 minutes for natural pressure release.
7. Open the pot and serve warm. Enjoy it with your loved one!

Oregano Lamb Shanks

Prep Time: 10 min.
Cooking Time: 35 min.
Number of Servings: 2
Ingredients:
- 2 garlic cloves, diced
- 1 large onion, chopped
- 1 tomato, diced
- 1 teaspoon oregano
- 1 cup red wine
- 3 carrots, diced
- 2 tablespoons tomato paste
- 2 pounds lamb shanks
- 4 tablespoons white flour
- 2 tablespoons olive oil
- ½ cup beef stock
- Pepper and salt as per taste preference

Directions:
1. In a bowl, mix the flour, salt, and pepper. Add the shanks and coat well with the flour.
2. Switch on the pot after placing it on a clean and dry platform. Press "Sauté" cooking function.

3. Open the pot lid; add the oil and lamb in the pot; cook for 2 minutes to cook well and browned. Set aside.
4. In the remaining hot oil, sauté the garlic and onion for 4-5 minutes. Mix in the tomato paste, tomato, red wine, and beef stock. Boil the mixture.
5. Add the shanks. Close the pot by closing the top lid. Also, ensure to seal the valve.
6. Press "Manual" cooking function and set cooking time to 25 minutes. It will start cooking after a few minutes. Let the pot mix cook under pressure until the timer reads zero.
7. Press "Cancel" cooking function and press "Natural release (NPR)" setting. It will take 8-10 minutes for natural pressure release.
8. Open the pot and serve warm. Enjoy it with your loved one!

Honey Glazed Pork Roast

Prep Time: 5 min.
Cooking Time: 35 min.
Number of Servings: 2
Ingredients:
- 2 tablespoons raw honey
- 1/2 tablespoon dry basil
- ½ tablespoon cornstarch
- ½ cup water
- ½ tablespoon garlic, minced
- ½ tablespoon olive oil
- 1 pound pork roast
- 2 tablespoons parmesan cheese, grated
- 1 tablespoon soy sauce
- Salt as per taste preference

Directions:
1. Switch on the pot after placing it on a clean and dry platform.
2. Open the pot lid and place the above-mentioned ingredients in the cooking pot area. Give the ingredients a little stir.
3. Close the pot by closing the top lid. Also, ensure to seal the valve.
4. Press "Meat" cooking function and set cooking time to 35 minutes. It will start cooking after a few minutes. Let the pot mix cook under pressure until the timer reads zero.
5. Press "Cancel" cooking function and press "Natural release (NPR)" setting. It will take 8-10 minutes for natural pressure release.
6. Open the pot and serve warm. Enjoy it with your loved one!

Classic Beef Bourguignon

Prep Time: 10 min.
Cooking Time: 40 min.
Number of Servings: 2
Ingredients:
- 1 medium onion, chopped
- 1 tablespoon thyme
- ½ cup beef stock

- ½ cup red wine
- 2 medium carrots, chopped
- 1 tablespoon parsley
- ½ pound beef stew meat
- 2 bacon slices
- 1 garlic clove, minced
- 1 large potato, cubed
- ½ tablespoon honey
- ½ tablespoon olive oil

Directions:
1. Switch on the pot after placing it on a clean and dry platform. Press "Sauté" cooking function.
2. Open the pot lid; add the oil and beef in the pot; cook for 3-4 minutes to cook well and evenly browned. Set aside.
3. Add the bacon and onion, and sauté until onion is translucent. Add beef and the rest of the ingredients.
4. Close the pot by closing the top lid. Also, ensure to seal the valve.
5. Press "Manual" cooking function and set cooking time to 30 minutes. It will start cooking after a few minutes. Let the pot mix cook under pressure until the timer reads zero.
6. Press "Cancel" cooking function and press "Natural release (NPR)" setting. It will take 8-10 minutes for natural pressure release.
7. Open the pot and serve warm. Enjoy it with your loved one!

Teriyaki Pork Meal

Prep Time: 8-10 min.
Cooking Time: 25 min.
Number of Servings: 5-6
Ingredients:
- 4 cloves garlic, minced
- ½ large onion, chopped
- 2 tablespoons olive oil
- 2-pounds pork tenderloin, make strips
- 3 red chili pepper, chopped
- 1 cup chicken broth
- ¼ cup brown sugar
- ¼ teaspoon black pepper
- ½ cup teriyaki sauce

Directions:
1. Take an Instant Pot; open the top lid.
2. Press "SAUTÉ" cooking function.
3. In the cooking pot area, add the oil and tenderloins. Stir-cook constantly for 5 minutes or until they become brown.
4. Add in garlic, onion, red chili pepper and black pepper. Add the remaining ingredients.
5. Close the top lid and make sure the valve is sealed.
6. Press "MEAT/STEW" cooking function. Adjust cooking time to 20 minutes.
7. Allow pressure to build and cook the ingredients for the set time.

8. After the set cooking time ends, press "CANCEL" and then press "NPR". Instant Pot will slowly and naturally release the pressure for 8-10 minutes.
9. Open the top lid, add the cooked mixture in serving plates.
10. Serve warm cooked rice (optional).

Beef Meatloaf Dinner

Prep Time: 8-10 min.
Cooking Time: 25 min.
Number of Servings: 4
Ingredients:
- 2 large egg whites
- ¼ cup seasoned Italian bread crumbs
- ¼ cup onion, chopped
- 1-pound lean ground beef
- ½ cup barbecue sauce

Directions:
1. In a mixing bowl, combine the onion, meat, egg whites, and bread crumbs. Mix in 1/4th of BBQ sauce.
2. Shape the mix into a log and place on a parchment paper.
3. Take an Instant Pot; open the top lid.
4. Pour the water and place steamer basket/trivet inside the cooking pot.
5. Arrange the log with parchment paper over the basket/trivet.
6. Close the top lid and make sure the valve is sealed.
7. Press "MANUAL" cooking function. Adjust cooking time to 25 minutes.
8. Allow pressure to build and cook the ingredients for the set time.
9. After the set cooking time ends, press "CANCEL" and then press "QPR". Instant Pot will quickly release pressure.
10. Open the top lid, add the cooked mixture in serving plates.
11. Serve warm with the remaining sauce on top.

Pineapple Steak Meal

Prep Time: 8-10 min.
Cooking Time: 20 min.
Number of Servings: 4
Ingredients:
- 2 pounds round steak, make chunks
- 1/2 teaspoon salt
- 1 tablespoon olive oil
- 1 large onion, chopped
- 1/8 teaspoon pepper
- 1 can pineapple chunks
- 1 can diced tomatoes
- 1 1/2 tablespoon Greek seasoning
- 2 large green peppers, chopped
- 1 can mild green chilies
- 1 cup water

- 2 tablespoons cornstarch + 1 tablespoon water

Directions:
1. Take an Instant Pot; open the top lid.
2. Press "SAUTÉ" cooking function.
3. In the cooking pot area, add the oil and onions. Cook until turn translucent and softened for 3 minutes.
4. Season the round steak with pepper and salt. Add to the pot; cook to brown for 4-5 minutes.
5. Add the pineapples, green pepper, chilis, and tomatoes. Mix in the Greek seasoning and then pour water on top.
6. Close the top lid and make sure the valve is sealed.
7. Press "MEAT/STEW" cooking function. Adjust cooking time to 15 minutes.
8. Allow pressure to build and cook the ingredients for the set time.
9. After the set cooking time ends, press "CANCEL" and then press "QPR". Instant Pot will quickly release pressure.
10. Open the top lid, add the cornstarch slurry and press the sauté button. Simmer until the sauce thickens.
11. Add the cooked mixture in serving plates.
12. Serve warm.

Chipotle Beef Roast

Prep Time: 8-10 min.
Cooking Time: 40 min.
Number of Servings: 7-8
Ingredients:
- 1 tablespoon ground cumin
- 1 lime, juiced
- 1/2 medium onion, chopped
- 5 cloves of garlic, minced
- 4 tablespoons chipotles in adobo sauce
- 1 cup water
- 3-pounds beef eye round roast, fat trimmed
- 1 tablespoon ground oregano
- 1/2 teaspoon ground cloves
- 2 1/2 teaspoon salt
- Black pepper as per taste
- 1 teaspoon oil
- 3 bay leaves

Directions:
1. Add the onion, garlic, cumin, lime juice, chipotles, oregano, and cloves in a blender. Add water and blend until smooth.
2. Season the beef with pepper and salt.
3. Take an Instant Pot; open the top lid.
4. Press "SAUTÉ" cooking function.
5. In the cooking pot area, add the oil and heat it.

6. Add the beef and cook for 5 minutes until it turns brown on all sides. Add the puree and bay leaves.
7. Close the top lid and make sure the valve is sealed.
8. Press "MANUAL" cooking function. Adjust cooking time to 35 minutes.
9. Allow pressure to build and cook the ingredients for the set time.
10. After the set cooking time ends, press "CANCEL" and then press "QPR". Instant Pot will quickly release pressure.
11. Open the top lid, remove the bay leave and shred the meat.
12. Add the cooked mixture in serving plates, adjust seasoning if needed. Serve warm.

Corn Potato Beef

Prep Time: 8-10 min.
Cooking Time: 25 min.
Number of Servings: 6-8
Ingredients:
- 3 cups beef broth
- 1 teaspoon olive oil
- Pepper and salt as needed
- 1-pound lean beef, make cubes
- 1 bay leaf
- ½ teaspoon dried oregano
- 1 onion, chopped
- 1 cup carrots, chopped
- 15-ounces tomato sauce
- 2 garlic cloves, minced
- 1 cup frozen corn, drained
- 1 cup celery, chopped
- 1 ½ cups red potatoes, cubed and skin removed

Directions:
1. Take an Instant Pot; open the top lid.
2. Press "SAUTÉ" cooking function.
3. In the cooking pot area, add the oil, garlic, dried oregano, and onions. Cook until turn translucent and softened for 1-2 minutes.
4. add the meat and cook for about 3–4 minutes to evenly brown.
5. Add the celery, carrots, pepper, and salt; stir-cook for more 3–4 minutes.
6. Add in the remaining ingredients; combine well.
7. Close the top lid and make sure the valve is sealed.
8. Press "MANUAL" cooking function. Adjust cooking time to 15-18 minutes.
9. Allow pressure to build and cook the ingredients for the set time.
10. After the set cooking time ends, press "CANCEL" and then press "NPR". Instant Pot will slowly and naturally release the pressure for 8-10 minutes.
11. Open the top lid, add the cooked mixture in serving plates.
12. Serve warm.

Beef Penne Meal

Prep Time: 8-10 min.
Cooking Time: 15 min.
Number of Servings: 5-6
Ingredients:
- 2 white onions, sliced
- 1 cup ground beef
- 3 tablespoons chives
- 8-ounces penne
- 1 teaspoon olive oil
- 1 teaspoon salt
- 2 tablespoons soy sauce
- 1 teaspoon turmeric
- 4 cups chicken stock
- ½ cup tomato sauce
- 1 teaspoon cilantro
- ½ tablespoon paprika

Directions:
1. Take an Instant Pot; open the top lid.
2. Press "SAUTÉ" cooking function.
3. In the cooking pot area, add the oil and onions.
4. Add the ground beef, salt, turmeric, cilantro, and paprika.
5. Stir the mixture well and sauté it for 4 minutes.
6. Remove the mixture from the pot and set aside.
7. In the pot, add the soy sauce, tomato sauce, and chives. Sauté the mixture for 3 minutes.
8. Add the pasta and chicken stock. Mix in the beef mixture.
9. Close the top lid and make sure the valve is sealed.
10. Press "MANUAL" cooking function. Adjust cooking time to 8 minutes.
11. Allow pressure to build and cook the ingredients for the set time.
12. After the set cooking time ends, press "CANCEL" and then press "QPR". Instant Pot will quickly release pressure.
13. Open the top lid, add the cooked mixture in serving plates.
14. Serve warm.

Classic Oregano Tenderloins

Prep Time: 8-10 min.
Cooking Time: 25 min.
Number of Servings: 6-8
Ingredients:
- 1 teaspoon onion powder
- 1 teaspoon garlic powder
- 2 teaspoons dried oregano
- 2 teaspoons dried thyme
- 1 teaspoon table salt
- 2 teaspoons olive oil
- 1 teaspoon black pepper

- 2-pounds lean pork tenderloin

Directions:
1. In a mixing bowl, mix together oregano, thyme, onion powder, garlic powder, salt, and pepper.
2. Coat the oil over the pork and sprinkle the herb mixture. Let it rest for 30 minutes to season.
3. Take an Instant Pot; open the top lid.
4. Pour 1 cup water and place steamer basket/trivet inside the cooking pot.
5. Arrange the pork over the basket/trivet.
6. Close the top lid and make sure the valve is sealed.
7. Press "MANUAL" cooking function. Adjust cooking time to 25 minutes.
8. Allow pressure to build and cook the ingredients for the set time.
9. After the set cooking time ends, press "CANCEL" and then press "QPR". Instant Pot will quickly release pressure.
10. Open the top lid, add the cooked mixture in serving plates.
11. Serve warm.

Worcestershire Pork Tenderloins

Prep Time: 8-10 min.
Cooking Time: 30 min.
Number of Servings: 5-6
Ingredients:
- 1 tablespoon chili powder
- 1 1/2 teaspoon ground cumin
- 1/4 teaspoon cayenne pepper
- 1 tablespoon paprika
- 2 tablespoons brown sugar
- 1 teaspoon salt
- 1 pepper, ground as per taste
- 1/4 cup apple cider vinegar
- 2 tablespoon molasses
- 1 1/2-pound pork tenderloin
- 1/3 cup ketchup
- 2 teaspoons Worcestershire sauce

Directions:
1. Prepare the rub by mixing the paprika, brown sugar, chili powder, cumin, cayenne pepper, salt, and black pepper.
2. Rub the spice mix on to the pork. Set aside 30 minutes to season.
3. Take an Instant Pot; open the top lid.
4. Pour 1 cup water and place steamer basket/trivet inside the cooking pot.
5. Arrange the pork over the basket/trivet.
6. Close the top lid and make sure the valve is sealed.
7. Press "MANUAL" cooking function. Adjust cooking time to 30 minutes.
8. Allow pressure to build and cook the ingredients for the set time.
9. After the set cooking time ends, press "CANCEL" and then press "QPR". Instant Pot will quickly release pressure.
10. Open the top lid, add the cooked mixture in serving plates.

11. Mix the remaining ingredients in a bowl and serve the pork with the bowl sauce on top.
12. Serve warm.

Cheesy Meat Pasta

Prep Time: 5 min.
Cooking Time: 8-10 min.
Number of Servings: 2
Ingredients:
- 4 ounces mozzarella cheese
- 1 cup pasta sauce
- 1 cup water
- ¼ pound ground beef
- ¼ pound ground pork
- 6 ounces ruffles pasta
- 4 ounces ricotta cheese
- Cooking oil

Directions:
1. Switch on the pot after placing it on a clean and dry platform. Press "Sauté" cooking function.
2. Open the pot lid; add the oil, pork, and beef in the pot; cook for 3-4 minutes to cook well and evenly browned.
3. Mix the water, pasta, and sauce.
4. Close the pot by closing the top lid. Also, ensure to seal the valve.
5. Press "Manual" cooking function and set cooking time to 5 minutes. It will start cooking after a few minutes. Let the pot mix cook under pressure until the timer reads zero.
6. Press "Cancel" cooking function and press "Quick release" setting.
7. Open the pot, mix the cheese and serve warm. Enjoy it with your loved one!

Honey Spiced Beef Ribs

Prep Time: 5-8min.
Cooking Time: 35 min.
Number of Servings: 4
Ingredients:
- ¼ cup honey
- ⅓ cup coconut aminos
- 1 teaspoon five spice powder
- 5 garlic cloves, minced
- 1 tablespoon ginger, grated
- ½ cup bone broth
- 2 pounds beef short ribs

Directions:
1. Switch on your instant pot after placing it on a clean and dry kitchen platform.
2. Open the pot lid and slowly start adding the above-mentioned ingredients in the pot. Give the ingredients a little stir.
3. Close the pot by closing the top lid. Also, ensure to seal the valve.

4. Press "Meat" cooking function and set cooking time to 35 minutes. It will start cooking after a few minutes. Let the pot mix cook under pressure until the timer reads zero.
5. Turn off and press "Cancel" cooking function. Allow the inside pressure to release naturally; it will take 8-10 minutes to release all inside pressure.
6. Open the pot and serve on a serving plate or bowl. Enjoy the Paleo dish!

Glazed Pepper Pork

Prep Time: 5-8min.
Cooking Time: 65-70 min.
Number of Servings: 3-4
Ingredients:
- 1 teaspoon dried sage
- ½ teaspoon black pepper
- 2 pounds boneless pork loin
- 1 garlic clove, minced
- ½ cup beef broth

Glaze:
- ½ cup coconut sugar
- ¼ cup balsamic vinegar
- 1 tablespoon arrowroot
- ½ cup water
- 2 tablespoon coconut aminos

Directions:
1. Mix the sage, garlic, and pepper in a small bowl. Rub this mixture into the meat.
2. Switch on your instant pot after placing it on a clean and dry kitchen platform.
3. Open the pot lid and slowly start adding the broth to the pot. Arrange the trivet inside it; arrange the meat over the trivet.
4. Close the pot by closing the top lid. Also, ensure to seal the valve.
5. Press "Manual" cooking function and set cooking time to 60 minutes. It will start cooking after a few minutes. Let the pot mix cook under pressure until the timer reads zero.
6. Turn off and press "Cancel" cooking function. Allow the inside pressure to release naturally; it will take 8-10 minutes to release all inside pressure.
7. Open the pot.
8. Mix the glaze ingredients in a bowl and add in your Instant Pot. Cook for 2 minutes on sauté.
9. Shred the meat and drizzle the glaze over. Serve warm!

Oregano Spiced Brisket

Prep Time: 8-10min.
Cooking Time: 65-70 min.
Number of Servings: 4
Ingredients:
- 1 teaspoon oregano
- 1 teaspoon ground ginger
- 1 teaspoon coconut sugar
- ½ cup beef broth

- ½ tablespoon liquid smoke
- 2 ½ pounds beef brisket
- 1 teaspoon cumin
- 1 teaspoon paprika
- ½ teaspoon pepper
- 1 tablespoon coconut oil

Directions:
1. Combine the spices in a bowl. Rub the spice mixture into the beef.
2. Switch on your instant pot after placing it on a clean and dry kitchen platform. Press "Saute" cooking function.
3. Open the pot lid; add the oil and beef in the pot; start cooking for 2-3 minutes per side to cook well and soften.
4. Combine the beef broth and liquid smoke and pour the mixture over the meat.
5. Close the pot by closing the top lid. Also, ensure to seal the valve.
6. Press "Manual" cooking function and set cooking time to 60 minutes. It will start cooking after a few minutes. Let the pot mix cook under pressure until the timer reads zero.
7. Turn off and press "Cancel" cooking function. Allow the inside pressure to release naturally; it will take 8-10 minutes to release all inside pressure.
8. Open the pot and serve on a serving plate or bowl. Enjoy the Paleo dish!

Classic Tomato Pork Ribs

Prep Time: 8-10min.
Cooking Time: 38-40 min.
Number of Servings: 3-4
Ingredients:
- ½ cup tomato sauce
- 2 racks of baby pork ribs
- 1 cup beef broth
- ½ tablespoon liquid smoke

Directions:
1. Cut the baby racks into quarters.
2. Switch on your instant pot after placing it on a clean and dry kitchen platform.
3. Pour the broth into the cooking pot area. Arrange the trivet inside it; arrange the meat over the trivet.
4. Close the pot by closing the top lid. Also, ensure to seal the valve.
5. Press "Meat" cooking function and set cooking time to 30 minutes. It will start cooking after a few minutes. Let the pot mix cook under pressure until the timer reads zero.
6. Turn off and press "Cancel" cooking function. Quick release pressure.
7. Open the pot.
8. In a bowl, mix the tomato sauce and liquid smoke; brush the mixture over the pork ribs.
9. Cook the ribs for about 4 minutes per side on saute mode. Serve and enjoy.

Lime Chili Roast

Prep Time: 8-10min.

Cooking Time: 65 min.
Number of Servings: 4
Ingredients:
- 4 garlic cloves, minced
- 2 pounds chuck roast
- 1 onion, sliced
- Juice of 2 limes
- 1 tablespoon oregano
- ½ teaspoon black pepper
- 1 tablespoon cumin
- ½ cup water
- 8 ounces canned green chilies, chopped

Directions:
1. Switch on your instant pot after placing it on a clean and dry kitchen platform.
2. Open the pot lid and slowly start adding the ingredients mentioned above in the pot. Give the ingredients a little stir.
3. Close the pot by closing the top lid. Also, ensure to seal the valve.
4. Press "Manual" cooking function and set cooking time to 60 minutes. It will start cooking after a few minutes. Let the pot mix cook under pressure until the timer reads zero.
5. Turn off and press "Cancel" cooking function. Quick release pressure.
6. Open the pot and shred the meat.
7. Choose the sauté mode and cook for about 4-5 minutes. Serve warm!

Classic Lamb & Figs

Prep Time: 8-10min.
Cooking Time: 20 min.
Number of Servings: 4
Ingredients:
- 2 tablespoons ground ginger
- 2 garlic cloves, minced
- 2 tablespoons apple cider vinegar
- 2 tablespoons coconut aminos
- 2 tablespoons coconut oil
- 4 lamb shanks
- 10 dried figs, halved lengthwise
- 1 ½ cups bone broth
- 1 onion, sliced

Directions:
1. Switch on your instant pot after placing it on a clean and dry kitchen platform. Press "Saute" cooking function.
2. Open the pot lid; add the 1 tablespoon of coconut oil and 2 shanks in the pot; start cooking for 3 minutes per side to cook well and soften. Set aside.
3. Repeat the process with the remaining shanks.
4. Add the ginger and onion in empty pot and cook for about 3 minutes. Mix in the rest of the ingredients.

5. Add all of the lamb shanks to the pot.
6. Close the pot by closing the top lid. Also, ensure to seal the valve.
7. Press "Manual" cooking function and set cooking time to 5 minutes. It will start cooking after a few minutes. Let the pot mix cook under pressure until the timer reads zero.
8. Turn off and press "Cancel" cooking function. Quick release pressure.
9. Open the pot and serve on a serving plate or bowl. Enjoy the Paleo dish!

Smoky Pork Roast

Prep Time: 8-10min.
Cooking Time: 70-75 min.
Number of Servings: 4
Ingredients:
- 2 tablespoons liquid smoke
- 2 tablespoons coconut sugar
- 2 tablespoons coconut aminos
- ½ cup water
- 2 pounds pork roast
- 1 tablespoon olive oil

Directions:
1. Switch on your instant pot after placing it on a clean and dry kitchen platform. Press "Saute" cooking function.
2. Open the pot lid; add the oil and meat in the pot; start cooking for 3 minutes per side to cook well and browned. Transfer the meat to a plate.
3. Combine all of the remaining ingredients in the pot and mix the meat.
4. Close the pot by closing the top lid. Also, ensure to seal the valve.
5. Press "Manual" cooking function and set cooking time to 60 minutes. It will start cooking after a few minutes. Let the pot mix cook under pressure until the timer reads zero.
6. Turn off and press "Cancel" cooking function. Allow the inside pressure to release naturally; it will take 8-10 minutes to release all inside pressure.
7. Open the pot and serve on a serving plate or bowl. Enjoy the Paleo dish!

Goat Tomato Curry

Prep Time: 10-15 min.
Cooking Time: 50 min.
Number of Servings: 5-6
Ingredients:
- 2 onions (diced)
- 3 cloves garlic (minced)
- 1 ½ inch knob fresh ginger (minced)
- 2 teaspoons salt
- 1 teaspoon turmeric powder
- ½ pound sweet potatoes (cut in half)
- 1 teaspoon spice mix
- 2-pound goat meat (or lamb) with bone
- 2 tablespoons avocado oil
- 4 cardamom pods

- 1 teaspoon cumin powder
- 1 tablespoon coriander powder
- 1 bay leaf
- 4 cloves (whole)
- 1 teaspoon paprika
- 1 teaspoon Kashmiri chili powder
- 2 cans organic tomatoes (diced)
- ½ cup water

Directions:
1. Switch on your instant pot after placing it on a clean and dry kitchen platform. Press "Saute" cooking function.
2. Open the pot lid; add the oil and meat in the pot; start cooking to brown the meat.
3. Add the ginger, diced onion, minced garlic, cloves, bay leaf, salt, cardamom, coriander, cumin, turmeric, Kashmiri chili powder, paprika, and spice mix.
4. Cook for about 3 minutes. Mix the sweet potatoes, diced tomatoes, and water.
5. Close the pot by closing the top lid. Also, ensure to seal the valve.
6. Press "Manual" cooking function and set cooking time to 45 minutes. It will start cooking after a few minutes. Let the pot mix cook under pressure until the timer reads zero.
7. Turn off and press "Cancel" cooking function. Allow the inside pressure to release naturally; it will take 8-10 minutes to release all inside pressure.
8. Open the pot and serve on a serving plate or bowl. Enjoy the Paleo dish!

Beef Tomato Meatballs

Prep Time: 8-10 min.
Cooking Time: 20 min.
Number of Servings: 6
Ingredients:
- 2 cups tomatoes, diced
- 2 large eggs
- 1 tablespoon olive oil
- 1 pound lean ground beef
- 3 tablespoons almond flour

Directions:
1. In a bowl (medium-large size), thoroughly mix the meat, eggs, and almond flour. Mix well and make meatballs of 1 ½ inch.
2. Grease a baking dish with some oil and add the meatballs. Add the tomatoes and tightly wrap with a foil.
3. Take your Instant Pot and place over dry kitchen surface; open its top lid and switch it on.
4. Pour 1 cup water in the cooking pot area. Arrange the trivet or steamer basket inside it; arrange the dish over the trivet/basket.
5. Close its top lid and make sure that its valve it closed to avoid spillage.
6. Press "MANUAL". Adjust the timer to 20 minutes.
7. Pressure will slowly build up; let the added ingredients to cook until the timer indicates zero.
8. Press "CANCEL". Now press "QPR" to quickly release pressure.
9. Open the top lid, transfer the cooked recipe in serving plates.
10. Serve the recipe warm.

Tomato Chili Pork

Prep Time: 8-10 min.
Cooking Time: 35 min.
Number of Servings: 8
Ingredients:

- 2 cups Roma tomatoes, whole
- 2 yellow bell peppers, make slices
- 2 cups beef stock, low-sodium
- 1 pound pork neck, fat removed and chopped
- 2 green chili peppers, diced

Directions:
1. Take your Instant Pot and place over dry kitchen surface; open its top lid and switch it on.
2. Press "SAUTÉ". Grease the pot with some cooking oil.
3. Add the peppers; cook for 3-4 minutes, stirring constantly.
4. Add the tomatoes and cook for 4-5 minutes. Season as needed and mix in the stock.
5. Close its top lid and make sure that its valve it closed to avoid spillage.
6. Press "MANUAL". Adjust the timer to 25 minutes.
7. Pressure will slowly build up; let the added ingredients to cook until the timer indicates zero.
8. Press "CANCEL". Now press "QPR" to quickly release pressure.
9. Open the top lid, transfer the cooked recipe in serving plates.
10. Serve the recipe warm.

Beef Green Beans

Prep Time: 8-10 min.
Cooking Time: 5 min.
Number of Servings: 4
Ingredients:

- 7 ounce green beans, canned
- 2 spring onions, chopped
- 1 tablespoon olive oil
- 10 ounce beef sirloin, fat removed
- 2 tablespoons soy sauce

Directions:
1. Take your Instant Pot and place over dry kitchen surface; open its top lid and switch it on.
2. Press "SAUTÉ". Grease the pot with some cooking oil.
3. Add the meat; stir-cook for 2-3 minutes to evenly brown.
4. Mix in the onions, and green beans. Add the soy sauce; cook for another 2-3 minutes, stirring constantly.
5. Serve warm.

Rosemary Lamb

Prep Time: 8-10 min.
Cooking Time: 50 min.
Number of Servings: 7-8
Ingredients:

- 2 onions, chopped
- 2 rosemary sprigs
- 3 cups beef broth, low-sodium
- 2 lamb shanks, about 1 pound each
- 2 bay leaves

Directions:
1. Take your Instant Pot and place over dry kitchen surface; open its top lid and switch it on.
2. Press "SAUTÉ". Grease the pot with some cooking oil.
3. Add the meat; stir-cook for 4-5 minutes to evenly brown. Set aside.
4. Add the onions; cook for 3-4 minutes until turn translucent and softened.
5. Add the meat and pour in the broth.
6. Add the remaining ingredients and stir well.
7. Close its top lid and make sure that its valve it closed to avoid spillage.
8. Press "MANUAL". Adjust the timer to 40 minutes.
9. Pressure will slowly build up; let the added ingredients to cook until the timer indicates zero.
10. Press "CANCEL". Now press "QPR" to quickly release pressure.
11. Open the top lid, transfer the cooked recipe in serving plates.
12. Remove the rosemary sprigs and bay leaves. Serve the recipe warm.

Beef Corn Chili

Prep Time: 8-10 min.
Cooking Time: 30 min.
Number of Servings: 8
Ingredients:
- 2 small onions, chopped (finely)
- 1/4 cup canned corn
- 1 tablespoon oil
- 10 ounce lean ground beef
- 2 small chili peppers, diced

Directions:
1. Take your Instant Pot and place over dry kitchen surface; open its top lid and switch it on.
2. Press "SAUTÉ".
3. In its cooking pot, add and heat the oil.
4. Add the onions, chili pepper, and beef; cook for 2-3 minutes until turn translucent and softened.
5. Add the 3 cups water in the cooking pot; combine to mix well.
6. Close its top lid and make sure that its valve it closed to avoid spillage.
7. Press "MEAT/STEW". Adjust the timer to 20 minutes.
8. Pressure will slowly build up; let the added ingredients to cook until the timer indicates zero.
9. Press "CANCEL". Now press "NPR" for natural release pressure. Instant Pot will gradually release pressure for about 8-10 minutes.
10. Open the top lid, transfer the cooked recipe in serving plates.
11. Serve the recipe warm.

Mushroom Beef Meal

Prep Time: 8-10 min.
Cooking Time: 40 min.
Number of Servings: 6
Ingredients:
- 2 cups button mushrooms, make slices
- 1 bacon slice, chopped
- 3 cups beef stock, low sodium
- 1 pound beef ribs, fat removed
- Salt as needed

Directions:
1. Season the meat with salt.
2. Take your Instant Pot and place over dry kitchen surface; open its top lid and switch it on.
3. Add the meat and stock in the cooking pot. Stir the ingredients to combine well.
4. Close its top lid and make sure that its valve it closed to avoid spillage.
5. Press "MANUAL". Adjust the timer to 30 minutes.
6. Pressure will slowly build up; let the added ingredients to cook until the timer indicates zero.
7. Press "CANCEL". Now press "NPR" for natural release pressure. Instant Pot will gradually release pressure for about 8-10 minutes.
8. Take out the meat; using a knife, shred it.
9. Add the shredded meat in the pot, add the bacon and mushrooms; gently stir to combine.
10. Press "MANUAL". Adjust the timer to 7 minutes.
11. Pressure will slowly build up; let the added ingredients to cook until the timer indicates zero.
12. Press "CANCEL". Now press "QPR" to quickly release pressure.
13. Open the top lid, transfer the cooked recipe in serving plates.
14. Serve the recipe warm.

Sausage Rice Meal

Prep Time: 8-10 min.
Cooking Time: 15 min.
Number of Servings: 6
Ingredients:
- 2 ounce chorizo sausage, thinly sliced
- 1 large red bell pepper, chopped
- 1 teaspoon butter
- 2 cups rice, cooked
- 2 large eggs, beaten

Directions:
1. Take your Instant Pot and place over dry kitchen surface; open its top lid and switch it on.
2. Press "SAUTÉ".
3. In its cooking pot, add and heat the butter.
4. Add the sausage; stir-cook for 2-3 minutes per side to evenly brown.
5. Mix in the beaten eggs; cook for 2-3 minutes.
6. Mix in the rice, and bell pepper. Stir-cook for 5 minutes; serve warm.

Lemon Beef Meal

Prep Time: 8-10 min.
Cooking Time: 10 min.
Number of Servings: 2
Ingredients:
- 2 tablespoons lemon juice
- 1 garlic clove, crushed
- 1 tablespoon oil
- 2 beef steaks, about 3 ½ ounce each
- ½ teaspoon garlic salt

Directions:
1. Take your Instant Pot and place over dry kitchen surface; open its top lid and switch it on.
2. Press "SAUTÉ".
3. In its cooking pot, add and heat the oil.
4. Add the meat and salt; stir-cook for 4-5 minutes to evenly brown.
5. Add the garlic and cook for 1-2 minutes.
6. Serve with lemon juice on top.

Sweet Potato Beef

Prep Time: 8-10 min.
Cooking Time: 40 min.
Number of Servings: 4
Ingredients:
- 1 tomato, roughly chopped
- 2 bell peppers, make slices
- 4 cups beef stock, low-sodium
- 1 pound lean beef stew meat
- 1 small sweet potato, diced

Directions:
1. Take your Instant Pot and place over dry kitchen surface; open its top lid and switch it on.
2. Press "SAUTÉ". Grease the pot with some cooking oil.
3. Add the meat; stir-cook to evenly brown.
4. Mix in the stock and vegetables.
5. Close its top lid and make sure that its valve it closed to avoid spillage.
6. Press "MANUAL". Adjust the timer to 35 minutes.
7. Pressure will slowly build up; let the added ingredients to cook until the timer indicates zero.
8. Press "CANCEL". Now press "NPR" for natural release pressure. Instant Pot will gradually release pressure for about 8-10 minutes.
9. Open the top lid, transfer the cooked recipe in serving plates.
10. Serve the recipe warm.

Pork Potato Lunch

Prep Time: 8-10 min.
Cooking Time: 25 min.
Number of Servings: 4
Ingredients:

- 10 ounce pork neck, fat removed and make small pieces
- 1 medium sweet potato, chopped
- 1 tablespoon oil
- 3 cups beef stock, low-sodium
- 1 onion, chopped (finely)

Directions:

1. Take your Instant Pot and place over dry kitchen surface; open its top lid and switch it on.
2. Press "SAUTÉ". Grease the pot with some cooking oil.
3. Add the onions; cook for 2 minutes until turn translucent and softened.
4. Add the meat; stir-cook for 4-5 minutes to evenly brown.
5. Mix in the stock and potatoes.
6. Close its top lid and make sure that its valve it closed to avoid spillage.
7. Press "MANUAL". Adjust the timer to 20 minutes.
8. Pressure will slowly build up; let the added ingredients to cook until the timer indicates zero.
9. Press "CANCEL". Now press "NPR" for natural release pressure. Instant Pot will gradually release pressure for about 8-10 minutes.
10. Open the top lid, transfer the cooked recipe in serving plates.
11. Serve the recipe warm.

Veal Cheese Meal

Prep Time: 8-10 min.
Cooking Time: 40 min.
Number of Servings: 8
Ingredients:

- 2 cups cherry tomatoes
- ¼ cup coconut milk, reduced fat
- 1 tablespoon olive oil
- 2 veal steaks, fat removed
- 3 tablespoons Cheddar cheese, grated

Directions:

1. Take your Instant Pot and place over dry kitchen surface; open its top lid and switch it on.
2. Press "SAUTÉ". Grease the pot with some cooking oil.
3. Add the meat; stir-cook for 3-4 minutes to evenly brown.
4. Add 1 cup water and mix well.
5. Close its top lid and make sure that its valve it closed to avoid spillage.
6. Press "MANUAL". Adjust the timer to 25 minutes.
7. Pressure will slowly build up; let the added ingredients to cook until the timer indicates zero.
8. Press "CANCEL". Now press "QPR" to quickly release pressure.
9. Open the top lid, drain the liquid, transfer the mix in a serving plate.
10. Empty the pot.

11. Press "SAUTÉ". Add the tomatoes and ¼ cup of water and cook for 8-10 minutes.
12. Stir the cheese and milk; cook until the cheese melts.
13. Add over the meat mixture and serve.

Beef Asparagus Salad

Prep Time: 8-10 min.
Cooking Time: 10 min.
Number of Servings: 4
Ingredients:
- 7 ounce asparagus, make small pieces
- 1 teaspoon dried thyme
- 2 teaspoons olive oil
- 7 ounce beef steaks, 2-3 pieces
- ½ teaspoon smoked salt
- Lemon juice as needed

Directions:
1. Coat the steak with salt and thyme.
2. Take your Instant Pot and place over dry kitchen surface; open its top lid and switch it on.
3. Press "SAUTÉ".
4. In its cooking pot, add and heat the oil.
5. Add the steak; stir-cook for 4-5 minutes to evenly brown.
6. Add the asparagus and cook for 4-5 minutes. Set aside the mix in a bowl.
7. Shred the meat and mix well. Top with the lemon juice and serve.

Hearty Beef Stew

Prep Time: 10 minutes
Cooking Time: 45 minutes
Number of Servings: 2
Ingredients:
- 1 pound chuck beef
- 1 teaspoon salt
- 1/2 teaspoon black pepper
- 2 tablespoons butter
- 1 onion, chopped
- 2 carrots, sliced
- 1 celery stalk, sliced
- 1 teaspoon thyme
- 1/2 teaspoon rosemary
- 2 tablespoons flour
- 1 tablespoon tomato paste
- 2 cups beef broth
- 1/2 pound potatoes, chopped

Directions:
1. Season the beef with salt and pepper. Melt the butter in the Instant Pot on Saute mode. Brown beef in butter. Remove to a plate.

2. Add onion, carrots, and celery to the pot. Cook until onion is translucent, then add thym, rosemary and toast 30 seconds. Add flour and stir until everything is well-coated.
3. Add tomato paste, then beef broth and scrape off anything stuck to the bottom of the pot. potatoes and replace beef in pot.
4. Close lid and set cooking time to 35 minutes on high pressure. Season to taste with salt and pepper.

Yankee Pot Roast

Prep Time: 10 minutes
Cooking Time: 45 minutes
Number of Servings: 6
Ingredients:
- 1 3-pound chuck roast
- 1 teaspoon salt
- 1/2 teaspoon black pepper
- 2 tablespoons olive oil
- 1 onion, chopped
- 2 carrots, sliced
- 2 stalks celery, sliced
- 1 can tomato paste
- 2 cups beef stock
- 2 thyme sprigs
- 2 bay leaves

Directions:
1. Season beef with salt and pepper. Heat olive oil in Instant Pot on Saute mode. Brown beef on all sides. Remove to a plate.
2. Add onion, carrots, and celery to the pot and brown in the droppings. Stir in tomato paste and beef stock. Replace beef in the pot. Add thyme and bay leaf.
3. Close lid and set cooking time to 45 minutes on high pressure.
4. Discard bay leaf and thyme. Serve pot roast with mashed potatoes.

American Chop Suey

Prep Time: 5 minutes
Cooking Time: 15 minutes
Number of Servings: 4
Ingredients:
- 1 tablespoon olive oil
- 1/2 pound ground beef
- 1 onion, diced
- 2 cloves garlic, minced
- 1 can whole tomatoes in their juice, crushed
- 1/2 cup beef stock
- 1 tablespoon Worcestershire sauce
- 1/2 teaspoon salt
- 1/2 teaspoon black pepper
- 1/2 pound uncooked macaroni
- 1 cup shredded mozzarella cheese

Directions:
1. Heat olive oil in Instant Pot on Saute mode. Brown beef and drain excess fat, then add onions and garlic.
2. Pour in tomatoes, stock, Worcestershire, salt, and pepper. Stir in pasta and half of the cheese.
3. Close lid and set cooking time to 8 minutes on high pressure. Use quick release to remove steam.
4. Sprinkle the remaining cheese over the pasta and close lid until the cheese is melted. Serve.

Sunday Beef Brisket

Prep Time: 10 minutes
Cooking Time: 1 hour
Number of Servings: 6
Ingredients:

- 1 3-pound brisket
- 1 teaspoon salt
- 1 teaspoon black pepper
- 2 tablespoons olive oil
- 3 carrots, sliced
- 1 onion, sliced
- 1 celery stalk, sliced
- 2 cups beef stock
- 2 tablespoons tomato paste
- 1 bay leaf

Directions:
1. Season beef with salt and pepper. Heat oil in Instant Pot on Saute mode. Brown brisket on both sides and transfer to a plate.
2. Add carrots, onion, and celery to the pot. Brown lightly, then add stock, tomato paste, and bay leaf. Replace beef in pot.
3. Close lid and set cooking time to 50 minutes.
4. Discard bay leaf and season sauce to taste with salt and pepper.

Applesauce Pork Chops

Prep Time: 10 minutes
Cooking Time: 8 minutes
Number of Servings: 4
Ingredients:
- 4 bone-in pork chops
- 1/2 teaspoon salt
- 1/2 teaspoon black pepper
- 1 apple, grated or cut into small pieces
- 1 onion, sliced
- 1 cup apple cider

Directions:
1. Season the pork chops with salt and pepper. Place in Instant Pot and cover with apple, onion, and cider.
2. Close lid and set cooking time to 8 minutes on high pressure. Use quick release to remove steam.

3. Transfer pork chops to a serving plate. Set Instant Pot to Saute. Mash the apples, reduce sauce to desired consistency, and season to taste.
4. Serve applesauce over pork.

Pork Carnitas

Prep Time: 5 minutes
Cooking Time: 30 minutes
Number of Servings: 6
Ingredients:
- 2 pounds pork shoulder
- 1 teaspoon salt
- 1 teaspoon cumin
- 1 teaspoon dried oregano
- 1/2 teaspoon black pepper
- 1 onion, chopped
- 2 garlic cloves, minced
- 1 bay leaf
- 2 cups chicken stock
- Juice of 1 orange
- Juice of 2 limes

Directions:
1. Rub pork with salt, cumin, oregano, and pepper. Place in Instant Pot with onion, garlic, bay leaf, chicken stock, and fruit juice.
2. Close lid and set cooking time for 30 minutes on high pressure.
3. Transfer pork to a serving dish, leaving the juice in the pot. Shred into strands using 2 forks.
4. Serve in tacos or burritos with limes for squeezing.

Barbecue Pork Ribs

Prep Time: 5 minutes
Cooking Time: 25 minutes
Number of Servings: 4
Ingredients:
- 1 rack baby back ribs
- 1 teaspoon salt
- 1 teaspoon black pepper
- 1 cup water
- 1/2 cup barbecue sauce

Directions:
1. Season ribs with salt and pepper. Place in Instant Pot with 1 cup water. Close lid and set cooking time for 20 minutes.
2. When ribs are finished, lay on a foil-lined baking sheet and brush with barbecue sauce. Place under broiler 5 minutes or until sauce bubbles and begins to brown.

Chapter 10: Warm Soups & Stews

Seafood Mix Stew

Prep Time: 5-8 min.
Cooking Time: 25 min.
Number of Servings: 6-7
Ingredients:
- ¼ teaspoon red pepper flakes
- ½ teaspoon pepper
- 2-pounds seafood medley (shrimps, scallops, crab legs, mussels, squid, fish etc.)
- 4 cups vegetable broth
- 1 can crushed tomatoes
- ½ teaspoon salt
- 1 teaspoon dried basil
- 1 teaspoon dried thyme
- ½ teaspoon celery salt
- 1 teaspoon dried cilantro
- ½ medium onion, diced
- 3 cloves garlic, minced

Directions:
1. Arrange your Instant Pot over a dry, clean platform. Plug it in power socket and turn it on.
2. Now press "Saute" mode from available options. In the cooking area, add the oil and garlic; cook for 1-2 minutes to soften.
3. Stir in onion and sauté until soft for 4-5 more minutes.
4. Mix the pepper flakes, pepper, salt, celery salt, cilantro, basil, and thyme. Cook for 1 more minute.
5. Add the tomatoes and cook until heated through for 5 more minutes. Add the broth and seafood medley.
6. Close the lid and lock. Ensure that you have sealed the valve to avoid leakage.
7. Press "Steam" mode from available cooking settings and set cooking time to 10 minutes. Instant Pot will start cooking the ingredients after a few minutes.
8. After the timer reads zero, press "Cancel" and quick release pressure.
9. Carefully remove the lid and serve the prepared keto dish warm!

Pork Veggie Soup

Prep Time: 10 min.
Cooking Time: 30 min.
Number of Servings: 5-6
Ingredients:
- 1 small onion, diced
- 3 baby carrots
- 4 cup water
- ½ chopped head cabbage
- 1 tablespoon olive oil

- 1 pound pork, ground
- Ground pepper, dry basil, garlic powder and salt as needed
- 2/3 cup coconut aminos
- 2 tablespoons arrowroot starch (optional)

Directions:
1. Arrange your Instant Pot over a dry, clean platform. Plug it in power socket and turn it on.
2. Now press "Saute" mode from available options. In the cooking area, add the oil and pork; cook until turn brown.
3. Add the onion and cook for 3 more minutes. Add all remaining ingredients.
4. Close the lid and lock. Ensure that you have sealed the valve to avoid leakage.
5. Press "Manual" mode from available cooking settings and set cooking time to 25 minutes. Instant Pot will start cooking the ingredients after a few minutes.
6. After the timer reads zero, press "Cancel"; press "NPR" to naturally release pressure. It takes about 8-10 minutes to release pressure naturally.
7. Carefully remove the lid and serve the prepared keto dish warm!

Kale Lentil Vegetarian Soup

Prep Time: 10-12 min.
Cooking Time: 25 min.
Number of Servings: 4
Ingredients:
- 2 cloves garlic, minced
- 1 can coconut milk
- 1 tablespoon coconut oil
- 1 can tomatoes, diced
- 1 ½ cups dry red lentils
- ½ teaspoon red pepper flakes
- 1 tablespoon ginger, minced
- 2 tablespoons curry powder
- 4 cups vegetable broth
- 1 large onion, chopped
- 2 tablespoons tomato paste
- 3 handfuls chopped kale
- Pepper and salt as needed

To Garnish:
- Chopped cilantro and sour cream

Directions:

1. Arrange your Instant Pot over a dry, clean platform. Plug it in power socket and turn it on.
2. Now press "Saute" mode from available options. In the cooking area, add the oil, ginger, garlic, and onions; cook for 2-3 minutes to soften.
3. Add the curry powder, paste and pepper flakes. Cook for 1-2 more minute. Mix the broth, tomatoes, milk, and lentils.
4. Close the lid and lock. Ensure that you have sealed the valve to avoid leakage.
5. Press "Manual" mode from available cooking settings and set cooking time to 20 minutes. Instant Pot will start cooking the ingredients after a few minutes.
6. After the timer reads zero, press "Cancel"; press "NPR" to naturally release pressure. It takes about 8-10 minutes to release pressure naturally.
7. Carefully remove the lid. Add the kale and season as needed.
8. Garnish with cilantro and sour cream.

Squash Chicken Mushroom Soup

Prep Time: 5-8 min.
Cooking Time: 15 min.
Number of Servings: 4
Ingredients:

- 2 cups chopped mushrooms
- 1 yellow summer squash, chopped
- 1 pound boneless, skinless chicken breast, make large chunks
- 2 ½ cups chicken broth
- 1 onion, make thin slices
- 3 garlic cloves, minced
- 1 teaspoon salt
- 1 teaspoon Italian seasoning or poultry seasoning
- 1 teaspoon (ground) black pepper
- 1 cup heavy (whipping) cream

Directions:

1. Take your Instant Pot; open the top lid. Plug it and turn it on.
2. In the cooking pot area, add the onion, garlic, mushrooms, squash, chicken, chicken broth, salt, pepper, and Italian seasoning. Using a spatula, stir the ingredients.
3. Close the top lid and seal its valve.
4. Press "MANUAL" setting. Adjust cooking time to 15 minutes.
5. Allow the recipe to cook for the set cooking time.
6. After the set cooking time ends, press "CANCEL" and then press "NPR (Natural Pressure Release)".
7. Instant Pot will slowly and naturally release the pressure.
8. Unlock the lid; transfer the chicken pieces to a bowl and set aside.
9. Using an immersion blender, purée the vegetables.
10. Shred the chicken and stir it back into the soup. Add the cream and stir well.
11. Serve warm.

Vietnamese Chicken Soup

Prep Time: 8-10 min.
Cooking Time: 40 min.
Number of Servings: 2-3
Ingredients:

- 1 small onion, make quarters
- ½ tablespoon coriander seeds, toasted
- 1-pound chicken pieces, bone in and skin on
- A small ginger piece, grated
- ½ teaspoon cardamom pods
- ½ lemongrass stalk, chopped
- ½ cinnamon stick
- ½ cardamom pods
- 2 cloves
- 2 tablespoons fish sauce
- ½ bok choy, chopped
- ½ daikon root, spiralized
- 1 tablespoon green onions, chopped

Directions:
1. Take an Instant Pot; open the top lid.
2. Add the chicken with ginger, onion, coriander seeds, cardamom, cloves, lemongrass, fish sauce, daikon, bok choy and water in the cooking pot. Using a spatula, gently stir to combine well.
3. Close the top lid and make sure the valve is sealed.
4. Press "MANUAL" cooking function. Adjust cooking time to 30 minutes.
5. Allow pressure to build and cook the ingredients for the set time.
6. After the set cooking time ends, press "CANCEL" and then press "QPR". Instant Pot will quickly release pressure.
7. Open the top lid, shred the chicken, add the cooked mixture in serving plates.
8. Serve warm with onions on top.

Creamy Lentil Stew

Prep Time: 8-10 min.
Cooking Time: 30 min.
Number of Servings: 5-6
Ingredients:

- ½ teaspoon sugar
- 2 carrots, chopped
- 2 cups lentils
- 5 cups beef stock
- 1 teaspoon salt
- 1 tablespoon ground black pepper
- 1 tablespoon sour cream
- ¼ cup thyme leaves, chopped
- ½ lemon, sliced

Directions:

1. Mix the salt, sugar, black pepper, and cream together in a mixing bowl.
2. Mix the thyme to the spice mixture.
3. Take an Instant Pot; open the top lid.
4. Add the lemon, lentils, and beef stock. Add the spice mixture in the cooking pot. Using a spatula, gently stir to combine well.
5. Close the top lid and make sure the valve is sealed.
6. Press "MANUAL" cooking function. Adjust cooking time to 30 minutes.
7. Allow pressure to build and cook the ingredients for the set time.
8. After the set cooking time ends, press "CANCEL" and then press "QPR". Instant Pot will quickly release pressure.
9. Open the top lid, add the cooked mixture in serving plates.
10. Serve warm.

Turkey Brown Rice Soup

Prep Time: 8-10 min.
Cooking Time: 10 min.
Number of Servings: 7-8
Ingredients:

- 1 (15 oz.) can of diced tomatoes
- 3 cups beef stock
- 1 (15 oz.) can of tomato sauce
- 1 tablespoon chili seasoning
- ½ teaspoon basil
- 1 cup cooked brown rice
- 1 cup chopped onion
- 1-pound lean ground turkey
- 2 cups chopped bell peppers

Directions:

1. Take an Instant Pot; open the top lid.
2. Press "SAUTÉ" cooking function.
3. Coat the pot with cooking spray. In the cooking pot area, add the onions, ground turkey and cook until brown.
4. Mix in the tomatoes, tomato sauce, stock, and spices.
5. Close the top lid and make sure the valve is sealed.
6. Press "MANUAL" cooking function. Adjust cooking time to 10 minutes.
7. Allow pressure to build and cook the ingredients for the set time.
8. After the set cooking time ends, press "CANCEL" and then press "QPR". Instant Pot will quickly release pressure.
9. Open the top lid, add cooked brown rice.
10. Stir well and let it sit for just 5 minutes. Serve warm.

Chicken Bean Soup

Prep Time: 8-10 min.
Cooking Time: 8 min.
Number of Servings: 3-4

Ingredients:
- 1 (15.5 oz.) can light kidney beans, drained
- 1 8 oz. can tomato sauce
- 1 small chopped onion
- 1 (15.5 oz.) can seasoned black beans, drained
- 10 oz. frozen corn
- 1 teaspoon cumin
- 1 teaspoon chili powder
- 2 10 oz. cans diced tomatoes with green chilis
- 1 packet taco seasoning
- 2 boneless, skinless chicken breast
- ½ cup water

Directions:
1. Take an Instant Pot; open the top lid.
2. Add the ingredients to the cooking pot. Using a spatula, gently stir to combine well.
3. Close the top lid and make sure the valve is sealed.
4. Press "MANUAL" cooking function. Adjust cooking time to 8 minutes.
5. Allow pressure to build and cook the ingredients for the set time.
6. After the set cooking time ends, press "CANCEL" and then press "NPR". Instant Pot will slowly and naturally release the pressure for 8-10 minutes.
7. Open the top lid, shred the meat, add the cooked mixture in serving plates.
8. Serve warm.

Mixed Bean Chicken Stew

Prep Time: 8-10 min.
Cooking Time: 10 min.
Number of Servings: 6
Ingredients:
- 1 ½ pounds chicken breast, skinless and boneless
- 15 oz. black beans
- 15 oz. corn
- 30 oz. great northern beans, rinsed
- 15 oz. kidney beans, rinsed
- 1 ½ cups diced celery stalks
- 1 tablespoon crushed red pepper
- 2 teaspoons garlic powder
- ½ cup chopped onions
- 3 cups water
- 2 teaspoons chili powder
- ½ teaspoon cumin

Directions:
1. Take an Instant Pot; open the top lid.
2. Press "SAUTÉ" cooking function.
3. Coat the pot with cooking spray. In the cooking pot area, add the celery and onions. Cook until turn translucent and softened for 1-2 minutes.

4. Add the beans, corn, water, and spices. Stir well and place the chicken on top.
5. Close the top lid and make sure the valve is sealed.
6. Press "MANUAL" cooking function. Adjust cooking time to 10 minutes.
7. Allow pressure to build and cook the ingredients for the set time.
8. After the set cooking time ends, press "CANCEL" and then press "NPR". Instant Pot will slowly and naturally release the pressure for 8-10 minutes.
9. Open the top lid, shred the meat; add the cooked mixture in serving plates.
10. Serve warm.

Bean Pepper Soup

Prep Time: 8-10 min.
Cooking Time: 40 min.
Number of Servings: 2-3
Ingredients:
- 1 red bell pepper, chopped
- 3-ounces tomatoes, chopped
- 1 small yellow onion, chopped
- 1 green bell pepper, chopped
- 1 celery stalk, chopped
- 1/3 teaspoon hot sauce
- ½ tablespoon chili powder
- ½ pound black beans
- A pinch of salt and black pepper
- 1 teaspoon paprika
- ½ tablespoon cumin
- 1 bay leaf
- 2 cups veggie stock

Directions:
1. Take an Instant Pot; open the top lid.
2. Add the onion with red bell pepper, green bell pepper, tomatoes, celery, black beans, salt, pepper, hot sauce, chili powder, cumin, paprika, bay leaf and stock in the cooking pot. Using a spatula, gently stir to combine well.
3. Close the top lid and make sure the valve is sealed.
4. Press "MANUAL" cooking function. Adjust cooking time to 40 minutes.
5. Allow pressure to build and cook the ingredients for the set time.
6. After the set cooking time ends, press "CANCEL" and then press "QPR". Instant Pot will quickly release pressure.
7. Open the top lid, add the cooked mixture in serving plates.
8. Serve warm.

Turkey Bean Soup

Prep Time: 8-10 min.
Cooking Time: 20 min.
Number of Servings: 5-6
Ingredients:
- 15 oz. tomatoes, diced

- 15 oz. red kidney beans, rinsed
- 1 cup red bell pepper, chopped
- ¼ teaspoon salt
- 1-pound turkey, lean ground
- 1 cup onion, diced
- ¼ teaspoon black pepper
- 2 tablespoons chipotle peppers, canned, chopped
- 1 cup crushed tomatoes
- 1 teaspoon chili powder
- 2 teaspoons garlic, make pieces
- 1 teaspoon ground cumin
- Lime wedges and radish slices to serve

Directions:
1. Season the turkey with pepper and salt.
2. Take an Instant Pot; open the top lid.
3. Press "SAUTÉ" cooking function.
4. Coat the pot with cooking oil. In the cooking pot area, add the turkey and cook to evenly brown.
5. Add in the other ingredients; combine well.
6. Close the top lid and make sure the valve is sealed.
7. Press "MANUAL" cooking function. Adjust cooking time to 10 minutes.
8. Allow pressure to build and cook the ingredients for the set time.
9. After the set cooking time ends, press "CANCEL" and then press "QPR". Instant Pot will quickly release pressure.
10. Open the top lid, add the cooked mixture in serving plates.
11. Serve with the lime wedges and radish slices.

Mushroom Steak Soup

Prep Time: 8-10 min.
Cooking Time: 15 min.
Number of Servings: 4
Ingredients:
- 1 cup crushed tomatoes
- 1 cup diced carrots
- 1 pound diced steak, fat trimmed
- 1 (8-oz) pack of sliced mushrooms
- 1 cup diced celery stalk
- 2 cups beef stock
- 2 cups water
- 1 cup sliced bell peppers
- ¾ cup diced onion
- 2 tablespoons garlic powder
- 2 teaspoons oregano
- 1 teaspoon thyme
- 1 bay leaf
- Salt as per taste

Directions:
1. Take an Instant Pot; open the top lid.
2. Press "SAUTÉ" cooking function.
3. Coat the pot with cooking spray. In the cooking pot area, add the beef and cook until brown.
4. Mix in the mushrooms, onions, carrots, celery, pepper, and cook until softened.
5. Mix in the water, stock, thyme, oregano, bay leaf, and salt.
6. Close the top lid and make sure the valve is sealed.
7. Press "SOUP" cooking function. Adjust cooking time to 15 minutes.
8. Allow pressure to build and cook the ingredients for the set time.
9. After the set cooking time ends, press "CANCEL" and then press "NPR". Instant Pot will slowly and naturally release the pressure for 8-10 minutes.
10. Open the top lid, add the cooked mixture in serving plates.
11. Serve warm.

Corn Cream Shrimp Soup

Prep Time: 8-10 min.
Cooking Time: 20 min.
Number of Servings: 5-6
Ingredients:
- 2 cups diced potatoes
- 1 cup low-fat milk
- 2 cups peeled and deveined shrimp
- 1 cups corn
- ½ cup chopped onion
- 2 tablespoons butter
- 5 cups veggie stock
- ¼ cup flour
- 1 minced garlic clove
- 1 bay leaf
- ½ teaspoon dried thyme

Directions:
1. Take an Instant Pot; open the top lid.
2. Press "SAUTÉ" cooking function.
3. In the cooking pot area, add the butter, corn, onions, and garlic; cook for 4 minutes.
4. Mix in the potatoes, bay leaf, and veggie stock.
5. Close the top lid and make sure the valve is sealed.
6. Press "MANUAL" cooking function. Adjust cooking time to 15 minutes.
7. Allow pressure to build and cook the ingredients for the set time.
8. After the set cooking time ends, press "CANCEL" and then press "QPR". Instant Pot will quickly release pressure.
9. Open the top lid, add the milk, flour, and stir well to combine.
10. Add the shrimp and close the lid again, and let it sit for 3-4 minutes.
11. Serve warm.

Chicken Coconut Spinach Soup

Prep Time: 8-10 min.
Cooking Time: 10 min.
Number of Servings: 5-6
Ingredients:

- ½ onion, finely diced
- 3 or 4 garlic cloves, crushed
- 1 (2-inch) piece ginger, finely chopped
- 1 pound boneless, skinless chicken thighs
- 1 ½ cups unsweetened coconut milk
- 1 cup sliced mushrooms, shitake or crimini
- 4-ounces baby spinach
- ½ teaspoon cayenne
- 1 teaspoon Spice mix or garam masala
- ¼ cup chopped fresh cilantro
- 1 teaspoon salt
- ½ teaspoon ground turmeric

Directions:

1. Take your Instant Pot; open the top lid. Plug it and turn it on.
2. In the cooking pot area, add the chicken, coconut milk, onion, garlic, ginger, mushrooms, spinach, salt, turmeric, cayenne, garam masala, and cilantro. Using a spatula, stir the ingredients.
3. Close the top lid and seal its valve.
4. Press "MANUAL" setting. Adjust cooking time to 10 minutes.
5. Allow the recipe to cook for the set cooking time.
6. After the set cooking time ends, press "CANCEL" and then press "NPR (Natural Pressure Release)".
7. Instant Pot will slowly and naturally release the pressure.
8. Open the top lid, take out the meat and shred it.
9. Add back to the mix and combine; add the cooked recipe mix in serving plates.
10. Serve and enjoy!

Herbed Turkey Stew

Prep Time: 10 min.
Cooking Time: 30 min.
Number of Servings: 5-6
Ingredients:

- 1 ½ pound turkey, ground
- 2 white onions
- 2 tablespoons Italian herbs
- 2 ½ cups chicken stock
- 2 cups chopped cauliflower
- 2 tablespoons paprika
- 2 tablespoons coconut oil

Directions:

1. Take your Instant Pot; open the top lid. Plug it and turn it on.
2. In the cooking pot area, add the ingredients. Using a spatula, stir the ingredients.
3. Close the top lid and seal its valve.
4. Press "STEW" setting. Adjust cooking time to 30 minutes.
5. Allow the recipe to cook for the set cooking time.
6. After the set cooking time ends, press "CANCEL" and then press "NPR (Natural Pressure Release)".
7. Instant Pot will slowly and naturally release the pressure.
8. Open the top lid, add the cooked recipe mix in serving plates.
9. Serve and enjoy!

Green Bean Beef Stew

Prep Time: 5-8 min.
Cooking Time: 8 min.
Number of Servings: 5-6
Ingredients:
- 2 tablespoons tomato paste
- 1 cup chicken broth
- 2 cups frozen green beans
- 1 pound 80% lean ground beef
- ½ cup tomato sauce
- 1 cup sliced onions
- 1 tablespoon soy sauce
- 1 teaspoon salt
- 3 tablespoons apple cider vinegar
- 2 teaspoons (ground) black pepper
- Juice of 1 lemon

Directions:
1. Take your Instant Pot; open the top lid. Plug it and turn it on.
2. Press "SAUTÉ" setting and the pot will start heating up.
3. In the cooking pot area, add the meat. Break up any clumps and cook for 2 to 3 minutes.
4. Stir in the tomato sauce, tomato paste, chicken broth, green beans, onions, vinegar, soy sauce, salt, and pepper.
5. Close the top lid and seal its valve.
6. Press "MANUAL" setting. Adjust cooking time to 5 minutes.
7. Allow the recipe to cook for the set cooking time.
8. After the set cooking time ends, press "CANCEL" and then press "NPR (Natural Pressure Release)".
9. Instant Pot will slowly and naturally release the pressure.
10. Open the top lid, add the cooked recipe mix in serving plates.
11. Stir in the lemon juice and serve.

Fish Cream Stew

Prep Time: 5-8 min.
Cooking Time: 8 min.
Number of Servings: 5-6
Ingredients:
- 2 celery stalks, diced
- 1 cup heavy cream
- 1-pound white fish fillets, chopped
- 3 cups fish broth
- 1 cup chopped broccoli
- 1 cup chopped cauliflower
- 1 onion, diced
- 1 carrot, sliced
- 1 cup chopped kale
- 2 tablespoons butter
- Pepper and salt, as needed

Directions:
1. Take your Instant Pot; open the top lid. Plug it and turn it on.
2. Press "SAUTÉ" setting and the pot will start heating up.
3. In the cooking pot area, add the butter and onions. Cook until starts becoming translucent and softened. Stir in between.
4. Stir all the ingredients, except for the cream.
5. Close the top lid and seal its valve.
6. Press "MANUAL" setting. Adjust cooking time to 5 minutes.
7. Allow the recipe to cook for the set cooking time.
8. After the set cooking time ends, press "CANCEL" and then press "NPR (Natural Pressure Release)".
9. Instant Pot will slowly and naturally release the pressure.
10. Open the top lid, add the cooked recipe mix in serving plates.
11. Stir in the heavy cream. Discard the bay leaf.
12. Serve and enjoy!

Cheesy Leek Squash Soup

Prep Time: 5-8 min.
Cooking Time: 5 min.
Number of Servings: 5-6
Ingredients:
- 1 cup chopped celery
- 2 tablespoons minced garlic
- 1 teaspoon dried oregano
- 1 teaspoon salt
- 3 cups finely sliced leeks
- 6 cups chopped rainbow chard, stems and leaves
- 2 teaspoons (ground) black pepper
- ¼ cup chopped parsley

- ¾ cup heavy (whipping) cream
- 3 cups chicken broth
- 2 cups sliced yellow summer squash, ½-inch slices
- 5 tablespoons grated Parmesan cheese

Directions:
1. Take your Instant Pot; open the top lid. Plug it and turn it on.
2. In the cooking pot area, add the leeks, chard, celery, 1 tablespoon garlic, oregano, salt, pepper, and broth. Using a spatula, stir the ingredients.
3. Close the top lid and seal its valve.
4. Press "MANUAL" setting. Adjust cooking time to 3 minutes.
5. Allow the recipe to cook for the set cooking time.
6. After the set cooking time ends, press "CANCEL" and then press "QPR (Quick Pressure Release)".
7. Instant Pot will quickly release the pressure.
8. Add the yellow squash, parsley, and remaining 1 tablespoon garlic and cook on "SAUTE" for 2-3 minutes.
9. Stir in the cream and ladle the soup into bowls. Sprinkle with the Parmesan and serve warm.

Beef Carrot Soup

Prep Time: 10 min.
Cooking Time: 25 min.
Number of Servings: 4
Ingredients:
- 2 tablespoons cooking oil
- 1 tablespoon tomato paste
- 6 thyme sprigs
- 4 garlic cloves
- 2 pounds beef stew meat
- 1 onion, sliced
- 3 cups beef broth
- 2 bay leaves
- 4 peeled carrots, sliced
- 1 cup water

Directions:
1. Season the beef with the pepper and salt.
2. Arrange your Instant Pot over a dry, clean platform. Plug it in power socket and turn it on.
3. Now press "Saute" mode from available options. In the cooking area, add the oil and meat; cook for 4-5 minutes to brown.
4. Add the garlic, carrots, and onions; cook for a few minutes. Add the thyme, bay leaves, paste, and broth into Instant Pot; stir well.
5. Close the lid and lock. Ensure that you have sealed the valve to avoid leakage.
6. Press "Manual" mode from available cooking settings and set cooking time to 30 minutes. Instant Pot will start cooking the ingredients after a few minutes.
7. After the timer reads zero, press "Cancel"; press "NPR" to naturally release pressure. It takes about 8-10 minutes to release pressure naturally.

8. Carefully remove the lid; season as needed and serve the prepared keto dish warm!

Cheesy Chicken Soup

Prep Time: 5 min.
Cooking Time: 15 min.
Number of Servings: 5-6
Ingredients:
- 15-ounce chicken stock
- 15 ounce canned low carb chunky salsa
- 1½ pounds and cubed chicken tights (boneless, skinless)
- 8 ounce Monterey jack cheese, shredded

Directions:
1. Arrange your Instant Pot over a dry, clean platform. Plug it in power socket and turn it on.
2. Open the lid from the top and put it aside; add the ingredients and gently stir them.
3. Close the lid and lock. Ensure that you have sealed the valve to avoid leakage.
4. Press "Manual" mode from available cooking settings and set cooking time to 15 minutes. Instant Pot will start cooking the ingredients after a few minutes.
5. After the timer reads zero, press "Cancel"; press "NPR" to naturally release pressure. It takes about 8-10 minutes to release pressure naturally.
6. Carefully remove the lid and serve the prepared keto dish warm!

Slow Cooked Spiced Squash Soup

Prep Time: 8-10 min.
Cooking Time: 7 hours 10-15 min.
Number of Servings: 6
Ingredients:
- 3 cups vegetable broth
- 1 cup coconut milk
- 1 spaghetti squash, skin removed, chopped
- ½ cup walnuts
- 1 green onion, minced
- 2 tablespoons ginger, grated
- 1 tablespoon pepper
- 1 teaspoon salt
- Coconut oil for cooking
- 1 tablespoon nutmeg

Directions:
1. Arrange your Instant Pot over a dry, clean platform. Plug it in power socket and turn it on.

2. Open the lid from the top and put it aside; add the ingredients and gently stir them.
3. Close the lid and lock. Ensure that you have sealed the valve to avoid leakage.
4. Press "Manual" mode from available cooking settings and set cooking time to 7 hours. Instant Pot will start cooking the ingredients after a few minutes.
5. After the timer reads zero, press "Cancel" and quick release pressure.
6. Carefully remove the lid. Transfer the soup mixture in a blender.
7. Blend well and serve the prepared keto dish warm!

Yummy Asparagus Ham Soup

Prep Time: 8-10 min.
Cooking Time: 50-55 min.
Number of Servings: 4-5
Ingredients:
- 3 tablespoons ghee
- 1/2 teaspoon thyme, dried
- 1 cup diced ham
- 1 white onion, diced
- 2 pounds asparagus, chopped
- 5 garlic cloves, pressed
- 4 cups chicken broth
- Pepper and salt to taste

Directions:
1. Arrange your Instant Pot over a dry, clean platform. Plug it in power socket and turn it on.
2. Now press "Saute" mode from available options. In the cooking area, add the ghee and onion; cook for 4-5 minutes to soften.
3. Add the broth, ham, and garlic. Cook for 2-3 minutes, then add asparagus and thyme.
4. Close the lid and lock. Ensure that you have sealed the valve to avoid leakage.
5. Press "Soup" mode from available cooking settings and set cooking time to 45 minutes. Instant Pot will start cooking the ingredients after a few minutes.
6. After the timer reads zero, press "Cancel"; press "NPR" to naturally release pressure. It takes about 8-10 minutes to release pressure naturally.
7. Carefully remove the lid.
8. Blend the mixture in a blender and serve the prepared keto dish warm!

Creamy Tomato Soup

Prep Time: 8-10min.
Cooking Time: 15 min.
Number of Servings: 4
Ingredients:
- 2 garlic cloves, minced
- 1 tablespoon olive oil
- 1 cup veggie stock
- ½ cup coconut cream
- 2 teaspoons thyme, chopped
- 1 tablespoon ghee, melted

- 4 ¼ cups tomatoes, chopped
- 1 yellow onion, chopped
- A pinch of pepper and salt

Directions:
1. Switch on your instant pot after placing it on a clean and dry kitchen platform. Press "Saute" cooking function.
2. Open the pot lid; add the oil, ghee, garlic, and onions in the pot; start cooking for 2-3 minutes to cook well and soften.
3. Add the tomatoes, thyme, stock, salt, and pepper; stir gently.
4. Close the pot by closing the top lid. Also, ensure to seal the valve.
5. Press "Manual" cooking function and set cooking time to 12 minutes. It will start cooking after a few minutes. Let the pot mix cook under pressure until the timer reads zero.
6. Turn off and press "Cancel" cooking function. Quick release pressure.
7. Open the pot and serve on a serving plate or bowl. Mix the cream, stir, and serve.

Spinach Lentil Soup

Prep Time: 10 min.
Cooking Time: 18 min.
Number of Servings: 2
Ingredients:
- 1/2 teaspoon turmeric, ground
- 1 teaspoon olive oil
- 1/2 cup yellow onion, chopped
- 1/3 cup celery, chopped
- 1 tablespoon garlic, minced
- 3 cup baby spinach
- 1/2 cup carrot, chopped
- 1 teaspoon cumin, ground
- 2 cup veggie stock
- 1/2 cup lentils
- 1/2 teaspoon thyme, dried
- A pinch of pepper and salt

Directions:
1. Take your 3-Quart Instant Pot; open the top lid. Plug it and turn it on.
2. Press "SAUTÉ" setting and the pot will start heating up.
3. In the cooking pot area, add the oil, carrot, celery, and onions.
4. Stir and cook for 5 minutes.
5. Mix the turmeric, garlic, cumin, thyme, salt, and pepper, and cook for 1 minute more.
6. Mix the lentils and stock.
7. Close the top lid and seal its valve.
8. Press "MANUAL" setting. Adjust cooking time to 12 minutes.
9. Allow the recipe to cook for the set cooking time.
10. After the set cooking time ends, press "CANCEL" and then press "QPR (Quick Pressure Release)".
11. Instant Pot will quickly release the pressure.

12. Open the top lid, add the cooked recipe mix in serving bowls.
13. Mix the spinach. Serve and enjoy!

Cheesy Tomato Soup

Prep Time: 10-15 min.
Cooking Time: 28 min.
Number of Servings: 2-3
Ingredients:
- 2 cups of chopped ripe tomatoes
- 2 tablespoons tomato paste
- 3 tablespoons olive oil, extra virgin
- 2 medium onions, chopped
- 2 medium carrots, peeled and chopped
- 3 large garlic cloves, finely chopped
- 1 tablespoon sugar
- 1 cup vegetable broth
- Pepper and salt as needed
- 1/2 cup Parmesan cheese, grated
- 1/2 cup heavy cream
- 4 basil leaves, as a garnish

Directions:
1. Take your 3-Quart Instant Pot; open the top lid. Plug it and turn it on.
2. Press "SAUTÉ" setting and the pot will start heating up.
3. In the cooking pot area, add the oil, carrot, and onions. Cook until starts becoming translucent and softened for 6-7 minutes. Stir in between.
4. Toss in the garlic and stir until fragrant.
5. Add in the tomato paste, tomatoes, broth, sugar, pepper and salt; stir gently.
6. Close the top lid and seal its valve.
7. Press "MANUAL" setting. Adjust cooking time to 20 minutes.
8. Allow the recipe to cook for the set cooking time.
9. After the set cooking time ends, press "CANCEL" and then press "NPR (Natural Pressure Release)".
10. Instant Pot will slowly and naturally release the pressure.
11. Open the top lid, add the cooked recipe mix in serving plates.
12. Pour in the cream, and puree the mix in a blender.
13. Garnish with torn basil leaves and cheese. Serve warm.

Italian Sausage Cream Soup

Prep Time: 5-8 min.
Cooking Time: 12 min.
Number of Servings: 2-3
Ingredients:
- 1 small yellow onion, finely chopped
- ½ pound Italian sausages

- 1 large russet potato, washed and sliced
- 3 cups chicken broth
- ¼ cup heavy cream
- 1 tablespoon olive oil
- 2 cloves garlic, minced
- Pepper and salt as needed

Directions:
1. Take your 3-Quart Instant Pot; open the top lid. Plug it and turn it on.
2. Press "SAUTÉ" setting and the pot will start heating up.
3. In the cooking pot area, add the oil, garlic, and onions. Cook until starts becoming translucent and softened for 3 minutes. Stir in between.
4. Stir in the sausage and cook for an extra 3 minutes.
5. Mix the potato, broth, a pinch black pepper and salt.
6. Close the top lid and seal its valve.
7. Press "MANUAL" setting. Adjust cooking time to 6 minutes.
8. Allow the recipe to cook for the set cooking time.
9. After the set cooking time ends, press "CANCEL" and then press "QPR (Quick Pressure Release)".
10. Instant Pot will quickly release the pressure.
11. Open the top lid, add the cooked recipe mix in serving bowls.
12. Serve and enjoy!

Marinara Turkey Soup

Prep Time: 8-10 min.
Cooking Time: 11 min.
Number of Servings: 2-3
Ingredients:
- 1/2 pound turkey, ground
- 1/2 tablespoon olive oil
- 1/2 cup cauliflower florets
- 1 garlic clove, crushed or minced
- 1/2 cup yellow onion, chopped
- 1/2 cabbage head, chopped
- 10 ounces marinara sauce
- 1 cup water
- 2 cups chicken stock

Directions:
1. Take your 3-Quart Instant Pot; open the top lid. Plug it and turn it on.
2. Press "SAUTÉ" setting and the pot will start heating up.
3. Add the oil, turkey, garlic, and onion, stir and sauté for 5 minutes.
4. Add the cauliflower, stock, water, marinara sauce and cabbage; stir gently.
5. Close the top lid and seal its valve.
6. Press "MANUAL" setting. Adjust cooking time to 6 minutes.
7. Allow the recipe to cook for the set cooking time.

8. After the set cooking time ends, press "CANCEL" and then press "QPR (Quick Pressure Release)".
9. Instant Pot will quickly release the pressure.
10. Open the top lid, add the cooked recipe mix in serving bowls.
11. Serve and enjoy!

Chicken Spiced Tropical Soup

Prep Time: 8-10 min.
Cooking Time: 40 min.
Number of Servings: 2-3
Ingredients:
- 1 garlic clove, crushed or minced
- 1 small red onion, chopped
- 1 carrot, chopped
- Lime wedges for serving
- 1/2 small red cabbage, chopped
- A pinch of pepper and salt
- 1/2 pound chicken pieces
- 1/3 pineapple, peeled and make medium size cubes
- 1/2 teaspoon cinnamon powder
- 1/2 teaspoon turmeric powder
- 1 sprigs onion, chopped
- 1/2 teaspoon ginger powder
- 1/2 teaspoon white peppercorns
- 1/2 tablespoon tamarind paste
- Juice from 1/3 lime

Directions:
1. Take your 3-Quart Instant Pot; open the top lid. Plug it and turn it on.
2. In the cooking pot area, add the carrot, red onion, chicken, salt, pepper, cabbage, garlic, peppercorns. Using a spatula, stir the ingredients.
3. Close the top lid and seal its valve.
4. Press "SOUP" setting. Adjust cooking time to 30 minutes.
5. Allow the recipe to cook for the set cooking time.
6. After the set cooking time ends, press "CANCEL" and then press "QPR (Quick Pressure Release)".
7. Instant Pot will quickly release the pressure.
8. Open the top lid, take out the meat and shred it.
9. Add back to the mix and combine.
10. In a bowl, mix 1 tablespoon soup with tamarind paste, stir and pour into the pot mix.
11. Mix the cinnamon, ginger, turmeric, pineapple and lime juice; stir the mix.
12. Press "SAUTÉ" setting and cook for 10 minutes more.
13. Ladle into bowls, top with the sprigs onion on top and serve with lime wedges on the side.

Wholesome Veggies Soup

Prep Time: 8-10 min.
Cooking Time: 8 min.
Number of Servings: 2-3
Ingredients:

- 2 tablespoons extra virgin olive oil
- 2 cloves garlic, crushed
- 2 large carrots, cut in 1/2 slices
- Pepper and salt, as needed
- 2 small potatoes, cut in ½-cubes
- 1 large onion, coarsely chopped
- 4 large zucchinis, cut in 1 slices
- 4 cups vegetable stock
- 1 tablespoon minced basil

Directions:
1. Take your 3-Quart Instant Pot; open the top lid. Plug it and turn it on.
2. Press "SAUTÉ" setting and the pot will start heating up.
3. In the cooking pot area, add the oil, garlic, and onions. Cook until starts becoming translucent and softened for 1 minutes. Stir in between.
4. Add the potatoes and sauté for another 1-2 minutes.
5. Add the remaining ingredients and stir to blend.
6. Close the top lid and seal its valve.
7. Press "MANUAL" setting. Adjust cooking time to 5 minutes.
8. Allow the recipe to cook for the set cooking time.
9. After the set cooking time ends, press "CANCEL" and then press "NPR (Natural Pressure Release)".
10. Instant Pot will slowly and naturally release the pressure.
11. Open the top lid, add the cooked recipe mix in serving plates.
12. Serve and enjoy!

Kale Beef Stew

Prep Time: 8-10 min.
Cooking Time: 45 min.
Number of Servings: 2
Ingredients:

- 1 small onion, chopped
- 2 carrots, peeled and chopped
- 1 cups kale leaves, trimmed and chopped
- 1 ½ cups beef broth
- 2 medium potatoes, chopped
- 1 celery stalk, chopped
- 1 tablespoon olive oil
- ½ pound beef stew meat, cut into cubes
- 1 tablespoon hot sauce
- ½ teaspoon garlic powder

273

- Pepper and salt as per taste preference

Directions:
1. Switch on the pot after placing it on a clean and dry platform. Press "Saute" cooking function.
2. Open the pot lid; add the oil and beef in the pot; cook for 4-5 minutes to cook well and turn browned evenly.
3. Mix in the remaining ingredients. Close the pot by closing the top lid. Also, ensure to seal the valve.
4. Press "Meat/Stew" cooking function and set cooking time to 40 minutes. It will start cooking after a few minutes. Let the pot mix cook under pressure until the timer reads zero.
5. Press "Cancel" cooking function and press "Quick release" setting.
6. Open the pot and serve warm. Enjoy it with your loved one!

Pork Cabbage Soup

Prep Time: 15 min.
Cooking Time: 30 min.
Number of Servings: 2
Ingredients:
- 1 small onion, chopped
- 1 cup carrot, peeled and shredded
- 2 cups low-sodium chicken broth
- 1 tablespoon soy sauce
- 1 ½ cups cabbage, chopped
- 1 tablespoon olive oil
- ½ pound ground pork
- ½ teaspoon ground ginger
- Fresh pepper as per taste preference

Directions:
1. Switch on the pot after placing it on a clean and dry platform. Press "Saute" cooking function.
2. Open the pot lid; add the oil and meat in the pot; cook for 4-5 minutes to cook well and turn browned evenly.
3. Mix in the remaining ingredients. Close the pot by closing the top lid. Also, ensure to seal the valve.
4. Press "Manual" cooking function and set cooking time to 25 minutes. It will start cooking after a few minutes. Let the pot mix cook under pressure until the timer reads zero.
5. Press "Cancel" cooking function and press "Quick release" setting.
6. Open the pot and serve warm. Enjoy it with your loved one!

Cashew Rice Soup

Prep Time: 8-10min.
Cooking Time: 45 min.
Number of Servings: 7-8
Ingredients:
- 3 cloves garlic, minced
- 1 ½ cups carrots, chopped
- 1 ½ cups onion, chopped

- 1 tablespoon olive oil
- 2 bay leaves
- 1 ½ cups wild rice
- 1 ½ cups celery stalks, chopped
- 1 ½ cups dried chickpeas, soaked in water overnight
- 1 ½ teaspoons dried thyme
- 7 ½ cups vegetable broth
- 1 cup water
- ¾ cup raw cashew, soaked in hot water for 30 minutes
- Pepper and salt as needed

Directions:
1. Take Instant Pot and carefully arrange it over a clean, dry kitchen platform. Turn on the appliance.
2. Find and press "Sauté" cooking function.
3. In the cooking pot area; add the oil and onions in the pot. Cook for 2 minutes to cook well and soften.
4. Stir in the garlic and sauté until fragrant. Stir in the carrots and celery and sauté for a couple of minutes.
5. Add the chickpeas, bay leaf, wild rice, thyme, and broth.
6. Close the pot lid and seal the valve to avoid any leakage. Find and press "Manual" cooking setting and set cooking time to 35 minutes.
7. Allow the recipe ingredients to cook for the set time, and after that, the timer reads "zero".
8. Press "Cancel" and press "NPR" setting for natural pressure release. It takes 8-10 times for all inside pressure to release.
9. Open the pot.
10. Add cashew and water to a blender and blend until smooth. Add the mix to the Instant Pot and combine well.
11. Mix the pepper and salt. Ladle into soup bowls and serve.

Corn Chickpea Curry

Prep Time: 5 min.
Cooking Time: 12-15 min.
Number of Servings: 5-6
Ingredients:
- 14.5 ounce diced tomatoes
- 30-ounce chickpeas, rinsed and drained
- 1 cup corn
- 2 tablespoons olive oil
- 1 cup kale leaves
- 1 onion, diced
- 2 large garlic cloves, minced
- 1 piece diced green bell pepper
- 1 tablespoon curry powder
- 1 tablespoon maple syrup
- 2 tablespoons cilantro leaves

- 1 cup vegetable broth
- Juice of 1 lime
- 1/4 teaspoon black pepper
- 1 teaspoons sea salt

Directions:
1. Take your Instant Pot and place it on a clean kitchen platform. Turn it on after plugging it into a power socket.
2. Put the pot on "Saute" mode. In the pot, add the oil and onions; cook for 2-3 minutes until the ingredients become soft.
3. Mix the garlic and bell pepper; cook for 2-3 minutes. Mix in the curry powder and cook for 30-40 seconds.
4. Now add the maple syrup, kale, broth, corn, tomatoes, and chickpeas.
5. Close the lid and lock. Ensure that you have sealed the valve to avoid leakage.
6. Press "Manual" mode and set timer for 5 minutes. It will take a few minutes for the pot to build inside pressure and start cooking.
7. After the timer reads zero, press "Cancel" and naturally release pressure. It takes about 8-10 minutes to naturally release pressure.
8. Carefully remove the lid; mix the lime juice, pepper, and salt.
9. Add cilantro on top. You can also serve the soup with steamed rice. (optional)

Wholesome Broccoli Soup

Prep Time: 5-8 min.
Cooking Time: 15 min.
Number of Servings: 4
Ingredients:
- ½ teaspoon garlic powder

- ¼ teaspoon paprika

- 3 peeled potatoes, make cubes

- ½ cup dry lentils, rinsed

- 1 medium head broccoli, make small florets

- 1 medium onion, chopped

- 3 sliced carrots

- 4 cups water

- 1 bay leaf

- ½ teaspoon thyme

Directions:
1. Take your Instant Pot and place it on a clean kitchen platform. Turn it on after plugging it into a power socket.

276

2. Open the lid from the top and put it aside; start adding the mentioned ingredients inside. Season as needed and gently stir them.
3. Close the lid and lock. Ensure that you have sealed the valve to avoid leakage.
4. Press "Manual" mode and set timer for 15 minutes. It will take a few minutes for the pot to build inside pressure and start cooking.
5. After the timer reads zero, press "Cancel" and naturally release pressure. It takes about 8-10 minutes to naturally release pressure.
6. Carefully remove the lid, take out the bay leaf and serve warm!

Cashew Carrot Soup

Prep Time: 5 min.
Cooking Time: 5 min.
Number of Servings: 4
Ingredients:
- 1/2 cup nutritional yeast
- 1 cup chopped carrots
- 1 teaspoon salt
- 1 teaspoon turmeric, chopped
- 1/2 cup raw cashews
- 1/2 cup onions, chopped
- 3 whole garlic cloves
- 2 cups peeled potatoes, chopped
- 2 cups water

Directions:
1. Take your Instant Pot and place it on a clean kitchen platform. Turn it on after plugging it into a power socket.
2. Open the lid from top and put it aside; start adding the mentioned ingredients inside and gently stir them.
3. Close the lid and lock. Ensure that you have sealed the valve to avoid leakage.
4. Press "Manual" mode and set timer for 5 minutes. It will take a few minutes for the pot to build inside pressure and start cooking.
5. After the timer reads zero, press "Cancel" and naturally release pressure. It takes about 8-10 minutes to naturally release pressure.
6. Carefully remove the lid and transfer the mix into a food processor, blend to make a creamy and smooth.
7. Serve warm.

Spinach Veggie Soup

Prep Time: 10 min.
Cooking Time: 30 min.
Number of Servings: 8
Ingredients:

- 2 pounds potatoes, peeled and make small cubes

- 1 cup onion, chopped

- 1 tablespoon ground flax or chia seed

- ¾ cup sliced baby carrots

- 1 cup vegetable broth

- ½ cup celery, chopped

- ½ cup chopped baby spinach leaves

- 18 ounces can roast garlic recipe starter

- ½ teaspoon salt

- 1/8 teaspoon paprika

- 1/8 teaspoon crushed red pepper

Directions:
1. Take your Instant Pot and place it on a clean kitchen platform. Turn it on after plugging it into a power socket.
2. Open the lid from the top and put it aside; start adding the mentioned ingredients inside and gently stir them.
3. Close the lid and lock. Ensure that you have sealed the valve to avoid leakage.
4. Press "Soup" mode and set timer for 30 minutes. It will take a few minutes for the pot to build inside pressure and start cooking.
5. After the timer reads zero, press "Cancel" and naturally release pressure. It takes about 8-10 minutes to naturally release pressure.
6. Carefully remove the lid and transfer the mixture in a blender to make it smooth. Serve warm!

Quinoa Mixed Bean Soup

Prep Time: 5min.
Cooking Time: 2 min.
Number of Servings: 3
Ingredients:

- 1 cup kidney beans or pinto beans
- 7.5 oz. canned diced tomatoes
- 1/4 tablespoon dried oregano
- Pepper and salt as needed
- 1/2 tablespoon dried basil

278

- 1/2 tablespoon hot sauce
- 2 tablespoons quinoa rinsed
- 1/2 tablespoon garlic, minced
- 6 oz. frozen vegetables
- 7.5 oz. cannelloni beans
- 1/2 teaspoon onion powder
- 1 1/2 cups boiling water

Directions:
1. Take Instant Pot and carefully arrange it over a clean, dry kitchen platform. Turn on the appliance.
2. In the cooking pot area, add the mentioned ingredients. Stir the ingredients gently.
3. Close the pot lid and seal the valve to avoid any leakage. Find and press "Manual" cooking setting and set cooking time to 2 minutes.
4. Allow the recipe ingredients to cook for the set time, and after that, the timer reads "zero".
5. Press "Cancel" and press "NPR" setting for natural pressure release. It takes 8-10 times for all inside pressure to release.
6. Open the pot and arrange the cooked recipe in serving plates. Enjoy the vegan recipe!

Broccoli Bean Soup

Prep Time: 5min.
Cooking Time: 5 min.
Number of Servings: 6
Ingredients:
- 1 cup shredded cabbage
- 1 cup broccoli florets
- ½ cup kidney beans
- 1 teaspoon oregano
- 1 tablespoon soy sauce
- 1 teaspoon onion powder
- ¼ cup quinoa
- 1 tablespoon vegetable oil
- 4 garlic cloves, minced
- 1 cup carrots, chopped
- 1 cup green bell pepper, chopped
- 4 cups vegetable broth
- ¼ teaspoon salt
- 2 tablespoons lemon juice
- Some ground pepper
- Some basil leaves

Directions:
1. Take Instant Pot and carefully arrange it over a clean, dry kitchen platform. Turn on the appliance.
2. Find and press "Sauté" cooking function. Heat the vegetable oil. Add minced garlic and sauté for about a minute.

3. Add remaining ingredients to the pot slowly, except for basil leaves and pepper. Stir to mix well.
4. Close the pot lid and seal the valve to avoid any leakage. Find and press "Manual" cooking setting and set cooking time to 5 minutes.
5. Allow the recipe ingredients to cook for the set time, and after that, the timer reads "zero".
6. Press "Cancel" and press "NPR" setting for natural pressure release. It takes 8-10 times for all inside pressure to release.
7. Open the pot and arrange the cooked recipe in serving plates. Season with some ground pepper and garnish with basil leaves.

Corn Peppery Chowder

Prep Time: 5min.
Cooking Time: 35 min.
Number of Servings: 4
Ingredients:
- 4 cups corn kernels
- 1 medium yellow onions, chopped
- 2 tablespoons olive oil
- 4 cups vegetable broth
- ½ teaspoon smoked paprika
- 1 teaspoon ground cumin
- 1 medium red bell peppers, chopped
- 3 medium gold potatoes, chopped
- ⅛ teaspoon cayenne pepper
- 1 cup almond milk
- Pepper as needed
- 1 scallion, chopped, to garnish

Directions:
1. Take Instant Pot and carefully arrange it over a clean, dry kitchen platform. Turn on the appliance.
2. Find and press "Sauté" cooking function.
3. In the cooking pot area; add the oil and onions in the pot. Cook for 2 minutes to cook well and soften.
4. Add the red bell pepper, 1 cup corn, potatoes, broth, salt, and spices.
5. Close the pot lid and seal the valve to avoid any leakage. Find and press "Manual" cooking setting and set cooking time to 15 minutes.
6. Allow the recipe ingredients to cook for the set time, and after that, the timer reads "zero".
7. Press "Cancel" and press "NPR" setting for natural pressure release. It takes 8-10 times for all inside pressure to release.
8. Open the pot. Blend in a blender until smooth. Add it back into the pot.
9. Add the remaining corn and almond milk.
10. Find and press "Sauté" cooking function; simmer for 15 minutes. Add the pepper and salt as needed and mixed well.
11. Ladle into soup bowls. Garnish with the scallions and red bell pepper.

Sweet Potato Lemongrass Soup

Prep Time: 8-10min.
Cooking Time: 15 min.
Number of Servings: 7-8
Ingredients:

- 2 cups sweet potatoes, peeled and chopped
- 4 cups vegetable broth
- 1 red chili, chopped
- 4 stalks lemongrass, halved
- 6 large carrots, peeled and chopped
- 2 large celery stalks, chopped
- 2 medium onions, chopped
- 2 cups coconut milk
- 4 cloves garlic, pressed
- 1-inch piece of ginger, minced
- Salt as needed
- Juice of a lime
- Cilantro leaves, chopped, to garnish
- Sesame seeds to garnish

Directions:
1. Take Instant Pot and carefully arrange it over a clean, dry kitchen platform. Turn on the appliance.
2. In the cooking pot area, add the mentioned ingredients. Stir the ingredients gently.
3. Close the pot lid and seal the valve to avoid any leakage. Find and press "Soup" cooking setting and set cooking time to 15 minutes.
4. Allow the recipe ingredients to cook for the set time, and after that, the timer reads "zero". Press "Cancel" and press "QPR" setting for quick pressure release.
5. Open the pot and discard lemongrass.
6. Cool for a while and blend with a hand blender. Add the lime juice while blending.
7. Ladle into bowls. Garnish with the cilantro and sesame seeds.

Classic Lentil Potato Stew

Prep Time: 5min.
Cooking Time: 25-30 min.
Number of Servings: 4
Ingredients:

- 1 small stalk celery, chopped
- 2 cups Swiss chard, chopped
- ½ tablespoon soy sauce
- 1 clove garlic, minced
- 1 ½ cups lentils, rinsed
- 2 medium gold potatoes, cubed
- 1 ½ tablespoons olive oil
- 1 medium onion, chopped
- 1 medium carrot, sliced

- 3 cups vegetable broth
- Pepper and salt as needed

Directions:
1. Take Instant Pot and carefully arrange it over a clean, dry kitchen platform. Turn on the appliance.
2. Find and press "Sauté" cooking function.
3. In the cooking pot area; add the oil, garlic, stems of Swiss chard, celery, and onions in the pot.
4. Add the rest of the ingredients except the Swiss chard leaves and stir.
5. Close the pot lid and seal the valve to avoid any leakage. Find and press "Soup" cooking setting with default cooking time.
6. Allow the recipe ingredients to cook for the set time, and after that, the timer reads "zero".
7. Press "Cancel" and press "NPR" setting for natural pressure release. It takes 8-10 times for all inside pressure to release.
8. Open the pot and add the Swiss chard leaves.
9. Press "saute" and simmer until the chard wilts. Ladle into soup bowls and serve.

Broccoli Cashew Soup

Prep Time: 5min.
Cooking Time: 25 min.
Number of Servings: 3
Ingredients:
- 1 cup broccoli, chopped into florets
- ½ teaspoon salt
- 6 tablespoons raw cashew, soaked in water for 4 hours
- 1 medium onion, chopped
- 2 medium carrots, chopped
- 2 cloves garlic, minced
- 3 cups water, divided
- 1 teaspoon olive oil
- 1 stalk celery, chopped
- Ground pepper as needed

Directions:
1. Take Instant Pot and carefully arrange it over a clean, dry kitchen platform. Turn on the appliance.
2. Find and press "Sauté" cooking function.
3. In the cooking pot area; add the oil, salt, and onions in the pot. Cook for 2 minutes to cook well and soften.
4. Stir in the carrots and celery and sauté for 2–3 minutes. Add the garlic and broccoli and sauté for a couple of minutes. Add 2 ½ cups water, pepper and salt.
5. Close the pot lid and seal the valve to avoid any leakage. Find and press "Soup" cooking setting and set cooking time to 20 minutes.
6. Allow the recipe ingredients to cook for the set time, and after that, the timer reads "zero".
7. Press "Cancel" and press "NPR" setting for natural pressure release. It takes 8-10 times for all inside pressure to release.
8. Open the pot and cool down the mix.

9. Blend it in a blender until smooth. Transfer the mix to a bowl.
10. Add the cashew into the blender with ½ cup water and blend until smooth. Pour into the soup mix and adjust seasoning and serve!

Kale Squash Stew

Prep Time: 8-10min.
Cooking Time: 15 min.
Number of Servings: 6
Ingredients:

- 2 15-ounce can navy beans
- 2 teaspoons smoked paprika
- 1 teaspoon dried basil
- 2 teaspoons dried oregano
- 1 teaspoon cumin
- 6 cloves garlic, minced
- 1 tablespoon vegetable oil
- 1 large onion, chopped
- 1 red bell pepper, chopped
- 1 15-ounce can diced tomatoes
- ½ cup cilantro leaves
- 1 pound winter squash, peeled and cubed
- 1 bunch of kale
- 1 teaspoon salt
- 5 cups water

Directions:
1. Remove the kale stems and finely slice. Tear the leaves into bits.
2. Take Instant Pot and carefully arrange it over a clean, dry kitchen platform. Turn on the appliance.
3. Find and press "Sauté" cooking function.
4. In the cooking pot area; add the oil and onions in the pot. Cook for 2 minutes to cook well and soften.
5. Add the garlic and cook until fragrant. Add everything else except cilantro.
6. Close the pot lid and seal the valve to avoid any leakage. Find and press "Manual" cooking setting and set cooking time to 10 minutes.
7. Allow the recipe ingredients to cook for the set time, and after that, the timer reads "zero".
8. Press "Cancel" and press "NPR" setting for natural pressure release. It takes 8-10 times for all inside pressure to release.
9. Open the pot.
10. Add cilantro and let stand 10 minutes before serving.

Zucchini Garlic Soup

Prep Time: 5-8 min.
Cooking Time: 20 min.
Number of Servings: 7-8
Ingredients:

- 1 tablespoon coconut oil or ghee

- 4 cloves garlic, sliced

- 5 medium zucchinis, make small chunks

- 2 onions, quartered

- 6 cups vegetable stock

- ½ cup coconut milk

- Ground pepper and salt as needed

Directions:
1. Take Instant Pot and carefully arrange it over a clean, dry kitchen platform. Turn on the appliance.
2. Find and press "Sauté" cooking function.
3. In the cooking pot area; add the oil, onions, zucchini, and garlic in the pot. Cook for 4-5 minutes to cook well and soften.
4. Add remaining ingredients except for coconut milk.
5. Close the pot lid and seal the valve to avoid any leakage. Find and press "Soup" cooking setting and set cooking time to 15 minutes.
6. Allow the recipe ingredients to cook for the set time, and after that, the timer reads "zero".
7. Press "Cancel" and press "NPR" setting for natural pressure release. It takes 8-10 times for all inside pressure to release.
8. Open the pot and add the coconut milk. Thoroughly blend the mixture with an immersion blender and serve warm!

Cauliflower Chickpea Soup

Prep Time: 5min.
Cooking Time: 10 min.
Number of Servings: 8
Ingredients:

- 1 15-ounce can tomatoes, diced
- 1 teaspoon salt
- 1 tablespoon peanut butter
- ¼ teaspoon cayenne
- 3 cups water
- 1 large cauliflower head
- 1 15-ounce can chickpeas
- Pinch of cinnamon
- 1 pound sweet potato, diced

284

- 4 cloves garlic, minced
- 1 tablespoon grated ginger
- 1 tablespoon curry seasoning
- 1 jalapeno, seeded and minced
- 4 cups vegetable broth
- 1 large onion, chopped

Directions:
1. Take Instant Pot and carefully arrange it over a clean, dry kitchen platform. Turn on the appliance.
2. Find and press "Sauté" cooking function.
3. In the cooking pot area; add the oil and onions in the pot. Cook for 3 minutes to cook well and soften.
4. Add the garlic and cook for 1 minute. Add the broth, potatoes, curry, and cinnamon.
5. Close the pot lid and seal the valve to avoid any leakage. Find and press "Manual" cooking setting and set cooking time to 5 minutes.
6. Allow the recipe ingredients to cook for the set time, and after that, the timer reads "zero". Press "Cancel" and press "QPR" setting for quick pressure release.
7. Open the pot and
8. Add everything else except peanut butter.
9. Close the pot lid and seal the valve to avoid any leakage. Find and press "Manual" cooking setting and set cooking time to 1 minutes.
10. Allow the recipe ingredients to cook for the set time, and after that, the timer reads "zero".
11. Press "Cancel" and press "NPR" setting for natural pressure release. It takes 8-10 times for all inside pressure to release.
12. Stir in peanut butter and serve.

Zucchini Instant Veggie Soup

Prep Time: 5 min.
Cooking Time: 30 min.
Number of Servings: 5-6
Ingredients:
- Juice of 1 lime

- 4 cloves garlic, crushed

- 6 stalks lemongrass, chopped

- 3 cups coconut milk

- 6 large peeled carrots, roughly chopped

- 2 zucchinis, roughly chopped

- 1-inch piece of ginger, minced

- 2 onions, roughly chopped

- Cilantro leaves, chopped

Directions:
1. Take your Instant Pot and place it on a clean kitchen platform. Turn it on after plugging it into a power socket.
2. Open the lid from the top and put it aside; start adding the mentioned ingredients inside and gently stir them. Do not add the zucchini.
3. Close the lid and lock. Ensure that you have sealed the valve to avoid leakage.
4. Press "Soup" mode and set timer for 15 minutes. It will take a few minutes for the pot to build inside pressure and start cooking.
5. After the timer reads zero, press "Cancel" and quick release pressure.
6. Carefully remove the lid and add the zucchini.
7. Press "Steam" mode and set timer for 15 minutes.
8. After the timer reads zero, press "Cancel" and quick release pressure. Cool for a while and blend the mixture in a blender or food processor.
9. Garnish with cilantro and serve warm!

Tomato Veggie Soup

Prep Time: 5-8 min.
Cooking Time: 10 min.
Number of Servings: 6-8
Ingredients:
- 3 tablespoon tomato paste

- 4 tablespoon vegan butter

- 28-ounce tomatoes, whole

- 1 potato, diced

- 1 carrot, chopped

- 1 chopped onion

- 3 tablespoon tomatoes (sun-dried), chopped

- 2 pinches black pepper

- 2 teaspoon salt

- 4 cups water

Directions:
1. Take your Instant Pot and place it on a clean kitchen platform. Turn it on after plugging it into a power socket.
2. Put the pot on "Saute" mode. In the pot, add the carrots, onions, pepper, and butter; cook for 5 minutes until the ingredients become soft.
3. Now mix in the salt, water, paste, potatoes, and both tomatoes.
4. Close the lid and lock. Ensure that you have sealed the valve to avoid leakage.

5. Press "Soup" mode and set timer for 5 minutes. It will take a few minutes for the pot to build inside pressure and start cooking.
6. After the timer reads zero, press "Cancel" and naturally release pressure. It takes about 8-10 minutes to naturally release pressure.
7. Carefully remove the lid and transfer the mixture in a blender to make it smooth.
8. Serve warm!

Squash Cranberry Soup

Prep Time: 8-10 min.
Cooking Time: 10 min.
Number of Servings: 5
Ingredients:
- 3 cups water

- 1/2 cup coconut milk

- 1 teaspoon curry powder

- 1 (3 pounds) peeled butternut squash, make small chunks

- 1 ½ teaspoon sea salt

- 1 teaspoon olive oil

- 1 chopped onion

- 2 garlic cloves, minced

- Dried cranberries (optional)

Directions:
1. Take your Instant Pot and place it on a clean kitchen platform. Turn it on after plugging it into a power socket.
2. Put the pot on "Saute" mode. In the pot, add the oil and onions; cook for 1-2 minutes until the ingredients become soft.
3. Mix in the curry powder and garlic; continue cooking for 1 minute.
4. Mix the squash, water, and salt.
5. Close the lid and lock. Ensure that you have sealed the valve to avoid leakage.
6. Press "Soup" mode and set timer for 10 minutes. It will take a few minutes for the pot to build inside pressure and start cooking.
7. After the timer reads zero, press "Cancel" and naturally release pressure. It takes about 8-10 minutes to naturally release pressure.
8. Carefully remove the lid and transfer the mixture in a blender to make it smooth.
9. Add the coconut milk; adjust the seasoning as needed. Top with dried cranberries and serve warm!

Wholesome Bean Potato Curry

Prep Time: 8-10 min.
Cooking Time: 25-30 min.
Number of Servings: 4-5
Ingredients:
- 3 tablespoons arrowroot powder
- 13 ounces coconut milk, full fat
- 2 cups green beans, make small pieces
- 2 cups water
- 1 yellow onion, chopped
- Cooking oil as needed
- 5 cups potatoes, make chunks
- 4 large garlic cloves, chopped finely
- 2 tablespoons curry powder
- Pepper and salt as needed

Directions:
1. Take your Instant Pot and place it on a clean kitchen platform. Turn it on after plugging it into a power socket.
2. Put the pot on "Saute" mode. In the pot, add the oil and onions; cook for 2-3 minutes until the ingredients become soft.
3. Add the garlic and cook for 1-2 more minutes. Add remaining ingredients inside and gently stir them. Do not add the green beans.
4. Close the lid and lock. Ensure that you have sealed the valve to avoid leakage.
5. Press "Manual" mode and set timer from 20 minutes. It will take a few minutes for the pot to build inside pressure and start cooking.
6. After the timer reads zero, press "Cancel" and naturally release pressure. It takes about 8-10 minutes to naturally release pressure.
7. Carefully remove the lid.
8. Put the pot on "Saute" mode. Add the beans, pepper, and salt; cook for 4-5 minutes until the beans turn tender.
9. Serve warm!

Zucchini Coconut Soup

Prep Time: 8-10 min.
Cooking Time: 20 min.
Number of Servings: 8
Ingredients:
- 5 medium zucchinis, make small pieces or chunks
- 1 tablespoon coconut oil
- 2 onions, quartered
- 6 cups vegetable stock

- 4 cloves garlic, sliced

- 1/2 cup coconut milk

- Salt and pepper as needed

Directions:
1. Take your Instant Pot and place it on a clean kitchen platform. Turn it on after plugging it into a power socket.
2. Put the pot on "Saute" mode. In the pot, add the oil, zucchini, garlic, and onions; cook for 4-5 minutes until the ingredients become soft.
3. Gradually add other ingredients inside and stir well. Do not add the milk.
4. Close the lid and lock. Ensure that you have sealed the valve to avoid leakage.
5. Press "Soup" mode and set timer for 15 minutes. It will take a few minutes for the pot to build inside pressure and start cooking.
6. After the timer reads zero, press "Cancel" and naturally release pressure. It takes about 8-10 minutes to naturally release pressure.
7. Carefully remove the lid and transfer the mixture in a blender to make it smooth.
8. Serve warm!

Mushroom Lentil Soup

Prep Time: 8-10 min.
Cooking Time: 10 min.
Number of Servings: 7-8
Ingredients:
- 1 ½ pounds red potatoes, cubed
- 1 yellow onion, chopped
- 8 cups veggie stock
- 2 cups green lentils
- Pepper and salt as needed
- 2 celery ribs, chopped
- 2 bay leaves
- 8 ounces mushrooms, make quarters
- 2 carrots, sliced
- 4 minced garlic cloves
- 1 teaspoon rosemary, dry
- ½ teaspoon sage, dry
- 2 teaspoons thyme, dry
- 1 tablespoon soy sauce

Directions:
1. Take your Instant Pot and place it on a clean kitchen platform. Turn it on after plugging it into a power socket.
2. Open the lid from the top and put it aside; start adding the mentioned ingredients inside and gently stir them.
3. Close the lid and lock. Ensure that you have sealed the valve to avoid leakage.

4. Press "Manual" mode and set timer for 10 minutes. It will take a few minutes for the pot to build inside pressure and start cooking.
5. After the timer reads zero, press "Cancel" and naturally release pressure. It takes about 8-10 minutes to naturally release pressure.
6. Carefully remove the lid, remove bay leaf and serve warm!

Instant Carrot Soup

Prep Time: 10-15 min.
Cooking Time: 22 min.
Number of Servings: 2
Ingredients:
- ½ teaspoon fresh ginger, minced
- 1 garlic clove, minced
- ½ pound carrots, peeled and chopped
- ½ tablespoon Sriracha
- ⅛ teaspoon brown sugar
- 7-ounce canned unsweetened coconut milk
- 1 cup chicken broth
- 1 tablespoon fresh cilantro, chopped
- 1 tablespoon unsalted butter
- 1 small onion, chopped
- Pepper and salt as per taste preference

Directions:
1. Switch on the pot after placing it on a clean and dry platform. Press "Saute" cooking function.
2. Open the pot lid; add the butter and onions in the pot; cook for 2-3 minutes to cook well and soften.
3. Add the ginger and garlic and cook for 1 minute. Add the carrots, salt, and black pepper and cook for another 2 minutes.
4. Mix in the coconut milk, broth, and Sriracha.
5. Close the pot by closing the top lid. Also, ensure to seal the valve.
6. Press "Manual" cooking function and set cooking time to 6 minutes. It will start cooking after a few minutes. Let the pot mix cook under pressure until the timer reads zero.
7. Press "Cancel" cooking function and press "Natural release (NPR)" setting. It will take 8-10 minutes for natural pressure release.
8. Open the pot and mix in the sugar. With an immersion blender, puree the soup.
9. Serve immediately; top with some cilantro.

Chicken Ginger Soup

Prep Time: 5 min.
Cooking Time: 15 min.
Number of Servings: 2
Ingredients:
- 1-teaspoon ginger
- 2 teaspoons minced garlic
- ½ cup chopped cilantro

- 1-teaspoon cinnamon
- 1-teaspoon coriander
- 1-tablespoon olive oil
- 1-tablespoon sugar
- 1 pound. chopped chicken
- ¼ cup chopped onion
- 3 cups low sodium chicken broth
- 1-tablespoon fish sauce
- ¾ teaspoon salt

Directions:
1. Switch on the pot after placing it on a clean and dry platform. Press "Sauté" cooking function.
2. Open the pot lid; add the butter, garlic, and onions in the pot; cook for 2-3 minutes to cook well and soften.
3. Mix in the chopped chicken, ginger, cilantro, sugar, cinnamon, coriander, fish sauce, and salt.
4. Pour chicken broth and stir gently.
5. Close the pot by closing the top lid. Also, ensure to seal the valve.
6. Press "Manual" cooking function and set cooking time to 15 minutes. It will start cooking after a few minutes. Let the pot mix cook under pressure until the timer reads zero.
7. Press "Cancel" cooking function and press "Natural release (NPR)" setting. It will take 8-10 minutes for natural pressure release.
8. Open the pot and serve warm. Enjoy it with your loved one!

Minestrone Pasta Soup

Prep Time: 5-8 min.
Cooking Time: 8 min.
Number of Servings: 2
Ingredients:
- 2 cups chicken broth
- ½ cup elbow pasta
- 14 ounces tomatoes, diced
- 1 cup cooked white beans
- 1 carrot, diced
- 1 teaspoon dried basil
- 1 tablespoon olive oil
- 1 teaspoon dried oregano
- 2 garlic cloves, minced
- 1 bay leaf
- 1 onion, diced
- ¼ cup fresh spinach
- Pepper and salt as per taste preference

Directions:
1. Switch on the pot after placing it on a clean and dry platform. Press "Saute" cooking function.
2. Open the pot lid; add the oil, carrot, onion, garlic, and celery in the pot; cook until turn tender and soft.

3. Add the oregano, basil, pepper, and salt. Mix the tomatoes, spinach, bone broth, pasta, and bay leaf.
4. Close the pot by closing the top lid. Also, ensure to seal the valve.
5. Press "Manual" cooking function and set cooking time to 6 minutes. It will start cooking after a few minutes. Let the pot mix cook under pressure until the timer reads zero.
6. Press "Cancel" cooking function and press "Natural release (NPR)" setting. It will take 8-10 minutes for natural pressure release.
7. Open the pot; add the beans and serve warm. Enjoy it with your loved one!

Spiced Black Bean Soup

Prep Time: 10-12 min.
Cooking Time: 35 min.
Number of Servings: 2
Ingredients:
- 1 tablespoon garlic paste
- 1 tablespoon ginger paste
- 1 teaspoon red chili powder
- ½ teaspoon ground turmeric
- ½ teaspoon garam masala
- 2 teaspoons ground coriander
- 1 tablespoon olive oil
- 1 teaspoon cumin seeds
- 1 medium onion, chopped
- Salt as per taste preference
- 1 cup black beans, soaked overnight and drained
- 2 cups water
- 1 teaspoon lemon juice

Directions:
1. Switch on the pot after placing it on a clean and dry platform. Press "Sauté" cooking function.
2. Open the pot lid; add the oil and cumin seeds in the pot; cook for 30 seconds.
3. Add the onion, garlic, spices, and ginger; cook for 3-4 minutes to cook well and soften.
4. Mix in the chickpeas and water. Close the pot by closing the top lid. Also, ensure to seal the valve.
5. Press "Bean/Chili" cooking function and set cooking time to 30 minutes. It will start cooking after a few minutes. Let the pot mix cook under pressure until the timer reads zero.
6. Press "Cancel" cooking function and press "Natural release (NPR)" setting. It will take 8-10 minutes for natural pressure release.
7. Open the pot; mix the lemon juice and serve warm. Enjoy it with your loved one!

Sweet Potato Chicken Stew

Prep Time: 8-10min.
Cooking Time: 35 min.
Number of Servings: 5-6
Ingredients:
- 1 yellow onion, chopped

- ¼ pound baby carrots, sliced
- ½ teaspoon thyme, dried
- 2 tablespoons tomato paste
- 2 cups chicken stock
- 1 celery stalk, chopped
- 6 chicken thighs
- 1 teaspoon olive oil
- A pinch of pepper and salt
- 15 ounces canned tomatoes, chopped
- 1 pound sweet potatoes, peeled and cubed

Directions:
1. Switch on your instant pot after placing it on a clean and dry kitchen platform. Press "Saute" cooking function.
2. Open the pot lid; add the oil, chicken, salt, and pepper in the pot; start cooking for 3-4 minutes on each side to cook well and brown.
3. Add the celery, onion, tomato paste, carrots, thyme, salt and pepper to your instant pot; stir and cook for 4-5 minutes.
4. Add the stock, return chicken, add tomatoes and potatoes; stir gently.
5. Close the pot by closing the top lid. Also, ensure to seal the valve.
6. Press "Manual" cooking function and set cooking time to 15 minutes. It will start cooking after a few minutes. Let the pot mix cook under pressure until the timer reads zero.
7. Turn off and press "Cancel" cooking function. Quick release pressure.
8. Open the pot and transfer chicken pieces to a cutting board, remove bones, shred meat and return it to the stew.
9. Divide into bowls and serve hot. Enjoy!

Carrot Coconut Soup

Prep Time: 5min.
Cooking Time: 20 min.
Number of Servings: 4
Ingredients:
- 2 tablespoons olive oil
- 2 garlic cloves, minced
- 2 ½ pounds carrots, chopped
- 2 tablespoons ginger, grated
- 4 ounces coconut milk
- 1 cup water
- 1 cup yellow onion, chopped
- 4 cups veggie stock
- 3 tablespoons ghee, melted
- Salt and pepper to the taste

Directions:
1. Switch on your instant pot after placing it on a clean and dry kitchen platform.

2. Open the pot lid and slowly start adding the ingredients mentioned above in the pot. Give the ingredients a little stir.
3. Close the pot by closing the top lid. Also, ensure to seal the valve.
4. Press "Manual" cooking function and set cooking time to 20 minutes. It will start cooking after a few minutes. Let the pot mix cook under pressure until the timer reads zero.
5. Turn off and press "Cancel" cooking function. Quick release pressure.
6. Open the pot and blend the mix using an immersion blender. Serve warm!

Turkey Chili Stew

Prep Time: 8-10min.
Cooking Time: 10 min.
Number of Servings: 4
Ingredients:
- 1 yellow onion, chopped
- 1 yellow bell pepper, chopped
- 1 and ½ teaspoons cumin, ground
- 12 ounces veggies stock
- 3 garlic cloves, minced
- 2 and ½ tablespoons chili powder
- 1 pound turkey meat, ground
- 5 ounces water
- A pinch of salt and cayenne pepper

Directions:
1. Switch on your instant pot after placing it on a clean and dry kitchen platform.
2. Open the pot lid and slowly start adding the meat and water in the pot. Give the ingredients a little stir.
3. Close the pot by closing the top lid. Also, ensure to seal the valve.
4. Press "Manual" cooking function and set cooking time to 5 minutes. It will start cooking after a few minutes. Let the pot mix cook under pressure until the timer reads zero.
5. Turn off and press "Cancel" cooking function. Quick release pressure.
6. Open the pot. Add the pepper, onion, garlic, chili powder, cumin, salt, cayenne, and veggie stock, stir gently.
7. Cover again and cook for 5 minutes more. Divide it between plates and serve warm!

Sweet Potato Fish Stew

Prep Time: 5min.
Cooking Time: 8-10 min.
Number of Servings: 7-8
Ingredients:
- 3 carrots, chopped
- 1 yellow onion, chopped
- 14 ounces chicken stock
- 1 pound halibut, boneless and cubed
- 1 red bell pepper, chopped
- 4 sweet potatoes, cubed

- 1 bay leaf
- ¼ teaspoon saffron powder
- 2 garlic cloves, minced
- ¼ cup parsley, chopped

Directions:
1. Switch on your instant pot after placing it on a clean and dry kitchen platform.
2. Open the pot lid and slowly start adding the stock, potatoes, carrots, onion, garlic, saffron, parsley and bay leaf ingredients in the pot. Give the ingredients a little stir.
3. Close the pot by closing the top lid. Also, ensure to seal the valve.
4. Press "Manual" cooking function and set cooking time to 4 minutes. It will start cooking after a few minutes. Let the pot mix cook under pressure until the timer reads zero.
5. Turn off and press "Cancel" cooking function. Quick release pressure.
6. Open the pot and add the fish and red bell pepper, cover and cook for 6 minutes more.
7. Discard bay leaf, and serve warm!

Beef Mushroom Stew

Prep Time: 8-10 min.
Cooking Time: 20-25 min.
Number of Servings: 6
Ingredients:
- 1 teaspoon rosemary, chopped
- 1 celery stalk, chopped
- 1 and ½ cups beef stock
- 1 yellow onion, chopped
- 2 tablespoons coconut flour
- 2 tablespoons ghee, melted
- 2 carrots, chopped
- 1 tablespoon olive oil
- 2-pound beef chuck, cubed
- 1-ounce porcini mushrooms, chopped
- A pinch of salt and black pepper

Directions:
1. Switch on your instant pot after placing it on a clean and dry kitchen platform. Press "Saute" cooking function.
2. Open the pot lid; add the oil and beef in the pot; start cooking for 5 minutes to cook well and brown evenly.
3. Mix the onion, celery, rosemary, salt, pepper, carrots, mushrooms, and stock.
4. Close the pot by closing the top lid. Also, ensure to seal the valve.
5. Press "Manual" cooking function and set cooking time to 15 minutes. It will start cooking after a few minutes. Let the pot mix cook under pressure until the timer reads zero.
6. Turn off and press "Cancel" cooking function. Quick release pressure.
7. Open the pot and press the simmer mode.
8. Heat up a saucepan; add the ghee, flour and 6 tablespoons cooking liquid from the stew, stir and add the mixture to the beef stew.
9. Simmer the Instant Pot for 5 minutes, divide into bowls and serve warm!

Beet Carrot Soup

Prep Time: 8-10min.
Cooking Time: 10 min.
Number of Servings: 4
Ingredients:

- 2 carrots, chopped
- 6 cups veggie stock
- ½ teaspoon thyme leaves, chopped
- 3 beets, chopped
- 3 bay leaves
- 1 tablespoon olive oil
- 1 red onion, chopped
- 1 and ½ tablespoons parsley, chopped
- Pepper and salt to the taste

Directions:

1. Switch on your instant pot after placing it on a clean and dry kitchen platform. Press "Saute" cooking function.
2. Open the pot lid; add the oil and onions in the pot; start cooking for 4-5 minutes to cook well and soften.
3. Add the carrots, beets, thyme, bay leaves, stock, salt, and pepper, stir gently.
4. Close the pot by closing the top lid. Also, ensure to seal the valve.
5. Press "Manual" cooking function and set cooking time to 5 minutes. It will start cooking after a few minutes. Let the pot mix cook under pressure until the timer reads zero.
6. Turn off and press "Cancel" cooking function. Quick release pressure.
7. Open the pot and discard bay leaves; blend using an immersion blender.
8. Mix the parsley, stir, divide into soup bowls and enjoy!

Chapter 11: Snacks & Appetizers

Queso Sauce with Chorizo

Prep Time: 2 minutes
Cooking Time: 5 minutes
Number of Servings: 6
Ingredients:
- 1/2 pound chorizo sausage
- 1 jalapeno, finely chopped
- 1 scallion, sliced
- 1 pound Mexican cheese blend, shredded

Directions:
1. Set the Instant Pot to Saute mode and add the sausage. Brown, then add the jalapeno and scallion, followed by the cheese.
2. Close the lid and set the cooking time for 5 minutes on high pressure.
3. Serve with tortilla chips.

Artichoke Dip with Nachos

Prep Time: 55-60 min.
Cooking Time: 20 min.
Number of Servings: 2
Ingredients:
- 8 medium sized artichokes, make halves
- 2 garlic cloves, minced
- ¾ cup plain yogurt
- ¾ teaspoon salt
- ¼ teaspoon ground pepper
- ½ cup grated ricotta cheese
- ½ lemon
- ½ cup cannellini beans, soaked for about 4 hours
- 1 cup vegetable broth
- Nachos to serve

Directions:
1. Boil artichokes in water for 30 minutes in a pan. Remove the leaves and discard the chokes.
2. Switch on the pot after placing it on a clean and dry platform.
3. Open the pot lid and place the garlic cloves, lemon, vegetable broth, artichokes, and beans in the cooking pot area. Give the ingredients a little stir.
4. Close the pot by closing the top lid. Also, ensure to seal the valve.
5. Press "Manual" cooking function and set cooking time to 20 minutes. It will start cooking after a few minutes. Let the pot mix cook under pressure until the timer reads zero.
6. Press "Cancel" cooking function and press "Natural release (NPR)" setting. It will take 8-10 minutes for natural pressure release.
7. Open the pot. Mix the yogurt, ground pepper, salt, and cheese and mix well.

8. Add these ingredients to a blender and combine until it forms a smooth paste. Serve along with some nachos.

Cheesy Asparagus

Prep Time: 8-10 min.
Cooking Time: 3 min.
Number of Servings: 2
Ingredients:
- ½ pound asparagus spears
- 5-ounces sliced prosciutto

Directions:
1. Wrap the prosciutto slices around the asparagus.
2. Switch on the pot after placing it on a clean and dry platform.
3. Pour 2 cups water into the pot. Arrange the trivet inside it; arrange the asparagus over the trivet.
4. Close the pot by closing the top lid. Also, ensure to seal the valve.
5. Press "Manual" cooking function and set cooking time to 3 minutes. It will start cooking after a few minutes. Let the pot mix cook under pressure until the timer reads zero.
6. Press "Cancel" cooking function and press "Natural release (NPR)" setting. It will take 8-10 minutes for natural pressure release.
7. Open the pot and serve warm. Enjoy it with your loved one!

Oregano Black Bean

Prep Time: 5-8min.
Cooking Time: 20 min.
Number of Servings: 6
Ingredients:
- 15 cherry tomatoes, sliced in half
- 1 teaspoon coriander
- 1 teaspoon oregano
- ½ teaspoon chili flakes
- 1 teaspoon cumin
- 1 teaspoon sea salt
- 2 tablespoons vegetable oil
- 1 teaspoon paprika
- 1 ½ cups dry black beans
- 3 garlic cloves, minced
- 1 large yellow onion
- 2 cubes vegetable bouillon

Directions:
1. Take Instant Pot and carefully arrange it over a clean, dry kitchen platform. Turn on the appliance.
2. In the cooking pot area; add beans and water to the pressure cooker and dissolve in bouillon cubes.
3. Close the pot lid and seal the valve to avoid any leakage. Find and press "Manual" cooking setting and set cooking time to 15 minutes.

298

4. Allow the recipe ingredients to cook for the set time and after that, the timer reads "zero".
5. Press "Cancel" and press "NPR" setting for natural pressure release. It takes 8-10 times for all inside pressure to release.
6. Open the pot and remove beans from the pot.
7. Place oil in the pot and using sauté setting, cook onion 3 minutes. Add garlic and cook 1 minute.
8. Put all remaining ingredients including the beans in the pot. Stir gently.
9. Close the pot lid and seal the valve to avoid any leakage. Find and press "Manual" cooking setting and set cooking time to 1 minutes.
10. Allow the recipe ingredients to cook for the set time, and after that, the timer reads "zero".
11. Press "Cancel" and press "NPR" setting for natural pressure release. It takes 8-10 times for all inside pressure to release.
12. Open the pot and arrange the cooked recipe in serving plates. Enjoy the vegan recipe!

Classic Potato Fries

Prep Time: 5min.
Cooking Time: 10-15 min.
Number of Servings:8
Ingredients:

- 2 pounds russet potatoes, peeled and slice to make fries

- 1/2 teaspoon baking soda

- 2 teaspoons kosher salt

- Canola oil to deep fry as needed

- 2 cups cold water

Directions:
1. Take Instant Pot and carefully arrange it over a clean, dry kitchen platform. Turn on the appliance.
2. Pour the water, soda and, salt in the cooking pot area. Arrange the trivet inside it; arrange the potatoes over the trivet.
3. Close the pot lid and seal the valve to avoid any leakage. Find and press "Manual" cooking setting and set cooking time to 2 minutes.
4. Allow the recipe ingredients to cook for the set time, and after that, the timer reads "zero".
5. Press "Cancel" and press "NPR" setting for natural pressure release. It takes 8-10 times for all inside pressure to release.
6. Open the pot and take out the fries.
7. Take a deep frying pan and add in the oil to a half depth of the pan size. Heat the pan over medium heat.
8. Add the fries in batches and fry until it is light golden brown. Enjoy the fries!

Chickpea Hummus

Prep Time: 5min.
Cooking Time: 10 min.
Number of Servings: 5-6
Ingredients:

- 1 tablespoon hot sauce of choice
- 1 tablespoon lemon juice
- 1 teaspoon salt
- 1 teaspoon black pepper
- ½ teaspoon smoked paprika
- 1 cup dry chickpeas, rinsed
- 3-4 tablespoons tahini
- 3 garlic cloves
- 3 cups water

Directions:
1. Take Instant Pot and carefully arrange it over a clean, dry kitchen platform. Turn on the appliance.
2. In the cooking pot area, add the beans and water.
3. Close the pot lid and seal the valve to avoid any leakage. Find and press "Manual" cooking setting and set cooking time to 10 minutes.
4. Allow the recipe ingredients to cook for the set time, and after that, the timer reads "zero". Press "Cancel" and press "NPR" setting for natural pressure release. It takes 8-10 times for all inside pressure to release.
5. Open the pot. Add chickpeas and garlic to food processor and pulse to form a crumbly mix. Add other ingredients and pulse to combine.
6. Gradually add water to get the desired consistency. Serve, or also you can refrigerate, and use it later.

Soy Sauce Tofu

Prep Time: 10min.
Cooking Time: 2 ½ hour
Number of Servings: 2
Ingredients:
- 1/2 tablespoon apple cider vinegar

- 1 tablespoon soy sauce

- 1/4 teaspoon garlic powder

- 1/4 teaspoon salt

- 1 container extra firm tofu, prepare 1-inch cubes

- 1/2 tablespoon red pepper flakes

- 3/4 cup ketchup

- 1 1/2 tablespoon brown sugar

Directions:
1. Take Instant Pot and carefully arrange it over a clean, dry kitchen platform. Turn on the appliance.
2. In the cooking pot area, add the mentioned ingredients. Stir the ingredients gently.

3. Close the pot lid and seal the valve to avoid any leakage. Find and press "Slow cook" cooking setting and set cooking time to 2 hours 30 minutes.
4. Allow the recipe ingredients to cook for the set time, and after that, the timer reads "zero".
5. Press "Cancel" and press "NPR" setting for natural pressure release. It takes 8-10 times for all inside pressure to release.
6. Cook for more time in the mix is too watery.
7. Open the pot and arrange the cooked recipe in serving plates. Enjoy the vegan recipe!

Honey Carrots

Prep Time: 10-15 min.
Cooking Time: 5 min.
Number of Servings: 2
Ingredients:
- 1 tablespoon Dijon mustard
- 1 tablespoon honey
- ¼ teaspoon paprika
- 1 teaspoon garlic, minced
- ½ teaspoon ground cumin
- ½ pound carrots
- 1 tablespoon butter
- Pepper and salt as per taste preference
- Dash of hot sauce

Directions:
1. Take the carrots and cut into quarters lengthwise and then cut each quarter in half.
2. Switch on the pot after placing it on a clean and dry platform.
3. Pour 1 cup water into the pot. Arrange the trivet inside it; arrange the carrots over the trivet.
4. Close the pot by closing the top lid. Also, ensure to seal the valve.
5. Press "Manual" cooking function and set cooking time to 2 minutes. It will start cooking after a few minutes. Let the pot mix cook under pressure until the timer reads zero.
6. Press "Cancel" cooking function and press "Quick release" setting.
7. Transfer carrots to a plate.
8. Empty the pot, pat the pot dry. Press "Sauté" cooking function.
9. Open the pot lid; add the butter and other in the pot; cook for 30 seconds.
10. Press "Cancel" and add the carrots. Toss well and serve!

Potato Buttermilk Appetizer

Prep Time: 8-10 min.
Cooking Time: 12 min.
Number of Servings: 6
Ingredients:
- 1/3 cup buttermilk, low-fat
- ½ teaspoon kosher salt
- ¼ cup sour cream
- 3 cups water
- 2-pound russet potatoes, peeled and make quarters

- 1 teaspoon salt
- 2 tablespoons butter
- Parsley as required, chopped
- Black pepper as needed

Directions:
1. Take an Instant Pot; open the top lid.
2. Add the water, salt, and potato in the cooking pot. Using a spatula, gently stir to combine well.
3. Close the top lid and make sure the valve is sealed.
4. Press "MANUAL" cooking function. Adjust cooking time to 10-12 minutes.
5. Allow pressure to build and cook the ingredients for the set time.
6. After the set cooking time ends, press "CANCEL" and then press "QPR". Instant Pot will quickly release pressure.
7. Open the top lid, drain water except for ½ cup and add the potatoes in a blender. Add ½ cup of water also.
8. Add in the remaining ingredients and blend to create a mash like consistency.
9. Serve warm.

Orange Glazed Potatoes

Prep Time: 8-10 min.
Cooking Time: 20 min.
Number of Servings: 7-8
Ingredients:
- 1 tablespoon cinnamon
- 1 tablespoon blackstrap molasses
- ½ cup orange juice
- 4 cups sweet potatoes, make small-sized pieces
- 1 teaspoon vanilla
- ¼ cup sugar

Directions:
1. In a heat-proof bowl, add the potatoes. Mix in the cinnamon, molasses, sugar, orange juice, and vanilla.
2. Take an Instant Pot; open the top lid.
3. Pour 1 cup water and place steamer basket/trivet inside the cooking pot.
4. Arrange the bowl over the basket/trivet.
5. Close the top lid and make sure the valve is sealed.
6. Press "MANUAL" cooking function. Adjust cooking time to 20-22 minutes.
7. Allow pressure to build and cook the ingredients for the set time.
8. After the set cooking time ends, press "CANCEL" and then press "NPR". Instant Pot will slowly and naturally release the pressure for 8-10 minutes.
9. Open the top lid, add the cooked mixture in serving plates.
10. Serve warm.

Broccoli Spinach Greens

Prep Time: 8-10 min.
Cooking Time: 5 min.
Number of Servings: 4-5
Ingredients:

- 2 cups kale, chopped
- 1/2 teaspoon cumin, ground
- 2 cups broccoli, chopped
- 2 cups baby spinach
- 1/2 teaspoon coriander, ground
- 2 cloves garlic, crushed or minced
- 2 tablespoons coconut oil
- 1 tablespoon ginger, minced

Directions:
1. Take an Instant Pot; open the top lid.
2. Press "SAUTÉ" cooking function.
3. In the cooking pot area, add the oil, garlic, ginger, and broccoli. Cook until turn translucent and softened for 4-5 minutes.
4. Add the remaining ingredients.
5. Cook until spinach and kale are wilted.
6. Add the cooked mixture in serving plates.
7. Serve warm.

Cheesy Artichokes

Prep Time: 8-10 min.
Cooking Time: 12 min.
Number of Servings: 4
Ingredients:

- 2 teaspoons minced garlic
- 4 washed artichokes, trimmed
- ¼ cup shredded parmesan cheese
- 4 teaspoons olive oil
- ½ cup vegetable broth

Directions:
1. Spread the garlic and oil over the artichokes. Top with the cheese.
2. Take an Instant Pot; open the top lid.
3. Pour the broth and place steamer basket/trivet inside the cooking pot.
4. Arrange the artichokes over the basket/trivet.
5. Close the top lid and make sure the valve is sealed.
6. Press "MANUAL" cooking function. Adjust cooking time to 8-12 minutes. For smaller artichokes, 8 minutes is adequate.
7. Allow pressure to build and cook the ingredients for the set time.
8. After the set cooking time ends, press "CANCEL" and then press "QPR". Instant Pot will quickly release pressure.
9. Open the top lid, add the cooked mixture in serving plates.

Bean Jalapeno Dip

Prep Time: 8-10 min.
Cooking Time: 30 min.
Number of Servings: 2
Ingredients:

- 1 cup dried pinto beans, rinsed
- ½ teaspoon paprika
- 1 jalapeno, seeded
- 2 cloves garlic, chopped
- ½ teaspoon chili powder
- ½ teaspoon cumin
- 1 medium onion, quartered
- ¼ teaspoon black pepper
- ¼ cup salsa
- ½ teaspoon salt
- 1 ½ cups water

Directions:
1. Switch on the pot after placing it on a clean and dry platform.
2. Open the pot lid and place the above-mentioned ingredients in the cooking pot area. Give the ingredients a little stir.
3. Close the pot by closing the top lid. Also, ensure to seal the valve.
4. Press "Manual" cooking function and set cooking time to 28 minutes. It will start cooking after a few minutes. Let the pot mix cook under pressure until the timer reads zero.
5. Press "Cancel" cooking function and press "Quick release" setting.
6. Open the pot and blend in a blender to make a smooth paste. Enjoy with your favorite crackers or tortilla chips.

Cashew Hummus

Prep Time: 5-8 min.
Cooking Time: 1 min.
Number of Servings: 5-6
Ingredients:

- 1 lemon, juiced
- 4 cloves garlic
- ½ teaspoon sea salt
- 1 teaspoon red pepper flakes
- 1 1/2 cups cashews
- ½ teaspoon cumin
- 2 tablespoons tahini
- ½ cup extra-virgin olive oil
- Handful of parsley

Directions:
1. Take your Instant Pot; open the top lid. Plug it and turn it on.
2. Press "SAUTÉ" setting and the pot will start heating up.
3. In the cooking pot area, add the oil and garlic. Cook for only 10 seconds.

4. Take a blender and add the cooked garlic and remaining ingredients.
5. Blend well and serve the hummus with vegetable sticks or low carb crackers.

Seasoned Peanut Mania

Prep Time: 8-10 min.
Cooking Time: 90 min.
Number of Servings: 5-6
Ingredients:

- ¼ cup kosher salt
- ¼ cup apple cider vinegar
- 1 pound raw peanuts with shells
- 1/3 cup Old Bay seasoning
- 1 tablespoon mustard seeds
- 1 bay leaf
- Water, as required

Directions:
1. Take your Instant Pot; open the top lid. Plug it and turn it on.
2. In the cooking pot area, add all the ingredients and enough water to cover all ingredients.
3. Close the top lid and seal its valve.
4. Press "MANUAL" setting. Adjust cooking time to 75-80 minutes.
5. Allow the recipe to cook for the set cooking time.
6. After the set cooking time ends, press "CANCEL" and then press "NPR (Natural Pressure Release)".
7. Instant Pot will slowly and naturally release the pressure.
8. Open the top lid, add the cooked recipe mix in serving plates.
9. Drain liquid and serve.

Cheddar Chicken Dip

Prep Time: 5 min.
Cooking Time: 15 min.
Number of Servings: 7-8
Ingredients:
- 16 ounces cheddar cheese
- 1 stick butter
- 1 packet ranch dip mix
- 1 cup cream cheese
- 1 pound chicken breast
- 1 cup hot sauce

Directions:
1. Arrange your Instant Pot over a dry, clean platform. Plug it in power socket and turn it on.
2. Open the lid from the top and put it aside; add the ranch, sauce, butter, cream cheese, and chicken and gently stir them.
3. Close the lid and lock. Ensure that you have sealed the valve to avoid leakage.

4. Press "Manual" mode from available cooking settings and set cooking time to 15 minutes. Instant Pot will start cooking the ingredients after a few minutes.
5. After the timer reads zero, press "Cancel" and quick release pressure.
6. Carefully remove the lid and shred up the chicken with a fork.
7. Mix the cheddar cheese and serve with low carb chips or veggies.

Zucchini Bites

Prep Time: 5-8 min.
Cooking Time: 2-3 min.
Number of Servings: 6
Ingredients:

- 1/2 teaspoon white pepper

- 1 cup coconut

- 3 tablespoons butter

- 1 teaspoon salt

- 4 tablespoons almond flour

- 1 medium size egg

- 1 zucchini, grated

Directions:
1. In a bowl (medium or large size), whisk the eggs. Add the almond flour, coconut, salt, and pepper.
2. Add the zucchini and mix well. Make small balls.
3. Arrange your Instant Pot over a dry, clean platform. Plug it in power socket and turn it on.
4. Coat the inner surface with the butter.
5. Now press "Saute" mode from available options. In the cooking area, add the balls; cook for a few minutes to brown the balls.
6. Enjoy them warm!

Boiled Cheese Peanuts

Prep Time: 5 min.
Cooking Time: 80 min.
Number of Servings: 4-6
Ingredients:
- 1/3 cup sea salt
- 1 pound raw peanuts
- Water as needed
- Shredded cheese of your choice

Directions:
1. Manually go through the peanuts and remove debris and broken pieces. Rinse them well and add to your pot.

2. Pour water to cover the peanuts and mix the salt.
3. If peanuts are floating, then set the trivet on top with a bowl to weight them down.
4. Press "Manual" mode from available cooking settings and set cooking time to 80 minutes. Instant Pot will start cooking the ingredients after a few minutes.
5. After the timer reads zero, press "Cancel" and quick release pressure.
6. Top the peanuts with shredded cheese of your choice.

Almond Zucchini Balls

Prep Time: 5 min.
Cooking Time: 4-8 min.
Number of Servings: 56
Ingredients:
- 1/2 teaspoon white pepper
- 1 cup coconut
- 4 tablespoons almond flour
- 3 tablespoons butter
- 1 teaspoon salt
- 1 egg
- 1 zucchini, grated

Directions:
1. In a bowl, whisk the eggs. Add the almond flour, coconut, salt, and white pepper.
2. Add the zucchini and combine; make small balls from the mix.
3. Take your Instant Pot; open the top lid. Plug it and turn it on.
4. Press "SAUTÉ" setting and the pot will start heating up.
5. In the cooking pot area, add the butter and balls.
6. Heat to brown the balls. Serve warm!

Turkey Meatball Snack

Prep Time: 5-8 min.
Cooking Time: 25 min.
Number of Servings: 7-8
Ingredients:

- ¼ teaspoon dried thyme
- ¼ teaspoon dried oregano
- ¼ teaspoon dried rosemary
- 1 pound lean ground turkey
- 1 organic egg
- ¼ teaspoon garlic powder
- Salt and (ground) black pepper, as needed
- 1½ cups sugar-free tomato sauce

Directions:
1. In a bowl, add all ingredients except tomato sauce and mix well. Make equal sized meatballs.
2. Take your Instant Pot; open the top lid. Plug it and turn it on.

3. In the cooking pot area, add the tomato sauce and meatballs. Using a spatula, stir the ingredients.
4. Close the top lid and seal its valve.
5. Press "MANUAL" setting. Adjust cooking time to 25 minutes.
6. Allow the recipe to cook for the set cooking time.
7. After the set cooking time ends, press "CANCEL" and then press "QPR (Quick Pressure Release)".
8. Instant Pot will quickly release the pressure.
9. Open the top lid, add the cooked recipe mix in serving plates.
10. Serve with some low carb dip of your choice.

Tangy Cashew Hummus

Prep Time: 8-10 min.
Cooking Time: 1 min.
Number of Servings: 6
Ingredients:
- 4 cloves garlic

- ½ cup olive oil, extra virgin

- 2 tablespoons tahini

- ½ teaspoon sea salt

- ½ teaspoon cumin

- Juice of 1 lemon

- 1 teaspoon red pepper flakes

- 1 1/2 cups cashews

- Handful Parsley

Directions:
1. Arrange your Instant Pot over a dry, clean platform. Plug it in power socket and turn it on.
2. Now press "Saute" mode from available options. In the cooking area, add the oil and garlic; cook for 10-15 seconds to soften the added ingredients.
3. Transfer the garlic in a blender and add the remaining ingredients.
4. Blend well to make a smooth mixture and serve with chips or vegetable sticks.

Garlic Brussels Sprouts

Prep Time: 5-8 min.
Cooking Time: 4 hours 30 min.
Number of Servings: 4-5
Ingredients:
- ¼ cup mayo
- 1 pound Brussels sprouts
- ¼ cup sour cream

- ¾ cup mozzarella, shredded
- 2 garlic cloves
- ¼ cup parmesan
- 4 ounces cream cheese
- ½ teaspoon thyme
- 1 tablespoon olive oil

Directions:
1. Preheat an oven to 400 degrees F.
2. Coat the sprouts with the oil, pepper, and salt. Add the garlic.
3. Bake the sprouts for 20-30 minutes. Flip halfway.
4. Remove skins from garlic, then mix everything in your pot.
5. Close the lid and lock. Ensure that you have sealed the valve to avoid leakage.
6. Press "Slow cook" mode from available cooking settings and set cooking time to 3-4 hours. Instant Pot will start cooking the ingredients after a few minutes.
7. After the timer reads zero, press "Cancel" and quick release pressure.
8. Carefully remove the lid and serve the prepared keto dish warm!

Scrumptious Coconut Cookies

Prep Time: 5-8 min.
Cooking Time: 10 min.
Number of Servings: 8
Ingredients:
- 1 cup sunflower seeds, crushed

- 1 cup coconut flour

- 4 tablespoons butter

- ¼ cup cream cheese

- ¼ teaspoon ground ginger

- 2 teaspoons stevia

- 1 teaspoon cinnamon

Directions:
1. In a bowl (medium or large size), mix the coconut flour, cinnamon, ginger, and seeds.
2. Add the cheese, butter, and sugar. Mix well. Make around 8 balls and roll up them.
3. Arrange your Instant Pot over a dry, clean platform. Plug it in power socket and turn it on.
4. Open the lid from the top and put it aside; add the cookies.
5. Close the lid and lock. Ensure that you have sealed the valve to avoid leakage.
6. Press "Manual" mode from available cooking settings and set cooking time to 10 minutes. Instant Pot will start cooking the ingredients after a few minutes.
7. After the timer reads zero, press "Cancel" and quick release pressure.
8. Carefully remove the lid and serve the prepared keto cookies warm!

Mayo Horseradish Snack

Prep Time: 10-15 min.
Cooking Time: 6 min.
Number of Servings: 5-6
Ingredients:
- 2 tablespoons white horseradish
- ½ teaspoon dill weed
- 6 large eggs
- ¼ cup mayonnaise
- ¼ teaspoon ground mustard
- Pinch of salt and (ground) black pepper
- Paprika, as needed

Directions:
1. Take your Instant Pot; open the top lid. Plug it and turn it on.
2. Pour 1 cup water and place steamer basket/trivet inside the pot; arrange the eggs over the basket/trivet.
3. Close the top lid and seal its valve.
4. Press "MANUAL" setting. Adjust cooking time to 6 minutes.
5. Allow the recipe to cook for the set cooking time.
6. After the set cooking time ends, press "CANCEL" and then press "QPR (Quick Pressure Release)".
7. Transfer eggs to a bowl of cold water to cool.
8. Take the eggs and remove yolks; add into a small bowl.
9. With a fork, mash the egg yolks. Add remaining ingredients except for paprika and mix well.
10. In a pastry bag, add the yolk mixture and pour into egg white halves evenly.
11. Sprinkle with paprika and serve.

Spinach Bacon Dips

Prep Time: 5-8 min.
Cooking Time: 4 min.
Number of Servings: 4
Ingredients:
- 1 teaspoon minced garlic
- 1/3 cup coconut milk
- 2 cups spinach, chopped
- 1/3 white onion, chopped
- 1-ounce bacon, chopped

Directions:
1. Take your Instant Pot; open the top lid. Plug it and turn it on.
2. In the cooking pot area, add all the ingredients. Using a spatula, stir the ingredients.
3. Close the top lid and seal its valve.
4. Press "MANUAL" setting. Adjust cooking time to 4 minutes.
5. Allow the recipe to cook for the set cooking time.
6. After the set cooking time ends, press "CANCEL" and then press "QPR (Quick Pressure Release)".

7. Instant Pot will quickly release the pressure.
8. Puree using a blender and serve with fresh vegetables or low carb crackers.

Classic Turnips Sticks

Prep Time: 5min.
Cooking Time: 5 min.
Number of Servings: 4
Ingredients:
- 2 pounds turnips, peeled and make sticks
- 1 teaspoon onion powder
- 1 teaspoon garlic powder
- ½ teaspoon oregano, dried
- 1 ½ tbs. cumin, ground
- ½ cup water
- 2 tbs. chili powder
- Finely ground pepper to the taste
- 2 tbs. olive oil

Directions:
1. In a mixing bowl, combine the chili powder with onion powder, garlic powder, oregano, cumin and parsnip sticks and toss.
2. Season with pepper, drizzle the oil and toss to coat well.
3. Switch on your instant pot after placing it on a clean and dry kitchen platform.
4. Pour the water into the cooking pot area. Arrange the trivet inside it; arrange the turnips over the trivet.
5. Close the pot by closing the top lid. Also, ensure to seal the valve.
6. Press "Manual" cooking function and set cooking time to 5 minutes. It will start cooking after a few minutes. Let the pot mix cook under pressure until the timer reads zero.
7. Turn off and press "Cancel" cooking function. Quick release pressure.
8. Open the pot and serve on a serving plate or bowl. Enjoy the Paleo dish!

Radish Lemon Snack

Prep Time: 5min.
Cooking Time: 12 min.
Number of Servings: 2
Ingredients:
- 1 tbs. chives, chopped
- ½ cup water
- 2 cups radishes, make quarters
- 1 tbs. lemon zest
- A pinch of salt and pepper
- 2 tbs. olive oil

Directions:
1. In a mixing bowl, combine the radishes with salt, pepper, chives, lemon zest and oil and toss to coat.
2. Switch on your instant pot after placing it on a clean and dry kitchen platform.

3. Pour the water into the cooking pot area. Arrange the trivet inside it; arrange the radishes over the trivet.
4. Close the pot by closing the top lid. Also, ensure to seal the valve.
5. Press "Manual" cooking function and set cooking time to 12 minutes. It will start cooking after a few minutes. Let the pot mix cook under pressure until the timer reads zero.
6. Turn off and press "Cancel" cooking function. Quick release pressure.
7. Open the pot and serve on a serving plate or bowl. Enjoy the Paleo dish!

Sweet Potato Lemon Spread

Prep Time: 8-10min.
Cooking Time: 12 min.
Number of Servings: 5-6
Ingredients:
- 2 tablespoons lemon juice
- ½ teaspoon cumin, ground
- 2 cups water+ 2 tablespoons water
- 5 garlic cloves, minced
- 2 cups sweet potatoes, peeled and chopped
- ¼ cup sesame seeds paste
- 1 tablespoon olive oil
- A pinch of salt

Directions:
1. Switch on your instant pot after placing it on a clean and dry kitchen platform.
2. Pour 2 cups water in the cooking pot area. Arrange the trivet inside it; arrange the potatoes over the trivet.
3. Close the pot by closing the top lid. Also, ensure to seal the valve.
4. Press "Manual" cooking function and set cooking time to 12 minutes. It will start cooking after a few minutes. Let the pot mix cook under pressure until the timer reads zero.
5. Turn off and press "Cancel" cooking function. Quick release pressure.
6. Open the pot and transfer potatoes to your food processor, add 2 tablespoons water, paste, lemon juice, garlic, oil, cumin and a pinch of salt. Pulse well.
7. Serve on a serving plate or bowl. Enjoy the Paleo dish!

Garlic Mushroom Snack

Prep Time: 8-10min.
Cooking Time: 10 min.
Number of Servings: 4
Ingredients:
- 16 oz. baby mushrooms
- Pepper to the taste
- 3 tbs. onion, dried
- 3 tbs. parsley flakes
- 1 teaspoon garlic powder
- 2 tbs. olive oil
- ½ cup water

Directions:
1. In a mixing bowl, mix the parsley flakes with onion, pepper, garlic powder, mushrooms and oil and toss.
2. Switch on your instant pot after placing it on a clean and dry kitchen platform.
3. Pour the water into the cooking pot area. Arrange the trivet inside it; arrange the mushrooms over the trivet.
4. Close the pot by closing the top lid. Also, ensure to seal the valve.
5. Press "Manual" cooking function and set cooking time to 10 minutes. It will start cooking after a few minutes. Let the pot mix cook under pressure until the timer reads zero.
6. Turn off and press "Cancel" cooking function. Quick release pressure.
7. Open the pot and serve on a serving plate or bowl. Enjoy the Paleo dish!

Cinnamon Almond

Prep Time: 8min.
Cooking Time: 10 min.
Number of Servings: 10-12
Ingredients:
- 4 and ½ cups almonds, raw
- 2 cups water
- 2 teaspoons vanilla extract
- 3 tablespoons cinnamon powder
- 3 tablespoons stevia

Directions:
1. In a mixing bowl, mix 1 cup water with vanilla extract and whisk. In another mixing bowl, mix the cinnamon with stevia and stir.
2. One by one, dip almonds in water, then in a cinnamon mix. Add them to a heatproof dish.
3. Switch on your instant pot after placing it on a clean and dry kitchen platform.
4. Add the rest of the water to your instant pot. Arrange the trivet inside it; arrange the dish over the trivet.
5. Close the pot by closing the top lid. Also, ensure to seal the valve.
6. Press "Manual" cooking function and set cooking time to 10 minutes. It will start cooking after a few minutes. Let the pot mix cook under pressure until the timer reads zero.
7. Turn off and press "Cancel" cooking function. Quick release pressure.
8. Open the pot and serve on a serving plate or bowl. Enjoy the Paleo dish!

Loaded Potato Skins

Prep Time: 10 minutes
Cooking Time: 20 minutes
Number of Servings: 6
Ingredients:
- 4 large potatoes, halved
- 1 cup water
- 1/4 cup flour
- 1/4 pound bacon
- 1 cup vegetable oil
- 1 cup shredded Cheddar cheese

- 1/2 cup sour cream
- 1/4 cup sliced scallions

Directions:
1. Pour 1 cup water into the Instant Pot and place a steamer basket over the pot. Arrange potatoes in the steamer basket. Close lid and set cooking time for 10 minutes.
2. Remove potatoes from pot. Hollow out the flesh and save it to make mashed potatoes. Set aside.
3. Wipe out the pot. With pot set to Saute mode, brown the bacon until most of the fat renders. Remove the bacon to a paper towel. When cool enough to handle, crumble into pieces. Set aside.
4. Pour the oil into the pot and heat to about 350℉. Dust the potato skins with flour. Place in the oil and cook until brown on all sides. Drain on a paper towel.
5. Fill the hot potato skins with cheese, followed by sour cream. Top with sliced scallions.

Cheese Fondue

Prep Time: 5 minutes
Cooking Time: 5 minutes
Number of Servings: 6
Ingredients:
- 1/2 pound Swiss cheese, cubed
- 1/2 pound Gruyere cheese, cubed
- 2 tablespoons flour
- 1 cup white wine
- 1 baguette, cubed

Directions:
1. Place cheese, flour, and wine in the Instant Pot. Close the lid and set the cooking time for 5 minutes on high pressure. When pressure is released, open the lid and stir until smooth.
2. Set Instant Pot to Keep Warm. Place the pot at the center of the table and use skewers to dip bread into the cheese.

Curried Cauliflower Bites with Dijonnaise

Prep Time: 3 minutes
Cooking Time: 3 minutes
Number of Servings: 6
Ingredients:
- 1 pound cauliflower, cut into bite-size chunks
- 1 tablespoon curry powder
- 1/4 teaspoon salt
- 2 tablespoons olive oil
- 1 cup water
- 1 cup mayonnaise
- 1/4 cup Dijon mustard

Directions:
1. Toss cauliflower with curry powder, salt, and oil.
2. Pour 1 cup water into the Instant Pot. Place a steamer basket over the water. Arrange the cauliflower in the basket.
3. Close the lid and set cooking time for 3 minutes. Use quick release to remove the steam.
4. Whisk together mayonnaise and mustard. Serve alongside the cauliflower.

Cocktail Meatballs

Prep Time: 10 minutes
Cooking Time: 10 minutes
Number of Servings: 6
Ingredients:
- 1 pound ground beef
- 1 egg
- 1/2 cup breadcrumbs
- 1 shallot, minced
- 1 cup grape jelly
- 1 cup Southern chili sauce

Directions:

1. In a bowl, mash together beef, egg, breadcrumbs, and shallot. Shape mixture into walnut-sized meatballs.
2. Stir together grape jelly and brown sugar in the Instant Pot. Arrange meatballs in the pot.
3. Close lid. Set cooking time for 10 minutes on high pressure. Turn meatballs to coat in sauce. Serve on a plate with toothpicks.

Deviled Eggs

Prep Time: 15 minutes
Cooking Time: 5 minutes
Number of Servings: 6
Ingredients:

- 1 dozen eggs
- 1/2 cup mayonnaise
- 1/2 tablespoon vinegar
- 1/2 tablespoon mustard
- 1/4 teaspoon salt
- 1/4 teaspoon black pepper
- 1/2 tablespoon paprika

Directions:
1. Pour water into Instant Pot and place steamer basket over the basket. Arrange the eggs in the basket and close lid. Set cooking time for 5 minutes.
2. Transfer eggs to a bowl of cold water. When cool enough to handle, remove shells. Cut the eggs in half and scoop the yolks into a bowl.
3. Add mayonnaise, vinegar, mustard, salt, and pepper to the yolks. Whisk together. Season to taste.
4. Transfer the yolk mixture to a piping bag and pipe the mixture into the egg whites. Sprinkle with paprika.

Stuffed Mushrooms

Prep Time: 10 minutes
Cooking Time: 4 minutes
Number of Servings: 4
Ingredients:

- 1 pound white mushrooms, stems removed
- 2 tablespoons olive oil
- 2 garlic cloves, minced
- 1/2 cup Italian seasoned breadcrumbs
- 1 cup shredded mozzarella cheese
- 1 cup water

Directions:
1. Mix together oil, garlic, breadcrumbs, and cheese. Stuff the mushrooms with the breadcrumb mixture.
2. Pour 1 cup water into the Instant Pot. Place the steamer basket over the water and arrange the mushrooms in the basket.
3. Close lid and set cooking time for 4 minutes.

Chapter 12: Desserts

Raisin Bread Pudding

Prep Time: 15 minutes
Cooking Time: 25 minutes
Number of Servings: 4
Ingredients:
- 6 slices day-old bread
- 1/4 cup butter, melted
- 3 eggs
- 3 cups milk
- 1/2 cup white sugar
- 1/2 cup brown sugar
- 1 teaspoon vanilla
- 1 teaspoon cinnamon
- 1/2 cup raisins

Directions:
1. Toss the bread with the butter. Sprinkle in raisins. Arrange the bread in a baking pan that fits in the Instant Pot.
2. Whisk together eggs, milk, sugars, vanilla, and cinnamon. Pour over the bread. Press down to help the bread absorb the liquid.
3. Place a trivet in the Instant Pot. Pour enough water into the Instant Pot to just reach the top of the trivet. Place the pan over the trivet.
4. Close the lid and set the cooking time for 25 minutes on high pressure. Serve warm or chilled.

Fudgy Brownies

Prep Time: 10 minutes
Cooking Time: 20 minutes
Number of Servings: 4
Ingredients:
- 1/2 cup butter
- 1 cup sugar
- 2 eggs
- 1 teaspoon vanilla
- 2/3 cup flour
- 1/3 cup cocoa powder
- 1/2 teaspoon baking powder
- 1/2 teaspoon salt

Directions:
1. Cream butter and sugar, then beat in eggs one at a time. Add vanilla last. In a separate bowl, whisk together flour, cocoa, baking powder, and salt. Fold dry ingredients into wet ingredients. Pour batter into a baking pan that fits into the Instant Pot.
2. Place a trivet in the Instant Pot. Add enough water to just reach the top of the trivet. Place the baking pan over the trivet.
3. Close the lid and set the cooking time to 20 minutes. Serve brownies warm or room temperature.

Cinnamon Rice Pudding

Prep Time: 10 minutes
Cooking Time: 10 minutes
Number of Servings: 4
Ingredients:
- 1 cup uncooked rice
- 2 cups milk
- 1 cup sugar
- 1 cup water
- 1 teaspoon vanilla
- 1 teaspoon cinnamon

Directions:
1. Add rice, milk, sugar, and water to the instant pot. Stir to combine. Close lid and set cooking time for 10 minutes on high pressure. Allow steam to naturally release for 10 minutes, then use quick release for the remaining steam.
2. Open the lid and stir in vanilla and cinnamon. Serve cold or warm.

New York Cheesecake

Prep Time: 10 minutes
Cooking Time: 25 minutes
Number of Servings: 4
Ingredients:
- 1 prepared graham cracker crust in aluminum pan
- 1 package cream cheese, softened
- 1/2 cup sour cream
- 2 eggs
- 2/3 cup sugar
- 2 tablespoons cornstarch
- 2 teaspoons vanilla

Directions:
1. Beat together cream cheese, sour cream, eggs, sugar, cornstarch, and vanilla. Pour into pie crust.
2. Place a trivet in the Instant Pot. Add enough water to reach the top of the trivet. Place the pie pan over the trivet.
3. Close lid and set cooking time for 25 minutes on high pressure. Chill before serving.

Apple Crisp

Prep Time: 10 minutes
Cooking Time: 8 minutes
Number of Servings: 4
Ingredients:
- 5 apples, peeled and chopped
- 1/2 cup apple cider
- 2 tablespoons maple syrup
- 1 teaspoon cinnamon
- 1/2 teaspoon nutmeg
- 3/4 cup rolled oats

- 1/4 cup flour
- 1/4 brown sugar
- 1/4 cup butter, melted

Directions:
1. Place apples in the Instant Pot. Pour apple cider and maple syrup over the apples. Sprinkle with cinnamon and nutmeg.
2. In a bowl, whisk together oats, flour, and sugar. Stir in melted butter. Drop spoonfuls of topping on the apples.
3. Close lid and set cooking time to 8 minutes on high pressure. Serve warm with ice cream.

Fruity Dessert Bowl

Prep Time: 8min.
Cooking Time: 40 min.
Number of Servings: 4
Ingredients:
- 2 pears, sliced
- 2 bananas. sliced
- 1 cup strawberries, halved
- 1 cup condensed coconut milk
- 2 apples, sliced
- 1 cup raspberries

Directions:
1. Add the coconut milk in a heat-proof jar.
2. Pour the water into the cooking pot area. Arrange the trivet inside it; arrange the jar over the trivet.
3. Close the pot by closing the top lid. Also, ensure to seal the valve.
4. Press "Manual" cooking function and set cooking time to 40 minutes. It will start cooking after a few minutes. Let the pot mix cook under pressure until the timer reads zero.
5. Turn off and press "Cancel" cooking function. Allow the inside pressure to release naturally; it will take 8-10 minutes to release all inside pressure.
6. Open the pot and cool down the mixture.
7. Combine the fruits in a bowl and divide them into serving bowls. Top each fruit bowl with the warm milk mixture. Enjoy.

Tangy Tapioca Treat

Prep Time: 8-10min.
Cooking Time: 10 min.
Number of Servings: 4
Ingredients:
- 1 and ¼ cup coconut milk
- 1 and ½ cups water
- 1/3 cup tapioca pearls
- Zest of ½ lemon
- 3 tablespoons stevia

Directions:
1. Add the tapioca pearls in a heatproof bowl, mix the milk, ½ cup water, lemon zest and stevia and stir well.
2. Switch on your instant pot after placing it on a clean and dry kitchen platform.
3. Put 1 cup water in your instant pot, add the steamer basket, add the dish with tapioca pudding.
4. Close the pot by closing the top lid. Also, ensure to seal the valve.
5. Press "Manual" cooking function and set cooking time to 10 minutes. It will start cooking after a few minutes. Let the pot mix cook under pressure until the timer reads zero.
6. Turn off and press "Cancel" cooking function. Quick release pressure.
7. Open the pot and serve on a serving plate or bowl. Enjoy the Paleo dish!

Banana Pie

Prep Time: 10min.
Cooking Time: 35 min.
Number of Servings: 4
Ingredients:
- ½ teaspoon vanilla
- ½ cup coconut cream
- 2 tbs. almond flour
- 1 medium banana
- ½ cup condensed coconut milk
- 1 tbs. coconut oil
- 2 cups coconut flour

Directions:
1. Meanwhile, combine the flours, oil, and vanilla. Add and press the mixture into the bottom of a lined baking dish.
2. Place the mixture in the fridge to chill. Add the milk to a heat-proof jar with a lid.
3. Switch on your instant pot after placing it on a clean and dry kitchen platform.
4. Open the pot lid. Fill the pot with water and place the jar inside.
5. Close the pot by closing the top lid. Also, ensure to seal the valve.
6. Press "Manual" cooking function and set cooking time to 35 minutes. It will start cooking after a few minutes. Let the pot mix cook under pressure until the timer reads zero.
7. Turn off and press "Cancel" cooking function. Quick release pressure.
8. Open the pot and cool down the mixture for about 25-30 minutes.
9. Slice the banana and place in a mixing bowl. Mix in the condensed milk. Enjoy the Paleo dish!

The Red Pears

Prep Time: 5min.
Cooking Time: 10 min.
Number of Servings:5-6
Ingredients:
- 1 clove
- A pinch of cinnamon
- 1 glass natural red grape juice
- 6 green pears
- 1 vanilla pod

- 7 ounces stevia

Directions:
1. Switch on your instant pot after placing it on a clean and dry kitchen platform.
2. Open the pot lid and slowly start adding the red grapes juice with stevia and cinnamon ingredients in the pot. Give the ingredients a little stir.
3. Add the clove and pears.
4. Close the pot by closing the top lid. Also, ensure to seal the valve.
5. Press "Manual" cooking function and set cooking time to 10 minutes.
6. It will start cooking after a few minutes. Let the pot mix cook under pressure until the timer reads zero.
7. Turn off and press "Cancel" cooking function. Quick release pressure.
8. Open the pot and serve on a serving plate or bowl. Enjoy the Paleo dish!

Nutty Chocolate Fudge Balls

Prep Time: 5 min.
Cooking Time: 5 min.
Number of Servings: 2
Ingredients:
- ½ cup walnuts
- ½ cup almonds
- 1 teaspoon vanilla
- 1 12-ounce package chocolate chips, semi-sweet
- 1 14-ounce can of condensed milk
- 2 cups water

Directions:
1. Combine the milk and chocolate chips in a medium bowl. Cover it with aluminum foil.
2. Switch on the pot after placing it on a clean and dry platform.
3. Pour the water into the pot. Arrange the trivet inside it; arrange the bowl over the trivet.
4. Close the pot by closing the top lid. Also, ensure to seal the valve.
5. Press "Manual" cooking function and set cooking time to 5 minutes. It will start cooking after a few minutes. Let the pot mix cook under pressure until the timer reads zero.
6. Press "Cancel" cooking function and press "Quick release" setting.
7. Remove the bowl and mix in the nuts and vanilla. Prepare unformed balls and arrange onto wax paper and allow to cool. Enjoy!

Mouthwatering Raisin Apples

Prep Time: 5 min.
Cooking Time: 10 min.
Number of Servings: 2
Ingredients:
- 3 tablespoons raisins
- ¼ cup sugar
- ¼ cup red wine
- 2 apples, cored
- ½ teaspoon cinnamon

Directions:
1. Switch on the pot after placing it on a clean and dry platform.
2. Open the pot lid and place the above-mentioned ingredients in the cooking pot area. Give the ingredients a little stir.
3. Close the pot by closing the top lid. Also, ensure to seal the valve.
4. Press "Manual" cooking function and set cooking time to 10 minutes. It will start cooking after a few minutes. Let the pot mix cook under pressure until the timer reads zero.
5. Press "Cancel" cooking function and press "Natural release (NPR)" setting. It will take 8-10 minutes for natural pressure release.
6. Open the pot and serve warm. Enjoy it with your loved one!

Chocolate Ramekins

Prep Time: 5-8 min.
Cooking Time: 10 min.
Number of Servings: 2
Ingredients:
- 2 ounces semi-sweet chocolate, chopped
- ½ teaspoon instant coffee
- ½ teaspoon vanilla extract
- 3 tablespoons all-purpose flour
- 1 egg yolk
- 1 egg
- ½ tablespoon sugar
- ¼ cup butter
- ½ cup confectioner's sugar
- ⅛ teaspoon salt

Directions:
1. Grease two ramekins and coat them with the sugar.
2. In a mixing bowl, mix the butter and chocolate. Add the confectioners' sugar and combine well.
3. Whisk in the egg yolk, egg, vanilla, and coffee. Add the salt and flour; combine again. Divide into the ramekins.
4. Switch on the pot after placing it on a clean and dry platform.
5. Pour 2 cups water into the pot. Arrange the trivet inside it; arrange the ramekins over the trivet.
6. Close the pot by closing the top lid. Also, ensure to seal the valve.
7. Press "Manual" cooking function and set cooking time to 9 minutes. It will start cooking after a few minutes. Let the pot mix cook under pressure until the timer reads zero.
8. Press "Cancel" cooking function and press "Quick release" setting.
9. Open the pot; take out the ramekins and top with some powdered sugar. Enjoy it with your loved one!

Wonder Wine Pears

Prep Time: 5 min.
Cooking Time: 10-12 min.
Number of Servings: 2
Ingredients:
- ¼ bottle of your choice of red wine

- 1 piece of ginger
- 1 clove
- 2 pears, peeled
- ½ cup sugar
- 1 cinnamon stick

Directions:
1. Switch on the pot after placing it on a clean and dry platform.
2. Open the pot lid and place the above-mentioned ingredients in the cooking pot area. Give the ingredients a little stir.
3. Close the pot by closing the top lid. Also, ensure to seal the valve.
4. Press "Manual" cooking function and set cooking time to 6 minutes. It will start cooking after a few minutes. Let the pot mix cook under pressure until the timer reads zero.
5. Press "Cancel" cooking function and press "Quick release" setting.
6. Open the pot and carefully take out the pears, setting them aside.
7. Switch the pot to sauté and let the liquid cook until it reduces by half quantity.
8. Drizzle the hot juice over the pears; serve warm!

Tangy Blueberry Lemon Delight

Prep Time: 8-10 min.
Cooking Time: 8 min.
Number of Servings: 2
Ingredients:
- 1/4 cup lemon juice
- 3 egg yolks, whisked
- 2/3 cup sugar
- 2 cup blueberries
- 1 1/2 cup water
- 2 teaspoons lemon zest, grated
- 4 tablespoons butter

Directions:
1. Take your 3-Quart Instant Pot; open the top lid. Plug it and turn it on.
2. Press "SAUTÉ" setting and the pot will start heating up.
3. Add the lemon juice and blueberries, stir and simmer for 2 minutes.
4. Strain the mix into a bowl, mash the ingredients. Mix in the sugar, butter, lemon zest and egg yolks, whisk well and add the mix into two ramekins.
5. Pour the water and place steamer basket/trivet inside the pot; arrange the ramekins over the basket/trivet.
6. Close the top lid and seal its valve.
7. Press "MANUAL" setting. Adjust cooking time to 6 minutes.
8. Allow the recipe to cook for the set cooking time.
9. After the set cooking time ends, press "CANCEL" and then press "QPR (Quick Pressure Release)".
10. Instant Pot will quickly release the pressure.
11. Chill the ramekins in refrigerator and serve chilled.

Cocoa Pudding Dessert

Prep Time: 8-10 min.
Cooking Time: 10-15 min.
Number of Servings: 2-3
Ingredients:
- 1 teaspoon vanilla extract
- 2 tablespoons cocoa powder
- 1 cup rice
- 5 cups coconut milk
- 1 cup sugar
- 1 tablespoon coconut oil
- 2 whole beaten eggs

Directions:
1. Take your 3-Quart Instant Pot; open the top lid. Plug it and turn it on.
2. In the cooking pot area, add the ingredients. Using a spatula, stir the ingredients.
3. Close the top lid and seal its valve.
4. Press "RICE" setting. It will automatically set cooking time.
5. After the set cooking time ends, press "CANCEL" and then press "NPR (Natural Pressure Release)".
6. Instant Pot will slowly and naturally release the pressure.
7. Open the top lid, add the cooked recipe mix in serving plates.
8. Serve and enjoy!

Avocado Choco Treat

Prep Time: 5-8 min.
Cooking Time: 10 min.
Number of Servings: 5
Ingredients:
- 1/4 teaspoon cinnamon
- 1 avocado, chopped and pitted
- 1 cup heavy cream
- 2 teaspoons sugar
- 1 medium size egg
- 1 ounce dark chocolate
- 1/4 tablespoon chia seeds

Directions:
1. Add the cream, sugar, and avocado in a blender. Blend to make a smooth mixture.
2. Beat the egg in a bowl and add it in the blender. Add the ground cinnamon and combine.
3. Ads the chocolate and blend the mixture.
4. Arrange your Instant Pot over a dry, clean platform. Plug it in power socket and turn it on.

5. Open the lid from the top and put it aside; add the mixture and top with the chia seeds.
6. Close the lid and lock. Ensure that you have sealed the valve to avoid leakage.
7. Press "Manual" mode from available cooking settings and set cooking time to 10 minutes. Instant Pot will start cooking the ingredients after a few minutes.
8. After the timer reads zero, press "Cancel" and quick release pressure.
9. Carefully remove the lid and serve the prepared keto dish warm!

Choco Almond Pudding

Prep Time: 5-8 min.
Cooking Time: 5 min.
Number of Servings: 4
Ingredients:
- 1 tablespoon agar powder
- ¼ cup almonds, finely chopped
- 2 tablespoons cocoa powder, unsweetened
- 1 cup unsweetened almond milk
- ¼ cup swerve
- 2 tablespoon chocolate chips, sugar-free
- 1 ¼ cup whipping cream
- ½ cup coconut cream
- 1 teaspoon vanilla extract

Directions:
1. Take your Instant Pot; open the top lid. Plug it and turn it on.
2. Press "SAUTÉ" setting and the pot will start heating up.
3. Pour in the milk, swerve, cocoa powder, coconut cream, and vanilla extract.
4. Bring it to a boil, stirring constantly, and then add the agar powder.
5. Continue to cook for 1-2 minutes.
6. Press "Cancel" button and mix the almonds.
7. Transfer the mix to a blender and pour in the whipping cream. Beat well on high speed for 2-3 minutes.
8. Add the mixture between serving bowls and chill in the refrigerator. Serve chilled.

Cashew Tapioca Pudding

Prep Time: 5-8min.
Cooking Time: 10 min.
Number of Servings:5-6
Ingredients:
- ½ cup maple syrup
- ½ cup tapioca pearls, soaked for at least 1 hour
- 3 tablespoons chopped cashews
- 1 cups coconut milk
- Some lemon zest
- 6 roasted cashews for garnishing

Directions:

1. Take Instant Pot and carefully arrange it over a clean, dry kitchen platform. Turn on the appliance.
2. In the cooking pot area, add the tapioca pearls, coconut milk, maple syrup, chopped cashews, and lemon zest. Stir the ingredients gently.
3. Close the pot lid and seal the valve to avoid any leakage. Find and press "Manual" cooking setting and set cooking time to 10 minutes.
4. Allow the recipe ingredients to cook for the set time, and after that, the timer reads "zero".
5. Press "Cancel" and press "NPR" setting for natural pressure release. It takes 8-10 times for all inside pressure to release.
6. Open the pot. Serve chilled with roasted cashews on top.

Stuffed Dessert Apples

Prep Time: 5min.
Cooking Time: 10 min.
Number of Servings: 6
Ingredients:
- 4 tablespoons maple syrup
- ½ cup cranberries
- 6 medium apples
- ½ cup walnuts, chopped
- ½ teaspoon ground cinnamon
- 1 cup water
- Some cashews, roasted and chopped
- ¼ teaspoon ground nutmeg

Directions:
1. Leave the bottom part of the apples as it is and core the apples. Slowly scoop out some more pulp from inside.
2. In a mixing bowl, mix rest of the ingredients except the cashews, and fill the mixture inside the apple.
3. Add water to the Instant Pot. Add the apples to the pot with bottom part resting on the surface of the pot.
4. Close the pot lid and seal the valve to avoid any leakage. Find and press "Manual" cooking setting and set cooking time to 10 minutes.
5. Allow the recipe ingredients to cook for the set time, and after that, the timer reads "zero".
6. Press "Cancel" and press "NPR" setting for natural pressure release. It takes 8-10 times for all inside pressure to release.
7. Open the pot. Sprinkle with cashews and serve hot.

Berry Dessert Mystery

Prep Time: 5 min.
Cooking Time: 2 min.
Number of Servings:7-8
Ingredients:
- 4 cups blackberries or blueberries
- 4 cups raspberries or strawberries, divide into halves

- 4 tablespoons lemon juice
- 4 tablespoons maple syrup or sweetener of your choice

Directions:
1. Take Instant Pot and carefully arrange it over a clean, dry kitchen platform. Turn on the appliance.
2. In the cooking pot area, add the strawberries, maple syrup, lemon juice and ⅓ of the blueberries. Stir the ingredients gently.
3. Close the pot lid and seal the valve to avoid any leakage. Find and press "Manual" cooking setting and set cooking time to 2 minutes.
4. Allow the recipe ingredients to cook for the set time, and after that, the timer reads "zero".
5. Press "Cancel" and press "NPR" setting for natural pressure release. It takes 8-10 times for all inside pressure to release.
6. Open the pot and chill in the refrigerator. Serve chilled!

Buckwheat Banana Treat

Prep Time: 5-8min.
Cooking Time: 8 min.
Number of Servings:7-8
Ingredients:
- 2 teaspoons ground cinnamon
- 6 cups rice milk
- 2 cups buckwheat groats, rinsed
- 2 bananas, sliced
- ½ cup raisins
- 1 teaspoon vanilla extract
- Chopped nuts for garnishing

Directions:
1. Take Instant Pot and carefully arrange it over a clean, dry kitchen platform. Turn on the appliance.
2. In the cooking pot area, add the mentioned ingredients. Stir the ingredients gently.
3. Close the pot lid and seal the valve to avoid any leakage. Find and press "Manual" cooking setting and set cooking time to 8 minutes.
4. Allow the recipe ingredients to cook for the set time, and after that, the timer reads "zero".
5. Press "Cancel" and press "NPR" setting for natural pressure release. It takes 8-10 times for all inside pressure to release.
6. Open the pot and arrange the cooked recipe in serving plates. Garnish with nuts and serve.

Cardamom Rice Pudding

Prep Time: 5-7 min.
Cooking Time: 40 min.
Number of Servings: 4
Ingredients:
- 2 cups brown rice, thoroughly rinsed
- 2 cinnamon sticks
- 6 ½ cups water

- 1 cup coconut sugar
- ½ cup coconut, shredded
- 5 cardamom pods
- 3 cloves

Directions:
1. Take your Instant Pot and place it on a clean kitchen platform. Turn it on after plugging it into a power socket.
2. Open the lid from top and put it aside; add the water, sugar, rice, cinnamon, cloves, and cardamom
3. Gently stir the added ingredients; close the lid and lock. Ensure that you have sealed the valve to avoid leakage.
4. Press "Manual" mode and set timer for 30 minutes. It will take a few minutes for the pot to build inside pressure and start cooking.
5. After the timer reads zero, press "Cancel" and quick release pressure. Discard cinnamon, cloves, and cardamom; add the coconut and stir well.
6. Close the lid again and cook for 5 more minutes on "Manual" mode.
7. Carefully remove the lid. Divide into dessert cups and serve!

Instant Fruit Bowl

Prep Time: 8-10 min.
Cooking Time: 10 min.
Number of Servings: 4
Ingredients:
- 1 apple, chopped
- 2 tablespoons granular stevia or sugar
- 1 plum, chopped
- 1 pear, chopped
- ½ teaspoon cinnamon
- 3 tablespoons coconut oil
- 1 cup water
- ¼ cup coconut, shredded
- ¼ cup pecans, chopped

Directions:
1. In a bowl (heatproof) of medium size, thoroughly mix the plum, apple, pear, coconut oil, coconut, cinnamon and stevia/sugar.
2. Take your instant pot and place it on a clean kitchen platform. Turn it on after plugging it into a power socket.
3. In the pot, slowly pour the water. Take the trivet and arrange inside it; place the bowl over it.
4. Close the lid and lock. Ensure that you have sealed the valve to avoid leakage.
5. Press "Manual" mode and set timer for 10 minutes. It will take a few minutes for the pot to build inside pressure and start cooking.
6. After the timer reads zero, press "Cancel" and quick release pressure.
7. Carefully remove the lid; divide into bowls and serve with pecans on top.

Yummy Wine Figs

Prep Time: 5 min.
Cooking Time: 3 min.
Number of Servings: 4
Ingredients:

- ½ cup pine nuts
- 1 cup red wine
- 1 pound figs
- Stevia or sugar as needed

Directions:
1. Take your Instant Pot and place it on a clean kitchen platform. Turn it on after plugging it into a power socket.
2. In the pot, slowly pour the wine and stevia/sugar. Take the trivet and arrange inside it; place the figs over it.
3. Close the lid and lock. Ensure that you have sealed the valve to avoid leakage.
4. Press "Manual" mode and set timer for 3 minutes. It will take a few minutes for the pot to build inside pressure and start cooking.
5. After the timer reads zero, press "Cancel" and quick release pressure.
6. Carefully remove the lid. Divide figs into bowls, and drizzle wine over them.
7. Top the pine nuts and enjoy the desserts.

Berry Dessert Cups

Prep Time: 5 min.
Cooking Time: 2 min.
Number of Servings: 5-6
Ingredients:

- 1 pound strawberries
- 1 pound blueberries
- 2 teaspoons lemon juice
- 4 tablespoons stevia or sugar as needed

Directions:
1. Take your Instant Pot and place it on a clean kitchen platform.
2. Open the lid from the top and put it aside; start adding the strawberries, blueberries and stevia/sugar. Set the pot aside for 20 minutes.
3. Turn it on after plugging it into a power socket.
4. Add the lemon juice and stir; close the lid and lock. Ensure that you have sealed the valve to avoid leakage.
5. Press "Manual" mode and set timer for 2 minutes. It will take a few minutes for the pot to build inside pressure and start cooking.
6. After the timer reads zero, press "Cancel" and quick release pressure.
7. Carefully remove the lid. Serve in small dessert cups. Enjoy!

Cherry Pecan Mousse

Prep Time: 10 min.
Cooking Time: 7 min.
Number of Servings: 5-6
Ingredients:

- 1 tablespoon pecans, minced
- ¼ cup erythritol
- 1 ½ cup whipping cream
- 5 large egg yolks, beaten
- ½ cup whole milk
- ½ cup coconut cream
- ½ teaspoon salt
- 2 teaspoon cherry extract

Directions:
1. Take your Instant Pot; open the top lid. Plug it and turn it on.
2. Press "SAUTÉ" setting and the pot will start heating up.
3. Add the whipping cream, egg yolks, erythritol, milk, salt, and coconut cream; boil the mix.
4. Cool down the mix and pour the mixture into heat-safe ramekins.
5. Sprinkle with pecans and wrap each ramekin with aluminum foil.
6. Take your Instant Pot; open the top lid. Plug it and turn it on.
7. Pour 1 cup water and place steamer basket/trivet inside the pot; arrange the ramekins over the basket/trivet.
8. Close the top lid and seal its valve.
9. Press "MANUAL" setting. Adjust cooking time to 7 minutes.
10. Allow the recipe to cook for the set cooking time.
11. After the set cooking time ends, press "CANCEL" and then press "QPR (Quick Pressure Release)".
12. Instant Pot will quickly release the pressure.
13. Open the top lid, cool down the ramekins.
14. Refrigerate for at least an hour before serving.

Creamy Strawberry Pudding

Prep Time: 8-10 min.
Cooking Time: 20 min.
Number of Servings: 4-5
Ingredients:
- 2 cups heavy cream
- 1 tablespoon butter
- 1/4 cup strawberries, mashed
- 1 tablespoon Erythritol
- 1 teaspoon chia seeds

- 1 tablespoon tapioca

Directions:
1. Arrange your Instant Pot over a dry, clean platform. Plug it in power socket and turn it on.
2. Now press "Saute" mode from available options. In the cooking area, add the cream; cook for 4-5 minutes to soften.
3. Add the tapioca and stir it well. Mix the Erythritol and butter.
4. In a bowl (medium or large size), mix the chia seeds and berries. Add the berry mixture to the pot and stir it gently.
5. Close the lid and lock. Ensure that you have sealed the valve to avoid leakage.
6. Press "Saute" mode from available cooking settings and set cooking time to 15 minutes. Instant Pot will start cooking the ingredients after a few minutes.
7. After the timer reads zero, press "Cancel" and quick release pressure.
8. Carefully remove the lid. Refrigerate and serve chilled!

Chocolate Cake

Prep Time: 10--15 min.
Cooking Time: 18-20 min.
Number of Servings: 5
Ingredients:
- ⅔ cup Erythritol

- 4 tablespoons cocoa powder, unsweetened

- ½ cup almond flour

- ¼ teaspoon vanilla extract

- 2 medium size eggs

- 4 tablespoons butter

- 2 tablespoons chocolate chips

Directions:
1. Melt the chips and butter in a microwave in a bowl (heat-safe) for 1 minute.
2. Add the Erythritol and whisk to combine. Add the vanilla and egg, and mix again.
3. Add the cocoa and flour; mix until blended. Add the mixture to ramekins; spread it gently.
4. Arrange your Instant Pot over a dry, clean platform. Plug it in power socket and turn it on.
5. Slowly pour the water into the pot order to avoid spilling out. Take the trivet and arrange in the pot; place the ramekins over the trivet.
6. Close the lid and lock. Ensure that you have sealed the valve to avoid leakage.
7. Press "Manual" mode from available cooking settings and set cooking time to 18 minutes. Instant Pot will start cooking the ingredients after a few minutes.
8. After the timer reads zero, press "Cancel" and quick release pressure.
9. Carefully remove the lid. Make squares and serve warm!

Vanilla Orange Muffins

Prep Time: 10 min.
Cooking Time: 10 min.
Number of Servings: 8
Ingredients:

- 1/2 teaspoon baking powder

- 1 tablespoon orange juice

- 1/4 cup cream cheese

- 5 tablespoons butter

- 3 tablespoons almond flour

- 4 tablespoons granular stevia or sugar

- 1 teaspoon vanilla extract

- 1 cup coconut flour

Directions:
1. Mix the butter and cheese in a blender. Mix in the baking powder and juice.
2. Mix in both the flours. Top the mixture of the stevia/sugar and vanilla extract.
3. Blend for 1 more minute to prepare a thick dough-like mixture. Pour into the lightly greased muffin tins.
4. Open the lid from the top and put it aside; add the tins and gently stir them.
5. Close the lid and lock. Ensure that you have sealed the valve to avoid leakage.
6. Press "Manual" mode from available cooking settings and set cooking time to 10 minutes. Instant Pot will start cooking the ingredients after a few minutes.
7. After the timer reads zero, press "Cancel" and quick release pressure.
8. Carefully remove the lid and serve the prepared keto dish warm!

Orange Choco Muffins

Prep Time: 10 min.
Cooking Time: 30 min.
Number of Servings: 4-5
Ingredients:

- 1 tablespoon chia seeds
- 1 tablespoon flaxseed meal
- ½ cup whole milk
- ½ cup almond flour
- ¼ cup almonds, roughly chopped
- 5 large eggs
- 1 tablespoon butter
- ¼ teaspoon bicarbonate of soda
- 1 tablespoon dark chocolate chips
- ½ teaspoon baking powder

- 1 teaspoon orange extract
- 2 teaspoons stevia powder
- ¼ teaspoon cinnamon, ground

Directions:
1. In a mixing bowl, combine the flour, almonds, chia seeds, flaxseed meal, baking powder, and bicarbonate soda.
2. Mix until well combined. Add the eggs, butter, milk, orange extract, stevia, and cinnamon.
3. Add the mix in a blender and make a smooth mix.
4. Divide into greased muffin molds. Top with the chocolate chips and set aside.
5. Take your Instant Pot; open the top lid. Plug it and turn it on.
6. Pour the water and place steamer basket/trivet inside the pot; arrange the molds over the basket/trivet.
7. Close the top lid and seal its valve.
8. Press "MANUAL" setting. Adjust cooking time to 30 minutes.
9. Allow the recipe to cook for the set cooking time.
10. After the set cooking time ends, press "CANCEL" and then press "QPR (Quick Pressure Release)".
11. Instant Pot will quickly release the pressure.
12. Open the top lid, cool down the molds.
13. Serve and enjoy!

Pure Pear Berry Cakes

Prep Time: 10-15 min.
Cooking Time: 35 min.
Number of Servings: 2-3
Ingredients:
- 1/4 teaspoon baking soda
- 1/4 teaspoon cardamom, ground
- 4 tablespoons milk
- 1 cup flour
- 3 tablespoons maple syrup
- 1 tablespoon flax seeds
- 4 tablespoons cranberries, chopped
- 1 1/2 cup water
- 1/4 teaspoon baking powder
- 1 tablespoon vegetable oil
- 1/2 cup pear, cored and chopped

Directions:
1. In a bowl, mix the baking soda, flour, cardamom, milk, flax seeds, baking powder, maple syrup and oil and stir well.
2. Add the chopped pear and cranberries, stir. Add the mix into a greased cake pan.
3. Pour the water and place steamer basket/trivet inside the pot; arrange the pan over the basket/trivet.
4. Close the top lid and seal its valve.
5. Press "MANUAL" setting. Adjust cooking time to 35 minutes.

6. Allow the recipe to cook for the set cooking time.
7. After the set cooking time ends, press "CANCEL" and then press "QPR (Quick Pressure Release)".
8. Instant Pot will quickly release the pressure.
9. Open the top lid, add the cooked recipe mix in serving plates.
10. Serve and enjoy!

Indian Pudding

Prep Time: 10 minutes
Cooking Time: 15 minutes
Number of Servings: 6
Ingredients:
- 1/2 cup cornmeal
- 1/4 cup flour
- 1 teaspoon salt
- 1 teaspoon cinnamon
- 1 teaspoon nutmeg
- 5 cups milk
- 1/2 cup molasses
- 3 eggs
- 1/3 cup sugar
- 1 cup raisins

Directions:
1. In a bowl, whisk together cornmeal, flour, salt, cinnamon, and nutmeg. In the Instant Pot, whisk together milk, molasses, eggs, and sugar. Stir dry ingredients into wet ingredients. Stir in raisins.
2. Close lid and set cooking time to 15 minutes on high pressure. Serve warm with ice cream.

Cream Brulee

Prep Time: 8-10 min.
Cooking Time: 10 min.
Number Servings: 4
Ingredients:
- ⅓ cup swerve sweetener
- 1 teaspoon pure vanilla extract
- 8 egg yolk
- 2 cups unsweetened coconut cream
- 1 ½ cups water

Directions:
1. In a mixing bowl (medium-large size), combine the cream, and sweetener. Stir well. Whisk in the yolks; mix well.
2. Mix in the vanilla extract.
3. Grease 4 ramekins with cooking spray. Pour in the mix.
4. Take an Instant Pot; open the top lid.
5. Pour the water and place steamer basket/trivet inside the cooking pot.
6. Arrange the ramekins over the basket/trivet.
7. Close the top lid and make sure the valve is sealed.

334

8. Press "MANUAL" cooking function. Adjust cooking time to 9 minutes.
9. Allow pressure to build and cook the ingredients for the set time.
10. After the set cooking time ends, press "CANCEL" and then press "NPR". Instant Pot will slowly and naturally release the pressure for 8-10 minutes.
11. Open the top lid.
12. Cool down and chill the ramekins in refrigerator 4 hours. Serve chilled.

Cocoa Almond Cake

Prep Time: 5 min.
Cooking Time: 2 min.
Number Servings: 1
Ingredients:
- ½ teaspoon pure vanilla extract
- 1 large egg
- 1 tablespoon almond butter, melted
- 1 teaspoon ghee
- 2 tablespoons swerve sweetener
- 1 tablespoon unsweetened coconut cream
- 2 tablespoons cocoa powder

Directions:
1. In a mixing bowl, combine all the above ingredients, except the almond butter.
2. Grease a ramekin with cooking spray. Pour in the batter.
3. Take an Instant Pot; open the top lid.
4. Pour 1 cup water and place steamer basket/trivet inside the cooking pot.
5. Arrange the ramekin over the basket/trivet.
6. Close the top lid and make sure the valve is sealed.
7. Press "MANUAL" cooking function. Adjust cooking time to 2 minutes.
8. Allow pressure to build and cook the ingredients for the set time.
9. After the set cooking time ends, press "CANCEL" and then press "QPR". Instant Pot will quickly release pressure.
10. Open the top lid, cool down the ramekin. Top with the butter.
11. Serve warm.

Basic Yogurt Recipe

Prep Time: 20 minutes
Cooking Time: 6-8 hours
Number of Servings: 6
Ingredients:
- 1/2 gallon milk
- 2 tablespoons plain probiotic yogurt

Directions:
1. Pour milk into Instant Pot. If your pot has a Yogurt function, use Yogurt More to heat milk to 180℉. If your pot does not have a Yogurt function, set the pot to Saute and use a thermometer to check when the milk reaches 180℉.
2. Turn off the heat and wait until the milk reaches about 110℉.

3. When the milk has cooled, pour about 1/2 cup into a bowl and whisk in the yogurt. Stir the thinned yogurt into the instant pot.
4. Use the Yogurt Normal function to ferment the yogurt. If your pot does not have a yogurt function, use the Slow Cook function. Do not open the lid for at least 6 hours.
5. When the yogurt reaches your desired level of fermentation, place in the refrigerator to chill.

Strained Greek Yogurt

Prep Time: 2 hours
Cooking Time: 0 minutes
Number of Servings:
Ingredients:
- 1/2 gallon Basic Yogurt (recipe above)
- 1 cheesecloth

Directions:
1. Arrange a double layer of cheesecloth over a fine mesh sieve. Place the sieve over a bowl.
2. Pour the yogurt into the cheesecloth. Allow the yogurt to strain at least 2 hours or until yogurt reaches your desired consistency.

Herbed Yogurt Cheese

Prep Time: 5 hours
Cooking Time: 0 minutes
Number of Servings: 6
Ingredients:
- 1/2 gallon Basic Yogurt (recipe above)
- 1 tablespoon dried thyme
- 1/2 tablespoon dried rosemary
- 1/4 cup olive oil

Directions:
1. Arrange a double layer of cheesecloth over a fine mesh sieve. Place the sieve over a bowl.
2. Pour the yogurt into the cheesecloth. Allow the yogurt to strain at least 4 hours in the refrigerator. Squeeze the cheesecloth to remove as much liquid as possible.
3. When yogurt is completely strained, twist together the open top of the cheesecloth and place the wrapped yogurt on a plate. Place another plate on top of the yogurt and put something heavy on top, such as a book. Allow to sit for 1 hour.
4. Roll yogurt cheese in the herbs. Drizzle with olive oil. Serve with crackers or toast.

Drinkable Yogurt Smoothies

Prep Time: 10 minutes
Cooking Time: 0 minutes
Number of Servings: 6
Ingredients:
- 4 cups Basic Yogurt (recipe above)
- 2 cup milk
- 2 cups fresh fruit
- Sugar or sweetener to taste

Directions:

1. Place yogurt, milk, and fruit in a blender. Blend until smooth.
2. Taste smoothie and add sugar or sweetener as desired. Refrigerate. Shake before serving.

Nutritional Values (Per Serving):
Calories - 165
Fat - 8.13 g
Carbohydrates - 15.22 g
Fiber - 1 g
Protein - 8.57 g

Coconut Milk Yogurt

Prep Time: 5 hours
Cooking Time: 6 hours
Number of Servings: 6
Ingredients:
*   2 cans coconut milk
*   1 tablespoon probiotic coconut milk yogurt

Directions:
1. Pour coconut milk into Instant Pot. If your pot has a Yogurt function, use Yogurt More to heat coconut milk to 180℉. If your pot does not have a Yogurt function, set the pot to Saute and use a thermometer to check when the coconut milk reaches 180℉.
2. Turn off the heat and wait until the coconut milk reaches about 110℉.
3. When the coconut milk has cooled, pour about 1/2 cup into a bowl and whisk in the coconut yogurt. Stir the thinned coconut yogurt into the instant pot.
4. Use the Yogurt Normal function to ferment the coconut yogurt. If your pot does not have a yogurt function, use the Slow Cook function. Do not open the lid for at least 6 hours.
5. When the coconut yogurt reaches your desired level of fermentation, place in the refrigerator to chill.

Vanilla Frozen Yogurt Recipe

Prep Time: 10 minutes plus freezing time
Cooking Time: 0 minutes
Number of Servings: 4
Ingredients:
*   2 cups Basic Yogurt (recipe above)
*   1 cup sugar
*   1 teaspoon vanilla

Directions:
1. Whisk together yogurt, sugar, and vanilla.
2. Churn yogurt in an ice cream machine until it reaches a soft-serve consistency. Transfer to a freezer-safe container and freeze at least 4 hours or overnight.

Nutritional Values (Per Serving):
Calories - 271
Fat - 3.98 g
Carbohydrates - 55.83 g
Fiber - 0 g
Protein - 4.25 g

Orange Honey Yogurt Panna Cotta

Prep Time: 25 minutes
Cooking Time: 1 minute
Number of Servings: 2
Ingredients:

- 1 cup Basic Yogurt (recipe above)
- 1/4 cup sugar
- 1 teaspoon vanilla
- 1 tablespoon hot water
- 1 teaspoon unflavored gelatin
- 1/4 cup honey
- Juice of 1 orange with pulp
- 1/4 teaspoon cardamom

Directions:
1. Whisk together yogurt, sugar, and vanilla.
2. Sprinkle gelatin over water and allow to soften. Whisk together until gelatin dissolves. Whisk gelatin mixture into yogurt mixture.
3. Pour yogurt mixture into two small ramekins or one large ramekin. Chill 2 hours.
4. Meanwhile, make a sauce. Combine honey, orange, and cardamom in the Instant Pot. Close lid and set cooking time to 1 minute. Chill completely.
5. When panna cotta is set, run a knife around the inside of the ramekin and invert onto a plate. Top with sauce.